WHAT HAPPENED IN CUBA?

WHAT HAPPENED
IN CUBA?

A Documentary History

by

ROBERT F. SMITH

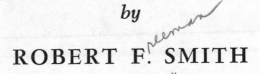

TWAYNE PUBLISHERS, INC.

NEW YORK

In memory of

MY FATHER,

and for

MY MOTHER;

parents who gave me many things, the most important
being the examples of Christian humanitarianism and the
courage to stand for what one believes to be right.

ACKNOWLEDGMENTS

THE EDITOR gratefully acknowledges the cooperation of authors, publishers, and individual holders of copyrights who have granted permission for the reprinting of copyrighted material as follows:

Mr. Stewart Alsop for permission to use excerpts from the article "Lessons of the Cuban Disaster," *Saturday Evening Post* (June 24, 1961). Copyright 1961 by the Curtis Publishing Company.

The Atlantic Monthly for permission to use excerpts from the article, "Is America Imperialistic?" by Sumner Welles.

The Carnegie Endowment for International Peace for permission to use excerpts from the following volumes:
International Conciliation (January 1934), "Relations Between Cuba and the U.S.," by Andres Lliteras.
William R. Manning, ed., *Diplomatic Correspondence of the United States: Inter-American Affairs, 1831–1860*, Vol. XI.

The Harvard University Press for permission to use excerpts from the following volumes:
Robert Bacon and James B. Scott, eds., *The Military and Colonial Policy of the United States: Addresses and Reports by Elihu Root.*
Elting E. Morison, *The Letters of Theodore Roosevelt*, Vols. I, II, IV, and V.

International Review Service for permission to use selections from *Cuba and the United States.*

David McKay Company for permission to use excerpts from the following volumes:
Allan Nevins, ed., *Polk: The Diary of a President, 1845–1849.*
Albert G. Robinson, *Cuba and the Intervention.*

J. B. Lippincott Company for permission to use a selection from John B. Moore, ed., *The Works of James Buchanan*, Vol. X.

The New York Times for permission to use the following selections:
Herbert Matthews' report on Fidel Castro, February 24, 1957.
Statement by President Eisenhower on signing the Cuban sugar quota bill, July 7, 1960.
President Eisenhower's statement announcing the break in relations with Cuba, January 4, 1961.

Ivan Obolensky Incorporated for permission to use excerpts from R. Hart Phillips, *Cuba: Island of Paradox.*

Lyle Stuart, Publisher, for permission to use excerpts from *History Will Absolve Me*, by Fidel Castro.

The Wall Street Journal for permission to use the following selections:
James N. Wallace, "Cuba Questions," February 16, 1961.
Manati Sugar Company's report on claims for property seizures in Cuba, February 16, 1961.

INTRODUCTION

THE CLOSING WORDS of the book of *Ecclesiastes* could well be para-
phrased and applied to certain literary productions of the last three
years: "Of the writing of books on Cuba there is no end, and any
attempt to read them all is a weariness of the flesh." This flow of
books has been produced by the dramatic developments in relations
between the United States and Cuba stemming from the Castro
Revolution. These recent events, however, did not develop in a
vacuum. Their roots lie deep in the past, and the tools of historical
scholarship must be utilized in order to achieve an understanding
of present developments.

The basic resource of the historian is the written document.
This is the raw material which must be utilized to reconstruct
the past. A collection of documents constitutes a unique approach
to the past. The reader is allowed to sample the nectar of history
before it has been distilled, blended, and bottled by the historian.
If such a collection is to have value, however, it must be illumi-
nated by editorial commentary which provides explanations and
background material. This is especially true for a one-volume work,
which is of necessity highly selective. Such a book is a guided
tour through the sources of history. And like all guided tours, this
approach has certain virtues and vices. Much depends upon the
guide. All battlefields and no cathedrals—or vice-versa—would constitute a distorted tour. I have tried to avoid as many of the vices
as possible by including material from a variety of sources. The
object of this volume is to illuminate the broad spectrum of United
States-Cuban relations by including documents from the areas of
economic, ideological, military, and political relations.

Although this volume deals with Cuba, the documents included
will also provide some insight into the relations between the United
States and the rest of the Caribbean area. Cuba has held a prominent place in the foreign policy of the United States since the early
days of the North American republic, and in some respects Cuba

has been a testing ground for the Caribbean and Central American policies of the United States. The economic and strategic importance of Cuba has been a rather consistent element in the official interpretations of the national interest of the United States. In addition, United States relations with the rest of Latin America and with various European nations has influenced United States–Cuban relations. Thus, a case study of Cuba as a focal point for United States interests in the Caribbean provides insights which help to explain other aspects of United States foreign and domestic policies.

I have used a rather broad criteria in selecting the documents in this volume. Most of the documents are written, contemporary evidence. A few are included for their interpretive value, and as examples of various points of view. The editorial comment is not primarily designed to evaluate each document, but to explain its context and to give the reader additional background material. While this volume is not a narrative history, it may be read as a survey of United States–Cuban relations. The source used for each document is given in the heading, and I have not altered the grammar, spelling, punctuation, or wording of any document. Explanatory notes are included for purposes of identification of persons and explanation of events, where these are needed to add clarity. Most of the documents are excerpts. Omissions inside selections are indicated, but omissions at the beginning or end of the excerpt are only indicated in cases where the excerpt begins or ends within a paragraph. A bibliographic essay is included for those readers who may wish to delve more deeply into the subject.

I would like to express my thanks to the following persons for the assistance which they have rendered in the preparation of this work: to Professor Hugo Gibson for assistance in translation; to Dr. Nettie Lee Benson (Latin American Collection of the University of Texas Library), Mr. Fred Folmer (Assistant Director of the University of Texas Library), and Miss Helen Hargrave (Law School Library of the University of Texas) for their most helpful assistance in locating and making available various sources; to Mr. Warren Lussky for his cooperation in securing various books; and to Dr. E. B. Everitt for his support of scholarly activity. No listing of debts of gratitude would be complete without a special note of appreciation for my wife and co-laborer, Alberta. If it were not for her typing, editing, proofreading, and general encouragement this book would still be only an ambition. Both our tasks were made easier due to the understanding cooperation of our children, Robin and Robert.

CONTENTS

13

Documents

CHAPTER II

EMPIRES IN CONFLICT AND THE CUBAN PROTECTORATE (1879–1918)

Documents

Documents

CHAPTER III

THE NEW DOLLAR DIPLOMACY BETWEEN WAR AND DEPRESSION (1919–1932)

15

Documents

CHAPTER IV

New Deal Diplomacy and the Cuban Settlement

Documents

17

CHAPTER V

WHAT HAPPENED IN CUBA?

CHAPTER I

EXPANSION, COMMERCE, AND THE
"NATURAL LAW OF POLITICAL GRAVITATION"
(1783–1878)

> But there are laws of political as well as of physical gravitation;
> and if an apple severed by the tempest from its native tree cannot
> choose but fall to the ground, Cuba, forcibly disjoined from its own
> unnatural connection with Spain . . . can gravitate only towards
> the North American Union, which by the same law of nature can-
> not cast her off from its bosom.
>
> —JOHN QUINCY ADAMS (1823)

COMMERCE, strategic trade routes, control of the Gulf of Mexico,
and expansion of the slave-plantation system were all elements in
the early history of relations between Cuba and North America.
The first links in the ever-growing chain of relations were forged
by merchants and shippers in the years preceding the American
Revolution. By 1775, the Spanish island colony was steadily growing in significance both as a market and as a source of raw materials
for the expanding mercantile economy of the enterprising British
colonials from the north. The British had taken Havana during the
Seven Years War, but had returned it to Spain in 1763 in exchange
for the Floridas. This decision to expand the North American
empire, rather than the West Indies empire, was to be highly significant for the expansion of the future United States.

The Spaniards periodically tried to cut the growing economic
ties between Cuba and North America. This proved to be impossible due to the interaction of several factors: (1) Spanish involve-
ment in the American Revolution and the Napoleonic Wars; (2)
the revolutions throughout the Spanish empire in Latin America;
and (3) Spanish internal political and economic weakness. Cuba
became increasingly dependent on imports from the United States

after 1793, and after Spain opened Cuban ports to international trade in 1818 the United States replaced Great Britain as the leading supplier of Cuban imports. By 1820 over one-half of Cuba's trade was with the United States. Spain, however, continued to harass United States traders throughout the nineteenth century by means of various duties, regulations, and *sub-rosa* payoffs.

After 1800 Cuba became the focal point for a three-cornered power struggle over the Gulf of Mexico. France, Great Britain, and the United States were interested in the control of Cuba for both commercial and strategic reasons. To the United States, Cuba appeared as a vital element controlling access to the Gulf and influence over trade routes to the south. This latter factor became even more important in the 1840's due to the development of the isthmian route to California. All three powers at various times concocted schemes to take Cuba, but the very nature of the power conflict tended to assure a compromise of ambitions which left Cuba under Spanish control.

The sectional controversy in the United States further complicated the situation. The Southern states became more and more interested in the acquisition of Cuba for reasons of commerce, domestic politics, and fear of a British-sponsored slave abolition movement in Cuba. Some Northern commercial support for Cuban annexation developed, but the increasing cold war between slave and free state—which had been complicated by the Mexican cession—stymied the annexationist drive to the south.

During these years various Cuban groups were growing restless under Spanish control, and some tried to enlist the aid of the United States; even to the point of advocating annexation to the United States. Annexationist sentiment in Cuba had almost disappeared, however, when the Cubans launched their first major drive to end Spanish control in 1868. The Ten Years War did momentarily fan a few embers of annexationist sentiment in the United States, but the Grant Administration generally confined its activities to the protection of the steadily increasing economic interests of the United States. The war did resurrect, however, a fundamental question for United States policy. Who should control the future destiny of Cuba? The Cubans—or more precisely, which Cubans—the United States, Spain or some other European power? The question would again be faced when the second round started in 1895.

Spain opened Cuban ports to trade with the North Americans in 1778, but this war-inspired gesture was terminated on May 30, 1783, when the Captain-General of Cuba again closed the island ports. Oliver Pollock, the newly appointed Commercial Agent of the United States, was unaware of this when he loaded two ships with merchandise in New Orleans and departed for Cuba. Pollock was given a cold reception. He was accused of smuggling, his goods were seized, and he was not given official recognition by the Spanish government. Trade between the United States and Cuba was completely dependent on the caprice of the colonial officials and, as Pollock predicted, even this limited trade practically disappeared after 1783. All foreigners were expelled from Cuba in 1785, but Pollock was detained for a year until his debts were paid.

DOCUMENT 1. Oliver Pollock (Commercial Agent of the United States in Havana) to the Secretary of Foreign Affairs, December 14, 1783. (Quoted in Herminio Portell Vilá, *Historia de Cuba: En Sus Relaciones con los Estados Unidos y España*. 4 vols.; Havana, 1938. I: 109.)

. . . The definitive treaty is not yet arrived here, or have the government received any answer from the court of Spain respecting my commission (copy of which they sent there soon after my arrival here); in consequence, what little commerce is carried on here, with the United States, is done upon the greatest uncertainties, totally depending upon the caprice, avarice, and abuses of the government, intendant and their officers.

I sincerely hope it will be in the power of the United States to remedy this.

Notwithstanding the aversion and jealousy that appear by the officers of the government against our trade, yet necessity now and then obliges them to admit a vessel with provisions, but this itself is not done upon generous principles, as they gather the cream into their own pockets exclusive of the difficulties and delays our vessels are subjected to, and at the same time persuade the owners they are granting them great favors.

Commerce on those terms cannot possibly flourish, but on the contrary it must dwindle away into nothing.

•   •   •

The Louisiana Purchase of 1803 did not solve the Florida boundary question or terminate the territorial ambitions of Thomas Jefferson. West Florida—which Spain held and Jefferson claimed as part of Louisiana—East Florida, Cuba, and the northeastern provinces of New Spain were on his list of future acquisitions. Conflict in Europe had prompted Napoleon Bonaparte to sell Louisiana, and Jefferson believed that this conflict could be utilized to pry even more territory from the European empires in America. In 1805–6 the French indicated a willingness to act as brokers for the sale of the Floridas, but the secret negotiations produced no results. Jefferson feared that the Floridas and Cuba might fall into the hands of France or Great Britain, thus creating a threat to the Southern states and to the trade routes emanating from the Mississippi Valley. This fear was aggravated by the revolutions which broke out in Spanish America in 1808, and—in the case of Cuba— influenced United States policy for several decades. In addition, Jefferson's view that Cuba was practically a part of North America was to become another major theme in the country's foreign policy.

DOCUMENT 2. Thomas Jefferson to James Madison (Secretary of State), August 16, 1807. (Paul L. Ford, ed., *The Writings of Thomas Jefferson*. 10 vols. New York, 1898. IX: 124–25.)

. . . As soon as we have all the proofs of the western intrigues, let us make a remonstrance & demand of satisfaction, and, if Congress approves, we may in the same instant make reprisals on the Floridas, until satisfaction for that & for spoliations, and until a settlemt [sic] of [the] boundary. I had rather have war against Spain than not, if we go to war against England. Our southern defensive force can take the floridas, volunteers for a Mexican army will flock to our standard, and rich pablum will be offered to our privateers in the plunder of their commerce & coasts. Probably Cuba would add itself to our confederation. . . .

DOCUMENT 3. Thomas Jefferson to President James Madison, April 27, 1809. (H. A. Washington, ed., *The Writings of Thomas Jefferson*. 9 vols. Washington, D.C., 1853. V: 444–45.)

. . . He [Napoleon Bonaparte] ought the more to conciliate our good will, as we can be such an obstacle to the new career opening on him in the Spanish colonies. That he would give us the Floridas to withhold intercourse with the residue of those colonies, cannot be doubted. But that is no price; because they are ours in the first moment of the first war; and until a war they are of no particular necessity to us. But, although with difficulty, he will consent to our receiving Cuba into our Union, to prevent our aid to Mexico and the other provinces. That would be a price, and I would immediately erect a column on the southernmost limit of Cuba, and inscribe on it a *ne plus ultra*[1] as to us in that direction. We should then have only to include the north in our Confederacy, which would be of course in the first war, and we should have such an empire for liberty as she has never surveyed since the creation; and I am persuaded no constitution was ever before so well calculated as ours for extensive empire and self-government. . . . It will be objected to our receiving Cuba, that no limit can then be drawn to our future acquisitions. Cuba can be defended by us without a navy, and this develops the principle which ought to limit our views. Nothing should ever be accepted which would require a navy to defend it.

•   •   •

The turmoil produced by the independence movement in Latin America made Cuba a focal point for conflict between France, Britain, and the United States. Some Creole planters in Cuba were interested in the idea of annexation to the United States since the Cuban liberals were advocating autonomy and the abolition of slavery. Advances were made to the United States in 1811, and these were revived in 1822. Opinion in the United States concerning annexation was mixed. Those who favored such a move represented diverse economic and political interests. John C. Calhoun and Charles Jared Ingersoll—one of the vice-presidents of the Pennsylvania Society for the Promotion of Manufactures—both supported annexation in 1822–23. Few, if any, of the pro-annexationists were willing to go to war to win Cuba, and the major problem became one of keeping Cuba free from British or French control. Influential Americans, such as John Quincy Adams and Thomas Jefferson, feared French interference and the possibility that Britain would demand Cuba as her price for supporting Spain against France.

Under these circumstances James Monroe, Jefferson, Adams, and Calhoun agreed that the most feasible policy was for weak Spain to retain the island. On several occasions the United States sought support from various European countries for its "No Transfer" policy. In 1823 the British Foreign Secretary proposed a mutual "self-denying" pledge—in regard to both Cuba and Mexico—as part of a joint declaration against European interference in Latin America. Secretary of State Adams did not want to enter into any agreement which would prevent the United States from annexing Cuba in the future. His views prevailed, and President Monroe delivered a unilateral statement of American policy in December 1823. Cuba was not the only, or even the major, factor behind what became known as the Monroe Doctrine. The struggle for influence in Latin America was an important factor, and Cuba continued to be a focal point in this struggle. The policy decisions behind the Monroe Doctrine were based, in part, on the belief that the United States should become the dominant power in the Caribbean, and these decisions became the cornerstone of the Cuban policy of the United States.

DOCUMENT 4.   Entry of February 7, 1823, *Diary of Charles Jared Ingersoll.* (John Bassett Moore, ed., *A Digest of International Law.* 8 vols. Washington, D.C., 1906. I: 582–83.)

I had some interesting conversation to-day with Mr. Poinsett[2] concerning . . . Cuba, where he has lately been on public service. . . . Cuba, he says, is ripe for union with the U.S. whenever Spain is forced to change her constitution. Even the old Spaniards, and the Creoles to a man—he had direct communications to this effect with many of their most influential characters. They do not, however, desire any change until Spain compels it by some radical alterations in her present constitution. Whenever she does Cuba will ask for our protection and for admission into the Union. If we reject them they will then apply to England. But at present, Mr. P. says, they are extremely averse to her superintendence. There have been two English agents at Havana for some time. Cuba has had an agent here in communication with our Government. His name is Morales.

It is a very momentous measure for the decision of this country. Much may be said against it. But I have long tho't that whenever

Cuba presents herself; without any forcing or manoeuvring on our part, we must e'en take the goods the Gods provide us. The Western States are all anxiety for it. To them Cuba in British hands would be intolerable. The Southern States have no objection. The middle and east would consent, tho' the latter perhaps not freely, as it would add immensely to a preponderance which they see with jealousy and dread already.

DOCUMENT 5. Secretary of State John Quincy Adams to Hugh Nelson (Minister to Spain), April 28, 1823. (W. C. Ford, ed., *The Writings of John Quincy Adams*. 7 vols. New York, 1913–17. VII: 372–79.)

Whatever may be the issue of this war, as between those two European powers [Spain and France], it may be taken for granted that the domination of Spain upon the American continents, North and South, is irrecoverably gone. But the islands of Cuba and of Porto Rico still remain nominally and so far really dependent upon her that she yet possesses the power of transferring her own domination over them, together with the possession of them, to others. These islands, from their local position, are natural appendages to the North American continent; and one of them, Cuba, almost in sight of our shores, from a multitude of considerations has become an object of transcendent importance to the political and commercial interests of our Union. Its commanding position with reference to the Gulf of Mexico and the West India seas; the character of its population; its situation midway between our southern coast and the island of San Domingo; its safe and capacious harbor of the Havana, fronting a long line of our shores destitute of the same advantage; the nature of its productions and of its wants, furnishing the supplies and needing the return of a commerce immensely profitable and mutually beneficial; give it an importance in the sum of our national interests, with which that of no other foreign territory can be compared, and little inferior to that which binds the different members of this Union together.

Such indeed are, between the interests of that island and of this country, the geographical, commercial, moral, and political relations, formed by nature, gathering in the process of time, and even now verging to maturity, that in looking forward to the probable course of events for the short period of half a century, it is scarcely possible to resist the conviction that the annexation of Cuba to our federal republic will be indispensable to the con-

tinuance and integrity of the Union itself. It is obvious however
that for this event we are not yet prepared. Numerous and formidable objections to the extension of our territorial dominations
beyond the sea present themselves to the first contemplation of
the subject. Obstacles to the system of policy by which it alone
can be compassed and maintained are to be foreseen and sur-
mounted, both from at home and abroad. But there are laws of
political as well as of physical gravitation; and if an apple severed
by the tempest from its native tree cannot choose but fall to the
ground, Cuba, forcibly disjoined from its own unnatural connection with Spain, and incapable of self-support, can gravitate only
towards the North American Union, which by the same law of
nature cannot cast her off from its bosom. . . .

Hitherto the wishes of this government have been that the
connection between Cuba and Spain should continue as it has
existed for several years. These wishes are known to the principal
inhabitants of the island, and instructions, copies of which are now
furnished you, were some months since transmitted to Mr. Forsyth,
authorizing him in a suitable manner to communicate them to the
Spanish government. These wishes still continue, so far as they
can be indulged with a rational foresight of events beyond our
control, but for which it is our duty to be prepared. If a government is to be imposed by foreign violence upon the Spanish nation,
and the liberties which they have assisted by their constitution are
to be crushed, it is neither to be expected nor desired that the
people of Cuba, far from the reach of the oppressors of Spain,
should submit to be governed by them. Should the cause of Spain
herself issue more propitiously than from its present prospects
can be anticipated, it is obvious that the trial through which she
must pass at home, and the final loss of *all* her dominions on the
American continents, will leave her unable to extend to the island
of Cuba that protection necessary for its internal security and its
outward defence.

Great Britain has formally withdrawn from the councils of the
European Alliance in regard to Spain. She disapproves the war
which they have sanctioned, and which is undertaken by France:
and she avows her determination to defend Portugal against the
application of the principles upon which the invasion of Spain
raises its only pretence of right.[3] To the war as it commences, she
has declared her intention of remaining neutral; but the spirit of
the British nation is so strongly and with so much unanimity pronounced against France, their interests are so deeply involved in
the issue, their national resentments and jealousies will be so

forcibly stimulated by the progress of the war, whatever it may be, that unless the conflict should be as short and the issue as decisive as that of which Italy was recently the scene, it is scarcely possible that the neutrality of Great Britain should be long maintained. The prospect is that she will be soon engaged on the side of Spain; but in making common cause with her, it is not to be supposed that she will yield her assistance upon principles altogether disinterested and gratuitous. As the price of her alliance the two remaining islands of Spain in the West Indies present objects no longer of much possible value or benefit to Spain, but of such importance to Great Britain, that it is impossible to suppose her indifferent to the acquisition of them.

The motives of Great Britain for desiring the possession of Cuba are so obvious, especially since the independence of Mexico, and the annexation of the Floridas to our Union; the internal condition of the island since the recent Spanish revolution, and the possibility of its continued dependence upon Spain, have been so precarious; the want of protection there; the power of affording it possessed by Great Britain, and the necessities of Spain to secure, by some equivalent, the support of Great Britain for herself; have formed a remarkable concurrence of predispositions to the transfer of Cuba; and during the last two years rumors have been multiplied, that it was already consummated. . . .

The transfer of Cuba to Great Britain would be an event unpropitious to the interests of this Union. This opinion is so generally entertained, that even the groundless rumors that it was about to be accomplished, which have spread abroad and are still teeming, may be traced to the deep and almost universal feeling of aversion to it, and to the alarm which the mere probability of its occurance has stimulated. The question both of our right and our power to prevent it, if necessary, by force, already obtrudes itself upon our councils, and the administration is called upon, in the performance of its duties to the nation, at least to use all the means within its competency to guard against and forefend it.

DOCUMENT 6.   Thomas Jefferson to James Monroe, June 11, 1823. (Ford, *The Writings of Thomas Jefferson.* X: 257–58.)

. . . With Europe we have few occasions of collision, and these, with a little prudence and forbearance, may be generally accommodated. Of the brethren of our own hemisphere, none are yet, or for an age to come will be, in a shape, condition, or disposition to war against us. And the foothold which the nations of Europe had in either America, is slipping from under them, so that we shall soon be rid of their neighborhood. Cuba alone seems at present to hold up a speck of war to us. Its possession by Great Britain would indeed be a great calamity to us. Could we induce her to join us in guaranteeing its independence against all the world, *except* Spain, it would be nearly as valuable to us as if it were our own. But should she take it, I would not immediately go to war for it; because the first war on other accounts will give it to us; or the island will give itself to us, when able to do so.. . .

DOCUMENT 7.   Thomas Jefferson to James Monroe, October 24, 1823. (Ford, *The Writings of Thomas Jefferson*. X: 278–79.)

But we have first to ask ourselves a question. Do we wish to acquire to our own confederacy any one or more of the Spanish provinces? I candidly confess, that I have ever looked on Cuba as the most interesting addition which could ever be made to our system of States. The control which, with Florida Point, this island would give us over the Gulf of Mexico, and the countries and isthmus bordering on it, as well as all those whose waters flow into it, would fill up the measure of our political well-being. Yet, as I am sensible that this can never be obtained, even with her own consent, but by war; and its independence, which is our second interest, (and especially its independence of England,) can be secured without it, I have no hesitation in abandoning my first wish to future chances, and accepting its independence, with peace and the friendship of England, rather than its association, at the expense of war and her enmity.

I could honestly, therefore, join in the declaration proposed,[4] that we aim not at the acquisition of any of those possessions, that we will not stand in the way of any amicable arrangement between them and the mother country; but that we will oppose, with all our means, the forcible interposition of any other power, as auxiliary, stipendiary, or under any other form or pretext, and most especially, their transfer to any power by conquest, cession or acquisition in any other way.. . .

DOCUMENT 8.   Diary Entry of November 7, 1823. (Charles Francis Adams, ed., *Memoirs of John Quincy Adams*. 12 vols. Philadelphia, 1875. VI: 177–79.)

Washington, November 7th. Cabinet Meeting at the President's from half-past one till four. Mr. Calhoun, Secretary of War, and Mr. Southard, Secretary of the Navy, present. The subject for consideration was, the confidential proposals of the British Secretary of State, George Canning, to R. Rush, and the correspondence between them relating to the projects of the Holy Alliance upon South America. There was much conversation, without coming to any definite point. The object of Canning appears to have been to obtain some public pledge from the Government of the United States, ostensibly against the forcible interference of the Holy Alliance between Spain and South America; but really or especially against the acquisition to the United States themselves of any part of the Spanish-American possessions.

Mr. Calhoun inclined to giving a discretionary power to Mr. Rush to join in a declaration against the interference of the Holy Allies, if necessary, even if it should pledge us not to take Cuba or the province of Texas; because the power of Great Britain being greater than ours to *seize* upon them, we should get the advantage of obtaining from her the same declaration we should make ourselves.

I thought the cases not parallel. We have no intention of seizing either Texas or Cuba. But the inhabitants of either or both may exercise their primitive rights, and solicit a union with us. They will certainly do no such thing to Great Britain. By joining with her, therefore, in her proposed declaration, we give her a substantial and perhaps inconvenient pledge against ourselves, and really obtain nothing in return. Without entering now into the enquiry of the expediency of our annexing Texas or Cuba to our Union, we should at least keep ourselves free to act as emergencies may arise, and not tie ourselves down to any principle which might immediately afterwards be brought to bear against ourselves.

•　　•　　•

After negotiating several bilateral treaties of alliance between Gran Colombia and several other new Latin American republics, Simón Bolívar proposed that a congress be held at Panama in 1826 to consider a number of questions. The formal agenda did not include the proposed Mexican-Colombian expedition to free Cuba and Puerto Rico, but it was generally known that the subject would be considered. Rumors concerning the expedition had been in the air since 1822, and the United States government had been working to block any such effort. In 1825 Secretary of State Henry

Clay tried to get Russia, Great Britain, and France to pressure Spain into making peace with her former colonies in order to prevent an invasion of Cuba. This effort failed, as did the British attempt to get the United States to enter into a joint agreement with Britain and France to guarantee Spanish control of Cuba.

After consultation with his cabinet, John Quincy Adams decided to send representatives to the Panama Congress. The threat to Spanish control of Cuba was one factor involved in this decision. In December 1825 he asked Congress to confirm his appointments and to make an appropriation for expenses. Some of the opponents of the Adams Administration took up the cudgels for a neutrality policy in the Caribbean in order to block United States participation at Panama. These supporters of Andrew Jackson, still angry as a result of the election of 1824, were determined to embarrass the administration at all costs. As part of their strategy the Jacksonites in the House proposed an amendment to the appropriations resolution which stated in part:

> The Ministers who may be sent shall attend at the said Congress in a diplomatic character merely; and ought not to be authorized to discuss, consider, or consult, upon any proposition of alliance, offensive or defensive, between this country and any of the Spanish American Governments, or any stipulation, compact, or declaration, binding the United States in any way, or to any extent, to resist interference from abroad ...; or any measure which shall commit the present or future neutral rights or duties of these United States, either as may regard European nations, or between the several States of Mexico and South America....[5]

An addition to this amendment would have prevented the United States from making any pledge to enforce Monroe's 1823 statement on future European colonization in the hemisphere.

Daniel Webster rose to attack this amendment (Document 9), and other attempts to hamper the administration's Latin American policy. Congress finally approved Adams' requests, but for a variety of reasons the American delegates did not arrive at Panama. In the instructions prepared for the delegates, Secretary of State Henry Clay expressed opposition to Cuban independence and to its annexation by any Spanish American country. As it turned out, the Panama Congress did not officially deliberate on Cuba, and

the plans for a joint expedition were abandoned by Mexico and
Colombia.

DOCUMENT 9. Speech: Upon the Panama Mission; Delivered in the House of Representatives of the United States,
April, 1826. (Daniel Webster, *Speeches and Forensic Arguments*. 2 vols. Boston, 1843. I: 330, 342–46.)

. . . Look, sir, to the very case of Cuba—the most delicate, and
vastly the most important point in all our foreign relations. Do
gentlemen think they exhibit skill or statesmanship, in laying such
restraints as they propose on our ministers, in regard to this subject, among others? It has been made matter of complaint, that the
Executive has not used, already, a more decisive tone towards
Mexico and Colombia, in regard to their designs on this Island.
Pray, sir, what tone could be taken, under these instructions? Not
one word—not one single word could be said on the subject. If
asked whether the United States would consent to the occupation
of that Island by those republics, or to its transfer by Spain to a
European power; or whether we should resist such occupation or
such transfer, what could they say? "That is a matter we cannot
discuss, and cannot consider—it would commit our neutral relations
—we are not at liberty to express the sentiments of our Government
on the subject: we have nothing at all to say." Is this, sir, what
gentlemen wish, or what they would recommend?

I now proceed, Mr. Chairman, to a few remarks on the subject
of Cuba, the most important point of our foreign relations. It is
the hinge on which interesting events may possibly turn. I pray
gentlemen to review their opinions on this subject before they fully
commit themselves. I understood the honorable member from South
Carolina to say, that if Spain chose to transfer this Island to any
power in Europe, she had a right to do so, and we could not interfere to prevent it. Sir, this is a delicate subject. I hardly feel competent to treat it as it deserves; and I am not quite willing to state
here all that I think about it. I must, however, dissent from the
opinion of the gentleman from South Carolina. The right of nations,
on subjects of this kind, are necessarily very much modified by circumstances. Because England or France could not rightfully complain of the transfer of Florida to us, it by no means follows, as the
gentleman supposes, that we could not complain of the cession of
Cuba to one of them. The plain difference is, that the transfer of

Florida to us was not dangerous to the safety of either of those nations, nor fatal to any of their great and essential interests. Proximity of position, neighborhood, whatever arguments the power of injuring and annoying, very properly belong to the consideration of all cases of this kind. The greater or less facility of access itself is of consideration in such questions, because it brings, or may bring, weighty consequences with it. It justifies, for these reasons, and on these grounds, what otherwise might never be thought of. By negotiation with a foreign power, Mr. Jefferson obtained a province. Without any alteration of our Constitution, we have made it part of the United States, and its Senators and Representatives, now coming from several States, are here among us. Now, sir, if, instead of being Louisiana, this had been one of the provinces of Spain proper, or one of her South American colonies, he must have been a madman, that should have proposed such an acquisition. A high conviction of its convenience, arising from proximity, and from close natural connexion, alone reconciled the country to the measure. Considerations of the same sort have weight in other cases.

An honorable member from Kentuckey, (Mr. Wickliffe,) argues, that although we might rightfully prevent another power from taking Cuba from Spain, by force, yet if Spain should choose to make the voluntary transfer, we should have no right whatever to interfere. Sir, this is a distinction without a difference. If we are likely to have contention about Cuba, let us first well consider what our rights are, and not commit ourselves. And, sir, if we have any right to interfere at all, it applies as well to the case of a peaceable, as to that of a forcible, transfer. If nations be at war, we are not judges of the question of right, in that war; we must acknowledge, in both parties, the mutual right of attack, and the mutual right of conquest. It is not for us to set bounds to their belligerant operations, so long as they do not affect ourselves. Our right to interfere, sir, in any such case, is but the exercise of the right of reasonable and necessary self-defence. It is a high and delicate exercise of that right; one not to be made but on grounds of strong and manifest reason, justice, and necessity. The real question is, whether the possession of Cuba by a great maritime power of Europe, would seriously endanger our own immediate security, or our essential interests. . . .

. . . It is not a slight injury to our interest; it is not even a great inconvenience, that makes out a case. There must be danger to our security, or danger, manifest and imminent danger, to our essential rights, and our essential interests. Now, sir, let us look at Cuba. I need hardly refer to its present amount of commercial connexion with the United States. Our statistical tables, I presume, would show us, that our commerce with the Havana alone is more in amount than our whole commercial intercourse with France and all her dependencies. But this is but one part of the case, and not the most important. Cuba, as is well said in the report of the Committee of Foreign Affairs, is placed in the mouth of the Mississippi. Its occupation by a strong maritime power would be felt, in the first moment of hostility, as far up the Mississippi and the Missouri, as our population extends. It is the commanding point of the Gulf of Mexico. See, too, how it lies in the very line of our coast wise traffic; interposed in the very highway between New York and New Orleans.

╱   ╱   ╱   ╱   ╱

But, sir, while some gentlemen have maintained, that on the subject of a transfer to any of the European powers, the President has said too much, others insist that on that of the Islands being occupied by Mexico or Colombia, he has said and done too little. I presume, sir, for my own part, that the strongest language has been directed to the source of greatest danger. Heretofore that danger was, doubtless, greatest, which was apprehended from a voluntary transfer. . . .

╱   ╱   ╱   ╱   ╱

Sir, what are the facts? This government saw fit to invite the Emperor of Russia to use his endeavors to bring Spain to treat of peace with her revolted colonies. Russia was addressed on this occasion as the friend of Spain; and, of course, every argument which it was thought might have influence, or ought to have influence, either on Russia or Spain, was suggested in the correspondence. Among other things, the probable loss to Spain, of Cuba and Porto Rico, was urged; and the question was asked, how it was, or could be, expected by Spain, that the United States could interfere, to prevent Mexico and Colombia from taking those Islands from her, since she was their enemy, in a public war, and since she pertinaciously, and unreasonably, as we think, insists on maintaining the war; and since these Islands offered an obvious object of attack? . . . We urged the proper motives to both parties. To Spain we urged the probable loss of Cuba; we showed her the dangers of its capture by the new States; and we asked her to inform us on what ground it was, that we could interfere to prevent such capture, since she was at war with these states, and they had an unquestionable right to attack her in any of her territories; and especially she was asked, how she could expect good offices from us, on this occasion, since she fully understood our opinion to be, that she was persisting in the war without, or beyond, all reason, and with a sort of desperation. This was the appeal made to the good sense of Spain, through Russia. But, soon afterwards, having reason to suspect that Colombia and Mexico were actually preparing to attack Cuba, and knowing that such an event would most seriously affect us, our government remonstrated against such meditated attack, and to the present time it has not been made. In all this, who sees anything either improper or inconsistent? For myself, I think the course pursued showed a watchful regard to our own interest, and is wholly free from any imputation, either of impropriety, or inconsistency.

•   •   •

With the major competing powers in tacit agreement concerning Spanish control of Cuba, a period of relative calm ensued after 1826. In 1830 Spain officially recognized the first Consul of the United States in Cuba—William Shaler—and for a time Americans enjoyed a privileged status. Immigrants from the United States invested in the sugar industry, American steam and railroad technology came to the island, and Cuban exports to the United States increased. Spain, however, initiated a tariff war in 1832, and trade between Cuba and the United States was curtailed. In addition, a law was enacted prohibiting Cuban men from going to the United States for their education. After 1835, however, shipowners from the United States took over most of the slave trade with Cuba; a development aided by the mutually profitable cooperation of Consul Nicholas P. Trist and Captain-General Miguel Tacón.

DOCUMENT 10.   Edward Livingston (Secretary of State) to William Shaler (Consul at Havana), September 1, 1832. (W. R. Manning, *Diplomatic Correspondence of the United States: Inter-American Affairs: 1831–1860*. 12 vols. Washington, D. C., 1939. XI 6–7.)[6]

It would be very important to procure a repeal or relaxation of the prohibition to send young men to the United States for their education. It is, I suppose, a measure of the local authorities; and as religion may have entered into the measure, it might in some

sort, perhaps, be counteracted by taking with you the advertise-
ments of the different Catholic Colleges in the United States, and
other publications relating to their situation, and the course of
studies to be pursued in them. I will request Mr. Brent to furnish
you with such as are within his reach.

The great objects of our Government in relation to Cuba, are,
a free and untrammeled trade, on its present footing, eased of the
discriminating duties,— to preserve it in the hands of Spain, even
at the expense of a war,— and only in the event of finding that impossible, to look to its annexation to our confederacy. To this last,
there are many objections, not the least of which is the supposed
want of information in the people to understand the principles, or
practice the reforms, of a Republican Government. This subject
is one of so much importance, and has so many bearings on the
vital interests of our country, that I must defer a further investigation of it until we meet, which I hope may be on your return.

•   •   •

From the early 1820's to the mid-1840's the United States government rather consistently supported Spanish control of Cuba,
and cooperated with Spain against Cuban internal revolts. In this
respect the administrations of John Quincy Adams, Andrew Jackson, Martin Van Buren, and John Tyler followed the same policy
toward Cuba. This situation changed in the 1840's when the
Democratic Party became the aggressive advocate of territorial
expansion. Stimulated by a variety of factors which appealed to
interests in all sections, the Democrats renewed the drive for
empire which resulted in the push to the Pacific. With this accomplished, President James K. Polk turned to Cuba in 1848.

The growing entanglement of territorial expansion with sectional antagonisms, however, acted to reduce the aggressiveness of
the push into the Caribbean. The Polk Administration offered Spain
$100 million for Cuba, but made no threat to use force to take it.
The North was becoming increasingly critical toward the addition
of new slave states, and the Whig Party tended to reflect this view.
This sectional and party conflict produced a domestic crisis which
was temporarily resolved by the Compromise of 1850. The Whig
administration of Zachary Taylor had withdrawn the purchase offer
a year earlier, and had generally reverted to the policy of the 1820's
and 1830's in regard to Spanish control of Cuba.

DOCUMENT 11.   Diary of James K. Polk—Entries of May 10,
May 30, and June 17, 1848. (Allan Nevins, ed., *Polk: The
Diary of a President.* New York, 1952: Pp. 321, 326, 327–
28.)[7]

Wednesday, 10th May, 1848.   I closed my doors at twelve
o'clock. Shortly after that hour Senator Douglas of Illinois called
with John O'Sullivan, Esq., of New York.[8] Their business with me
was to urge that I take early measures with a view to the purchase
of the island of Cuba from Spain. I heard their views but deemed
it prudent to express no opinion on the subject. Mr. O'Sullivan read
to me and left with me a paper embodying his views in favor of
the measure. Though I expressed no opinion to them I am decidedly in favor of purchasing Cuba and making it one of the States
of the Union.

✓   ✓   ✓   ✓   ✓

Tuesday, 30th May, 1848.   I informed the Cabinet today that I
desired to invite their attention, not for the purpose of immediate
decision, but for consideration, to the important question whether
a proposition should not be made to Spain to purchase the island of
Cuba. The subject was freely discussed. The great importance of
the island to the United States, and the danger, if we did not
acquire it, that it might fall into the hands of Great Britain, were
considered. Mr. Walker, the Secretary of the Treasury, was earnestly in favor of making the attempt to purchase it, and was willing
to pay one hundred millions of dollars for it. Mr. Mason, the Secretary of the Navy, concurred in opinion with Mr. Walker. Mr.
Johnson, the Postmaster-General, had objections to incorporating
the Spanish population of Cuba into our Union, and did not seem
to favor the idea of purchasing it. Mr. Buchanan, the Secretary of
State, expressed a general wish to acquire Cuba, but thought there
were objections to making the attempt at this time. He feared if it
became known that such a step was contemplated, that it might act
prejudicially to the Democratic party in the next Presidential election. He said he would reflect on the subject and be prepared to
give me his advice upon the subject hereafter. I intimated my
strong conviction that the effort should be made without delay to
purchase the island.

✓   ✓   ✓   ✓   ✓

Saturday, 17th June, 1848.   The Cabinet met at the usual hour;
all the members present. Mr. Buchanan read the despatch to Mr.

Saunders, United States Minister to Spain, on the subject of the purchase of Cuba, which he prepared in pursuance of the decision made at a previous Cabinet meeting (see this diary of the 9th June, 1848). It was an able and well-written despatch. It authorized Mr. Saunders to inform the Spanish Minister of Foreign Affairs of the Secretary of State's despatch to the United States consul at Havana for the purpose of satisfying him of the good faith of the United States towards Spain. He was authorized to inform him in conversation that the United States could never permit Cuba to pass into the hands of any European Power and that whilst the Island remained a possession of Spain the United States would in no way interfere with it. He was authorized, after having done this, to signify to him in a detailed manner that the United States would be willing to purchase the Island if it would be agreeable to Spain to cede it for a pecuniary consideration to the United States. In his confidential instructions he was authorized to stipulate to pay one hundred millions of dollars in convenient installments for the island. He was furnished with full powers to make a treaty to this effect. The whole matter was profoundly confidential, and the knowledge of it was to be confined to the Cabinet alone. I will not even make known the result of the Cabinet deliberation on the subject to Mr. J. L. O'Sullivan of New York, who first suggested to me the idea of purchasing Cuba, and who takes much interest in the subject.

DOCUMENT 12. James Buchanan (Secretary of State) to Romulus M. Saunders (Minister to Spain), June 17, 1848. (Manning, *Inter-American Affairs: 1831–1860*. XI: 54–59, 61–64.)

By direction of the President, I now call your attention to the present condition and future prospects of Cuba. The fate of this Island must ever be deeply interesting to the people of the United States. We are content that it shall continue to be a Colony of Spain. Whilst in her possession we have nothing to apprehend. Besides, we are bound to her by the ties of ancient friendship, and we sincerely desire to render these perpetual.

But we can never consent that this Island shall become a Colony of any other European power. In the possession of Great Britain or any strong naval power, it might prove ruinous both to our domestic and foreign commerce, and even endanger the Union of the States. The highest and first duty of every independent nation is to provide for its own safety: and acting upon this principle we should be compelled to resist the acquisition of Cuba by any powerful maritime State with all the means which Providence has placed at our command.

Cuba is almost within sight of the coast of Florida. Situated between that State and the Peninsula of Yucatan and possessing the deep, capacious and impregnable fortified harbor of the Havana, if this Island were under the domination of Great Britain, she could command both the inlets to the Gulf of Mexico. She would thus be enabled in time of war effectively to blockade the mouth of the Mississippi and to deprive all the western States of this Union, as well as those within the Gulf, teeming as they are with an industrious and enterprising population, of a foreign market for their immense productions. But this is not the worst. She could, also destroy the commerce by sea between our ports on the Gulf and our Atlantic ports;— a commerce of nearly as great a value as the whole of our foreign trade.

Is there any reason to believe that Great Britain desires to acquire the Island of Cuba?

We know that it has been her uniform policy throughout her past history to seize upon every valuable commercial point throughout the world whenever circumstances have placed this in her power. And what point so valuable as the Island of Cuba? The United States are the chief commercial rival of Great Britain. Our tonnage at the present moment is nearly equal to hers: and it will be greater within a brief period, if nothing should occur to arrest our progress. Of what vast importance would it then be to her to obtain the possession of an Island from which she could at any time destroy a very large proportion both of our foreign and coasting trade. Besides, she well knows that if Cuba were in our possession, her West India Islands would be rendered comparatively valueless. From the extent and fertility of this Island and from the energy and industry of our people, we should soon be able to supply the markets of the world with tropical productions at a cheaper rate than these could be raised in any of her possessions.

The disposition of Great Britain to extend her dominion over the most important commercial positions of the globe has been clearly manifested on a recent occasion. . . .

    ✔   ✔   ✔   ✔   ✔

The northern boundary of the Belize, is only about two hundred miles from the western extremity of Cuba: and if she could acquire the sovereignty over this Island, in addition to what she has already accomplished and is now struggling to obtain along the Coasts of the Caribbean Sea, our commerce on that Sea, as well as in the Gulf, would be placed at her mercy.

It must be admitted that Great Britain has a much more plausible pretext for acquiring possession of the Island of Cuba than she had, as the assumed protector of the Kingdom of Mosquito, for seizing upon the Coasts of the Caribbean Sea....[9]

✓   ✓   ✓   ✓   ✓

But let me present another view of the subject. If Cuba were annexed to the United States, we should not only be relieved from the apprehensions which we can never cease to feel for our own safety and the security of our commerce whilst it shall remain in its present condition; but human foresight cannot anticipate the beneficial consequences which would result to every portion of our Union. This can never become a local question.

1. With suitable fortifications at the Tortugas, and in possession of the strongly fortified harbor of Habana as a naval station on the opposite Coast of Cuba, we could command the outlet of the Gulf of Mexico between the Peninsula of Florida and that Island. This would afford ample security both to the foreign and coasting trade of the Western and Southern States which seek a market for their surplus productions through the Ports on the Gulf.

2. Under the Government of the United States, Cuba would become the richest and most fertile Island of the same extent throughout the world. . . .

✓   ✓   ✓   ✓   ✓

Were Cuba a portion of the United States it would be difficult to estimate the amount of bread-stuffs, rice, cotton and other agricultural, as well as manufacturing and mechanical productions;—of lumber, of the products of our fisheries and of other articles, which would find a market in that Island, in exchange for their coffee, sugar, tobacco and other productions. This would go on, increasing with the increase of its population and the development of its resources: and all portions of the Union would be benefitted by the trade.

Desirable, however, as the possession of this Island may be to the United States, we would not acquire it except by the free consent of Spain. Any acquisition not sanctioned by justice and honor, would be too dearly purchased. Whilst such is the determination of the President, it is supposed, that the present relations between Cuba and Spain might incline the Spanish Government to cede the Island to the United States, upon the payment of a fair and full consideration. We have received information from various

sources, both official and unofficial, that among the Creoles of
Cuba, there has long existed a deep rooted hostility to Spanish
domination. The revolutions which are rapidly succeeding each
other throughout the world, have inspired the Cubans with an
ardent and irrepressible desire to achieve their independence. Indeed, we are informed by the Consul of the United States at the
Havana that "there appears every probability that the Island will
soon be in a State of civil war." He, also, states, that "efforts are
now being made to raise money for that purpose in the United
States, and there will be attempts to induce a few of the volunteer
regiments now in Mexico to obtain their discharge and join the
Revolution."

I need scarcely inform you that the Government of the United
States has had no agency whatever in exciting the spirit of dis-
affection among the Cubans. Very far from it. A short time after we
received this information from our Consul, I addressed a despatch
to him, of which I transmit you a copy, dated on the 9th Instant,
from which you will perceive that I have warned him to keep a
watchful guard both upon his words and actions, so as to avoid
even the least suspicion that he had encouraged the Cubans to rise
in insurrection against the Spanish Government. I stated, also that
the relations between Spain and the United States had long been
of the most friendly character; and both honor and duty required
that we should take no part in the struggle which he seemed to
think was impending.

I informed him that it would certainly "become the duty of this
Government to use all proper means to prevent any of our volunteer regiments, now in Mexico, from violating the neutrality of
the country by joining in the proposed civil war of the Cubans
against Spain."

Since the date of my despatch to him, this duty had been
performed. . . .

ſ   ſ   ſ   ſ   ſ

Upon the whole, the President would not hesitate to stipulate
for the payment of one hundred millions of dollars, in convenient
installments, for a cession of the Island of Cuba, if it could not be
procured for a less sum.

The apprehensions which existed for many years after the
origin of this Government, that the extension of our federal system
would endanger the Union, seem to have passed away. Experience
has proved that this system of confederated Republics, under
which the Federal Government has charge of the interests com-

mon to the whole, whilst local Governments watch over the concerns of the respective States, is capable of almost indefinite extension, with increasing strength. This, however, is always subject to the qualification that the mass of the population must be of our own race, or must have been educated in the school of civil and religious liberty. With this qualification, the more we increase the number of confederated States, the greater will be the strength and security of the Union; because the more dependent for their mutual interests will the several parts be upon the whole and the whole upon the several parts.

✓   ✓   ✓   ✓   ✓

But the acquisition of Cuba would greatly strengthen our bond of Union. Its possession would secure to all the States within the valley of the Mississippi and the Gulf of Mexico, free access to the ocean; but this security could only be preserved whilst the ship-building and navigating States of the Atlantic shall furnish a navy sufficient to keep open the outlets from the Gulf to the Ocean. Cuba, justly appreciating the advantages of annexation, is now ready to rush into our arms. Once admitted, she would be entirely dependent for her prosperity, and even existence, upon her connexion with the Union; whilst the rapidly increasing trade between her and the other States, would shed its benefits and its blessings over the whole. Such a state of mutual dependence, resulting from the very nature of things, the world has never witnessed. This is what will insure the perpetuity of our Union.

With all these considerations in view, the President believes that the crisis has arrived when an effort should be made to purchase the Island of Cuba from Spain, and he has determined to entrust you with the performance of this most delicate and important duty. The attempt should be made, in the first instance, in a confidential conversation with the Spanish Minister for Foreign Affairs. A written offer might produce an absolute refusal in writing, which would embarrass us, hereafter, in the acquisition of the Island. . . .

✓   ✓   ✓   ✓   ✓

The President would be willing to stipulate for the payment of one hundred millions of dollars for the Island, and its dependencies, in ten equal annual installments. This, however, is the maximum price: and if Spain should be willing to sell, you will use your best efforts to purchase it at a rate as much below that sum as practicable. In case you should be able to conclude a Treaty, you may adopt as your model, so far as the same may be applicable, the two Conventions of April 30th, 1803, between France and the United States for the sale and purchase of Louisiana. The Seventh and Eighth Articles of the first of these Conventions, ought, if possible, to be omitted; still if this should be indispensable to the accomplishment of the object, articles similar to them may be retained.[10]

I transmit you a Full Power to conclude such a Treaty.

You will be careful to make a full and faithful report to this Department of all the conversations and proceedings on this subject between yourself and the Spanish Minister of Foreign Affairs.

Should you succeed in accomplishing the object, you will associate your name with a most important and beneficial measure for the glory and prosperity of your country.

DOCUMENT 13.   John M. Clayton (Secretary of State) to Daniel M. Barringer (Minister to Spain), August 2, 1849. (Manning, *Inter-American Affairs: 1831–1860*. XI: 69–70.)

. . . The President cannot comprehend or appreciate the motives or expediency of openly declaring to Spain that the whole power of the United States, would be employed to prevent the occupation in whole or in part of Cuba, from passing into other hands; because he has reason to believe that this declaration on our part has led to counter-declarations, being made to Spain, against us, of a similar character, by other interested powers.—

Whilst this Government is resolutely determined that the Island of Cuba, shall never be ceded by Spain to any other power than the United States, it does not desire, in future, to utter any threats, or enter into any guaranties, with Spain, on that subject.—Without either guaranties or threats, we shall be ready, when the time comes, to act.—The news of the cession of Cuba to any foreign power would, in the United States, be the instant signal for war.— No foreign power would attempt to take it, that did not expect a hostile collision with us as an inevitable consequence.—

As to the purchase of Cuba from Spain, we do not desire to renew the proposition made by the late Administration on this subject.— It is understood that the proposition, made by our late Minister at Madrid, under instructions from this Department, or from the late President of the United States, was considered by the Spanish Ministry as a national indignity, and that the sentiment of the Ministry was responded to by the Cortes.— After all that has occurred, should Spain desire to part with the Island, the proposition, for its cession to us, should come from her;—and in case she should make any, you will content yourself with transmitting the same to your Government for consideration.—

You will exert yourself by every means in your power to procure, from the Government at Madrid, the abolition of the discriminating duties against our commerce, which are imposed or collected in the Islands of Cuba and Porto Rico.— Every consideration of sound policy should induce the Spanish Government to abandon these duties.—This has been so much the subject of conversation between us, that it is hardly necessary for me to dilate upon it in this note.— It is highly desirable to procure relaxations of the Spanish restrictive system, as affecting our navigation and commerce in general, and you will, no doubt, use every proper effort, within your power, to effect that object.— . . .

•   •   •

In 1848 General Narciso López—a Venezuelan who had served in the Carlist Wars and as an official in Cuba—emerged as the leader of a renewed drive for revolt against Spanish rule. Many Cubans in this movement also wanted annexation to the United States. The Cuban Council in New York City declared for annexation in 1849, and Cubans in the same city published an annexationist newspaper—*La Verdad*—from 1848 to 1853.

Although the United States government tried to enforce the neutrality laws, López managed to launch two expeditions against Cuba. The first, in 1850, set out from New Orleans with some 750 men. One ship made it to Cuba, but López and his followers had to race back to the United States when the expected uprising did not materialize. The other two ships were captured, but the men were later pardoned by the Queen of Spain. López was arrested and brought to trial for violation of the neutrality laws, but a sympathetic Southern jury would not convict him. In 1851 López sailed from New Orleans with about four hundred men. This time he was captured also, and was garroted in the Havana public square. Some of his followers were shot, and about 160 others were sent to prison in Spain. These pleaded for diplomatic intercession on the grounds that they had been misled by López. They were pardoned in 1852.

DOCUMENT 14. Angel Calderón de la Barca (Spanish Minister to the United States) to Daniel Webster (Secretary of State), August 2, 1850. (Manning, ed., *Inter-American Affairs: 1831–1860.* XI: 528–35.)

The rapidity with which the idea is gaining ground in some of the States of the Union, of seizing upon the Island of Cuba, in spite of all law, and without any other reasons than the promptings of self-interests;— and the facility, also, with which, in some of those States, armed expeditions have been set on foot, for the purpose of carrying this contemplated act of usurpation into effect, have kept that Spanish province in a perpetual state of uneasiness which affects her prosperity to a considerable extent, and compels the Spanish Government to preserve an attitude there, involving great expense, and more embarrassing even, than an absolute state of war.

In the year 1845, a proposition for annexing the Island of Cuba to the United States, was brought for the first time before the Senate, by Senator Levy, (Yulee.)—[11] In the same year, the Honorable Mr. Dallas, who was then Vice President of the Republic, made the incorporation of the aforesaid Island, the subject of a toast at a public entertainment; and later still, in 1849, he published a letter in which he declared himself in favor of its annexation, as the crowning act in the scheme of National prosperity, and national aggrandizement. Sentiments like these, uttered publicly, and by persons occupying elevated stations in life, could not fail to give a character of durability to those daily controversies, which, from that time, have been carried on upon this subject, and to those alarming rumors, which although absurd in themselves, were yet put in circulation.

. . . Scarcely a year has elapsed, since there was organized on the soil of the Republic, in the face of the whole world, and amidst the congratulations of that portion of the press which is inimical to Spain, the first expedition against the Island of Cuba. It is true that the sailing of the expedition was prevented by the illustrious and loyal General Taylor, whose noble sentiments were well-known to, and appreciated by Her Majesty's government; but those composing the aforesaid expedition were allowed to go free, with their arms and ammunition, without being subjected to the punishment which the laws of the Republic provide in all such cases. This impunity has produced results which it was easy to have anticipated. In the undertaking of last year, it was only sought to prevent those connected with this seditious conspiracy from sailing from any ports of the Union with arms; consequently, in the attempt made this year, the final point of meeting and departure was fixed out of the limits of the United States.

. . . A second expedition, armed and equipped in the United States, was landed on the coast of Cuba, for the purpose of spilling the blood of her loyal inhabitants, to plunder the public funds, to burn down her edifices and to commit every species of atrocity. Having returned to the United States, these pirates,— so styled in the very treaty of 1795,— are now following the example of their confederates of last year, boasting of their criminal designs, if not absolutely concerting plans for a third expedition, which, according to information received by the Undersigned, and forwarded by him to the Hon Daniel Webster by date of the 26th inst, they are now hatching without disguise.

The government of Her Catholic Majesty has been extremely surprised to find, that the Traitor López was instantly set free at Savannah, in consequence of some legal quibbling, which is a mockery of the law itself, in as much as it was a question of a man who had just returned from a criminal expedition, and who, not only, did not deny the act, but actually boasted of it publicly; and with a perfect contempt for law and treaties, had harangued the people, promising them never to desist from his nefarious designs, but to consecrate all his life to the object he had in view. . . .

. . . Ever since 1826, when the United States Government protested against the schemes of the Government of Venezuela, declaring, that it would uphold the rights of Spain over the Island of Cuba and Porto Rico, with all its power,— until this day, many have been the occasions when the same language has been held by every successive administration; even the Undersigned has received assurances, which he has hastened to communicate to his government, that López and his accomplices should be prosecuted and the laws vindicated. But, in as much as, notwithstanding these assurances, the invasion of Cuba has actually taken place, her Majesty's government finds itself in a position which it considers much more embarrassing than a positive state of war;—because it is a war *de facto*, in the midst of official peace. In this position, that government can no longer remain; and, consequently, it desires to know, what it has to expect, in order that it may adopt such measures, as prudence shall dictate. It desires to know whether the United States are able, legally to suppress, these military expeditions, which are fitting out in their own territory, for the purpose of invading the colonies of Spain?—What is the opinion of the American Government in regard to the neutrality stipulated for, in existing treaties, and to what extent they are willing to act, in order to enforce its observance?—In short, it desires to know, whether these violations of treaty obligations can be suppressed on American soil, and those concerned in them punished? The opportunity for deciding in the affirmative is now at hand: let the projectors of the criminal attempt which has just been made against the Island of Cuba be severely dealt with. Her Majesty's government solemnly demands, and has instructed the Undersigned to demand, this just reparation.

DOCUMENT 15. Charles A. Downer, Joel D. Hughes, Fenton B. Hough, and James St. Levy (U.S. citizens imprisoned at Cadiz) to Daniel M. Barringer (Minister to Spain), October [?], 1851. (Manning, *Inter-American Affairs: 1831–1860*. XI: 639.)

We the undersigned, American citizens now prisoners in Spain on account of our participation in the late expedition against the Island of Cuba under the command of Gen'l López, take the liberty of addressing you a statement of facts, and praying you to intercede with the heads of the Government of Spain in our behalf. The following are [sic] a plain & truthful statement of facts as they occurred.

Some time during the month of April or May last the newspapers of the city of New Orleans commenced the circulation of reports purporting to be Cuban correspondence, stating that a revolution was about to take place on that Island; such reports continued in circulation until sometime in July, when the so said correspondant [sic] reported that a Revolution *had taken place*, and that on the 4th of July a Declaration of Independence had been issued, that the whole Island was in arms, that some eight or ten of the principal cities on the Island had revolted, that several Regiments of Spanish troops had joined the Patriots, and that in fact the Revolution was in a state of prosperity.

Gen. López, being at New Orleans during this time, and being desirous to embark & join in this affair, procured meetings to be held, stating that the standard of Liberty had been planted on the Island, and that the aid of Americans was solicited. These meetings produced an excitement rarely if ever before seen in New Orleans. To induce us to join it was stated that we were to be merely a body guard to Gen. López—and that once disembarked on the Island he would be joined by thousands of Patriots.

In all this we were deceived, for once landed we found no friends but on the contrary found an enemy in every house.

The people who had been described to us as unhappy & oppressed, we found as near as we could judge contented and happy —having no wish for a change of their Government. Could we have left the expedition many of us would have abandoned it on the third and fourth day, but our steamer left us immediately on our disembarking and our means were cut off. As regards the truth of this statement I can only refer to Mr. Laborde—Spanish Consul from New Orleans who will I have no doubt vouch for it.

•   •   •

The governments of Great Britain and France believed that the United States was ready to take Cuba. Aggressive expansionist declarations in the press and the López expeditions prompted these governments to send naval vessels to Cuban waters. In 1852 both governments proposed that the United States join with them in a tripartite agreement pledging all three to respect Spanish sovereignty in Cuba. President Millard Fillmore and Secretary of State Webster expressed their approval of such a measure, but requested that talks be postponed until after the November election.

The Whigs were walking a political tightrope in 1852. The party was divided over the expansion issue, and faced with the problem of maintaining its national character in the face of sectional tensions. The party leaders wanted to pursue a cautious policy in regard to expansion, but they were also afraid to antagonize the South and the expansionist "Young Americans." Fillmore also wanted the Hawaiian Islands included in a tripartite guarantee, but the President and Webster decided to wait for the election returns before entering into any discussions.

Webster died in October, and the Whigs lost the election in November. Edward Everett became Secretary of State and drafted a resounding, nationalistic rejection to the tripartite proposal. It is possible that the Whigs were attempting to steal the Democrat's thunder in preparation for the election of 1856. Stephen A. Douglas applauded the note, even though it was, in part, a bid for national support on the part of the Whigs. The Whig attempt to straddle the expansion issue did not save the party.

DOCUMENT 16.   Edward Everett (Secretary of State) to the Count Sartiges (French Minister to the United States), December 1, 1852. (Moore, *Digest of International Law*. VI: 460–65, 468–70.)

That note, and the instruction of M. de Turgot of the 31st March, with a similar communication from the English minister, and the *projet* of a convention between the three powers relative to Cuba, have been among the first subjects to which my attention has been called by the President.

The substantial portion of the proposed convention is expressed in a single article in the following terms:

"The high contracting parties hereby, severally and collectively, disclaim, now and for hereafter, all intention to obtain possession of the island of Cuba, and they respectively bind themselves to discountenance all attempt to that effect on the part of any power or individuals whatever."

"The high contracting parties declare, severally and collectively, that they will not obtain or maintain for themselves, or for any one of themselves any exclusive control over the said island, nor assume nor exercise any dominion over the same."

The President has given the most serious attention to this proposal, to the notes of the French and British ministers accompanying it, and to the instructions of M. de Turgot and the Earl of Malmesbury, transmitted with the project of the convention, and he directs me to make known to you the view which he takes of this important and delicate subject.

The President fully concurs with his predecessors, who have on more than one occasion authorized the declaration referred to by M. de Turgot and Lord Malemsbury, [*sic*] that the United States could not see with indifference the island of Cuba fall into the possession of any other European Government than Spain; not, however, because we should be dissatisfied with any natural increase of territory and power on the part of France or England. France has, within twenty years, acquired a vast domain on the northern coast of Africa, with a fair prospect of indefinite extension. England, within half a century, has added very extensively to her Empire. These acquisitions have created no uneasiness on the part of the United States.

In like manner, the United States have, within the same period, greatly increased their territory. The largest addition was that of Louisiana, which was purchased from France. These accessions of territory have probably caused no uneasiness to the great European powers, as they have been brought about by the operation of natural causes, and without any disturbance of the international relations of the principal states. They have been followed, also, by a great increase of mutually beneficial commercial intercourse between the United States and Europe.

But the case would be different in reference to the transfer of Cuba from Spain to any other European power. That event could not take place without a serious derangement of the international system now existing, and it would indicate designs in reference to this hemisphere which could not but awaken alarm in the United States.

We should view it in somewhat the same light in which France and England would view the acquisition of some important island in the Mediterranean by the United States, with this difference, it is true; that the attempt of the United States to establish themselves in Europe would be a novelty, while the appearance of a European power in this part of the world is a familiar fact. But this difference in the two cases is merely historical, and would not diminish the anxiety which, on political grounds, would be caused by any great demonstration of European power in a new direction in America.

M. de Turgot states that France could never see with indifference the possession of Cuba by *any* power but Spain, and explicitly declares that she has no wish or intention of appropriating the island to herself; and the English minister makes the same avowal on behalf of his Government. M. de Turgot and Lord Malmesbury do the Government of the United States no more than justice in remarking that they have often pronounced themselves substantially in the same sense. The President does not covet the acquisition of Cuba for the United States; at the same time, he considers the condition of Cuba as mainly an American question. The proposed convention proceeds on a different principle. It assumes that the United States have no other or greater interest in the question than France or England; whereas it is necessary only to cast one's eye on the map to see how remote are the relations of Europe, and how intimate those of the United States, with this island.

The President, doing full justice to the friendly spirit in which his concurrence is invited by France and England, and not insensible to the advantages of a good understanding between the three powers in reference to Cuba, feels himself, nevertheless, unable to become a party to the proposed compact, for the following reasons:

It is, in the first place, in his judgment, clear (as far as the respect due from the Executive to a coordinate branch of the Government will permit him to anticipate its decision) that no such convention would be viewed with favor by the Senate. Its certain rejection by that body would leave the question of Cuba in a more unsettled position than it is now. This objection would not require the President to withhold his concurrence from the convention if no other objection existed, and if a strong sense of the unity of the measure rendered it his duty, as far as the executive action is concerned, to give his consent to the arrangement. Such, however, is not the case.

The convention would be of no value unless it were lasting: accordingly its terms express a perpetuity of purpose and obligation. Now, it may well be doubted whether the Constitution of the United States would allow the treaty-making power to impose a permanent disability on the American Government for all coming time, and prevent it under any further change of circumstances, from doing what has been so often done in times past. In 1803 the United States purchased Louisiana of France; and in 1819 they purchased Florida of Spain. It is not within the competence of the treaty-making power in 1852 effectually to bind the Government in all its branches; and, for all coming time, not to make a similar purchase of Cuba. A like remark, I imagine, may be made even in reference both to France and England, where the treaty-making power is less subject than it is with us to the control of other branches of the Government.

There is another strong objection to the proposed agreement. Among the oldest traditions of the Federal Government is an aversion to political alliances with European powers. . . .

But the President has a graver objection to entering into the proposed convention. He has no wish to disguise the feeling that the compact, although equal in its terms, would be very unequal in substance. France and England, by entering into it, would disable themselves from obtaining possession of an island remote from their seats of government, belonging to another European power, whose natural right to possess it must always be as good as their own—a distant island in another hemisphere, and one which by no ordinary or peaceful course of things could ever belong to either of them. If the present balance of power in Europe should be broken up, if Spain should become unable to maintain the island in her possession, and France and England should be engaged in a death struggle with each other, Cuba might then be the prize of the victor. Till these events all take place, the President does not see how Cuba can belong to any European power but Spain.

The United States, on the other hand, would, by the proposed convention, disable themselves from making an acquisition which might take place without any disturbance of existing foreign relations, and in the natural order of things. The island of Cuba lies at our doors. It commands the approach to the Gulf of Mexico, which washes the shores of five of our States. It bars the entrance of that great river which drains half the North American continent, and with its tributaries forms the largest system of internal water-communication in the world. It keeps watch at the door-way of our intercourse with California by the Isthmus route. If an island like Cuba, belonging to the Spanish Crown, guarded the entrance of the Thames and the Seine, and the United States should propose a convention like this to France and England, those powers would assuredly feel that the disability assumed by ourselves was far less serious than that which we asked them to assume.

The opinion of American statesmen, at different times, and under varying circumstances, have differed as to the desirableness of the acquisition of Cuba by the United States. Territorially and commercially it would, in our hands, be an extremely valuable possession. Under certain contingencies it might be almost essential to our safety. Still, for domestic reasons, on which, in a communication of this kind, it might not be proper to dwell, the President thinks that the incorporation of the island into the Union at the present time, although effected with the consent of Spain, would be a hazardous measure; and he would consider its acquisition by force, except in a just war with Spain, (should an event so greatly to be deprecated take place), as a disgrace to the civilization of the age.

*   *   *   *   *

That a convention such as is proposed would be a transitory arrangement, sure to be swept away by the irresistible tide of affairs in a new country, is, to the apprehension of the President, too obvious to require a labored argument. The project rests on principles applicable, if at all, to Europe, where international relations are, in their basis, of great antiquity, slowly modified, for the

most part, in the progress of time and events; and not applicable
to America, which, but lately a waste, is filling up with intense
rapidity, and adjusting on natural principles those territorial relations which, on the first discovery of the continent, were in a good
degree fortuitous.

*   *   *   *   *

Spain, meantime, has retained of her extensive dominions in
this hemisphere but the two islands of Cuba and Porto Rico. A
respectful sympathy with the fortunes of an ancient ally and a
gallant people, with whom the United States have ever maintained
the most friendly relations, would, if no other reason existed, make
it our duty to leave her in the undisturbed possession of this little
remnant of her mighty trans-Atlantic empire. The President desires
to do so; no word or deed of his will ever question her title or
shake her possession. But can it be expected to last very long? Can
it resist this mighty current in the fortunes of the world? Is it
desirable that it should do so? Can it be for the interest of Spain
to cling to a possession that can only be maintained by a garrison
of twenty-five or thirty thousand troops, a powerful naval force,
and an annual expenditure for both arms of the service of at least
twelve millions of dollars? Cuba, at this moment, costs more to
Spain than the entire naval and military establishment of the
United States costs the Federal Government. . . .

I will but allude to an evil of the first magnitude: I mean the
African slave-trade, in the suppression of which France and England take a lively interest—an evil which still forms a great re-
proach upon the civilization of Christendom, and perpetuates the
barbarism of Africa, but for which it is to be feared there is no
hope of a complete remedy while Cuba remains a Spanish colony.

But, whatever may be thought of these last suggestions, it
would seem impossible for anyone who reflects upon the events
glanced at in this note to mistake the law of American growth and
progress, or think it can be ultimately arrested by a convention
like that proposed. In the judgment of the President, it would be
as easy to throw a dam from Cape Florida to Cuba, in the hope
of stopping the flow of the Gulf Stream, as to attempt, by a compact like this, to fix the fortunes of Cuba "now and for hereafter:"
or, as expressed in the French text of the convention, "for the
present as for the future," (*pour le present comme pour l'avenir,*)
that is, for all coming time. The history of the past—of the recent
past—affords no assurance that twenty years hence France or
England will even wish that Spain should retain Cuba; and a

century hence, judging of what will be from what has been, the pages which record this proposition will, like the record of the family compact between France and Spain, have no interest but for the antiquary.[12]

For these reasons, which the President has thought it advisable, considering the importance of the subject, to direct me to unfold at some length, he feels constrained to decline respectfully the invitation of France and England to become a party to the proposed convention. He is persuaded that these friendly powers will not attribute this refusal to any insensibility on his part to the advantages of the utmost harmony between the great maritime states on a subject of such importance. As little will Spain draw any unfavorable inference from this refusal; the rather, as the emphatic disclaimer of any designs against Cuba on the part of this Government, contained in the present note, affords all the assurance which the President can constitutionally, or to any useful purpose, give of a practical concurrence with France and England in the wish not to disturb the possession of that island by Spain.

•   •   •

Franklin Pierce came to the presidency in 1853 determined to pursue an aggressive foreign policy as a device for soothing the festering sectional conflict. The administration, however, started out with a cautious approach to the Cuban problem. This changed early in 1854 when the *Black Warrior* affair stirred up nationalistic protests against Spain and put new heat into the expansionist's desire for Cuba. In the South this ambition was further inflamed by renewed reports of British schemes to abolish slavery in Cuba, and to set up an "Africanized" republic aimed at creating instability in the United States.

Secretary of State William L. Marcy instructed the Minister to Spain—Pierre Soulé—to renew the purchase offer, but also hinted broadly that the United States would aid the Cubans in any efforts which they might make to overthrow Spanish control (Document 19). This was a most welcome opportunity to the red-hot expansionist from New Orleans. Soulé had already broached the subject to Queen Isabella, and was convinced that Spain would give up Cuba if the United States took an aggressive position. The Minister, however, pushed the Cuban issue beyond the bounds of diplomatic propriety. He had gained a kind of notoriety by wounding the French Ambassador in a duel, and he further displayed his impetuous nature by meddling in Spanish politics and by antagonizing the Spanish government.

The administration hoped to take advantage of the Crimean War and Spanish internal difficulties, but plans for appointing a special commission to negotiate with Spain were opposed by Congress. As an alternative the administration instructed Soulé to confer with James Buchanan and John Mason—the ministers to England and France. The three were told to formulate recommendations, and the result was the "Ostend Manifesto" which was signed at Aix-la-Chapelle. Soulé thought that this report was too weak, and in a private letter to Marcy advocated the use of force (Document 24).

Pierce and Marcy, however, had retreated from the aggressive posture taken in April. The Kansas-Nebraska controversy had broken out in the interim, and Soulé's diplomacy, coupled with the "Ostend Manifesto," had further inflamed sectional feeling. Some who favored the acquisition of Cuba joined in the protests directed at Soulé's aggressive actions, and blamed the minister—and his Southern friends—for driving Spain into complete rejection of any American offers (Document 22). Marcy, in effect, rebuked Soulé and stated that the administration did not favor a coercive policy. Soulé resigned, but the Northern opponents of the administration continued to hammer away at the Democrats as the party of aggressive slavocracy.

DOCUMENT 17. William L. Marcy (Secretary of State) to Pierre Soulé (Minister to Spain), July 23, 1853. (Manning, *Inter-American Affairs: 1831–1860*. XI: 160–63.)

. . . The Island of Cuba, on account of its magnitude, situation, fine climate and rich production,— far superior in all respects to any in the West India group,— is a very desirable possession to Spain, and, for the same reasons, very difficult for her to retain in its present state of dependence. The opinion generally prevails among the European nations that the Spanish dominion over it is insecure. This was clearly evinced by the alacrity with which both England and France, on occasion of the late disturbances in Cuba, volunteered their aid to sustain the Spanish rule over it, and by their recent proposition to the United States for a tripartite Convention to guarantee its possession to Spain. Without an essential change in her present policy—such a change as she will most likely be unwilling to make—she cannot, it is confidently believed, long sustain, unaided, her present connection with that Island. What will be its destiny after it shall cease to be a dependency of Spain, is a question with which some of the principal powers of Europe have seen fit to concern themselves, and in which the United States have a deep and direct interest.

The policy of the Government of the United States in regard to Cuba, in any contingency calling for our interposition, will depend in a great degree upon the peculiar circumstances of the case, & cannot, therefore, now be presented with much precision beyond what is indicated in the instructions before referred to. Nothing will be done on our part to disturb its present connection with Spain, unless the character of that connection should be so changed as to affect our present or prospective security. While the United States would resist at every hazard the transferrence of Cuba to any European nation, they would exceedingly regret to see Spain resorting to any Power for assistance to uphold her rule over it. Such a dependence on foreign aid would in effect invest the auxiliary with the character of a protector, and give it a pretext to interfere in our affairs and also generally in those of the North American Continent. In case of collision with the United States, such protecting power would be in a condition to make nearly the same use of that Island to annoy us, as it could do if it were the absolute possessor of it. We have recently learned in the instance of Central America what a protectorate means, and to what uses it may be devoted. There is not a very great difference between the protector and the possessor of a territory, and when the possessor is weak and the protector strong, the distinction we apprehend would in effect be annihilated. The one in reality furnishes the same pretext for interfering in the concerns of neighboring nations as the other. While Spain remains in fact as well as in name the sovereign of Cuba, she can depend upon our maintaining our duty as a neutral nation towards her, however difficult it may be. . . .

In the present aspect of the case the President does not deem it proper to authorize you to make any proposition for the purchase

of that island. There is now no hope, as he believes, that such a
proposition would be favorably received, and the offer of it might,
and probably would, be attended with injurious effects. Without
making approaches to the Spanish authorities upon this subject,
you may be able to get information that may be important in
shaping our future policy in regard to Cuba. It is very desirable
for this government to know, and your position may enable you to
ascertain, what arrangements have been made with Great Britain
and France in regard to sustaining the present dominion of Spain
over Cuba, & how far they, or either of them, are urging a change
in the internal condition of the island, particularly in regard to
the slaves now there, or to the present system of labor.

ᐧ   ᐧ   ᐧ   ᐧ   ᐧ

If Cuba could be emancipated from a European domination,
the United States would probably be relieved from all the anxieties
they now feel in regard to its future destiny. It would in that case
fall necessarily into the American Continental system, and contribute to its stability, instead of exposing it to danger. You will,
if a fair occasion be offered, favor this view of the case, but, at the
same time, take special care not to excite suspicions of sinister
views on the part of this government nor to wound the sensibility
of an ancient and proud nation. The United States would cordially
favor such a voluntary separation and, if necessary to effect it,
would be willing to contribute something more substantial than
their good will towards an object so desirable to them; but what
they would do in furtherance of it cannot be precisely specified
until it is more distinctly seen what would be required on their
part to secure its accomplishment. On this interesting subject this
Department is very desirous of obtaining early and full information, not only of the views of the government of Spain and the
people of Cuba, but of the disposition of European powers to favor
or obstruct a measure of vast political and commercial importance. . . .

DOCUMENT 18. William L. Marcy to Charles W. Davis
(United States Special Agent to Cuba), March 15, 1854.
(Manning, *Inter-American Affairs: 1831–1860.* XI: 170–72.)

It has been repeatedly represented to this Department recently,
through official and other channels, that the Africanization of Cuba
is in contemplation by Spain, and that she is even engaged in mak-

ing arrangements to carry the measure into effect. The President desirous of obtaining minute and reliable information upon the subject, has selected you to proceed to that Island to ascertain whether the intelligence received is correct. You will, therefore, repair with the least possible delay to Havana, where your duties will commence.

     ✓   ✓   ✓   ✓   ✓

The attitude of Spain towards the United States is beginning to assume an aspect threatening to the peace of the two countries. Wrong after wrong has been so long submitted to in Cuba, without a hostile demonstration on our part, that it would seem as if the Cabinet at Madrid was impressed with a belief that we are indisposed to making a preemptory demand for redress.

Unless a change of policy ensue, whereby our rights are to be rigorously respected and our future completely guarded against the influences of bad neighborhood, the day of retributive justice must soon arrive. Injury to our citizens and insult to our flag, have been of such frequent occurrence, that our forbearance is ceasing to be a virtue.

Spain, it is believed, has been encouraged by Great Britain to adopt a policy adverse to the well being of this country. The British Government after abolishing slavery in its own possessions, has been incessantly engaged in endeavoring to cause its abolition elsewhere. . . .

     ✓   ✓   ✓   ✓   ✓

The ostensible motive of Great Britain for desiring the abolition of slavery is the promotion of philanthropy, but the real one doubtless is to benefit her planting and other interests.

DOCUMENT 19. William L. Marcy to Pierre Soulé, April 3, 1854, *Confidential*. (Manning, *Inter-American Affairs: 1831–1860*. XI: 176–77.)

Should circumstances present a favorable opportunity, you are directed by the President to renew the attempt to purchase that Island. He is aware that this will be a delicate and difficult negotiation, and the manner of conducting it is left wholly to your discretion. The maximum sum which our Minister, Mr. Saunders, was authorized to offer on a former occasion was $100,000,000. This is regarded by the President as a liberal price, yet the acquisition of that Island is so very desirable that he would not have the negotiation fail if an additional amount of 20 or 30 millions were required to effect that object.

The difficulties of a direct purchase were discussed in our interviews before you left the United States; they may have been diminished, if not removed, by the events which have since taken place in the internal condition of Spain. The change of policy in Cuba, particularly in regard to supplying the demand for agricultural labor, has increased discontent and created alarm among people of that Island, and made them more averse to the continuance of Spanish rule, and more willing to come under the protection of the United States.

Should you, however, become convinced that Spain will not, for any consideration you are authorized to offer, entertain a proposition for a transfer of the sovereignty of Cuba to the United States, you will then direct your efforts to the next most desirable object, which is to detach that Island from the Spanish dominion and from all dependence on any European power. If Cuba were relieved from all transatlantic connection and at liberty to dispose of herself as her present interest and prospective welfare would indicate, she would undoubtedly relieve this government from all anxiety in regard to her future condition.

Though the pride of Spain might revolt at the proposition to sell the Island of Cuba to a foreign power, it has been suggested that she might be induced to consent to its independence, and that the United States might essentially contribute to such a result. In any conceivable arrangement of this kind the people of Cuba must necessarily be a party to it. There is now no political organization in the Island which can act for the people, nor is it possible there can be under its present system of government. No body of men are permitted to associate for the purpose of accepting or offering terms. Should the despotic rule now established be so far relaxed as to allow of any such association, the United States would readily countenance and aid its efforts to release the Island from dependence on Spain. Any assistance this country might give to the people of Cuba to enable them to induce Spain to consent to their independence might be fully compensated by advantages which they would be able to secure to the United States.

This government would look with favor upon such an arrangement, and aid in any useful way to bring it about; but without knowing whether anything can be done to effect that object, or what part the United States could properly take in furtherance of it, it is not possible to give you any special instructions for your action in such a contingency.

DOCUMENT 20.   Pierre Soulé to William L. Marcy, July 18, 1854. (Manning, *Inter-American Affairs: 1831–1860.* XI: 799.)

Madrid is at last in full insurrection. . . .
What a moment for taking in our own hands that question of Cuba, which it seems almost impossible we may hereafter be able to adjust in any other way than by force of arms!

DOCUMENT 21.   William L. Marcy to Pierre Soulé, August 16, 1854. (Manning, *Inter-American Affairs: 1831–1860.* XI: 193.)

I am directed by the President to suggest to you a particular step from which he anticipates much advantage to the negotiations with which you are charged on the subject of Cuba.

It is not believed that Great Britain would interpose in any hostile sense to prevent the cession of Cuba to the United States. Yet she might be disposed to obstruct this as she did the annexation of Texas.

But the present government of France is less responsible to public opinion than that of Great Britain, it is not checked by any effective parlimentary influence and it has already indicated a tendency to intermeddle in the affairs of the American Continent.

These and other considerations which will readily occur to you, suggest that much may be done at London and Paris either to promote directly the great object in view, or at least to clear away impediments to its successful consummation.

Under these circumstances it seems desirable that there should be a full and free interchange of views between yourself, Mr. Buchanan and Mr. Mason, in order to secure a concurrence in reference to the general object.

The simplest and only very apparent means of attaining this end is for the three Ministers to meet as early as may be at some convenient central point, (say Paris,) to consult together, to compare opinions as to what may be advisable, and to adopt measures for perfect concert of action in aid of your negotiations at Madrid.

While the President has, as I have before had occasion to state, full confidence in your own intelligence and sagacity, he conceives that it cannot be otherwise than agreeable to you and to your colleagues in Great Britain and France, to have the consultation sug-

gested, and thus bring your common wisdom and knowledge to
bear simultaneously upon the negotiations at Madrid, London and
Paris.

DOCUMENT 22. Horatio J. Perry (Chargé d'Affaires *ad
interim* at Madrid) to William L. Marcy, September 6, 1854.
(Manning, *Inter-American Affairs: 1831–1860.* XI: 806, 808–
10, 813.)

Sir, the policy which Mr. Soulé has represented at this Court
and urged with all his talent and all his resources is a complete
and utter failure. He has not an individual of any influence in any
party who supports him at this moment, or who would listen to
any proposition from him. He has not a friend or a dependent
even, who could serve him for anything in politics. He is isolated
in Spain and forced to retire or fail in every consideration he owes
to his own dignity and personal character.

The peaceable cession of the Island of Cuba by Spain to us at
this time is impossible, still more impossible, now, if I can say *more,*
than before the revolution which has begun.

The present Ministry could not in any way attempt it, even if
the opinion of all its members were unanimous in its favor. It could
not be done otherwise than as an act deliberately determined on
and voted by the Spanish people in Cortes as the will of the whole
nation.

There is no Cabinet, there is no Minister possible, who could
dream of proposing that measure in the present state of affairs
with respect to us. There is no Cortes possible who would consider
it. There is no people who would not instantly hurl Minister &
Cortes to destruction for having touched it.

I beg to be understood. I do not say that such a cession will
never be made, or that it may not perhaps be made within a quite
limited period; on the contrary I consider the offer of such a cession
to us most highly probable, provided meantime we ourselves do
nothing to impede it.

Cuba will be ours. She may become so as Louisiana became
ours, and as I am told the Russian possessions in America may now
become ours, & for similar reasons. Because geographically, commercially, and strategically the connexion of Cuba is naturally

with us and not with any other power, & because independently
of us and for reasons with which we have nothing to do, Spain in
the same way as France, now already has, and may be expected
to have in an increasing degree, the strongest motives for wishing
to exchange her possessions on our coast for a value which can be
used at home.

✦   ✦   ✦   ✦   ✦

Our industry must stimulate and develop the industry of Spain,
whilst at the same time reaping richly its own reward. The right
of our citizens to be and to do all this, should be guaranteed by
effective provisions, sanctioned by a solemn international compact.
In short, Sir, your own wise and far-seeing policy with regard to
Canada and the fisheries, should be extended to Cuba also, and the
issue is undubitable.[13] The time of its consummation may not be
distinctly seen, but it cannot be very long, and meantime with all
the interests of the United States guarded and fostered, we can
afford to wait.

All this can be done and done immediately, but it must be done
intelligently, and with the single patriotic aim of serving the interests of the whole Union and them alone.

Mr. Soulé cannot do it. General Quitman and the Cuban Junta
cannot do it. The State of Louisiana, Mississippi and Alabama can
do little towards it. They *may* ruin this natural, fair and fruitful
policy of the United States, but they cannot aid it. They may pre-
cipitate the nation into a war for the conquest of Cuba, but they
cannot purchase it, so long as they threaten that alternative. They
and their daring Minister at this Court may give to the world a
repetition of the style of proceedings adopted by Prince Menschi-
coff at Constantinople: but it is with sorrow that I confess to you
my profound conviction, that, if they be sustained in that course,
the consequences also will only too closely resemble those which
have followed upon that famous embassy—[14]

I know this people and their faults; fear is not one of them.
Ignorance and a stubborn, unyielding, uncompromising hostility
to whomsoever they may come to believe is their enemy, whether
it be an individual or a nation, is one of their characteristics. The
United States might gain every battle, carry victory from every
field and every sea in a war with Spain, and yet they would not
be able to force her to peace or to a cession of Cuba to us, under
a sense of injury—never—

✦   ✦   ✦   ✦   ✦

But Mr. Soulé is desirous of effecting a rupture with this Government. Lately all his efforts are directed towards that end. For that reason I oppose him, and for that alone. No man can know Mr. Soulé as a friend without being drawn to him by strong sympathies. He is in many respects a superior man, but as a diplomatist he has mistaken his career. His ideas are fanciful, and his projects if put in execution would be fatal to the interests of our country.

DOCUMENT 23. James Buchanan, J. Y. Mason, Pierre Soulé to William L. Marcy, "The Ostend Conference," October 18, 1854. (*House Executive Documents,* No. 93, 33rd Cong., 2nd Sess. Washington, D. C., 1855. Pp. 127–32.)

Sir: The undersigned, in compliance with the wish expressed by the President in the several confidential dispatches you have addressed to us, respectively, to that effect, have met in conference, first at Ostend, in Belgium, on the 9th, 10th, and 11th instant, and then at Aix la Chapelle, in Prussia, on the days next following, up to the date hereof. . . .

We have arrived at the conclusion, and are thoroughly convinced, that an immediate and earnest effort ought to be made by the government of the United States to purchase Cuba from Spain at any price for which it can be obtained, not exceeding the sum of ——.

The proposal should, in our opinion, be made in such a manner as to be presented through the necessary diplomatic forms to the Supreme Constituent Cortes about to assemble. On this momentous question, in which the people of both Spain and the United States are so deeply interested, all our proceedings ought to be open, frank, and public. They should be of such a character as to challenge the approbation of the world.

We firmly believe that, in the progress of human events, the time has arrived when the vital interests of Spain are as seriously involved in the sale, as those of the United States in the purchase, of the island and that the transaction will prove equally honorable to both nations.

Under these circumstances we cannot anticipate a failure, unless possibly through the malign influence of foreign powers who possess no right whatever to interfere in the matter.

We proceed to state some of the reasons which have brought us to this conclusion, and, for the sake of clearness, we shall specify them under two distinct heads:

1. The United States ought, if practicable, to purchase Cuba with as little delay as possible.

2. The probability is great that the government and cortes of Spain will prove willing to sell it, because this would essentially promote the highest and best interest of the Spanish people.

Then, 1. It must be clear to every reflecting mind that, from the peculiarity of its geographical position, and the considerations attended on it, Cuba is as necessary to the North American republic as any of its present members, and that it belongs naturally to the great family of States of which the Union is the providential nursery. . . .

The natural and main outlet to the products of this entire population, the highway of their direct intercourse with the Atlantic and the Pacific States, can never be secure, but must ever be endangered whilst Cuba is a dependency of a distant power in whose possession it has proved to be a source of constant annoyance and embarrassment to their interests.

Indeed, the Union can never enjoy repose, nor possess reliable security, as long as Cuba is not embraced within its boundaries.

Its immediate acquisition by our government is of paramount importance, and we cannot doubt but that it is a consummation devotedly wished for by its inhabitants.

The intercourse which its proximity to our coasts begets and encourages between them and the citizens of the United States, has, in the progress of time, so united their interests and blended their fortunes that they now look upon each other as if they were one people and had but one destiny.

Considerations exist which render delay in the acquisition of this island exceedingly dangerous to the United States. . . .

Cuba has thus become to us an unceasing danger, and a permanent cause of anxiety and alarm.

But we need not enlarge on these topics. It can scarcely be apprehended that foreign powers, in violation of international law, would interpose their influence with Spain to prevent our acquisition of the island. . . .

Besides, the commercial nations of the world cannot fail to perceive and appreciate the great advantages which would result to their people from a dissolution of the forced and unnatural connexion between Spain and Cuba, and the annexation of the latter to the United States. The trade of England and France with Cuba would, in that event, assume at once an important and profitable character, and rapidly extend with the increasing population and prosperity of the island.

2. But if the United States and every commercial nation would be benefited by this transfer, the interests of Spain would also be greatly and essentially promoted.

She cannot but see what such a sum of money as we are willing to pay for the island would effect in the development of her vast natural resources. . . .

Should Spain reject the present golden opportunity for developing her resources, and removing her financial embarrassments, it may never again return. . . .

Under no probable circumstances can Cuba ever yield to Spain one per cent on the large amount which the United States are willing to pay for its acquisition. But Spain is in imminent danger of losing Cuba, without remuneration. . . .

It is not improbable, therefore, that Cuba may be wrested from Spain by a successful revolution; and in that event she will lose both the island and the price which we are now willing to pay for it—a price far beyond what was ever paid by one people to another for any province.

It may also be remarked that the settlement of this vexed question, by the cession of Cuba to the United States, would forever prevent the dangerous complications between nations, to which it may otherwise give birth.

It is certain, that should the Cubans themselves organize an insurrection against the Spanish government, and should other independent nations come to the aid of Spain in the contest, no human power could, in our opinion, prevent the people and government of the United States from taking part in such a civil war in support of their neighbors and friends.

But if Spain, dead to the voice of her own interest, and actuated by stubborn pride and a false sense of honor, should refuse to sell Cuba to the United States, then the question will arise, What ought to be the course of the American government under such circumstances?

Self-preservation is the first law of nature, with States as well as with individuals. All nations have, at different periods, acted upon this maxim. Although it has been made the pretext for committing flagrant injustice, as in the partition of Poland and other similar cases which history records, yet the principle itself, though often abused, has always been recognized. . . .

Our past history forbids that we should acquire the island of Cuba without the consent of Spain, unless justified by the great law of self-preservation. We must, in any event, preserve our own conscious rectitude and our own self-respect.

Whilst pursuing this course we can afford to disregard the censures of the world, to which we have been so often unjustly exposed.

After we shall have offered Spain a price for Cuba far beyond its present value, and this shall have been refused, it will then be time to consider the question, does Cuba, in the possession of Spain, seriously endanger our internal peace and the existence of our cherished Union?

Should this question be answered in the affirmative, then, by every law, human and divine, we shall be justified in wresting it from Spain if we possess the power; and this upon the very same principle that would justify an individual in tearing down the burning house of his neighbor if there were no other means of preventing the flames from destroying his own home.

Under such circumstances, we ought neither to count the cost nor regard the odds which Spain might enlist against us. We forbear to enter into the question, whether the present condition of the island would justify such a measure? We should, however, be recreant to our duty, be unworthy of our gallant forefathers, and commit base treason against our posterity, should we permit Cuba to be Africanized and become a second St. Domingo, with all its attendant horrors to the white race, and suffer the flames to enter to our own neighboring shores, seriously to endanger or actually to consume the fair fabric of our Union.

We fear that the course and current events are rapidly tending towards such a catastrophe. We, however, hope for the best, though we ought certainly to be prepared for the worst. . . .

DOCUMENT 24.   Pierre Soulé to William L. Marcy, October 20, 1854. (Manning, *Inter-American Affairs: 1831–1860*. XI: 826.)

The question of the acquisition of Cuba, by us, is gaining ground as it grows to be more seriously agitated and considered. Now is the moment for us to be done with it; for if we delay its solution we will certainly repent that we let escape the fairest opportunity we could ever be furnished with, of bringing it to a decisive test.

Present indications would seem to encourage the hope that we may come to that solution peaceably.

But, if it were otherwise, if it is to bring upon us the calamity of a war, let it be now, while the great powers of this continent are engaged in that stupendous struggle which cannot but engage all their strength and tax all their energies, as long as it lasts, and may before it ends, convulse them all.[15]

Neither England nor France would be likely to interfere with us.

England could not bear to be suddenly shut out of our market and see her manufactures paralysed even by a temporary suspension of her intercourse with us.

And France, with the heavy task now on her hands, and when she so eagerly aspires to take her seat as the acknowledged chief of the European family, would have no inducement to assume the burthen of another war, nor any motive to repine at seeing that we took in our keeping the destinies of the new World, as she will soon have those of the old.

DOCUMENT 25.   William L. Marcy to Pierre Soulé, November 13, 1854. (Manning, *Inter-American Affairs: 1831–1860*. XI: 196–97.)

. . . By a free and friendly intercourse among official and influential men you will be enabled to determine the proper course to be pursued in regard to opening a negotiation for the acquisition of Cuba. Should you find persons of position or influence disposed to converse on the subject, the considerations in favor of a cession are so many and so strong, that those who can be brought to listen would very likely become converts to the measure. But should you have reason to believe that the men in power are averse to entertaining such a proposition,—that the offer of it would be offensive to the national pride of Spain, and that it would find no favor in any considerable class of the people, then it will be but too evident that the time for opening or attempting to open such negotiation has not arrived. It appears to the President that nothing could be gained and something might be lost by an attempt to push on a negotiation against such a general resistance. This view of the case is taken on the supposition that you shall become convinced that a proposition for the cession of Cuba would certainly be rejected.

The language of some part of the Report might, perhaps, be so construed as to sustain the inference that you and your associates in the conference were of opinion that the proposition should be made though there should be no chance of its being entertained, and that it should be accomplished with the open declaration or a significant suggestion that, the United States were determined to have the Island and would obtain it by other means if their present advances, so advantageous to Spain, be refused by her; but other parts of the Report repel this inference. The remark in that document that if Spain should refuse these proposals of the United States, then "the question will arise, What ought to be the course of the American Government under such circumstances?" clearly shows that it was not intended by yourself and colleagues to recommend to the President to offer to Spain the alternative of cession or seizure. The conclusion that the members of the conference were against such an alternative proposition is also drawn from the following passage.—"After we shall have offered Spain a price for Cuba far beyond its present value, and this shall have been refused, it will then be time to consider the question, does Cuba in the possession of Spain seriously endanger our internal peace and the existence of our cherished Union?". The President concurs in this view of the subject. But to conclude that on the rejection of a proposition to cede seizure should ensue, would be to assume that self-preservation necessitates the acquisition of Cuba by the United State,— that Spain has refused and will persist in refusing our reclamations for injuries and wrongs inflicted, and that she will make no arrangement for our future security against the recurrence of similar injuries and wrongs.

•　　•　　•

New Orleans and New York were the major centers of the Cuban annexation movement. A combination of commercial and political motives, tied together in the ideology of Manifest Destiny, provided a common bond of interest represented, in part, by the Democratic Party. Western expansionists, such as Stephen A. Douglas, completed the mosaic of imperial Americans. The commercial interests of Northeastern businessmen even provided an expansionist wing within the Whig Party before its demise in the 1850's. The prospect of increased markets to the south, protection for trade routes, and bases for future economic expansion linked the sections together with a common goal; and Cuba was the main focal point.

The Southern states had an additional interest, however, which complicated an otherwise neat picture. Southerners not only feared the establishment of a Negro Republic in Cuba—under British influence—but also desired the addition of Cuba as another slave state. Cuba, as well as Mexico, were seen as profitable areas for the expansion of Southern slave-owners, or potential slave-owners. The New Orleans publication edited by the expansionist J. D. B. De Bow voiced all of the reasons listed (Document 26).

Some expansionists took a more exalted view, and wrote about the extension of republican institutions and freedom (Document 27). Exporting the American Revolution to overthrow European tyranny went hand-in-hand with profits and strategic advantage. For the Continentalists Cuba was part of North America, and the "garden of the world" theme was given a Caribbean setting.

The new Republican Party, however, opposed the expansion of slavery and thus opposed the annexation of Cuba in the 1850's (Document 28). This sectional party initially became the political home for those groups which viewed expansion in terms of the slavery issue.

DOCUMENT 26. George Fitzhugh, "Destiny of the Slave States." (*De Bow's Review*, September, 1854. Pp. 281–84.)

It is not saying too much to say that if we hold Cuba, in the next fifty years we will hold the destiny of the richest and most increased commerce that ever dazzled the cupidity of men. And with that commerce we can control the power of the world. Give us this, and we can make the public opinion of the world.

✓   ✓   ✓   ✓   ✓

It is by war you conquer the barbarian race, and by slavery you reduce them to labor and arts of civilized life. Slavery and war have thus been the two great forerunners of civilization.

✓   ✓   ✓   ✓   ✓

A general rupture in Europe would force upon us the undisputed sway of the Gulf of Mexico and the West Indies, with all their rich and mighty productions. Guided by our genius and enterprise, a new world would rise there, as it did before under the genius of Columbus. With Cuba and St. Domingo we could control the productions of the tropics and with them the commerce of the world, and with that the power of the world. . . . Our destiny is onward, until many more rich and prolific regions are to be wrapt under the broad folds of our national banner. The spread of our population and peculiar organization will be more rapid and triumphant than the conquest of the Roman eagles in their proudest day, or the British lion upon the Burampoota or the Ganges.

DOCUMENT 27.   Maturin M. Ballou, *History of Cuba:* or, *Notes of a Traveller in the Tropics.* (New York, 1854. Pp. 216–17, 220–21, 225–30.)

. . . The existence, almost under the shadow of the flag of the freest institutions the earth ever knew, of a government as purely despotic as that of the autocrat of all the Russias, is a monstrous fact that startles the most indifferent observer. It must be seen to be realized. To go hence to Cuba is not merely passing over a few degrees of latitude in a few days' sail,— it is a step from the nineteenth century back into the dark ages. In the clime of sun and endless summer, we are in the land of starless political darkness. Lying under the lee of a land where every man is a sovereign, is a realm where the lives, liberties, and fortunes of all are held at the tenure of the will of a single individual, and whence not a single murmur of complaint can reach the ear of the nominal ruler more than a thousand leagues away in another hemisphere. In close proximity to a country where the taxes, self-imposed, are so light as to be almost unfelt, is one where each free family pays nearly four hundred dollars per annum for the support of a system of bigoted tyranny, yielding in the aggregate an annual revenue of twenty-five millions of dollars for which they receive no equivalent, —no representation, no utterance, for pen and tongue are alike proscribed,— no honor, no office, no emolument; while their industry is crippled, their intercourse with other nations hampered in every way, their bread literally snatched from their lips, the freedom of education denied, and every generous, liberal aspiration of the human soul stifled in its birth. And this in the nineteenth century, and in North America.

Such are the contrasts, broad and striking, and such the reflections forced upon the mind of the citizen of the United States in Cuba. Do they never occur to the minds of the Creoles? We are told that they are willing slaves. Spain tells us so, and she extols to the world with complacent mendacity the loyalty of her *"siempre fielissima isla de Cuba."* But why does she have a soldier under arms for every four white adults? We were about to say, white male citizens, but there are no citizens in Cuba. A proportionate military force in this country would give us a standing army of more than a million bayonets, with an annual expenditure, reckoning each soldier to cost only two hundred dollars per annum, of more than two hundred millions of dollars. And this is the peace establishment of Spain in Cuba—for England and France and the United States are all her allies, and she has no longer to fear the roving buccaneers of the Gulf who once made her tremble in her island fastness. For whom then is this enormous warlike preparation? Certainly for no external enemy,— there is none. The question answers itself,— it is for her very loyal subjects, the people of Cuba, that the queen of Spain makes all this warlike show.

If Cuba lies at present under the armed heel of despotism we may be sure that the anguish of her sons is keenly aggravated by their perfect understanding of our own liberal institutions, and an earnest if fruitless desire to participate in their enjoyment. It is beyond the power of the Spanish government to keep the people of the island in a state of complete darkness, as it seems to desire to do. The young men of Cuba educated at our colleges and schools, the visitors from the United States, and American merchants established on the island, are all so many apostles of republicanism, and propagandists of treason and rebellion. Nor can the captains-general with all their vigilance, exclude what they are pleased to call incendiary newspapers and documents from pretty extensive circulation among the "ever faithful." That liberal ideas and hatred of Spanish despotism are widely entertained among the Cubans is a fact no one who has passed a brief period among them can truthfully deny. The writer of these pages avers, from his personal knowledge, that they await only the means and the opportunity to rise in rebellion against Spain. We are too far distant to see more than the light smoke, but those who have trodden the soil of Cuba have sounded the depths of the volcano. The history of the unfortunate Lopez expedition proves nothing contrary to this. . . .

It is difficult for a republic and a despotism, situated like the United States and Cuba, to live on neighborly terms; and to control the indignation of the citizens of the former, proud and high spirited, conscious of giving no offence, and yet subjected to repeated insults, is a task almost too great for the most adroit and pacific administration. When we add to this feeling among our people a consciousness that Cuba, the source of all this trouble, is in unwilling vassalage to Spain, and longing for annexation to the United States, that under our flag the prosperity of her people would be secured, a vast addition made to our commercial resources, an invaluable safeguard given to our southern frontier, and the key to the Mississippi and the great west made secure forever, we can no longer wonder at the spread of the conviction that Cuba should belong to this country, and this too as soon as can be honorably brought about. Had she possessed more foresight and less pride, Spain would have long since sold the island to the United States, and thereby have relieved herself of a weighty care and a most dangerous property.

"So far from being really injured by the loss of the island," says Hon. Edward Everett, in his able and well known letter to the British minister rejecting the proposition for the tripartite convention, "there is no doubt that, were it peacefully transferred to the United States, a prosperous commerce between Cuba and Spain, resulting from ancient associations and common language and tastes, would be far more productive than the best contrived system of colonial taxation. Such, notoriously, has been the result to Great Britain of the establishment of the independence of the United States."

If it be true that the American minister at Madrid has been authorized to offer a price nothing short of a royal ransom for the island, we cannot conceive that the greedy queen, and even the Cortes of Spain, would reject it, unless secretly influenced by the powers which had the effrontery to propose for our acceptance the tripartite treaty, by which we were expected to renounce forever all pretension to the possession of Cuba. It is difficult to believe that France and England could for a moment seriously suppose that such a ridiculous proposition would be for one moment entertained by this government, and yet they must so have deceived themselves, or otherwise they would not have made the proposition as they did.

Of the importance, not to say necessity, of the possession of Cuba by the United States, statesmen of all parties are agreed; and they are by no means in advance of the popular sentiment; indeed, the class who urge its immediate acquisition, at any cost, by any means, not as a source of wealth, but as a political necessity, is by no means inconsiderable. It would be foreign to our purpose to quote the opinions of any ultraists, nor do we design, in these closing remarks, to enter the field of politics, or political discussion. We have endeavored to state facts only, and to state them plainly, deducing the most incontrovertible conclusions.

We find the following remarks in a recent conservative speech
of Mr. Latham, a member of Congress, from California. They
present, with emphasis, some of the points we have lightly touched
upon:

"I admit that our relations with Spain, growing out of that
island (Cuba), are of an extremely delicate nature; that the fate of
that island, its misgovernment, its proximity to our shores, and the
particular institutions established upon it, are of vast importance
to the peace and security of this country; and that the utmost
vigilance in regard to it is not only demanded by prudence, but an
act of imperative duty on the part of our government. The island
of Cuba commands, in a measure, the Gulf of Mexico. In case of a
maritime war, in which the United States may be engaged, its possession by the enemy might become a source of infinite annoyance
to us, crippling our shipping, threatening the great emporium of
our southern commerce, and exposing our whole southern coast,
from the capes of Florida to the mouth of the Rio Grande, to the
enemy's cruisers. The geographical position of Cuba is such that
we cannot, without a total disregard to our own safety, permit it
to pass into the hands of any first-class power; nay, that it would
be extremely imprudent to allow it to pass even into the hands of
a power of the second rank, possessed of energy and capacity for
expansion."

If Cuba come into our possession peaceably, as the fruits of a
fair bargain, or as a free-will offering of her sons, after a successful
revolution, we can predict for her a future as bright as her past
has been desolate and gloomy; for the union of a territory with a
foreign population to our confederacy is no new and doubtful
experiment. Louisiana, with her French and Spanish Creoles, is
one of the most reliable states of the Union; and, not long after her
admission, she signed, with her best blood, the pledge of fealty to
the common country.

More recently, we all remember how, when Taylor, in the
presence of the foe up the Rio Grande, called for volunteers, the
gallant Creoles rushed to arms, and crowded to his banner. The
Creoles of Cuba are of the same blood and lineage—Spaniards in
chivalry of soul, without the ferocity and fanaticism of the descen-
dants of the Cid. We are sure, from what they have shown in the
past, that liberal institutions will develop latent qualities which
need only free air for their expansion. They will not want com-
panions, friends and helpers. A tide of emigration from the States
will pour into the island, the waste lands will be reclaimed, and
their hidden wealth disclosed; a new system of agricultural econ-

omy will be introduced; the woods of the island will furnish material for splendid ships; towns and villages will rise with magical
celerity, and the whole surface of the "garden of the world" will
blossom like the rose.

"Rich in soil, salubrious in climate, varied in productions, the
home of commerce," says the Hon. O. R. Singleton, of Mississippi,
"Cuba seems to have been formed to become 'the very button on
Fortune's cap.' Washed by the Gulf-stream on half her borders,
with the Mississippi pouring out its rich treasures on one side, and
the Amazon, destined to become a 'cornucopia,' on the other,— with
the ports of Havana and Matanzas on the north, and the Isle of
Pines and St. Jago de Cuba on the south, Nature has written upon
her, in legible characters, a destiny far above that of a subjugated
province of a rotten European dynasty. Her home is in the bosom
of the North American confederacy. Like a lost Pleiad, she may
wander on for a few months or years in lawless, chaotic confusion;
but, ultimately, the laws of nature and of nations will vindicate
themselves, and she will assume her true social and political condition, despite the diplomacy of statesmen, the trickery of knaves,
or the frowns of tyrants. Cuba will be free. The spirit is abroad
among her people; and, although they dare not give utterance to
their thoughts, lest some treacherous breeze should bear them to
a tyrant's ears, still they think and feel, and will act when the
proper time shall arrive. The few who have dared 'to do or die'
have fallen, and their blood still marks the spot where they fell.
Such has been the case in all great revolutionary struggles. Those
who lead the van must expect a sharp encounter before they
break through the serried hosts of tyranny, and many a good man
falls upon the threshold of the temple. . . ."

DOCUMENT 28. Republican National Platform, 1856. (Political Text-Book for 1860. New York, 1860. P. 22.)

Resolved, That the highwayman's plea, that "might makes
right", embodied in the Ostend Circular, was in every respect unworthy of American diplomacy, and would bring shame and dis-
honor upon any government or people that gave it their sanction.

DOCUMENT 29. Democratic National Platform, 1856. (Political Text-Book for 1860. P. 25.)

Resolved, That the Democratic Party will expect of the next administration that every proper effort be made to insure our ascendency in the Gulf of Mexico, and to maintain permanent protection to the great outlets through which are emptied into its waters the products raised out of the soil and the commodities created by the industry of the people of our western valleys and of the Union at large.

•   •   •

President James Buchanan tried to purchase Cuba on several occasions between 1857 and 1860. Congress refused to appropriate the necessary funds, in spite of his attempt to soften the measure by stressing the influence such a move would have in ending the slave trade. This latter argument was connected with the renewed British effort to stop the slave trade. The British were stopping and searching American ships off the coast of Africa and in the Gulf of Mexico. Thus, Buchanan saw the Cuban problem as part of the problem of American rights on the sea, since most of the slave vessels went to Cuba. Spanish harassment of the increasing United States trade with Cuba was another irritating factor.

At the Democratic convention in Charleston, South Carolina in 1860, the Northern and Southern wings produced separate platforms. The planks concerning the acquisition of Cuba revealed the more militant attitude of the Southern wing, but a compromise platform put the two together. When the party split over other issues the two original planks on Cuba reappeared in the new platforms.

DOCUMENT 30.   President James Buchanan to Christopher Fallon (Minister to Spain), December 14, 1857, *Private and Confidential.* (John B. Moore, ed., *The Works of James Buchanan.* 12 vols. Philadelphia, 1910. X: 165.)[16]

In reference to our conversation of yesterday respecting Cuba, I desire to say that the Government of the United States is as willing now to obtain the Island by fair purchase as it was in 1848. You are well acquainted with the efforts made in that year to accomplish the object, & the cause of their failure. It is now, I think, manifest that a transfer of the Island to the United States for a reasonable & fair price would greatly promote the interest of both countries. You are, therefore, authorized to ascertain whether Spain is willing to sell, & upon what terms; & should your report be encouraging, you shall immediately receive more formal instructions. I shall be glad to hear from you on the subject as soon as you can furnish me with any reliable information as to the prospect of success. Both you & those with whom you converse may rely with confidence upon my silence & discretion.

DOCUMENT 31.   President James Buchanan; Second Annual Message to Congress, December 6, 1858. (*Messages and Papers of the Presidents*. 20 vols. Bureau of National Literature edition, New York, n.d. VII: 3040–42.)

Spanish officials under the direct control of the Captain-General of Cuba have insulted our national flag and in repeated instances have from time to time inflicted injuries on the persons and property of our citizens. These have given birth to numerous claims against the Spanish Government, the merits of which have been ably discussed for a series of years by our successive diplomatic representatives. Notwithstanding this, we have not arrived at a practical result in any single instance, unless we may except the case of the *Black Warrior*, under the late Administration, and that presented an outrage of such character as would have justified an immediate resort to war. All our attempts to obtain redress have been baffled and defeated. The frequent and oft-recurring changes in the Spanish ministry have been employed as reasons for delay. We have been compelled to wait again and again until the new minister shall have had time to investigate the justice of our demands.

Even what had been denominated "the Cuban claims," in which more than 100 of our citizens are directly interested, have furnished no exception. These claims were for the refunding of duties unjustly exacted from American vessels at different custom-houses in Cuba so long ago as the year 1844. The principles upon which they rest are so manifestly equitable and just that, after a period of nearly ten years, in 1854 they were recognized by the Spanish Government. . . .

✓   ✓   ✓   ✓   ✓

The truth is that Cuba, in its existing colonial condition, is a constant source of injury and annoyance to the American people.

It is the only spot in the civilized world where the African slave trade is tolerated, and we are bound by treaty with Great Britain to maintain a naval force on the coast of Africa, at much expense both of life and treasure, solely for the purpose of arresting slaves bound to that island. The late serious difficulties between the United States and Great Britain respecting the right of search, now so happily terminated, could never have arisen if Cuba had not afforded a market for slaves. As long as this market shall remain open there can be no hope for the civilization of benighted Africa. Whilst the demand for slaves continues in Cuba wars will be waged among the petty and barbarous chiefs of Africa for the purpose of seizing subjects to supply this trade. In such a condition of affairs it is impossible that the light of civilization and religion can ever penetrate these dark abodes.

It has been made known to the world by my predecessors that the United States have on several occasions endeavored to acquire Cuba from Spain by honorable negotiations. If this were accomplished, the last relic of the African slave trade would instantly disappear. We would not, if we could, acquire Cuba in any other manner. This is due to our national character. All the territory which we have acquired since the origin of the Government has been by a fair purchase from France, Spain, and Mexico or by the free and voluntary act of the independent State of Texas in blending her destinies with our own. This course we shall ever pursue, unless circumstances should occur which we do not now anticipate, rendering a departure from it clearly justifiable under the imperative and overruling law of self-preservation.

The island of Cuba, from its geographical position, commands the mouth of the Mississippi and the immense and annually increasing trade, foreign and coastwise, from the valley of that noble river, now embracing half the sovereign States of the Union. With that island under the domination of a distant foreign power this trade, of vital importance to these States, is exposed to the danger of being destroyed in time of war, and it has hitherto been subjected to perpetual injury and annoyance in time of peace. Our relations with Spain, which ought to be of the most friendly character, must always be placed in jeopardy whilst the existing colonial government over the island shall remain in its present condition.

Whilst the possession of the island would be of vast importance to the United States, its value to Spain is comparatively unimportant. Such was the relative situation of the parties when the great Napoleon transferred Louisiana to the United States. Jealous as he ever was of the national honor and interests of France, no person throughout the world has imputed blame to him for accepting a pecuniary equivalent for this cession.

The publicity which has been given to our former negotiations upon this subject and the large appropriation which may be required to effect the purpose render it expedient before making another attempt to renew the negotiation that I should lay the whole subject before Congress. This is especially necessary, as it may become indispensable to success that I should be intrusted with the means of making an advance to the Spanish Government immediately after the signing of the treaty, without awaiting the ratification of it by the Senate. I am encouraged to make this suggestion by the example of Mr. Jefferson previous to the purchase of Louisiana from France and by that of Mr. Polk in view of the acquisition of territory from Mexico. I refer the whole subject to Congress and commend it to their careful consideration.

DOCUMENT 32. Democratic National Platform, 1860; First Majority Report (Became the plank of the Southern wing). (*Political Text-Book for 1860.* P. 29.)

Resolved, That it is the duty of the Government of the United States to acquire Cuba at the earliest practicable moment.

DOCUMENT 33. Democratic National Platform, 1860; First Minority Report (Became the plank of the Northern, or Douglas, wing). (*Political Text-Book for 1860.* P. 32.)

Resolved, That the Democratic Party are in favor of the acquisition of the island of Cuba, on such terms as shall be honorable to ourselves and just to Spain.

DOCUMENT 34. Democratic National Platform, 1860; Compromise Platform Reported by the Majority. (*Political Text-Book for 1860.* P. 31.)

Fourth, That the Democratic party are in favor of the acquisition of the Island of Cuba, on such terms as shall be honorable to ourselves and just to Spain, at the earliest practicable moment.

•   •   •

Secession and civil war became the major problems of the United States in 1861. Expansion was no longer a major issue, but it was not completely forgotten. There were expansionists in the Republican Party, such as Secretary of State William Seward, who still entertained dreams of territorial additions. Seward, in fact, proposed that the United States declare war on Spain and France as a means of unifying the country. A war with Spain would have certainly meant an attack on Cuba and Puerto Rico. President Abraham Lincoln rejected this proposal, but Seward still believed that the United States should acquire both Cuba and Puerto Rico (Document 36).

The Southern states, however, reversed positions on the expansion issue. The Confederacy desired Spanish recognition and the use of Cuban ports, so the new government was anxious to assure Spain that it had no aggressive designs on Cuba. George Fitzhugh and *De Bow's Review* reflected the shift, and both argued that Cuba should remain under Spanish control to prove the universal validity of slavery.

DOCUMENT 35. William Seward to Carl Schurz (Minister to Spain), April 27, 1861. (Moore, *Digest of International Law*. I: 589.)

The United States "have constantly indulged the belief that they might hope at some day to acquire those islands [Cuba and Porto Rico] by just and lawful means, with the consent of their sovereign."

DOCUMENT 36. George Fitzhugh, "Cuba: The March of Empire and the Course of Trade." (*De Bow's Review*, January, 1861. Pp. 33–34.)

The only thing in this admirable book with which we do not concur, is the suggestion that it is desirable that we should own Cuba. Spain, Brazil, and the South, are the only slaveholding countries. If Cuba were detached from Spain, the cause of slavery would be weakened, not only by the loss of one of the greatest powers of Europe as its friend, but still more, by converting that rising nation into its irreconcilable enemy. . . . Did we own Cuba, her prosperity would be at once attributed to the Anglo-Saxon race, and to American institutions. This would narrow and weaken the argument in favor of the institution of negro slavery.

• • •

The first major Cuban revolt against Spanish control began in 1868. The repercussions of the Ten Years War were soon felt by the United States, since American-owned properties in Cuba were attacked. The United States government offered its good offices to mediate the conflict. The proposal also contained a veiled hint that, if Spain refused, the United States would recognize the belligerent rights of the rebels. The Cubans rejected the armistice terms offered by Spain, however, and the war continued. President Ulysses S. Grant signed a proclamation recognizing Cuban belligerency, but Secretary of State Hamilton Fish suppressed it and the neutrality policy was maintained.

In effect, neutrality was difficult to enforce. The Cuban junta in New York received aid from American citizens, and numerous filibustering expeditions provided the rebels with arms, supplies, and volunteers. In October 1873 one of the main ships engaged in this activity—the *Virginius*—was captured by a Spanish gunboat, and fifty-three passengers and crewmen were executed. The rest were saved by the timely intervention of a British naval vessel. Some Americans demanded war, but the administration alternated between caution and belligerency. The Navy was put on a war basis, and plans were made for an attack on Havana. Grant and Fish, however, were not anxious to fight, and at last a compromise agreement was reached. The *Virginius* was released and Spain paid $80,000 to the families of the executed men.

The war continued to exert an adverse effect on American trade and investments. Having rejected recognition of either Cuban belligerency or independence, the administration finally proposed a joint intervention plan to several European nations. The plan was rejected, however. There was little support in the United States for war or expansion, so the neutrality policy was pursued until the war ended in 1878.

DOCUMENT 37.   Ulysses S. Grant; Annual Message to Congress, December 1, 1873. (*Messages and Papers of the Presidents.* IX: 4196.)

The embargoing of American estates in Cuba, cruelty to American citizens detected in no act of hostility to the Spanish Government, the murdering of prisoners taken with arms in their hands,
and, finally, the capture upon the high seas of a vessel sailing under
the United States flag and bearing a United States registry have
culminated in an outburst of indignation that has seemed for a
time to threaten war. Pending negotiations between the United
States and the Government of Spain on the subject of this capture,
I have authorized the Secretary of the Navy to put our Navy on a
war footing, to the extent, at least, of the entire annual appropriation for that branch of the service, trusting to Congress and the
public opinion of the American people to justify my action.

DOCUMENT 38.   Ulysses S. Grant; Annual Message to Congress, December 7, 1875. (*Messages and Papers of the Presidents.* IX: 4290–94.)

The past year has furnished no evidence of an approaching
termination of the ruinous conflict which has been raging for
seven years in the neighboring island of Cuba. The same disregard
of the laws of civilized warfare and of the just demands of humanity which has heretofore called forth expressions of condemnation
from the nations of Christendom has continued to blacken the
sad scene. . . .

          ✔   ✔   ✔   ✔   ✔

The protracted continuance of this strife seriously affects the
interests of all commercial nations, but those of the United States
more than others, by reason of close proximity, its larger trade
and intercourse with Cuba, and the frequent and intimate personal
and social relations which have grown up between its citizens and
those of the island. Moreover, the property of our citizens in Cuba
is large, and is rendered insecure and depreciated in value and in
capacity of production by the continuance of the strife and the
unnatural mode of its conduct. The same is true, differing only in
degree, with respect to the interests and people of other nations;
and the absence of any reasonable assurance of a near termination

of the conflict must of necessity soon compel the States thus suffering to consider what the interests of their own people and their duty toward themselves may demand.

I have hoped that Spain would be enabled to establish peace in her colony, to afford security to the property and the interests of our citizens, and allow legitimate scope to trade and commerce and the natural productions of the island. Because of this hope, and from an extreme reluctance to interfere in the most remote manner in the affairs of another and a friendly nation, especially of one whose sympathy and friendship in the struggling infancy of our own existence must ever be remembered with gratitude, I have patiently and anxiously waited the progress of events. . . .

While conscious that the insurrection in Cuba has shown a strength and endurance which make it at least doubtful whether it be in the power of Spain to subdue it, it seems unquestionable that no such civil organization exists which may be recognized as an independent government capable of performing its international obligations and entitled to be treated as one of the powers of the earth. A recognition under such circumstances would be inconsistent with the facts, and would compel the power granting it soon to support by force the government to which it had really given its only claim of existence. In my judgment the United States should adhere to the policy and the principles which have heretofore been its sure and safe guides in like contests between revolted colonies and their mother country, and, acting only upon the clearest evidence, should avoid any possibility of suspicion or of imputation.

A recognition of the independence of Cuba being, in my opinion, impracticable and indefensible, the question which next presents itself is that of the recognition of belligerent rights in the parties to the contest.

. . . Considered as a question of expediency, I regard the accordance of belligerent rights still to be as unwise and premature as I regard it to be, at present, indefensible as a measure of right. Such recognition entails upon the country according the rights which flow from its difficult and complicated duties, and requires the exaction from the contending parties of the strict observance of their rights and obligations; it confers the right of search upon the high seas by vessels of both parties; it would subject the carrying of arms and munitions of war, which now may be transported freely and without interruption in the vessels of the United States, to detention and to possible seizure; it would give rise to countless vexatious questions, would release the parent Government from responsibility for acts done by the insurgents, and would invest Spain with the right to exercise the supervision recognized by our treaty of 1795 over our commerce on the high seas, a very large part of which, in its traffic between the Atlantic and the Gulf States and between all of them and the States on the Pacific, passes through the waters which wash the shores of Cuba. The exercise of this supervision could scarce fail to lead, if not to abuses, certainly to collisions perilous to the peaceful relations of the two States. There can be little doubt to what result such supervision would before long draw this nation. . . . The recognition of independence or of belligerency being thus, in my judgment, equally inadmissible, it remains to consider what course shall be adopted should the conflict not soon be brought to an end by acts of the parties themselves, and should the evils which result therefrom, affecting all nations, and particularly the United States, continue. In such event I am of opinion that other nations will be compelled to assume the responsibility which devolves upon them, and to seriously consider the only remaining measures possible—mediation and intervention.

At the same time, while thus impressed I do not at this time recommend the adoption of any measure of intervention. I shall be ready at all times, and as the equal friend of both parties, to respond to a suggestion that the good offices of the United States will be acceptable to aid in bringing about a peace honorable to both. It is due to Spain, so far as this Government is concerned, that the agency of a third power, to which I have adverted, shall be adopted only as a last expedient. Had it been the desire of the United States to interfere in the affairs of Cuba, repeated opportunities for so doing have been presented within the last few years; but we have remained passive, and have performed our whole duty and all international obligations to Spain with friendship, fairness, and fidelity, and with a spirit of patience and forbearance which negatives every possible suggestion of desire to interfere or to add to the difficulties with which she has been surrounded.

CHAPTER II

EMPIRES IN CONFLICT AND
THE CUBAN PROTECTORATE
(1879–1918)

> It seems to me that God, with infinite wisdom and skill, is training
> the Anglo-Saxon race for an hour sure to come in the world's
> future. . . . If I read not amiss, this powerful race will move down
> upon Mexico, down upon Central and South America, out upon
> the islands of the sea, over upon Africa and beyond. And can any
> one doubt that the result of this competition of races will be the
> "survival of the fittest"?
>
> —REVEREND JOSIAH STRONG (1885)

INCREASINGLY IN THE 1880's a new generation of expansionists
were speaking out in the United States. Their "new" Manifest
Destiny was a revised version of the older ideology readjusted to
a world context. A veritable potpourri of emotions, ideas, and
beliefs were combined with a mixture of economic-strategic interests to complete the system. The Reverend Josiah Strong in
1885 published a manifesto of the American mission entitled, *Our
Country*. This handy guide to an aggressive, moralistic foreign
policy was a best-seller. In it Reverend Strong compounded a
mixture of Darwinian evolution, political reform, the "White Man's
Burden," moral uplift at home, evangelizing the world in "this
generation," the frontier hypothesis, anti-Catholicism, and the
vision of prosperity based on a vastly increased export trade.
Captain Alfred Thayer Mahan was another prominent advocate of
an aggressive foreign policy. Mahan placed much emphasis on
naval factors, but the end product of his arguments was much the
same as that of the Congregationalist clergyman.

Underlying these arguments were the problems posed by the
changing economy and society of the United States. Depressions

were becoming more severe, and fears of revolution were ever present after the railroad upheavals of 1877. Poor working conditions, slum problems, corrupt political machines, powerful business combinations, and rumblings of discontent from the farmers of the South and West were part of the confusing and frightening new world. Industrial and urban America was maturing, and the solutions and verities of an agrarian age were showing signs of wear. The old wineskins had to be replaced or patched since industrialization and urbanization produced a potent brew. The advocates of the revived Manifest Destiny were trying to devise solutions for these problems, and thus to patch and reform the existing economic and political containers. This helps to explain why many proponents of the Social Gospel and political progressivism invoked overseas expansion as an outlet for surplus energy and goods.

Many businessmen arrived at the same end via a more restricted road. Leaders in industries producing an increasing surplus began to demand a foreign policy which would protect existing overseas markets, and help to open new ones. This commercial interest was fused into the broader Manifest Destiny movement in the crucible of the Spanish-American War. The result was a policy of imperial expansion based upon an interlocking foundation of ideas and interests.

An important element in the development of this revived expansionism was the technological revolution of the nineteenth century. Nations were drawn closer together by the steam engine, and the leading navies of the world were greatly increasing their power through the adoption of steel, steam, and vastly improved armaments. The expansion of European nations in Africa and the Far East seemed to be a reflection of these changes combined with a mad race for markets, sources of raw materials, and national prestige. American imperialists, such as Mahan, were firmly convinced that the United States must join the race for empire or be forever isolated with a stagnating economy and an indefensible strategic position. Economics and strategy were two sides of the same coin, since national power and security depended on a prosperous economy. As the Reverend Strong stated; "Commerce follows the missionary."[1]

In addition, Captain Mahan, Theodore Roosevelt, and others believed that modern technology would turn the so-called "barbarian" groups of the world—especially of Asia—into a powerful force threatening Western civilization. Civilizing and Christianizing the "backward" areas of the world would tie them to the "Anglo-Saxon" world, and create a world order in which the ideas, institutions, prosperity, and safety of the United States would be protected. Captain Mahan compared the late nineteenth century to the latter days of the Roman Empire. To Mahan, European and American civilization constituted an "oasis set in the midst of a desert of barbarism," and he concluded: "Our Pacific slope, and the Pacific colonies of Great Britain, with an instinctive shudder have felt the threat, which able Europeans have seen in the teeming multitudes of central and northern Asia."[2] These fears, ideas, and interests set the stage for the aggressive foreign policy of the 1890's.

The island of Cuba could hardly escape the effects of these developments in the United States. Trade and investments linked the Spanish colony even more closely to the United States. American exports to Cuba were valued at approximately $105,000,000 in 1894, and in 1896 American investments in sugar and mining properties totaled $50,000,000. By 1897 such industrial giants as Carnegie Steel, the American Sugar Refining Company, and Standard Oil had important stakes in the Cuban economy. In addition, Cuba sold a large share of its sugar to refiners in the United States. Spain, however, continued its harassment of the United States-Cuban trade through taxes, duties, and various restrictions. The United States government agitated for a more liberal trade policy, and for a short period following the enactment of the McKinley Tariff in 1890 Spanish policy became more flexible. In 1894 the Wilson-Gorman Tariff removed sugar from the free list, and Spain canceled the reciprocity agreement between Cuba and the United States. These moves combined with the depression in the United States to drastically cut the market for Cuban sugar.

The poor condition of the Cuban economy helped to set the stage for the final war of independence. After 1878 groups of Cubans had continued to plot the overthrow of Spanish rule, and sporadic outbursts of violence had characterized the uneasy armistice. Under the leadership of José Martí, Tomás Estrada Palma, Antonio Maceo, Máximo Gómez, and Calixto García the Cubans launched their war against Spain in 1895.

For three years the United States government was torn by debates concerning the steps the country should take. Presidents Grover Cleveland and William McKinley were subjected to a variety of conflicting pressures and opinions. The suffering, turmoil, and property destruction in Cuba produced much concern in the United States. Until April 1898, however, both administrations generally followed a policy of offering mediation in the struggle and pressing for some kind of peaceful settlement.

The showdown between the United States and Spain came close on the heels of the sinking of the U.S.S. *Maine* in the harbor of Havana on February 15, 1898. The war fever produced by this event was a complex mixture of humanitarian, political, imperialistic, economic, and nationalistic forces. The war was officially declared on April 25, and was practically over by the last of July.

Complete Cuban independence did not come as rapidly. An American military government was created for Cuba, and ruled the island until 1902. American forces withdrew, however, only after a quasi-protectorate had been established by the addition of the Platt Amendment to the new constitution of Cuba.

From 1902 to 1918 the United States utilized a combination of military force and economic tools to maintain a stable, orderly, and friendly Cuba. This policy was a vital part of American hegemony in the Caribbean which was designed to protect the combined economic-strategic interests of the United States. The United States intervened in Cuba in 1906, and administered the affairs of the island until 1909. During the "race war" of 1912 Marines were landed on numerous occasions to protect American property, and in 1917 a relatively large contingent of American Marines was sent to Cuba to help prevent a revolt and to safeguard property.

American trade with Cuba and the value of American investments in Cuba rapidly increased after 1899. The Platt Amendment and the Reciprocity Treaty of 1903 greatly facilitated both of these developments. By 1914 Cuba ranked sixth among the customers of the United States, and Cuba sold 50.4 per cent of its sugar to the United States. By 1915 American investments in Cuba were valued at $265,000,000, and during World War I American investments became predominant. The declining position of European capital continued until 1960.

By 1918 Cuba was closely bound to the United States by economic and political ties. In fact, the Cuban policy of the United States was regarded by American officials as the model policy for the Caribbean area and Central America. In spite of this rather sanguine view, however, United States-Cuban relations were far from settled.

In order to end the Ten Year War Spain promised various reforms to the Cubans. Little was done, however. Spain finally abolished slavery in Cuba in 1886, but most of the old problems remained. Commercial relations between Cuba and the United States was one of these. To the Cuban sugar planter it was one of the more important problems. Spain finally consented to the negotiation of a commercial treaty to liberalize trade arrangements between the United States and the two remaining Spanish colonies. This treaty was concluded in January 1884 (Document 1). As far as the United States was concerned the most important part of the treaty was the supposed elimination of the "differential flag system." Under this system highly discriminatory duties were levied on goods brought to Cuba by non-Spanish ships. In actual practice the authorities in Cuba evaded the terms of the treaty, and in 1886 President Cleveland threatened to reimpose the retaliatory duties on Spanish ships. The Spaniards concluded another agreement with the United States in October 1886. This agreement provided for reciprocity and the suspension of all discriminating duties of tonnage and impost on trade between the United States and the Spanish colonies. Official evasion characterized the life of this agreement also.

In 1890 the United States Congress passed the McKinley Tariff Act which provided for commercial reciprocity and placed sugar on the free list. Cuban sugar interests pressured the Spanish government, and in 1891 a new reciprocity treaty was signed. Trade between the United States and Cuba increased until 1894, when the Wilson-Gorman Tariff reimposed duties on sugar and Spain canceled the reciprocity agreement.

DOCUMENT 1. Agreement Concerning Commercial Relations between the United States and the Spanish Colonies of Cuba and Porto Rico. Concluded January 2, 1884. (William M. Malloy, ed., *Treaties, Conventions, International Acts, Protocols and Agreements Between the United States of America and Other Powers: 1776-1909*. 2 vols. Washington, D.C., 1910. II: 1680–81.)

Article 1.

In virtue of the authorization given to the Spanish Government by article 3 of the law of the 20th of July, 1882, the duties of the third column of the customs tariffs, of Cuba and Porto Rico, which implies the suppression of the differential flag duty, will at once be applied to the products of, and articles proceeding from, the United States of America.

Article 2.

In consequence of this agreement the Royal Order of the 13th March, 1882, which imposes a special duty on live fish imported into Cuba under a foreign flag, is void for the United States.

Article 3.

The Spanish consular officers in the United States will cease to impose or collect tonnage fees on the cargoes of vessels leaving the ports of the United States for Cuba and Porto Rico.

Article 4.

The Government of the said United States will remove the extra duty of ten *per cent, ad valorem* which it has imposed on the products and articles proceeding from Cuba and Porto Rico under the Spanish flag.

Article 5.

Perfect equality of treatment between the said Spanish provinces and the United States is established, thus removing all extra duties or discrimination not general as to other countries having the treatment of the most favored nations.

Article 6.

The custom houses of the United States will furnish to the respective Spanish consuls, whenever they may request them, certificates of the cargoes of sugar and tobacco brought in vessels proceeding from both the Spanish Antilles, stating the quantities of said articles received.

Article 7.

The preceding stipulations shall go into effect both in the United States and in the provinces of Cuba and Porto Rico on the first day of March, 1884.

Article 8.

Both Governments bind themselves to begin at once negotiations for a complete treaty of commerce and navigation between the United States of America and the said provinces of Cuba and Porto Rico.

• • •

The renewal of hostilities in Cuba produced various reactions in the United States. Many Americans were genuinely sympathetic to the aspirations of the Cuban revolutionaries, and some—such as Horatio Rubens—worked with the Cuban junta (Document 6). The sufferings of the Cuban people added a humanitarian element to this segment of opinion. Some Americans supported a hands-off policy, and opposed any type of intervention. Men such as Senator Orville H. Platt held this view for several reasons. Platt believed that American meddling would lead to war, and he had great doubts concerning the ability of the Cubans to govern themselves.

The American business community was also divided over Cuban policy. Some businessmen wanted American intervention by force —August Belmont was one of this group—while others wanted peace and order in Cuba but not war with Spain. Edwin F. Atkins held important sugar properties in Cuba, and his views reflect an important tendency among those men whose property was actually threatened. Atkins wanted the restoration of peace and order under the old regime, if at all possible. He opposed Cuban independence or the recognition of Cuban belligerent rights, but he believed that military intervention was absolutely necessary in the event the United States adopted either of these policies (Documents 3 and 5).

Some groups of Americans wanted an aggressive policy in the Caribbean to advance American economic and strategic interests. Captain Alfred Thayer Mahan, Theodore Roosevelt, Senator Henry

Cabot Lodge, and Senator John T. Morgan were the more important figures demanding a get-tough-with-Spain policy even at the cost of a war. A study of Midwestern newspaper opinion revealed that this point of view was also prevalent outside the circle of the Washington imperialists.[3] Some of the advocates of this policy wanted the annexation of Cuba, but the acquisition of a Cuban colony does not seem to have been of major importance to most. Roosevelt and Lodge expressed annexation sympathies at various times, but their major colonial ambitions tended to focus on Asia. Roosevelt believed that the United States could exercise control over the Caribbean through a "protection" policy. Thus, the annexation of Cuba was not necessary in order for the United States to exercise control over it after Spanish rule had been ended (Documents 7 and 8). This helps to explain why this segment of American opinion later acquiesced rather easily to those who would support a war only when combined with Cuban independence.

The Cleveland Administration faced these various pressures and tried to encourage Spain to grant reforms. Cleveland offered the mediatory services of the United States, but Spain objected to foreign interference in a crisis which threatened the prestige of the nation. Cleveland's main object was to restore peace in Cuba, but various groups demanded a more vigorous policy. Only a small group wanted military intervention at this time, but larger, and more vocal, groups called for the recognition of Cuban independence or the granting of belligerent rights to the Cuban rebels. In April 1896, both houses of Congress overwhelmingly passed a concurrent resolution declaring that the insurgents were entitled to belligerent rights, and that the good offices of the United States should be used to obtain Spanish recognition of Cuban independence (Document 4). Cleveland ignored this action, and the Republican Party tried to make political capital out of the Cuban situation. The Republican national platform in 1896 called for the government to "actively use its influence and good offices to restore peace and give independence to the islands." After the inauguration of President William McKinley, however, the Republicans generally pursued the policy established by Cleveland. The imperialist element in the party remained just as frustrated under McKinley as it had been under Cleveland. The strategic difference was that now they were among the insiders.

DOCUMENT 2. Senator Orville H. Platt of Connecticut to
Isaac H. Bromley, New York *Tribune,* December 18, 1895.
(Louis A. Coolidge, *An Old-Fashioned Senator—Orville H.
Platt.* New York, 1910. Pp. 265–66.)

Your articles in the *Tribune* about Cuba are in accord with my
judgment. But if the sober, thoughtful business interests of the
country don't want a resolution passed through Congress recognizing "the independence of the republic of Cuba" they must
speak out and speak quickly and loudly. This false devotion to the
cause of liberty, the uneasiness which prevails, and the desire for
patriotic notoriety is acting and reacting on members of the
Senate and House who are usually level-headed, and things are
being worked up to a frenzy that is sweeping such men off their
feet. It seems to be pretty much understood that our Senate Committee on Foreign Relations is going to report such a resolution,
and if it does, the great probability now is that it would pass the
Senate. It is hard to stem the water when the dam breaks away.
There is no republic of Cuba, and the people there who claim
there is have not established their independence any more than
the Armenians have theirs in Turkey. The newspaper rot about
what is going on there, though published one day and contradicted
the next, seems to stir up all the aggressive spirit in the minds
of the people, and the Cuban junta or legation, or whatever it is
called, is active and pestiferous in circulating its views of the situation. It is a case of Naboth's vineyard. Men whose love of humanity was not fluttered when in Texas about a year ago a negro was
covered with kerosene oil and burned to death on a public platform in the presence of 7000 yelling people, are shedding tears
over the sad fate of Maceo. So I repeat what I said in the first
place, that if those who do not want a war with Spain (because
if we recognize an independence which does not exist, we ought
to go and establish it and should probably be forced into a war
anyway) had better bestir themselves. . . .

DOCUMENT 3. Edwin F. Atkins to General William F.
Draper (Congressman from Massachusetts), February 24,
1896. (Edwin F. Atkins, *Sixty Years in Cuba: Reminiscences
of Edwin F. Atkins.* Cambridge, Mass., 1926. Pp. 208–10.)

Up to about November 29th, the insurgents had announced their policy of respecting foreign property, but on or about that date a number of American properties were attacked, including our own, and General Campos responded immediately to our request to send troops there and established a permanent guard of twenty-five men, giving us permission to arm an additional force, the Government furnishing arms. This guard has prevented the destruction of our factory buildings up to the present time. . . .

✶   ✶   ✶   ✶   ✶

Our own case is simply one instance of many, and the question now arises, in case the House and Administration follow the lead of the Senate Committee and recognize belligerency or independence, to whom can the American property-holders look for protection? We could hardly expect that Spain would continue to defend our rights; the insurgents are not in position to do so, even if they were disposed, and in my opinion the only alternative would be the landing of United States troops. Whether the country would be prepared to take such extreme action is a question that should be considered, and whether the sentimental feeling of sympathy with the Cubans should outweigh the property interests amounting to $30,000,000 of United States citizens in Cuba.

It would seem to me that before going further, the United States should decide exactly what she means to do; whether or not she will protect her property interests, and if not, she should advise their abandonment while there is time to save the lives of the Americans in charge. For without any armed protection and subject to the suspicions and attacks of both combatants, few, if any, would be safe.

The losses sustained by Americans in Cuba up to the present time are, in my opinion, of minor importance as compared with what still remains at stake; and whatever action is taken by the United States, it seems to me that due consideration to our future security should be accorded us by our own Government.

DOCUMENT 4. Concurrent Resolution on Cuban Belligerency, 54th Cong., 1st Sess., April 6, 1896. (Fitzhugh Lee, *Cuba's Struggle Against Spain*. New York, 1899. P. 163.)

Resolved by the Senate (the House of Representatives concurring therein), That, in the opinion of Congress, a condition of public war exists between the Government of Spain and the government proclaimed and for some time maintained by force of arms by the people of Cuba; and that the United States of America should maintain a strict neutrality between the contending powers, according to each all the rights of belligerents in the ports and territory of the United States.

Resolved Further, That the friendly offices of the United States should be offered by the President to the Spanish Government for the recognition of the independence of Cuba.

DOCUMENT 5. Edwin F. Atkins to Secretary of State Richard Olney, May 5, 1896. (Atkins, *Sixty Years in Cuba.* Pp. 235–36.)

During my visit I took advantage of every opportunity of getting the views of various classes of people in regard to the insurrection, and its possible solution. A long residence in Cuba and an extended acquaintance among the people enabled me to do this while attending to my own business interests. Among those with whom I talked were General Weyler and General Pando, the heads of some of the largest banking and commercial houses in Havana (American, German, Spanish, and Cuban), as well as many planters both Spanish and Cuban from various districts, also working and country men of both classes. I found among the people having interests in the Island an almost universal feeling that some compromise measure should be sought to bring the war to a speedy termination. . . .

In seeking opinion regarding the possible solution of the troubles, I found a very general feeling both among Spanish residents and native Cubans favoring autonomy (home rule). It is fair to say that the Spaniards do not think that the Cubans would accept anything short of independence, while the Cubans do not believe that the Spaniards would grant any concessions. Yet personally individuals of both classes favored autonomy as a solution. The most intelligent of these people expressed a wish that the United States might use its friendly services to such end. Among the more conservative Spaniards, those having interests at stake, I found an inclination to annexation, although few believed in its practicability. . . .

Upon the insurgent side, the Negro element, together with adventurers from abroad (of whom there are many) who are seeking power or gain, are not inclined to settle the matter short of

absolute independence of the Island; and it is from the intermediate class of both Spaniards and Cubans, the property-owners
and the peaceable citizens, that a solution by means of compromise
must be expected. These are already more than anxious for an
early termination of the war upon any reasonable basis, as they
are fully aware that the resources of the country will soon be
entirely destroyed if the present deplorable condition of affairs
continues.

DOCUMENT 6. The Activities of Horatio Rubens and the
Cuban Junta, 1896–1897. (Horatio S. Rubens, *Liberty: The
Story of Cuba*. New York, 1932. Pp. 204–6.)

The New York reporters visited the Junta offices at 4 o'clock
each afternoon. When I was in the city I met them, answering
their questions if possible and giving them whatever news items
the facts warranted. No matter what the leanings of his paper, I
knew of none who was not personally sympathetic to Cuba in her
trouble. Gradually the meeting came to be known as "The Peanut
Club" for, though each reporter brought his own tobacco, it was
understood that I would contribute a large box of peanuts, a sort
of substitute afternoon tea.

As time passed innumerable volunteers appeared with schemes
and advice. Women who later became active in the woman's
suffrage campaign took a vigorous interest in Cuba's plight. Among
these were Carrie Chapman Catt, and Mrs. Margarita Arlina
Hamm. American women sympathizers organized fairs and bazaars
and, while no great sums of money were raised, many friends were
made for Cuba.

The largest single contribution of American source came in
New York from Tammany Hall. William Astor Chanler had a
preliminary conference with the then Sachem, Richard Croker,
and subsequently, when i called on him, he asked me how much
I wanted, adding that the recent election had left an unexpected
sum in the treasury. I replied that whatever balance there was
would do. Croker, an impassive man, just stared at me, doubtless
because the sum, as I heard later, was nearly $80,000.

It was agreed, then, that I would bring a small committee of
Cubans to a meeting he should call, but he warned me that he
wanted no speeches from any of them.

As usual on formal occasions, the Cubans were all dressed in black. Croker looked around the circle and remarked, in a hoarse aside, "They look like a lot of undertakers!"

We barely arrived on time, for someone had discovered at the last moment that Estrada Palma's cuffs were frayed to a fringe and the rest of us must wait until the damage could be camouflaged.

Croker having prepared for the meeting, a district leader quickly proposed that, out of the unexpended campaign funds, $30,000 be donated to "the sick and wounded Cubans." The motion quietly passed. Croker shook hands with each "undertaker," received their thanks and told me to see the treasurer next morning.

Estrada Palma was stunned and asked me if I thought we would actually receive the money next day. Still later, when I delivered the check to him, he was speechless with delight and wonder. Another expedition could now be dispatched to Cuba.

DOCUMENT 7. Captain Alfred Thayer Mahan, "The Strategic Features of the Gulf of Mexico and the Caribbean Sea," June, 1897. (Captain Alfred Thayer Mahan, *The Interest of America in Sea Power, Present and Future*. Boston, 1898. Pp. 280–82, 288–89, 299, 301–5, 310–12.)

In the Caribbean, likewise, the existence of numerous important ports, and a busy traffic in tropical produce grown within the region itself, do but make more striking the predominance in interest of that one position known comprehensively, but up to the present somewhat indeterminately, as the Isthmus. Here again the element of decisive value is the crossing of the roads, the meeting of the ways, which, whether imposed by nature itself, as in the cases before us, or induced, as sometimes happens, in a less degree, by simple human dispositions, are prime factors in mercantile or strategic consequence. For these reason the Isthmus, even under the disadvantages of land carriage and transshipment of goods, has ever been an important link in the communications from East to West, from the days of the first discoverers and throughout all subsequent centuries, though fluctuating in degree from age to age; but when it shall be pierced by a canal, it will present a maritime centre analogous to the mouth of the Mississippi. They will differ in this, that in the latter case the converging water routes on one side are interior to a great state whose resources they bear, whereas the roads which on either side converge upon the Isthmus lie wholly upon the ocean, the common

possession of all nations. Control of the latter, therefore, rests
either upon local control of the Isthmus itself, or, indirectly, upon
control of its approaches, or upon a distinctly preponderant navy.
In naval questions the latter is always the dominant factor, exactly
as on land the mobile army—the army in the field—must dominate
the question of fortresses, unless war is to be impotent.

We have thus the two centres round which revolve all the military study of the Caribbean Sea and the Gulf of Mexico. The
two sheets of water, taken together, control or affect the approaches
on one side to these two supreme centres of commercial, and therefore of political and military, interest. The approaches on the
other side—the interior communications of the Mississippi, that is,
or the maritime routes in the Pacific converging upon the Isthmus—
do not here concern us. These approaches, in terms of military
art, are known as the "communications." Communications are
probably the most vital and determining element in strategy, military or naval. They are literally the most radical; for all military
operations depend upon communications, as the fruit of a plant
depends upon communication with its root. We draw therefore
upon the map the chief lines by which communication exists
between these two centres and the outside world. Such lines represent the mutual dependence of the centres and the exterior, by
which each ministers to the others, and by severance of which
either becomes useless to the others. It is from their potential
effect upon these lines of communication that all positions in the
Gulf or the Caribbean derive their military value, or want of value.

It is in this respect that the pre-eminent intrinsic advantages
of Cuba, or rather of Spain in Cuba, are to be seen; and also, but
in much less degree, those of Great Britain in Jamaica. Cuba,
though narrow throughout, is over six hundred miles long, from
Cape San Antonio to Cape Maysi. It is, in short, not so much an
island as a continent, susceptible, under proper development, of
great resources—of self-sufficingness. In area it is half as large
again as Ireland, but, owing to its peculiar form, is much more
than twice as long. Marine distances, therefore, are drawn out to
an extreme degree. Its many natural harbors concentrate themselves, to a military examination, into three principal groups,
whose representatives are, in the west, Havana; in the east, Santiago; while near midway of the southern shore lies Cienfuegos.
The shortest water distance separating any two of these is 335
miles, from Santiago to Cienfuegos. To get from Cienfuegos to
Havana 450 miles of water must be traversed and the western point

of the island doubled; yet the two ports are distant by land only a little more than a hundred miles of fairly easy country. Regarded, therefore, as a base of naval operations, as a source of supplies to a fleet, Cuba presents a condition wholly unique among the islands of the Caribbean and of the Gulf of Mexico; to both which it, and it alone of all the archipelago, belongs. It is unique in its size, which should render it largely self-supporting, either by its own products, or by the accumulation of foreign necessaries which naturally obtains in a large and prosperous maritime community; and it is unique in that such supplies can be conveyed from one point to the other, according to the needs of a fleet, by interior lines, not exposed to risks of maritime capture. The extent of the coast-line, the numerous harbors, and the many directions from which approach can be made, minimize the dangers of total blockade, to which all islands are subject. Such conditions are in themselves advantageous, but they are especially so to a navy inferior to its adversary, for they convey the power—subject, of course, to conditions of skill—of shifting operations from side to side, and finding refuge and supplies in either direction.

For, granting that the Isthmus is in the Caribbean the predominant interest, commercial, and therefore concerning the whole world, but also military, and so far possessing peculiar concern for those nations whose territories lie on both oceans, which it now severs and will one day unite—of which nations the United States is the most prominent—granting this, and it follows that entrance to the Caribbean, and transit across the Caribbean to the Isthmus, are two prime essentials to the enjoyment of the advantages of the latter. Therefore, in case of war, control of these two things becomes a military object not second to the Isthmus itself, access to which depends upon them; and in their bearing upon these two things the various positions that are passed under consideration must be viewed—individually first, and afterwards collectively.

In a very literal sense the Caribbean is a mediterranean sea; but the adjective must be qualified when comparison is made with the Mediterranean of the Old World or with the Gulf of Mexico. The last-named bodies of water communicate with the outer oceans by passages so contracted as to be easily watched from near-by positions, and for both there exist such positions of exceptional strength—Gibraltar and some others in the former case, Havana and no other in the latter. The Caribbean, on the contrary, is

enclosed on its eastern side by a chain of small islands, the passages
between which, although practically not wider than the Strait of
Gibraltar, are so numerous that entrance to the sea on that side
may be said correctly to extend over a stretch of near 400 miles.
The islands, it is true, are so many positions, some better, some
worse, from which military effort to control entrance can be
exerted; but their number prevents that concentration and that
certainty of effect which are possible to adequate force resting
upon Gibraltar or Havana.

On the northern side of the sea the case is quite different. From
the western end of Cuba to the eastern end of Puerto Rico extends
a barrier of land for 1200 miles—as against 400 on the east—broken
only by two straits, each fifty miles wide, from side to side of which
a steamer of but moderate power can pass in three or four hours.
These natural conditions, governing the approach to the Isthmus,
reproduce as nearly as possible the strategic effect of Ireland upon
Great Britain. There a land barrier of 300 miles, midway between
the Pentland Firth and the English Channel—centrally situated,
that is, with reference to all the Atlantic approaches to Great
Britain—gives to an adequate navy a unique power to flank and
harass either the one or the other, or both. Existing political conditions and other circumstances unquestionably modify the importance of these two barriers, relatively to the countries affected
by them. Open communication with the Atlantic is vital to Great
Britain, which the Isthmus, up to the present time, is not to the
United States. There are, however, varying degrees of importance
below that which is vital. Taking into consideration that of the
1200-mile barrier to the Caribbean 600 miles is solid in Cuba, that
after the 50-mile gap of the Windward Passage there succeeds 300
miles more of Haiti before the Mona Passage is reached, it is in-
disputable that a superior navy, resting on Santiago de Cuba or
Jamaica, could very seriously incommode all access of the United
States to the Caribbean mainland, and especially to the Isthmus.

In connection with this should be considered also the influence
upon our mercantile and naval communication between the Atlantic
and the Gulf coasts exercised by the peninsula of Florida, and by
the narrowness of the channels separating the latter from the
Bahama Banks and from Cuba. The effect of this long and not
very broad strip of land upon our maritime interests can be realized
best by imagining it wholly removed, or else turned into an island
by a practicable channel crossing its neck. In the latter case the
two entrances to the channel would have indeed to be assured; but
our shipping would not be forced to pass through a long, narrow

waterway, bordered throughout on one side by foreign and possibly hostile territories. In case of war with either Great Britain or Spain, this channel would be likely to be infested by hostile cruisers, close to their own base, the very best condition for a commerce-destroying war; and its protection by us under present circumstances will exact a much greater effort than with the supposed channel, or than if the Florida Peninsula did not exist. The effect of the peninsula is to thrust our route from the Atlantic to the Gulf 300 miles to the southward, and to make imperative a base for control of the strait; while the case is made worse by an almost total lack of useful harbors. On the Atlantic, the most exposed side, there is none; and on the Gulf none nearer to Key West than 175 miles, where we find Tampa Bay. There is, indeed, nothing that can be said about the interests of the United States in an Isthmian canal that does not apply now with equal force to the Strait of Florida. The one links the Atlantic to the Gulf, as the other would the Atlantic to the Pacific. It may be added here that the phenomenon of the long, narrow peninsula of Florida, with its strait, is reproduced successively in Cuba, Haiti, and Puerto Rico, with the passages dividing them. The whole together forms one long barrier, the strategic significance of which cannot be overlooked in its effect upon the Caribbean; while the Gulf of Mexico is assigned to absolute seclusion by it, if the passages are in hostile control.

The aim of any discussion such as this should be to narrow down, by a gradual elimination, the various factors to be considered, in order that the decisive ones, remaining, may become conspicuously visible. The trees being thus thinned out, the features of the strategic landscape can appear. The primary processes in the present case have been carried out before seeking the attention of the reader, to whom the first approximations have been presented under three heads. First, the two decisive centres, the mouth of the Mississippi and the Isthmus. Second, the four principal routes, connecting these two points with others, have been specified; these routes being, 1, between the Isthmus and the Mississippi themselves; 2, from the Isthmus to the North American coast, by the Windward Passage; 3, from the Gulf of Mexico to the North American coast by the Strait of Florida; and 4, from the Isthmus to Europe, by the Anegada Passage. Third, the principal military positions throughout the region in question have been laid down, and their individual and relative importance indicated.

From the subsequent discussion it seems evident that, as "communications" are so leading an element in strategy, the position or positions which decisively affect the greatest number or extent of the communications will be the most important, so far as situation goes. Of the four principal lines named, three pass close to, and are essentially controlled by, the islands of Cuba and Jamaica, namely, from the Mississippi to the Isthmus by the Yucatan Channel, from the Mississippi to the Atlantic coast of America by the Strait of Florida, and from the Isthmus to the Atlantic coast by the Windward Passage. The fourth route, which represents those from the Isthmus to Europe, passes nearer to Jamaica than to Cuba; but those two islands exercise over it more control than does any other one of the archipelago, for the reason that any other can be avoided more easily, and by a wider interval, than either Jamaica or Cuba.

Regarded as positions, therefore, these two islands are the real rivals for control of the Caribbean and of the Gulf of Mexico; and it may be added that the strategic centre of interest for both Gulf and Caribbean is to be found in the Windward Passage,[4] because it furnishes the ultimate test of the relative power of the two islands to control the Caribbean.

DOCUMENT 8.   Theodore Roosevelt to William Astor Chanler, December 23, 1897. (Elting E. Morison, ed., *The Letters of Theodore Roosevelt*. 8 vols., Cambridge, Mass., 1951–54. I: 746–47.[5])

. . . I wish we had a perfectly consistent foreign policy, and that this policy was that ultimately every European power should be driven out of America, and every foot of American soil, including the nearest islands in both the Pacific and the Atlantic, should be in the hands of independent American states, and so far as possible in the possession of the United States or under its protection. With this end in view I should take every opportunity to oust each European power in turn from this continent, and to acquire for ourselves every military coign of vantage. . . . Now, our people are not up as yet to following out this line of policy in its entirety, and the thing to be done is to get whatever portion of it is possible at the moment. . . . At present, owing mainly to the change in the Spanish policy, it is not possible at the moment to do anything about Cuba, but it is possible to get Hawaii. . . . If we don't take Hawaii it will pass into the hands of some strong nation, and the chance of our taking it will be gone forever. If we fail to take Cuba it will remain in the hands of a weak and decadent nation, and the chance to take it will be just as good as ever. . . . I do not believe that Cuba can be pacified by autonomy and I earnestly hope that events will so shape themselves that we must interfere some time in the not distant future. . . . You ought to get Mahan's last book on America's interest in Sea Power.

•　　•　　•

In his annual message to Congress of December 1897, President McKinley expressed cautious hopes that a peaceful settlement of the Cuban insurrection would be effected by Spain. After the assassination of the Spanish Premier Antonio Canovas in August 1897, the new Premier—the liberal Praxedes Sagasta—introduced a more moderate policy. General Valeriano Weyler was recalled, and the brutal "reconcentration" policy was modified. In addition, the Spanish government informed McKinley that plans were being made to grant limited autonomy to Cuba.

Two events occurred in February 1898 which greatly strengthened the hand of those Americans that wanted war with Spain. A private letter written by the Spanish Minister, Dupuy de Lôme, was stolen by agents of the Cuban junta and published in William Randolph Hearst's *New York Journal*. This letter contained some rather blunt statements concerning McKinley, and served to convince some that Spain was not sincere in its dealings with the United States. The sinking of the *Maine* followed by a week, and was a godsend to the jingoes. "Remember the Maine, to hell with Spain," became the slogan of the day as the Hearst press— and its many imitators—declared the guilt of Spain.

War fever was in the air and the red-ink headlines of American newspapers fanned the flames of this very profitable crisis. Congress unanimously voted $50 million for military expenditures, and Theodore Roosevelt preached the necessity of war to McKinley so many times that the President told him to stay away. McKinley still hoped that a peaceful solution could be found, but pressure for war was building rapidly. The President based his hopes for averting war on an armistice in Cuba, to be followed by autonomy. The Cuban insurgents, however, wanted neither and Spain was not prepared to accept Cuban independence. Horatio Rubens stressed the policy of the insurgents in an interview with McKinley (Document 10), and this information may have played a part in the President's decision in April to ignore the Spanish armistice proposals.

Faced with an apparently irreconcilable conflict in Cuba, Mc-Kinley was, at the same time, being subjected to various pressures in the United States. Lodge, Roosevelt, and other advocates of the "large policy" for imperial expansion were now ringing tocsin for *"Cuba libre"* as a lever to move the country down the imperial road (Document 9). Public opinion generally was inflamed by humanitarianism, nationalism, and the desire to end the chaos in Cuba. Republican Party leaders were also concerned over the Southern and Midwestern clamors for war. William Jennings Bryan and many of the old Populist leaders were speaking out for Cuban independence, and visions of "Free Silver" and "Free Cuba" as a Democratic Party slogan in 1900 caused anguish among the Republicans. The President was also under pressure from business groups to effect a speedy end to the situation which was harming trade and investments. McKinley considered a plan to purchase Cuban independence, but this was dropped due to the belief that the Senate would not approve. On March 27, 1898, the United States submitted its final proposals to Spain. Specifically, these concerned an immediate armistice, the revocation of the concentration decree, and United States mediation. The Spanish government was also informed that complete independence for Cuba was what Americans wanted. The first Spanish reply was a rejection of these proposals, but, on April 10, Spain agreed to the specific proposals.

On April 11, McKinley sent his famous message to Congress requesting authorization to use military force to bring peace to Cuba (Document 11). In this message he referred to the Spanish note of April 10, but to McKinley and the Congress this was no longer the answer. The Spanish government said nothing about Cuban independence, and McKinley knew that the Cuban insurgents would not agree to an armistice without independence. Thus, in terms of American opinion for Cuban independence and the restoration of peace coupled with the insurgents' policy, the Spanish note was "too little, and too late." The Spanish decision would probably not have brought peace to Cuba. McKinley's message was partly based on political realities, and partly on his decision that only American force could restore peace to Cuba. He did, however, leave the door ajar for another attempt at mediation if Congress wished to give the new Spanish policy a trial. Congress promptly slammed the door, and gave Spain the alternatives of Cuban independence or war (Document 12).

The "splendid little war" was short and complete. The United States stole the show from the Cuban insurgents—as the name of the war indicates—and would not even allow the insurgent leaders to be present at the final capitulation of the Spanish forces in Cuba. The American press played down the activities of the insurgents, and concentrated on the military engagements of American naval and land forces (Document 14). The Cubans were presented with a quick victory, but the insurgents were not too sure what the consequences would be.

The treaty of peace was concluded in December 1898, and the Senate gave its approval in February 1899 (Document 15). As a result the United States obtained the Philippine Islands, Guam, Puerto Rico, and the right to occupy Cuba for an indefinite period. The Spanish commissioners at Paris tried to persuade the United States to annex Cuba, but the American delegates upheld the Teller Amendment pledging Cuban independence. Spain gave up its title to Cuba, and the island was theoretically free. How free was an unanswered question.

DOCUMENT 9. Theodore Roosevelt to Robert Bacon, April 8, 1898. (Morison, *Letters of Theodore Roosevelt*. II: 814.)

If it is in any way possible, the President and Congress must act together. But I do not feel that there is any honorable escape from war. We should not haggle over matters separately. Let us treat the whole question as an entirety and put Spain out of the western hemisphere. I am perfectly willing to follow the policy of intervening without recognizing independence, although I think it a mistake; for I should be very doubtful about annexing Cuba in any event, and should most emphatically oppose it unless the Cubans wished it. I care nothing about recognizing the present government if only we emphatically state that we will recognize the independence of Cuba. I don't want it to seem that we are engaged merely in a land-grabbing war. Let us fight on the broad grounds of securing the independence of a people who, whether

they amount to much or not, have been treated with hideous brutality by the oppressors; upon the further ground of putting a
medieval power once for all out of the western world; and, finally,
with the determination to get the only satisfaction we can for our
murdered men, not by taking blood money for them, but by securing the two objects outlined above.

DOCUMENT 10[6]. Horatio S. Rubens (Attorney for the Cuban
Junta) confers with President William McKinley, January
or February, 1898. (Rubens, *Liberty: The Story of Cuba.*
Pp. 326–29.)

As it became more evident that the proposed autonomy would
not satisfy the Cubans, it occurred to McKinley and Woodford that
the solution could be found, if fighting were to cease.

McKinley called me to the White House and when I got there
he wasted no words. His piercing black eyes were alight with
ominous fires, taking on an eagle look under his shaggy, heavy
brows. He walked restlessly around his private office and the very
tails of his frock coat seemed to swing with a warrior determination.

"You must," he clipped out at me, "accept an immediate armistice with Spain."

"To what end, Mr. President?"

"To settle the strife in Cuba," he cried.

"But is Spain ready to grant Cuba independence?" I asked.

"That isn't the question now," he exclaimed, his voice rising.
"We may discuss that later. The thing for the moment is an armistice."

"But, Mr. President, we can talk here, while they continue to
fight down there."

"No no," he said, sharply; "that cannot be thought of. The loss
of life and property must stop at once."

"We can treat on one basis and one basis only," I reminded
him. "The absolute independence of Cuba. We are willing to follow the example of the United States, for the battle of New
Orleans was fought after the treaty of peace was signed between
England and the United States."

The President looked like a man abruptly stopped at the jump.

In a tone modified by a sort of plaintive perplexity he said, "But
why do the Cubans refuse what might be as effective as independence? Why don't they come together with Spain?"

"Because, Mr. President, they are separated by a river of blood which, flowing now for thirteen years, cannot coagulate."

"But why can't the flow be stopped now, at least? What reason is there, other than sentiment—or obstinacy—to refuse an armistice?"

"The reason is a practical one, Mr. President. Nothing you could propose would be so beneficial to Spain and so detrimental to Cuba as an armistice. If an armistice is carried out in good faith, it means the dissolution and disintegration of the Cuban army. There is no commissary for it even now; it must live, poorly and precariously, on the country. If armistice is accepted the army cannot even obtain its food supplies; it will starve. Furthermore, in the natural uncertainty pending negotiations, the men would scatter, going to their homes. Spain would certainly prolong the negotiations until this happened. If, on the other hand, having accepted the armistice, the Cubans continued to live on the country, they would be loudly charged with breach of faith, even by you, Mr. President. In the last analysis, therefore, you propose to do what over 200,000 Spanish soldiers have not been able to do to the Cuban army; you propose to wipe it out."

"But how can we let the terrible struggle continue?" he pleaded.

"If the Cubans fail to obtain their objective untold lives have been uselessly sacrificed. If success is not obtained now, it means another war for the children and grandchildren of those suffering now in the field, because the only justification for bringing on the war in the first place lies in the fundamental principle of liberty, and the willingness of men to die in pursuit of it,—because, if we fail, everyone who has participated in this revolution will be called bandit, assassin, incendiary, instead of patriot."

The President stood looking out over the South grounds. "One thing I don't understand," he said, at length; "that is, what is the Cuban? Is he not a Spanish descendant, though born in Cuba? And if he is, why is he so good that we must sympathize with him, and the Spaniard so bad that we must detest him?"

The only answer I could make was a simple one. "There is the difference between Cuban and Spaniard today, Mr. President, that there was between Colonial and Englishman in '76."

The President stared at me and then turned abruptly to look out the window again. "Isn't this a beautiful view of the river?" he said.

"Beautiful, Mr. President," I agreed. And that was the only point of agreement between us that day.

Being a trifle conscience stricken at so blunt a thrust as com-

paring the English with the Spaniards, I said, "Perhaps if you look
at these photographs, you will see that I have gratuitously maligned
the English by comparing them with the Spaniards." I had brought
some enlarged photographs of Cuban Reconcentrados.

McKinley bent over them at the table, looking gingerly at them
at first; then he looked more closely; finally, I noticed, tears began
to course down his face.

When he could trust his voice he said, "I hope you will say
nothing of the effect of this sight on me."

I assured him that it did him too much credit, and that I would
not allow his sentiment to be exploited.

Then the President's mind reverted to the subject of the armistice.

"You are certain your friends will not have an armistice?" he
asked.

"Quite certain, Mr. President."

Suddenly he was the eagle again. "Then listen to me; I know
what you want; you want us to go to war in behalf of Cuba. But
that won't be. I have conferred with every man in Congress, Democrat and Republican, and I have a majority with me. You do not
realize the thousands of lives and millions of treasure war means.
I have you beaten." He strode up and down before me, gazing at
me with an indomitable triumph.

"You must excuse me if I dispute you, Mr. President," I
answered. "We do not ask you to go to war; we only ask for your
neutrality, for the recognition of Cuban belligerent rights. What
you offer is not neutrality, but an armistice which would annihi-
late the Cuban Army of Liberation. One thing more, Mr. President.
As you realize, an armistice is only possible anyhow between belligerents; and the price of recognizing Cuban belligerency is their
sanction to a means of their own disappearance."

Bankers and business men, through certain Cubans, had pressed
Estrada Palma for the support of this eleventh hour salvation, an
armistice. The Delegate had politely but firmly explained that,
knowing the temper of his people, he could not possibly propose
such a solution.

When I had left the President, his words, "I have you beaten!"
kept recurring to me. I conferred with newspaper friends, Hearst,
Bradford Merrill, men from the *New York Sun* and other papers,
for it occurred to me that we were now at the point of an action
which placed the American people and the McKinley Administration in a controversial position. The next Fall would see the election of members of Congress; the people could then be aroused

to vote for those friendly to Cuba. Meanwhile, "I have you beaten" meant now, in the present Congress.

DOCUMENT 11. William McKinley; Special Message to the Congress of the United States, April 11, 1898. (*Messages and Papers of the President*, XIII: 6281–82, 6284, 6292.)

Obedient to that precept of the Constitution which commands the President to give from time to time to the Congress information of the state of the Union and to recommend to their consideration such measures as he shall judge necessary and expedient, it becomes my duty to now address your body with regard to the grave crisis that has arisen in the relations of the United States to Spain by reason of the warfare that for more than three years has raged in the neighboring island of Cuba.

I do so because of the intimate connection of the Cuban question with the state of our own Union and the grave relation the course which it is now incumbent upon the nation to adopt must needs bear to the traditional policy of our Government if it is to accord with the precepts laid down by the founders of the Republic and religiously observed by succeeding Administrations to the present day.

Our people have beheld a once prosperous community reduced to comparative want, its lucrative commerce virtually paralyzed, its exceptional productiveness diminished, its fields laid waste, its mills in ruins, and its people perishing by tens of thousands from hunger and destitution. We have found ourselves constrained, in the observance of that strict neutrality which our laws enjoin and which the law of nations commands, to police our own waters and watch our own seaports in prevention of any unlawful act in aid of the Cubans.

Our trade has suffered, the capital invested by our citizens in Cuba has been largely lost, and the temper and forbearance of our people have been so sorely tried as to beget a perilous unrest among our own citizens, which has inevitably found its expression from time to time in the National Legislature, so that issues wholly external to our own body politic engross attention and stand in the way of that close devotion to domestic advancement that becomes a self-contained commonwealth whose primal maxim has been the avoidance of all foreign entanglements. All this must needs awaken, and has, indeed, aroused, the utmost concern on the part of this Government, as well during my predecessor's term as in my own.

In this state of affairs my Administration found itself confronted with the grave problem of its duty. My message of last December reviewed the situation and narrated the steps taken with a view to relieving its acuteness and opening the way to some form of honorable settlement. The assassination of the prime minister, Canovas, led to a change of government in Spain. The former administration, pledged to subjugation without concession, gave place to that of a more liberal party, committed long in advance to a policy of reform involving the wider principle of home rule for Cuba and Puerto Rico.

The overtures of this Government made through its new envoy, General Woodford, and looking to an immediate and effective amelioration of the condition of the island, although not accepted to the extent of admitted mediation in any shape, were met by assurances that home rule in an advanced phase would be forthwith offered to Cuba, without waiting for the war to end, and that more humane methods should thence forth prevail in the conduct of hostilities. Coincidentally with these declarations the new government of Spain continued and completed the policy, already begun by its predecessor, of testifying friendly regard for this nation by releasing American citizens held under one charge or another connected with the insurrection, so that by the end of November not a single person entitled in any way to our national protection remained in a Spanish prison.

The long trial has proved that the object for which Spain has waged the war can not be attained. The fire of insurrection may flame or may smolder with varying seasons, but it has not been and it is plain that it can not be extinguished by present methods. The only hope for relief and repose from a condition which can no longer be endured is the enforced pacification of Cuba. In the name of humanity, in the name of civilization, in behalf of endangered American interests which give us the right and duty to speak and to act, the war in Cuba must stop.

In view of these facts and of these considerations I ask the Congress to authorize and empower the President to take measures to secure a full and final termination of hostilities between the Government of Spain and the people of Cuba, and to secure in the island the establishment of a stable government, capable of maintaining order and observing its international obligations, insuring peace and tranquillity and the security of its citizens as well as our own, and to use the military and naval forces of the United States as may be necessary for these purposes.

And in the interest of humanity and to aid in preserving the lives of the starving people of the island I recommend that the distribution of food and supplies be continued and that an appropriation be made out of the public Treasury to supplement the charity of our citizens.

The issue is now with the Congress. It is a solemn responsibility. I have exhausted every effort to relieve the intolerable condition of affairs which is at our doors. Prepared to execute every obligation imposed upon me by the Constitution and the law, I await your action.

Yesterday, and since the preparation of the foregoing message, official information was received by me that the latest decree of the Queen Regent of Spain directs General Blanco, in order to prepare and facilitate peace, to proclaim a suspension of hostilities, the duration and details of which have not yet been communicated to me.

This fact, with every other pertinent consideration, will, I am sure, have your just and careful attention in the solemn deliberations upon which you are about to enter. If this measure attains a successful result, then our aspirations as a Christian, peace-loving people will be realized. If it fails, it will be only another justification for our contemplated action.

DOCUMENT 12. Joint Resolution of Congress for the Recognition of the Independence of Cuba, April 20, 1898. (*Messages and Papers of the Presidents*. XIII: 6297–98.)

Whereas the abhorrent conditions which have existed for more than three years in the island of Cuba, so near our own borders, have shocked the moral sense of the people of the United States, have been a disgrace to Christian civilization, culminating, as they have, in the destruction of a United States battle ship, with 266 of its officers and crew, while on a friendly visit in the harbor of Havana, and cannot longer be endured, as has been set forth by the President of the United States in his message to Congress of April 11, 1898, upon which the action of Congress was invited: Therefore,

Resolved by the Senate and House of Representatives of the United States of America in Congress assembled, First. That the people of the island of Cuba are and of right ought to be free and independent.

Second. That it is the duty of the United States to demand, and the Government of the United States does hereby demand, that the Government of Spain at once relinquish its authority and government in the island of Cuba and withdraw its land and naval forces from Cuba and Cuban waters.

Third. That the President of the United States, be and hereby is, directed and empowered to use the entire land and naval forces of the United States and to call into the actual service of the United States the militia of the several States to such extent as may be necessary to carry these resolutions into effect.

Fourth. That the United States hereby disclaims any disposition or intention to exercise sovereignty, jurisdiction, or control over said island except for the pacification thereof, and asserts its determination, when that is accomplished, to leave the government and control of the island to its people.

DOCUMENT 13. Declaration of War with Spain, April 25, 1898. (*Messages and Papers of the Presidents*. XIII: 6348.)

AN ACT declaring that war exists between the United States of America and the Kingdom of Spain.

Be It enacted by the Senate and House of Representatives of the United States of America in Congress assembled, First. That war be, and the same is hereby, declared to exist, and that war has existed since the 21st day of April, A.D. 1898, including said day, between the United States of America and the Kingdom of Spain.

Second. That the President of the United States be, and he hereby is, directed and empowered to use the entire land and naval forces of the United States and to call into the actual service of the United States the militia of the several States to such extent as may be necessary to carry this act into effect.

DOCUMENT 14. Mr. Dooley, "On Our Cuban Allies." (Finley Peter Dunne, *Mr. Dooley in Peace and In War*. Boston, 1898. Pp. 63–67.)

"Well, sir," said Mr. Dooley, "dam thim Cubians! If I was Gin'ral Shafter, I'd back up th' wagon in front iv th' dure, an' I'd say to Gin'ral Garshy,[7] I'd say, 'I want you'; an' I'd have thim all down at th' station an' dacently booked be th' desk sergeant befure th' fall iv night. Th' impydince iv thim!"

"What have they been doin'?" Mr. Hennessy asked.

"Failin' to undherstand our civilization," said Mr. Dooley. "Ye see, it was this way. This is th' way it was: Gin'ral Garshy with wan hundherd thousan' men's been fightin' bravely f'r two years f'r to liberyate Cubia. F'r two years he's been marchin' his sivinty-five thousan' men up an' down th' island, desthroyin' th' haughty Spanyard be th' millyons. Whin war was declared, he offered his own sarvice an' th' sarvices iv his ar-rmy iv fifty thousan' men to th' United States; an', while waitin' f'r ships to arrive, he marched at th' head iv his tin thousan' men down to Sandago de Cuba an' captured a cigar facthry, which they soon reyjooced to smokin' ruins. They was holdin' this position—Gin'ral Garshy an' his gallant wan thousan' men—whin Gin'ral Shafter arrived. Gin'ral Garshy immedjitly offered th' sarvices iv himsilf an' his two hundred men f'r th' capture iv Sandago; an', when Gin'ral Shafter arrived, there was Gin'ral Garshy with his gallant band iv fifty Cubians, r-ready to eat at a minyit's notice.

"Gin'ral Shafter is a big, coorse, two-fisted man fr'm Mitchigan, an', whin he see Gin'ral Garshy an' his twinty-five gallant followers, 'Fr-ront,' says he. 'This way,' he says, 'step lively,' he says, 'an' move some iv these things,' he says. 'Sir,' says Gin'ral Garshy, 'd'ye take me f'r a dhray?' he says. 'I'm a sojer,' he says, 'not a baggage car,' he says. 'I'm a Cubian pathrite, an' I'd lay down me life an' the lives iv iv'ry wan iv th' eighteen brave men iv me devoted ar-rmy,' he says; 'but I'll be dam'd if I carry a thrunk,' he says. 'I'll fight whiniver 'tis cool,' he says, 'an they ain't wan iv these twelve men here that wudden't follow me to hell if they was awake at th' time,' he says; 'but,' he says, 'if 'twas wurruk we were lookin' f'r, we cud have found it long ago,' he says. 'They'se a lot iv it in this counthry that nobody's usin',' 'he says. 'What we want,' he says, 'is freedom,' he says; 'an', if ye think we have been in th' woods dodgin' th' savage corryspondint f'r two year,' he says, 'f'r th' sake iv r-rushin' yer laundhry home,' he says, ''tis no wundher,' he says, 'that th' r-roads fr'm Marinette to Kalamazoo is paved with goold bricks bought be th' people iv ye'er native State,' he says.

"So Shafter had to carry his own thrunk; an' well it was f'r him that it wasn't Gin'ral Miles,' the weather bein' hot. An' Shafter was mad clear through; an', whin he took hold iv Sandago, an' was sendin' out invitations, he scratched Garshy. Garshy took his gallant band iv six back to th' woods; an' there th' three iv thim ar-re now, ar-rmed with forty r-rounds iv canned lobster, an' ready to raysist to th' death. Him an' th' other man has written to Gin'ral

Shafter to tell him what they think iv him, an' it don't take long."

"Well," said Mr. Hennessy, "I think Shafter done wrong. He might've asked Garshy in f'r to see th' show, seein' that he's been hangin' ar-round f'r a long time, doin' th' best he cud."

"It isn't that," explained Mr. Dooley. "Th' trouble is th' Cubians don't understand our civilization. Over here freedom means hard wurruk. What is th' ambition iv all iv us, Hinnissy? 'Tis ayether to hold our job or to get wan. We want wurruk. We must have it. D'ye reymimber th' sign th' mob carrid in th' procession las' year? 'Give us wurruk, or we perish,' it said. They had their heads bate in be polismen because no philanthropist'd come along an' make thim shovel coal. Now, in Cubia, whin th' mobs turns out, they carry a banner with the wurrds, 'Give us nawthin' todo, or we perish.' Whin a Cubian somes home at night with a happy smile on his face, he don't say to his wife an' childher, 'Thank Gawd, I've got wurruk at last!' He says, 'Thank Gawd, I've been fired.' An' th' childher go out, and they say, 'Pah-pah has lost his job,' And Mrs. Cubian buys hersilf a new bonnet; and where wanst there was sorrow an' despair all is happiness an' a cottage organ.

"Ye can't make people here undherstand that, an' ye can't make a Cubian undherstand that freedom means th' same thing as a pinitinchry sintince. Whin we thry to get him to wurruk, he'll say: 'Why shud I? I haven't committed anny crime.' That's goin' to be th' throuble. Th' first thing we know we'll have another war in Cubia whin we begin disthributin' good jobs, twelve hours a day, wan sivinty-five. Th' Cubians ain't civilized in our way. I sometimes think I've got a touch iv Cubian blood in me own veins."

DOCUMENT 15.   Treaty of Paris Ending the Spanish-American War; Concluded December 10, 1898; Proclaimed April 11, 1898. (Malloy, *Treaties, Conventions . . . Between the United States of America and Other Powers*. II: 1691–92, 1695.)

Article I.

Spain relinquishes all claim of sovereignty over and title to Cuba.

And as the island is, upon its evacuation by Spain, to be occupied by the United States, the United States will, so long as such occupation shall last, assume and discharge the obligations that may under international law result from the fact of its occupation, for the protection of life and property.

✓   ✓   ✓   ✓   ✓

Article VII.

The United States and Spain mutually relinquish all claims for indemnity, national and individual, of every kind of either Government, or of its citizens or subjects, against the other Government, that may have arisen since the beginning of the late insurrection in Cuba and prior to the exchange of ratifications of the present treaty, including all claims for indemnity for the cost of the war.

The United States will adjudicate and settle the claims of its citizens against Spain relinquished in this article.

Article XVI.

It is understood that any obligations assumed in this treaty by the United States with respect to Cuba are limited to the time of its occupancy thereof; but it will upon the termination of such occupancy, advise any Government established in the island to assume the same obligations.

•   •   •

The United States military forces in Cuba made a rapid conversion from fighting to the administration of civil affairs. The military governors between 1898 and 1902, carried out a program which consisted of organizing the government of Cuba at all levels, eradicating yellow fever, demobilizing the Cuban insurgents, and carrying out relief projects. In addition, an extensive program was created for the rehabilitation of schools, hospitals, the penal system, the judiciary, and charitable institutions (Documents 19 and 20). The military government definitely smoothed the transition from war-ravaged colony to independent state.

In 1898 the future status of Cuba was not completely clear. Independence was declared to be an objective of the war by virtue of the Teller Amendment to the resolution of April 20, 1898, but the degree of independence was a hotly debated subject. Many American officials thought in terms of "controlled" independence, and few thought it wise to turn the island over to the insurgents. In general, the policy of the McKinley Administration was to establish a peaceful, orderly Cuban government that would be friendly to the United States and protect property. This was consistent with McKinley's prewar policy and with his declarations of April 11, 1898. Men of diverse prewar viewpoints such as

Edwin F. Atkins, Orville H. Platt, and Theodore Roosevelt could agree on these objectives (Documents 16, 17, 24, and 25).

The problem at hand was the degree of control the United States should exercise, and the method of implementing it. Annexation was held by Senator Albert Beveridge and General James Wilson to be the best solution. Both, however, stated that such a policy should only be followed if the Cubans requested it. Few, if any, Americans wanted to see Cuba as an exploited colony. The annexationists talked in terms of possible statehood (Document 18), and many officials stated the need for some kind of privileged economic status for Cuba.

The end product of these debates was the Platt Amendment; a joint product of Senator Orville H. Platt and Secretary of War Elihu Root (Document 21). This was a compromise arrangement (Document 24) which Root made more flexible in an interpretation aimed at overcoming Cuban opposition (Documents 22 and 23). The Platt Amendment was in keeping with the policy of insuring stability by placing the Cuban government in the hands of conservative, property owners. As such, it was a logical step based on prewar policy of the United States and the dominant political philosophy of both major parties.

Thus, Cuba became a semi-independent republic in 1902. The Platt Amendment was written into the constitution of Cuba and into a treaty between the two countries in 1903. The Cubans most objected to the "right-of-intervention" clause, but Elihu Root gave it a very broad interpretation which satisfied many Cubans. The meaning of the Amendment was far from settled, however, and American officials would continue to give it various interpretations until its abrogation in 1934.

DOCUMENT 16.   Edwin F. Atkins to President William Mc-Kinley, March 7, 1899. (Atkins, *Sixty Years in Cuba*. Pp. 306–7.)

The cities and larger towns are very quiet, being occupied by United States troops and under American authority, but the back country towns are entirely under the control of armed insurgents, principally blacks, who are collecting taxes and managing affairs quite independent of other authority. These are less disposed to disarm as time goes on, and less disposed to return to work.

It is probably no exaggeration to say that three fourths of the property interests are in the hands of foreigners, classing the Spaniards as such, and taking into consideration the personal indebtedness of Cuban estate owners. The insurgent independent party (wishing to be rid of American control) represent no property interest as a class, and their control of affairs is equally feared by the Cuban property-holders, Spaniards, and foreigners.

Reports from Washington indicate a possibility of the withdrawal of troops in the near future. Should such a course be decided upon, I very much fear that a condition bordering upon anarchy would very soon prevail. It is this fear, which is very general, that leads me to address you at the present time.

DOCUMENT 17. Theodore Roosevelt to Secretary of State John Hay, July 1, 1899. (Morison, *Letters of Theodore Roosevelt*. II: 1024–27.)

I am uneasy at the way things seem to be going both in the Philippines and in Cuba, and also at the mutterings of discontent with what we have done in those islands, which can be heard here and there throughout the country even now. A series of disasters at the very beginning of our colonial policy would shake this administration, and therefore our party, and might produce the most serious and far-reaching effects upon the nation as a whole, for if some political cataclysm was the result, it might mean the definite abandonment of the course upon which we have embarked—the only course I think fit for a really great nation. . . .

. . . In Cuba we may lay up for ourselves infinite trouble if we do not handle the people with a proper mixture of firmness, courtesy and tact. . . . Both in Cuba and in the Philippines what we obviously need, and need at once, is to have some man put in supreme command, in whom we can absolutely trust and to whom we give the widest liberty of action.

. . . I most earnestly urge the wisdom of the President putting Major General Leonard Wood in immediate command of all Cuba, with a complete liberty to do what he deems wisest in shaping our policy for the island, and with complete control over every other military and civil officer. . . .

. . . Wood is a born diplomat. . . . He has peculiar faculty for getting on with the Spaniards and Cubans. They like him, trust him, and down in their hearts are afraid of him. He always pays deference not only to their principles but to their prejudices. He is scrupulously courteous and polite. He undestands [sic] their needs, material and moral, and he also understands their sensitiveness and their spirit of punctilio. Finally, he is able, while showing them entire courtesy and thoughtful consideration, to impress upon them the fact that there can be no opposition when once he has made up his mind.

. . . With Wood in command I venture the assertion that you would speedily have part of the regular force now in Cuba footloose for the Philippine campaign; that you would have necessary administrative reform inaugurated; and that the island would speedily be on the path to content and prosperity.

DOCUMENT 18.   Report of General James H. Wilson (Commander of the Department of Matanzas and Santa Clara) on Conditions in Cuba, September 7, 1899. (U. S. Army, *Civil Report of Major-General John R. Brooke, U. S. Army, Military Governor, Island of Cuba.* Washington, 1900. P. 339.)

. . . It is stated by European writers that "it [trade of Cuba] exceeded that of any other tropical area of its size in the world." When this is considered in connection with the further fact that the trade of the United States with tropical countries amounts to about 65 per cent of its total trade with the remainder of the world, it will be seen that the establishment of proper economic condition in this island, and of proper trade relations with the United States, is of even greater importance than the establishment of proper political institutions.

The solution of the sugar question, and of the other questions of trade affecting this island, is the first step toward the successful solution of every other question. As it has been well said by a European writer, "This is not a question of the relative merits of any race amongst civilized people; it is simply and purely a question of the ultimate business relations" of Cuba with the United States and with the rest of the world.

Obviously, annexation under the Constitution of the United States, whether Cuba becomes a Territory or a State, would settle all economic questions, because it would entitle the Cubans to the free and unrestricted exchange of their natural and manufactured products with the United States, but this course, for the present at least, seems to be absolutely prohibited by the terms of the joint resolution of Congress which resulted in the war with Spain. It would, therefore, appear to be the duty of those in authority, and especially of the Congress of the United States, to settle upon some other method of insuring a condition of peace, and the re-establishment of agriculture and commerce in the island.

From the best study I have been enabled to give to the subject, I am strongly of the opinion, as fully set forth in my official report of June 20, that the line of least resistance will be found in the establishment of a local independent government, republican in form, and, as soon thereafter as practicable, in the negotiation of a treaty of alliance and commerce between Cuba and the United States, which shall give practical effect to the Monroe doctrine, define the rights, privileges, and duties of both the contracting parties on all subjects of common interest, and leave Cuba free and independent in all other matters. That such an arrangement as this would give almost instantaneous relief to Cuba, can hardly be doubted. That it would put matters on the best possible footing for the ultimate absorption of the latter into the Union by natural, voluntary, and progressive steps, honorable alike to both parties, seems to be equally probable. It would give time for the Cubans to show that they are not tropical and revolutionary, not a mongrel and vicious race, and not disqualified by religion or impaired social efficiency from carrying on a peaceful and stable government, or becoming American citizens.

In my opinion, whatever may be their merits or political condition, they will never reach the highest freedom and independence of which they are capable till they are free to enter the Great Republic on a just and equal footing; and that will depend not altogether upon them, but upon the American people, who are justly jealous of their citizenship, and of the inestimable privileges which the Constitution guarantees to Territories and States, as well as to all their inhabitants.

✔   ✔   ✔   ✔   ✔

It is believed that the establishment and maintenance of a pacific and stable government, and the negotiation of a treaty which would permit the free entrance of sugar and other natural and manufactured products of Cuba into the United States and establish close and reciprocal relations between the two countries, would instantly restore confidence, create an inflow of capital, and

bring about such a state of prosperity as would inevitably make
this island, at no distant day, one of the richest and most prosperous countries in the Western Hemisphere, if not in the world.

DOCUMENT 19.   Report of the Secretary of War, Elihu Root,
for 1899. (Robert Bacon and James B. Scott, ed., *The Military and Colonial Policy of the United States: Addresses
and Reports by Elihu Root.* Cambridge, Mass., 1916. Pp.
190–91.)[8]

Since the Spanish evacuation there have been no strictly military operations, and the officers of the army in Cuba have been
largely occupied in conducting, under the direction of the military
governor and the department commanders, a general civil administration for which no other governmental machinery existed, and
in aiding the existing municipal governments in the performance
of their duties. . . .

In all these respects satisfactory progress has been made. The
use of troops to maintain order was necessary for but a short
period. Forces of civil police organized from the people of the
island have been substituted, and are performing their duties
efficiently. The part played by our troops in the maintenance of
order is now substantially but the restraining influence of their
presence. . . .

The sanitary conditions of the cities and towns throughout the
island were found to be as bad as it is possible to conceive. Thorough and systematic inspections were made, sanitary corps were
organized, streets were cleaned, sewers were opened, cesspools
and sinks were emptied, public and private buildings were disin-
fected, methods of disposing of refuse were adopted, water supplies were improved, and rules were established and enforced to
prevent a recurrence of similar conditions. In the larger cities a
thoroughly good sanitary condition will require the establishment
of grades, the construction of adequate sewer systems, and increase
of water supplies. . . .

The city of Havana is now undergoing a house-to-house renovation and disinfection. Some two thousand houses have already
been treated, and the work continues at the rate of one hundred
and twenty to one hundred and twenty-five houses per day. The
reports show that in no case has the process of disinfection failed
to eradicate the infection, and no case of fever has occurred except

from a fresh infection. The total deaths from yellow fever in Havana for the first ten months of each year since 1889 have been as follows:

1890	314	1895	512
1891	318	1896	950
1892	272	1897	991
1893	469	1898	134
1894	369	1899	63

The deaths from all causes in Havana during the first few months after our occupation were numerous, owing to the great number of sick and dying who were there at the time of the Spanish evacuation. The rate has been steadily decreased until in September it was brought down to the annual rate of 27 per thousand and in October to 26.6 per thousand.

DOCUMENT 20. The Organization of Civil Government in Cuba: Report of the Secretary of War, Elihu Root, for 1900. (Bacon and Scott, *Military and Colonial Policy of the United States*. Pp. 193–94, 197–200.)

The conduct of affairs in Cuba during the year has been a continuance of the process of aiding the Cuban people in the development of a Cuban government in such a way that when fully organized it shall be stable and efficient. This has been done by guiding the Cubans in the first steps of systematic self-government and by introducing, mainly through the instrumentality of Cuban officers, such reforms in the various branches of administration as shall serve to put the business of government in fairly good condition when a complete Cuban administration finally assumes control of government in the island.

✓   ✓   ✓   ✓   ✓

The census having been completed and the period given for Spanish residents to make their election as to citizenship having expired on April 11, 1900, steps were immediately taken for the election of municipal governments by the people. In view of the fact that sixty-six per cent of the people could not read and write, it was not deemed advisable that absolutely unrestricted suffrage should be established, and, after very full conference with leading Cubans, including all the heads of the great departments of state, a general agreement was reached upon a basis of suffrage, which provided that every native male Cuban or Spaniard who had elected to take Cuban citizenship, of full age, might vote if he either could read or write, or owned real estate or personal property to the value of $250, or had served in and been honorably discharged from the Cuban army; thus according a voice in the government of the country to every one who had the intelligence to acquire the rudiments of learning, the thrift to accumulate property, or the patriotism to fight for his country.

On the eighteenth of April an election law, which aims to apply the best examples of our American election statutes to the existing conditions of Cuba, was promulgated for the guidance of the proposed election. On the sixteenth of June an election was held throughout the island in which the people of Cuba in all the municipalities, which include the entire island, elected all their municipal officers. The boards of registration and election were composed of Cubans selected by the Cubans themselves. No United States soldier or officer was present at or in the neighborhood of any polling place. There was no disturbance.

After the newly elected municipal officers had been installed and had commenced the performance of their duties, an order was made enlarging the powers of the municipal governments and putting into their hands as much of the government of the people as was practicable. . . .

✓   ✓   ✓   ✓   ✓

Especial attention has been given by the military government to the development of primary education. The enrollment of the public schools of Cuba immediately before the last war shows 36,306 scholars, but an examination of the reports containing these figures indicates that probably less than half the names enrolled represented actual attendance. There were practically no separate school buildings, but the scholars were collected in the residences of the teachers. There were few books, and practically no maps, blackboards, desks, or other school apparatus.

The instruction consisted largely in learning by rote, the catechism being the principal text-book, and the girls occupying their time chiefly in embroidery. The teachers were allowed to eke out their unpaid salaries by accepting fees from the pupils, and since less than one-tenth of the children of school age could be accommodated, the result of the fee system was that the children of the poor were either excluded or wholly neglected. Even those poor apologies for public schools were, to a great extent, broken up by the war, and in December, 1899, the entire public-school enrollment of the island numbered 21,435. . . . In June, 1900, it had grown to 143,120.

✓ ✓ ✓ ✓ ✓

All over the island the old Spanish barracks and barracks occupied by the American troops, which had been withdrawn, are being turned into schoolrooms after thorough renovation. The pressure for education is earnest and universal. The appropriations of this year from the insular treasury for that purpose will amount to about four and a half million dollars; but great as the development has been, it will be impossible, for a long time yet to come, to meet fully with the resources of the island the demand for the learning so long withheld. . . .

During the past summer, through the generosity of Harvard University and its friends, who raised a fund of $70,000 for that purpose, 1,281 Cuban teachers were enabled to attend summer school of instruction at Cambridge, designed to fit them for their duties. They were drawn from every municipality and almost every town in the island. . . .

✓ ✓ ✓ ✓ ✓

The issue of rations which characterized the first year of American occupation has been discontinued and has been succeeded by an extensive reëstablishment, renovation, and reorganization of the charitable institutions of the island. These were left at the close of the war without funds or supplies, and, with comparatively few exceptions, consisting mainly of the Sisters of the religious orders, without attendance. Such of them as were not closed were dilapidated, filthy, and unsanitary. The hospitals were practically without apparatus, medicines, or physicians. The children in the asylums were receiving but little education, insufficient food, and insufficient care.

A comprehensive law governing the department of charities was adopted on the seventh of July last, and, under the able direction of Major Edwin St. J. Greble, the head of the department, has been put into effective operation. . . . All of the buildings have been cleaned and renovated and receive regular and systematic support.

There are now receiving Government aid in Cuba thirty-eight hospitals, four asylums for the aged, twelve orphan asylums, two dispensaries for the poor, one insane asylum, three leper hospitals, two reform schools, one training school for boys, one for girls, and one emergency hospital in Santiago de Cuba. In the orphan asylums a strong effort has been made to secure the placing of chil-

dren in private families through the island, and the effort has met
with great success.

✓   ✓   ✓   ✓   ✓

The hospitals have been supplied with medicines and surgical
apparatus and attendance, and trained nurses brought from the
United States are engaged in the instruction of trained nurses in
Cuba. At the civil hospital No. 1 in Havana there are five American
trained nurses, and a training school for nurses has been started
for women with accommodations for forty scholars. At the civil
hospital in Matanzas there are four American nurses and a training
school for nurses with accommodations for thirty scholars. At the
civil hospital in Cienfuegos there is one American trained nurse
and about sixteen scholars; at Remedios, one American trained
nurse and eighteen scholars.

✓   ✓   ✓   ✓   ✓

The condition of the insane was particularly distressing. They
were confined in cells in the jails all over the island, filthy and
ragged, and treated literally like wild beasts. All these unfortunates
have been collected and taken to the large insane asylum in Havana, which has been put in good order, and they are cared for
in accordance with the dictates of modern humanity.

The prisons in the island were filled to overflowing with
wretched creatures living in indescribable filth and squalor. An
early inspection of the woman's prison in Havana disclosed the
fact that the women had no other place to sleep than on the
floor, and were unable to appear in a body because they were
without clothes to cover their nakedness; and they came before
the inspector one by one, passing the same garment from one to
another.

The cruelty of these conditions is more impressive from the
fact that many of the unfortunate inmates had never been tried,
or convicted of any offense. As the simplest way of dealing with
the evil, a board of pardons was constituted in January, which
visited all the prisons and examined the inmates. They found many
who had been for long periods waiting trial, and in one instance
this period had extended for eleven years. So far as the offenses
with which they were charged could be ascertained, a large part
of these people had been punished far more severely, whether
they were innocent or guilty, than they could have been upon
conviction. . . .

✓   ✓   ✓   ✓   ✓

PUBLIC WORKS

There has been great activity in public works. Our officers have been renovating, repairing, and reconstructing public buildings, building extensive and enduring roads and sewers and waterworks, and inspecting and cleansing private and public buildings and paving streets in most of the cities and towns of the island. . . .

DOCUMENT 21.   The Platt Amendment, 1902. (*U. S. Statutes at Large*. XXI: 897–98.)

That in fulfilment of the declaration contained in the joint resolution approved April twentieth, eighteen hundred and ninety-eight, entitled "For the recognition of the independence of the people of Cuba, demanding that the Government of Spain relinquish its authority and government in the island of Cuba, and to withdraw its land and naval reserve forces from Cuba and Cuban waters, and directing the President of the United States to use the land and naval forces of the United States to carry these resolutions into effect," the President is hereby authorized to "leave the government and control of the island of Cuba to its people" so soon as a government shall have been established in said island under a constitution which, either as a part thereof or in an ordinance appended thereto, shall define the future relations of the United States with Cuba, substantially as follows:

I. That the government of Cuba shall never enter into any treaty or other compact with any foreign power or powers which will impair or tend to impair the independence of Cuba, or in any manner authorize or permit any foreign power or powers to obtain by colonization or, for military or naval purposes or otherwise, lodgment in or control over any portion of said island.

II. That said government shall not assume or contract any public debt, to pay the interest upon which, and to make reasonable sinking fund provision for the ultimate discharge of which, the ordinary revenues of the island, after defraying the current expenses of government shall be inadequate.

III. That the government of Cuba consents that the United States may exercise the right to intervene for the preservation of Cuban independence, the maintenance of a government adequate for the protection of life, property, and indvidual liberty, and for discharging the obligations with respect to Cuba imposed by the

Treaty of Paris on the United States, now to be assumed and undertaken by the government of Cuba.

IV. That all Acts of the United States in Cuba during its military occupancy thereof are ratified and validated, and all lawful
rights acquired thereunder shall be maintained and protected.

V. That the government of Cuba will execute and as far as
necessary extend, the plans already devised or other plans to be
mutually agreed upon, for the sanitation of the cities of the island,
to the end that a recurrence of epidemic and infectious diseases
may be prevented, thereby assuring protection to the people and
commerce of Cuba, as well as to the commerce of the southern
ports of the United States and of the people residing therein.

VI. That the Isle of Pines shall be omitted from the proposed
constitutional boundaries of Cuba, the title thereto being left to
future adjustment by treaty.

VII. That to enable the United States to maintain the independence of Cuba, and to protect the people thereof, as well as
for its own defence, the government of Cuba will sell or lease to
the United States land necessary for coaling or naval stations at
certain specified points, to be agreed upon with the President of
the United States.

VIII. That by way of further assurance the government of Cuba
will embody the foregoing provisions in a permanent treaty with
the United States.

DOCUMENT 22. Report of the Committee on Relations of
the Cuban Constitutional Convention, February 27, 1901.
(Albert G. Robinson, *Cuba and the Intervention*. New York,
1905. P. 238.)

. . . We are the delegates of the people of Cuba. Therefore our
primary duty lies in interpreting the will and serving the necessities
of our people. It was apparent that the intimations of the American
Executive contained only the expression of what, in *his* judgment,
the people of Cuba ought to desire in the matter of future relations.
. . . It is clear and plain that this is sufficient reason for our giving
them [the opinions of the American Executive] a careful consideration. . . . But we have a complete right to accept or reject them,
to select from them that which we think fit, to add to them or to
subtract from them, or to substitute for them others according to
the dictates of our consciences, holding always before us our duty

to reconcile all that may be a legitimate interest or a rational proposal of the people of the United States, with our own highest interest and sacred rights.

The undersigned committee, while accepting the starting point of the American Executive—which provides that the independence of Cuba shall remain absolutely guaranteed—is of the opinion that some of these stipulations are not acceptable, inasmuch as they modify the independence and sovereignty of Cuba. Our duty consists in making Cuba independent of all other nations, including the great and noble American nation; and if we bind ourselves to ask the consent of the United States to our international treaties; if we allow them to retain the right to intervene in our country to support or displace administrations, and to fulfil rights which only concern the Cuban Government; and if, lastly, we concede to them the right to acquire and maintain any title over any lands whereon they may establish naval stations, it is plain that we should appear to be independent of the rest of the world, but surely we should never be so with relation to the United States.

DOCUMENT 23. Elihu Root (Secretary of War) to General Leonard Wood (Military Governor of Cuba), April 3, 1901: The Root Interpretation of the Platt Amendment. (U. S. Department of State, *Foreign Relations of the United States, 1932.* 5 vols. Washington, 1948. V: 545.)

You are authorized to state officially that in the view of the President the intervention described in the third clause of the Platt Amendment is not synonymous with intermeddling or interference with the affairs of the Cuban Government, but the formal action of the Government of the United States, based upon just and substantial grounds, for the preservation of Cuban independence, and the maintenance of a government adequate for the protection of life, property, and individual liberty, and adequate for discharging the obligations with respect to Cuba imposed by the Treaty of Paris on the United States.

DOCUMENT 24. Senator Orville H. Platt to Edwin F. Atkins, June 11, 1901. (Coolidge, *An Old-Fashioned Senator.* Pp. 348–49.)

Personally, I was in favor of very much more stringent measures requiring much more as to our future relations, but in legislation you have got to consider the preponderance of public sentiment. As you say, it is difficult enough to bring those Cuban delegates to an acceptance of the terms we propose. If we had proposed more stringent terms, we should not only have had that difficulty vastly increased but we should have had a party in the United States and in Congress giving aid and comfort to the Cuban radicals. My own judgment is that when they conceded to us the right of intervention and naval stations, as set forth in the Amendment, the United States gets an effective and moral position which may become something more than a moral position and which will prevent trouble there. It is easy to say that we ought to insist on more, it was impossible to pass through Congress anything more drastic than we did. It is a mistake, if I may say so, for the people of Cuba who are conservative and who have property interests to be cared for to refuse to exert their influence to make the new government of Cuba what it ought to be. I think I recognize all the difficulties of the situation, but it does seem to me that the able, forceful, and conservative men of Cuba must do something to help themselves and I think they will finally see this. At any rate, the United States will always, under the so-called Platt Amendment, be in a position to straighten out things if they get seriously bad. I see nothing for it except to try the experiment of an independent republican government in Cuba, and, while I see the dangers, I think we may hope some day that the experiment will be fairly successful.

DOCUMENT 25. Senator Orville H. Platt on Relations with Cuba—from an article in *World's Work,* May, 1901. (Coolidge, *An Old-Fashioned Senator.* Pp. 345-47.)

Two solutions only are possible. One, the annexation of the island by the United States; the other, the establishment of an independent republic there in which the vital and just interest both of Cuba and the United States shall be defined and maintained.

The project of annexation may, and ought to be, dismissed. It should not for a moment be considered except in case of the direst necessity. The people of Cuba, by reason of race and characteristics, cannot be easily assimilated by us. In these respects they have little in common with us. Their presence in the American union, as a state, would be most disturbing, and we have already asserted, as the deliberate conclusion of Congress, that they ought to be free and independent. There is nothing to be gained, much, even honor, to be lost, by the annexation of Cuba.

The real question, then, is, how can an independent republic be established there under conditions and circumstances which shall best subserve the interests of the people both of Cuba and of the United States? That our people have interests in Cuba which must be subserved and protected, goes without saying. We can not, and will not, permit any European Power, much less a hostile or unfriendly Power, to acquire rights or privileges in Cuba to our disadvantage. The essence of the Monroe Doctrine asserted, and justly insisted upon for nearly eighty years, forbids it. Nor can the United States permit the existence of a government in Cuba in which peace and order, the protection of life and property, and the maintenance of all international obligations are not observed. In respect to the future government of Cuba our interests and those of the Cuban people are identical; the government of Cuba must be stable, as well as republican in form. Again, our obligation to the world at large, created and assumed by the act of intervention, demand of us that we become responsible both for the character and maintenance of the new government. If duty required us to see to it that Cuba was free, duty equally requires us to see to it that the Cuba of the future shall be both peaceful and prosperous. . . .

    ✓   ✓   ✓   ✓   ✓

The new government of Cuba will have neither an army nor a navy. There are something like six millions of dollars of Spanish bonds outstanding, for which the revenues of Cuba were pledged at the time of their issue. These bonds are held largely in Germany and France. It is entirely probable that Cuba being left without any means of defence, these governments on behalf of their citizens would demand and endeavor to enforce their assumption. Cuba's only guarantee against this will be the fact that any nation attempting to compel it to pay this indebtedness will understand that it has the United States to deal with. Between revolutionists and Spaniards and Cubans who were loyal to Spain there is little love. With no army to repress disorder, it is certainly within the limit of reasonable probability that the revolutionary and turbulent party may attempt the destruction or confiscation of Spanish and Cuban property which the new government would be utterly powerless to prevent. We most certainly owe a duty to our own citizens in Cuba that they shall be protected in the enjoyment of their property and kept free from the dangers which attend revolutionary uprisings. Indeed, any one who knows public senti-ment in Cuba is aware that it is expected by Cuban people that if difficulty, either foreign or domestic, shall arise, the United States will be called upon to meet it. Even those who insist that nothing should be put into the Constitution recognizing our right to do so, say that the United States will do it as a matter of course. . . . The United States needs this mutual arrangement because, for its own defence, it cannot permit any foreign power to dominate, control, or obtain a foothold in this hemisphere or its adjacent territory, and cannot tolerate such revolutions or disorders upon an island so near our coast, as frequently occur in southern American republics; more than all, because it stands pledged in honor to its own citizens, to the citizens of Cuba, and to all the world to maintain quiet and peace and good government in Cuba. In a word, Cuba needs self-government, peace, tranquillity and pros-perity. The United States asks for nothing more than this, but it recognizes its obligation and insists upon its right to see that such results are to be permanently secured.

•   •   •

In order to help persuade the Cuban Constitutional Convention to accept the Platt Amendment, some officials indicated that the United States would reciprocate by granting special consideration to Cuban sugar. Officials such as General Wilson, General Wood, and Elihu Root were convinced that the economic rehabilitation of Cuba and political stability were intimately linked to the sugar market in the United States. President McKinley supported this policy, but an administration measure to admit sugar and molasses duty-free from Cuba and Puerto Rico was tabled by Congress in 1900. Theodore Roosevelt recommended tariff concessions in De-cember 1901, and his request for authority to negotiate a reciprocal trade agreement provoked a heated fight in Congress. The sup-porters of the domestic beet sugar industry won the first round, but Roosevelt proceeded to negotiate a treaty with Cuba anyway (Document 27). After another battle the treaty was approved, and became effective in December 1903. The fact that the American Sugar Refining Company had gained control of some of the beet refineries during 1902 may have helped to swing the necessary support. The reciprocity treaty granted Cuban sugar a 20 per cent preferential reduction in the American tariff, and various American products received from 20 to 40 per cent reductions in the Cuban tariff.

One article of the Platt Amendment stated that Cuba would "sell or lease" to the United States sites for coaling stations and naval bases. In 1903 a lease agreement was approved (Document 26), and later that year Cuba leased the sites of Bahia Honda and Guantánamo to the United States. A naval base was constructed at the latter site, but the United States gave up its rights to Bahia Honda in 1912 in return for increased advantages at Guantánamo Bay.

DOCUMENT 26. Agreement for the Lease to the United States of Lands in Cuba for Coaling and Naval Stations, February 1903. (Malloy, *Treaties, Conventions . . . Between the United States of America and Other Powers.* I: 359.)

Article II.

The grant of the foregoing Article shall include the right to use and occupy the waters adjacent to said areas of land and water, and to improve and deepen the entrances thereto and the anchorages therein, and generally to do any and all things necessary to fit the premises for use as coaling or naval stations only, and for no other purpose.

Vessels engaged in the Cuban trade shall have free passage through the waters included within this grant.

Article III.

While on the one hand the United States recognizes the continuance of the ultimate sovereignty of the Republic of Cuba over the above described areas of land and water, on the other hand the Republic of Cuba consents that during the period of the occupation by the United States of said areas under the terms of this agreement the United States shall exercise complete jurisdiction and control over and within said areas with the right to acquire (under conditions to be hereafter agreed upon by the two Governments) for the public purposes of the United States any land or any other property therein by purchase or by exercise of eminent domain with full compensation to the owners thereof.

DOCUMENT 27. Theodore Roosevelt's Message on Cuban Reciprocity to the Special Session of Congress, November 10, 1903. (*Messages and Papers of the Presidents.* XIV: 6741–43.)

I have convened the Congress that it may consider the legislation necessary to put into operation the commercial treaty with Cuba, which was ratified by the Senate at its last session, and subsequently by the Cuban Government. I deem such legislation demanded not only by our interest, but by our honor. We can not with propriety abandon the course upon which we have so wisely embarked. When the acceptance of the Platt amendment was required from Cuba by the action of the Congress of the United States, this Government thereby definitely committed itself to the policy of treating Cuba as occupying a unique position as regards this country. It was provided that when the island became a free and independent republic she should stand in such close relations with us as in certain respects to come within our system of international policy; and it necessarily followed that she must also to a certain degree become included within the lines of our economic policy. Situated as Cuba is, it would not be possible for this country to permit the strategic abuse of the island by any foreign military power. It is for this reason that certain limitations have been imposed upon her financial policy, and that naval stations have been conceded by her to the United States. The negotiations as to the details of these naval stations are on the eve of completion. They are so situated as to prevent any idea that there is the intention ever to use them against Cuba, or otherwise than for the protection of Cuba from the assaults of foreign foes, and for the better safeguarding of American interests in the waters south of us.

These interests have been largely increased by the consequences of the war with Spain, and will be still further increased by the building of the isthmus canal. They are both military and economic. The granting to us by Cuba of the naval stations above alluded to is of the utmost importance from a military standpoint, and is proof of the good faith with which Cuba is treating us. Cuba has made great progress since her independence was established. She has advanced steadily in every way. She already stands high among her sister republics of the New World. She is loyally observing her obligations to us; and she is entitled to like treatment by us.

The treaty submitted to you for approval secures to the United States economic advantages as great as those given to Cuba. Not an American interest is sacrificed. By the treaty a large Cuban market is secured to our producers. It is a market which lies at our doors, which is already large, which is capable of great expansion, and which is especially important to the development of our export trade. It would be indeed shortsighted for us to refuse to take advantage of such an opportunity, and to force Cuba into making arrangements with other countries to our disadvantage.

This reciprocity treaty stands by itself. It is demanded on considerations of broad national policy as well as by our economic interest. It will do harm to no industry. It will benefit many industries. It is in the interest of our people as a whole, both because of its importance from the broad standpoint of international policy, and because economically it intimately concerns us to develop and secure the rich Cuban market for our farmers, artisans, merchants, and manufacturers. Finally, it is desirable as a guaranty of the good faith of our Nation towards her young sister Republic to the south, whose welfare must ever be closely bound with ours. We gave her liberty. We are knit to her by the memories of the blood and the courage of our soldiers who fought for her in war; by memories of the wisdom and integrity of our administrators who served her in peace and who started her so well on the difficult path of self-government. We must help her onward and upward; and in helping her we shall help ourselves.

The foregoing considerations caused the negotiation of the treaty with Cuba and its ratification by the Senate. They now with equal force support the legislation by the Congress which by the terms of the treaty is necessary to render it operative. A failure to enact such legislation would come perilously near a repudiation of the pledged faith of the Nation.

I transmit herewith the treaty, as amended by the Senate and ratified by the Cuban Government.

DOCUMENT 28. Congressman Sereno E. Payne of New York Defends Cuban Reciprocity, November 16, 1903. (*Congressional Record*. 58th Cong., 1st Sess., 1903. Vol. XXXVII, pp. 263–64.)

Sir, let Cuba become prosperous, with closer trade relations with the United States, making the conditions down there stable for five years or as much longer as this treaty shall remain in force. Let American capital go down there to develop the island and employ the islanders. Let there be a demand for better things and more of them. Multiply the buying capacity of the people as we have multiplied it in the last five years in the United States under the Dingley tariff law, so that the people want more, buy more, and are ready to give bigger prices, because they get larger wages. Under such improved conditions what shall be the future of our imports into Cuba? Shall the amount be barely $60,000,000 as during the past year, for all imports, running up to $100,000,000 in the days preceding the war; or shall it be what Colonel Bliss, of the United States Army, a careful and impartial observer, says in his report on Cuba—$300,000,000 a year bought from the United States to supply the needs and the capacities of the people down there? Why there are millions in this bill to the farmers and manufacturers of the United States. . . .

. . . Why should we allow the nations from across the seas to come here, right to Cuba, within 80 miles of the United States, and take her trade in articles that we could furnish? Let us branch out, and when we have conquered the Cuban trade let our merchants go a little farther down into the South American States and follow up the vantage ground we have gained, and when the numberless ships that shall traverse the ocean from the United States to Cuba under the American flag find it a little dull, let them go down as far as Brazil—yes, take in the whole of South America—and pick up the trade that our people are willing and anxious to furnish the material for and give further employment to our people and our artisans and our capital. . . .

● ● ●

The Cuban experience became the model for United States policy in the Caribbean and Central America as the policy makers of the country increasingly pushed for hegemony over the area. The acquisition of the isthmian canal route through Panama in 1903 was an important factor in this development, and the United States placed even more emphasis on preserving stability, order, and pro-American regimes in this area. The proposed canal would be a combined trade and military route, and the economic-strategic interests of the United States formed an interlocking set of interests to be protected and fostered. In order to protect these interests Roosevelt developed an expanded version of the Monroe Doctrine which decreed that the United States was the "protector" and "policeman" of the Caribbean and Central America. Combined with this was the added feature that the protection of property and creditors was now included in the Monroe Doctrine.

It is significant that the first specific statement of the "Roosevelt Corollary" to the Monroe Doctrine was made in a letter which Roosevelt sent to Root for presentation at a dinner celebrating the anniversary of the founding of the Cuban Republic (Document 29). The Cuban experience was now to be applied to the rest of the area.

Roosevelt's optimism in regard to the Cuban settlement was disrupted two years later. Strife erupted after the re-election of President Tomás Estrada Palma in 1905, but Roosevelt was quite reluctant to intervene. Palma wanted armed support from the United States, as did Consul General Frank Steinhart. Roosevelt sent a commission headed by William Howard Taft to attempt to work out a peaceful solution. Palma and his cabinet resigned, and Taft took over as provisional governor. He was later replaced by Charles E. Magoon, who administered Cuba until the end of the "Second Intervention" in 1909.

Enterprisers from the United States swarmed to Cuba after 1902 to engage in various kinds of economic endeavors. As a group, these resident investors looked to the United States government for protection and support. Frank Steinhart was a good example of this type. He became involved in utilities and banking while serving as Consul General in Cuba for the United States. Steinhart had much to do with the Intervention of 1906, and made good use of his official connections. Close and useful ties between United States officials in Cuba and resident investors became an important element in relations between the two countries (Document 31).

Not all of Cuba's troubles were due to American interference. Domestic economic, political, and social problems contributed to instability and corruption. A perceptive account written by Irene Wright in 1912 pointed out these problems, and indicated with prophetic insight the probable consequences of a policy which cooperated with this status quo (Document 32). The quasi-protectorate policy resulted in enough meddling by the United States to cause resentment in Cuba, but this meddling was concerned with the protection of a kind of political stability and not with basic reforms. To promote the latter, however, the United States would have had to interfere in Cuba on a much more intensive scale, thus resurrecting the opposition to colonialism. This dilemma has not been solved.

DOCUMENT 29.   Theodore Roosevelt to Elihu Root, May 20, 1904. (Morison, *Letters of Theodore Roosevelt.* IV: 801.)

My dear Mr. Root: Through you I want to send my heartiest greetings to those gathered to celebrate the second anniversary of the Republic of Cuba. I wish that it were possible to be present with you in person. I rejoice in what Cuba has done and especially in the way in which for the last two years her people have shown their desire and ability to accept in a serious spirit the responsibilities that accompany freedom. Such determination is vital, for those unable or unwilling to shoulder the responsibility of using their liberty aright can never in the long run preserve such liberty.

As for the United States, it must ever be a source of joy and gratification to good American citizens that they were enabled to play the part they did as regards Cuba. We freed Cuba from tyranny; we then stayed in the island until we had established civil order and laid the foundations for self-government and prosperity; we then made the island independent, and have since benefited her inhabitants by making closer the commercial relations between us. I hail what has been done in Cuba not merely for its own sake, but as showing the purpose and desire of this nation toward all the nations south of us. It is not true that the United States has any land hunger or entertains any projects as regards other nations, save such as are for their welfare.

All that we desire is to see all neighboring countries stable, orderly and prosperous. Any country whose people conduct themselves well can count upon our hearty friendliness. If a nation shows that it knows how to act with decency in industrial and political matters, if it keeps order and pays its obligations, then it need fear no interference from the United States. Brutal wrongdoing, or an impotence which results in a general loosening of the ties of civilized society, may finally require intervention by some civilized nation, and in the Western Hemisphere the United States cannot ignore this duty; but it remains true that our interests, and those of our southern neighbors, are in reality identical. All that we ask is that they shall govern themselves well, and be prosperous and orderly. Where this is the case they will find only helpfulness from us.

Tonight you are gathered together to greet a young nation which has shown hitherto just these needed qualities; and I congratulate not only Cuba but also the United States upon the showing which Cuba has made.

DOCUMENT 30. Theodore Roosevelt to George Otto Trevelyan, September 9, 1906. (Morison, *Letters of Theodore Roosevelt*. V: 401.)

In Cuba, what I have dreaded has come to pass in the shape of a revolt or revolution. We of course kept everything straight and decent in the island while we were running the government, and for the four years that it has been independent the push that we gave enabled them to go on along the same path. Now a revolution has broken out, and not only do I dread the loss of life and property, but I dread the creation of a revolutionary habit, and the creation of a class of people who take to disturbance and destruction as an exciting and pleasant business, steadily, altho intermittently, to be followed. In confidence I tell you that I have just been notified by the Cuban Government that they intend to ask us forcibly to intervene in the course of this week, and I have sent them a most emphatic protest against their doing so, with a statement that I am not prepared to say what I will do if the request is made. On the one hand we cannot permanently see Cuba a prey to misrule and anarchy; on the other hand I loathe the throught of assuming any control over the island such as we have over Porto Rico and the Philippines. We emphatically do not want it; and tho nothing but direst need could persuade us to take it, once that we did so we should firmly convince most nations that really we had been intriguing to put ourselves in possession of it. As a matter of fact, what I have been ardently hoping for has been, not that we should have to reduce Cuba to the position of the Philippines, but that the Philippines would make such progress that we could put them in the position of Cuba.

DOCUMENT 31. Enoch Crowder to Henry P. Fletcher, October 29, 1921. (U. S. Department of State, General Files: 837.51/632⅚.)[9]

I am, of course, a frequent caller at the home of our mutual friend of many years standing, Frank Steinhart. . . .

    ✓   ✓   ✓   ✓   ✓

Undoubtedly he was a man of great influence with the Wood administration. In the second intervention, he actually controlled Magoon and was the invisible Government. He bids for the same kind of control with every American Minister appointed here, and he generally acquires it. Ordinarily, he deals with Ministers anxious to defend their tenure, and you know the value in that regard of his friendship.

DOCUMENT 32. The Problems of Cuba in 1912. (Irene Wright, *Cuba*. New York, 1912. Pp. 166–67, 190–92.)

We have, then, in Cuba, a country owned by foreigners, the government of which is supported by foreigners, but administered by Cubans, after such a fashion, however (foreigners have not the suffrage), that these Cubans in office are not answerable to the real source of their salaries for the disbursement of these or other revenues, paid in by the foreigners, nor in any legitimate manner can they be obligated to consider the welfare of the country (owned by foreigners) or of the business conducted (by foreigners) within its boundaries. As at present constituted this is the most expensive government on earth, and those who operate it (the Cuban office-holding class) have every reason to labor to make it even more so, since its extravagances run to salaries, which they receive, and to even more outrageous contracts and concessions, on which they get liberal "rake-offs." While they enjoy these profits on their independence, the bills for the maintenance of the government, which is the sole evidence of the existence of that independence, fall for payment not to them, but to the foreigner, and, through him, on the "ultimate consumer," who, again, although he is Cuban in part . . . is not in the majority the Cuban office-holding class. He is, instead, the unhappy "Cuban of the country,"— the petty planter, tobacco grower, charcoal burner, pig-herder, perhaps, and humble wage earner in hamlet and small town, in whose name that fabric of government stands which is crushing the life out of him.

This situation is the reason why only professional politicians, who hold the "jobs" and accumulate the "rake-offs," advocate the continued maintenance of this so-called Republic of Cuba, as against the property holders, the business men of every class and condition, and the miscellaneous population of the island, destined, some day, to become its "people" who the first two directly, and the last one indirectly, pay the exorbitant cost of this republic's upkeep, protestingly, because they do not receive any benefits from it to make the excessive expenditure seem worth while.

ᶠ   ᶠ   ᶠ   ᶠ   ᶠ

. . . The reform, like charity, which, to Cuba it would prove to be, must begin at home,—in Washington. The United States has acquired dependencies. Cuba is one of them; no legal fiction can alter the fact that she is. It is a little late in the day to discuss whether or not we want dependencies: the fact stands that we have them on our hands. Here they are, and we can't get rid of them. Having them, we must administer them, and to do it properly we need a colonial department. . . .

Once we have a proper colonial department, with men not biased by political considerations at the head of it, the future of our possessions will brighten like the east at sunrise, for such men will have inclination, ability, and opportunity to consider what those dependencies need, and time to carry out the projects so intelligently formulated. They will discover for instance that the "crisis" which seems to exist, eternal and omnipresent, in Cuba is not . . . political at all, but economic. Having discovered this . . . they will have tenure in their office assured them long enough to permit them to remedy basic evils. . . .

At Roosevelt's command (and not by the will of a non-existent Cuban people) the Cuban republic arose in a night, on soil owned by others than its electors, swarming with a bureaucracy these foreigners and producing Cubans have had to support ever since. There it stands, tottering, and pregnant with militant trouble as was the Trojan horse of old; when finally it collapses to its inevitable destruction let Americans on hearing the crash recall distinctly, that this is not a creature of Cubans,— it was neither fashioned by them nor by them upheld—but on the contrary, it is of all-American manufacture. Americans built it. Americans set it up again when once it fell flat. American influence is all that sustains it to this moment. If they discover anything to criticise in it, or its failure, let Americans remember in so criticising that they are dealing with the work of their own hands.

•   •   •

President Woodrow Wilson continued the basic policy toward the Caribbean and Central America which had been developed by his Republican predecessors. When William Jennings Bryan stepped down as Secretary of State in 1915 his memorandum outlining United States policy declared the Platt Amendment to be the model for policy in this area (Document 33).

Early in 1917 disturbances broke out in Cuba, and the United States landed detachments of Marines on numerous occasions to protect American-owned property. As property destruction increased, the State Department decided to send a large body of troops. The decision was made in May, but Cuban objections had to be overcome before a regiment of Marines was dispatched in August (Document 35). Public pronouncements declared this to be a war measure, but protection of property and stability were the underlying causes. The Marines remained in Cuba until 1922.

The Cuban sugar economy was closely regulated by the United States during World War I. The International Sugar Committee was organized by Herbert Hoover under the auspices of the Food Administration. The Cubans objected to the price set by the committee—since it controlled all Allied sugar purchases—but economic pressure was used to gain Cuban cooperation (Document 36). Import licenses from the Food Administration were needed in order for Cuba to buy wheat and coal from the United States. These were not issued until after Cuba approved the contract for sugar purchases.

In 1917 the Cuban government also began negotiations with the United States for a fifteen-million-dollar loan. The State Department used the loan as a lever to induce the Cuban government to settle the claims of the Cuba Railroad and the Ports Company of Cuba. Both were controlled by American capital. Settlement agreements were made in 1918, and the loan was made.

The use of "Dollar Diplomacy"— described by Taft as using "dollars instead of bullets"— had been utilized in Cuba since the Reciprocity Treaty of 1903. This technique had been supplemented by the use of military force, and Wilson had made extensive use of the armed intervention. By 1918, however, the State Department was beginning to place a new emphasis on the use of economic devices to insure order and stability in the Caribbean. A memorandum written by Boaz Long in 1918 presented a lengthy discussion of the use of loans, trade, and investments to secure this end. Long stated armed intervention should be used only in extreme cases, and that "aid of a practical character" would insure the hegemony of the United States with fewer repercussions in Latin America. Cuban policy was cited as the example to be followed (Document 37).

DOCUMENT 33. William Jennings Bryan to Robert Lansing, June 15, 1915. (U. S. Department of State, General Files: 111.11/74.)

My experience with the Latin-American countries has convinced me that the most important service that we can render to them (excepting the under-writing of their loans) is like that we rendered to Cuba under the Platt amendment. The fact that we stand ready to assist in the preserving of order will usually make it unnecessary for us to take any action. We are like the "big brother" whose presence is a silent protection to the little brother. We have this arrangement with Cuba and Santo Domingo. I believe that Haiti and Nicaragua are the only other countries that now need the benefit of the Platt amendment.

DOCUMENT 34. Robert Lansing (Secretary of State) to William Gibbs McAdoo (Secretary of the Treasury), August 13, 1917. (U. S. Department of State, *Foreign Relations of the United States, 1918*. Washington, 1930. P. 299.)

In connection with the matter of the loan, it is necessary to take into consideration the present political situation in Cuba.

The revolution which occurred in February of this year, and which may be considered to be at an end as an organized movement, although certain unrest still prevails in the eastern end of

Cuba, brought in its train great destruction of property of foreigners and of Cubans and for which large claims will be presented to the Cuban government. The entrance of Cuba into the war as an ally of the United States has occasioned her a considerable outlay of money for equipment of troops and repair and refitting of ships. For both of these reasons it would seem that Cuba would be in need of much greater funds than she now possesses.

Nevertheless, the financial and the political situations are so closely interwoven that I feel that no step should be taken in the present situation without the careful consideration and cooperation of the Treasury Department and the State Department, both on account of the provisions of the Platt amendment and the political questions involved.

Two pertinent political questions are the settlement of the Cuban Ports Company matter and the payment of certain part of the claims of the Cuba Railroad Company against the Government for property destroyed in the revolution, in order to enable this company to put its road in condition to haul the sugar crop which is of such great importance to the United States and to the Entente Allies.

The matter of the Cuban Ports Company, a corporation in which both American and British capital is interested, has been a most vexatious one for several years and a few weeks ago the Cuban Congress authorized the President of Cuba to make a settlement of the question, the President having expressed his desire on various occasions to make an equitable settlement of this matter if Congress would authorize him to do so.

It is felt that it would be particularly useful at this time if a settlement could be made of the Ports question, inasmuch as Cuba, Great Britain, and the United States are now all fighting side by side against the German Government, but this settlement may not be forthcoming unless certain pressure is brought to bear on the President of Cuba, possibly through the approval for a loan, in view of the fact that he has decided not to make a settlement himself but has appointed a commission to decide the case, certain members of which are openly known to be very hostile to the Ports Company.

In order that the Cuba Railroad may be in a position to haul the sugar crop it may also be necessary to make an arrangement with the Cuban Government before the loan is authorized for a monthly payment to the railroad of part of its claims. A payment of $300,000 per month for four months has been suggested by the company.

DOCUMENT 35. William E. Gonzales (Minister to Cuba) to
Robert Lansing, July 14, 1917. (U. S. Department of State,
General Files: 837.00/1395.)

Your July 12, 7 p.m. received midnight July thirteenth. Saw
President[10] at his country place today and presented matter, passing lightly over necessities of such force in Oriente which is now
not manifest and stressing wisdom of plan as war measure. He gives
his cordial approval.

The President also authorized me to offer United States sites
for training camps in other parts of Cuba if it should be considered
desirable to send troops to train in mild winter climate. Should it
at anytime appear advisable to impress eastern Cuba with the fact
of presence of United States troops this offer could open the way
for tactful commander arrange for extensive practice marches from
Guantanamo station.

DOCUMENT 36. Herbert Hoover (United States Food Ad-
ministrator) to President Woodrow Wilson, November 24,
1917. (*Foreign Relations of the United States, 1918*. Pp. 349–
50.)

Dear Mr. President: As you know, we have formed a joint committee with the Allies for the united purchase and division of
Cuban and other foreign sugars. In the meantime, we have fixed
a price agreement with our own sugar producers. On the basis of
our domestic price the International Committee should pay approximately $4.80 per 100, delivered New York, for Cuban sugar. This
is an increase of $1.30 per 100 pounds over 1913, the year before
the war, and an increase of 25 cents over 1917, and in our view
fully takes account of any increased production costs in Cuba and
leaves a very wide margin of profit to the producers.

The English members of our committee contended for a price
of about $4.30 New York, but, in an effort to conciliate, we offered
and persuaded the English members to agree with us in offering
the excessive amount of $4.90.

President Menocal has intervened and is endeavoring to force
a price which works out from $5.05 to $5.25 New York and has
dispatched a committee to New York to negotiate.

The President of Cuba, we understand, refuses to accede and claims he will force us to agree through the American Government. We have endeavoured to keep the entire matter simply a commercial transaction, but they insist on interjection of governmental pressure.

I feel that we can not, in justice to our consumers or to our own producers, accede to their demands. It means on maximum figures demanded, about $40,000,000 to our people, and likewise a large increase of similar amounts to our Allies, which we will probably have to finance. Cuba only obtains a minor part of this huge sum because an increased price to them automatically raises the price of all the sugar of the whole world.

I trust we will, if the matter arises, have your support in our views.

DOCUMENT 37. "Memorandum and Arguments Relating to Constructive Steps Which Should be Taken in Central America Before the Close of the European War," Boaz Long to Robert Lansing, February 15, 1918. (U. S. Department of State, General Files: 711.13/55.)

The total trade of Cuba with the United States just prior to the end of the Spanish rule over that island (1897) amounted to about twenty-seven million dollars per annum. During the decade following the termination of our war with Spain, the island of Cuba, guided by American influence, increased her trade with us by leaps and bounds and brought it to the startling total in 1917 of something over four hundred and thirty million dollars. This unprecedented development of Cuba may serve as an illustration of what probably would take place in the Central American countries provided this Government extended to them aid of a practical character as it did to Cuba.

It must be apparent to those familiar with the political situation in the various Central American countries that it would not be possible under present day conditions to insert a Platt Amendment into the agreements or practical arrangements which should now be made to give new life to these small neighboring Republics. It is respectfully submitted that the adoption of other means, possibly something along the lines of those used in the Haitian situation, might produce the favorable effects desired.

•   •   •

CHAPTER III

THE NEW DOLLAR DIPLOMACY
BETWEEN WAR AND DEPRESSION
(1919-32)

He who goes in to the hilt on the "bull" side of inter-American cooperation stands with Calvin Coolidge, Charles Evans Hughes, Leo S. Rowe, Victor M. Cutter, John L. Merrill, Henry Ford and a growing host of shrewd, keen, businessmen, statesmen, and diplomats. And he links hands with the Ferraras and Machados of Cuba. . . .

—WALLACE THOMPSON (1928)

THE WORLD DEMAND for sugar after World War I produced a monumental boom in Cuba. The "Dance of the Millions" was performed to the feverish tune of soaring prices, a tidal wave of credit from United States bankers, and wild speculative ventures. The bottom fell out of the boom in mid-1920, and the repercussions brought economic and political turmoil to the island.

The revival of political difficulties resulted in revolutionary threats. The presidential campaign in the fall of 1920 was characterized by violent agitation and hints of coming civil strife. The Wilson Administration had generally been attempting since 1918 to settle Caribbean problems by means other than armed force, and Wilson hoped to effect a Cuban settlement by peaceful means. Minister Long's request for additional Marines was turned down, but a division of Army troops was secretly assembled in case of revolution. Alfredo Zayas was narrowly elected to the presidency in November, but the opposition brought fraud charges in numerous districts. The political situation was complicated by the virtual prostration of the economy and the poor financial condition of the Cuban government.

Early in 1921, Wilson sent General Enoch Crowder back to

Cuba to advise the government and to help settle the political and financial problems. After the election issue was peacefully resolved, Crowder began to press for various administrative and fiscal changes. The "moralization" program quickly became entangled with the Cuban government's negotiations for a loan from New York bankers. Crowder would have preferred to base his demands on military threats, but the use of dollars had produced results peacefully in the past and the Wilson Administration had increasingly utilized economic tools. Charles Evans Hughes continued this technique, and the State Department and J. P. Morgan and Company worked together in setting conditions for the Cuban government to meet.

Early in 1923 the Cuban government received a fifty-million-dollar loan from a syndicate headed by the Morgan Company, and later that year President Zayas began to unravel the "moralization" program. A measure of stability had returned to Cuba, however, and the election of 1924 was relatively peaceful. Gerardo Machado became President in 1925, and most United States officials and businessmen believed that Cuba was in good hands. Machado had business connections with United States investors, and was viewed as a Cuban Calvin Coolidge. Rising Cuban nationalism had become a problem, since it involved anti-United States attitudes, but Machado was able to manipulate this nationalism and still protect the interests of the United States. The Republican administrations in Washington cooperated by pushing the Isle of Pines Treaty—which had been negotiated in 1904—through the Senate in 1925.

A semblance of prosperity and stability prevailed in Cuba during these years, and Machado became the symbol of the new "Dollar Diplomacy." Business Pan-Americanism flourished during the 1920's, as United States capital poured into Latin America. Machado was highly extolled by American business interests for his pro-business policy, and American bankers competed vigorously for the public works bonds which Machado issued. This stability, however, was more apparent than real. Capital from the United States temporarily covered some of the cracks in the Cuban economy, but by 1928 even these financial transfusions were unable to bolster the sagging sugar economy. Political unrest grew more intense after 1928, and Machado became increasingly tyrannical in his efforts to retain power. The situation in Cuba deteriorated rapidly after the United States fell into the spreading world depression, and the Cuban government again faced bankruptcy.

The United States government and American businessmen with Cuban interests continued to back Machado. These groups believed that as long as the Cuban Army remained loyal, the President represented the best hope for order and stability. Machado generally preserved order and protected American property. The uprising of 1931 was quickly suppressed—with indirect help from the United States—and payments on the foreign debt were maintained with help from the bankers. American interests believed that if Machado could be tided over until the Depression ran its course that all would return to normal. Ambassador Harry Guggenheim and some officials of the Chase National Bank tried to persuade Machado to work out a compromise settlement with the leaders of the conservative opposition, but his policies became even more repressive in 1932–33.

Since the end of World War I the United States government had generally followed a policy of substituting diplomatic and economic tools for armed force in the Caribbean and Central America. In the case of Cuba, the Platt Amendment had been given a less aggressive slant by the revival of the Root Interpretation. Herbert Hoover continued the retreat from armed intervention and from aggressive diplomatic interference in the internal affairs of governments in this area. As a result the State Department was caught with its policies down when revolutions and turmoil began to erupt after 1929. Committed to noninterference on the one hand, and to the maintenance of the status quo on the other, the State Department did virtually nothing. The New York bankers were asked to take the initiative in supporting Machado, but many Cubans still blamed the United States government for Machado's terrorism. "Guggenado and Machadoheim," was the way the Cubans expressed the supposed connection between their President and Ambassador Guggenheim.

Some Americans wanted to intervene in Cuba in order to reform the government, but the Hoover Administration feared that such action would shake the status quo which had symbolized stability. Hoover hoped that the Depression would soon give way to prosperity, and United States policy toward Cuba continued to hang on the horns of the dilemma until the summer of 1933.

The business-oriented stability embodied by Machado was tied up with the vast increase in United States investments in Cuba after World War I. Such companies as Electric Bond and Share, and International Telephone and Telegraph bought controlling interests in Cuban utilities and various banks handled portfolio investments for private businesses and the government. In addition, some banks went into the sugar business after the loan defaults following the collapse of the sugar market in 1920. By 1928 various estimates placed American control of Cuban sugar production between 70 and 75 per cent. By 1929 total American investments in Cuba had grown to an estimated $1,525,900,000, or 27.31 per cent of the total Latin American investment of United States interests.

The domestic tariff policy followed by Congress complicated the international financial policies of the government. Congress raised the tariff on sugar in 1921, 1922, and 1930. These victories by agricultural and industrial groups interested in the domestic market complicated the economic problems of Cuba and American groups involved in the Cuban economy. This dispute between economic groups in the United States further complicated the problems of the policy makers. By 1931 the Depression in the United States had struck a vital blow at the intimate economic ties between the United States and Cuba. Loans and investments had obscured the flaws in this system after 1920, but when the New York capital market collapsed in 1929 the connection between investments, trade, and Cuban stability became readily apparent. As a result, many Americans became convinced that the status quo in Cuba, the value of American investments, and the Cuban market for American goods were all dependent upon the market for Cuban sugar in the United States. The experience of the period 1919–33 proved that the protection of American interests in Cuba depended upon the development of positive economic policies by the United States government.

The postwar sugar boom in Cuba produced gilded dreams of profits to be made by investing in the island. As American capital poured into Cuba, the trend toward consolidation in the sugar industry was accelerated. American investors vastly underestimated the recuperative power of the world's sugar industry, however, and by 1920 world production was ahead of consumption. The European beet sugar industry recovered rapidly, and other producing areas expanded production to meet the supposed market needs. United States beet sugar producers expanded their output, and when the market collapsed cries for increased tariff protection resounded from this group.

The end of the sugar boom also contributed to consolidation as bankers and stronger companies took over many small producers. American investors still hoped for favorable market conditions after 1920, and the flow of capital was only temporarily slowed. Between 1913 and 1928 United States investments in Cuba increased 536 per cent.

DOCUMENT 1. The National City Bank of New York Surveys the Cuban Economy, 1919. (National City Bank, *Cuba, Review of Commercial, Industrial and Economic Conditions in 1919.* New York, 1919. Pp. 3–6.)

While this large increase in sugar production in Cuba and in the share which she supplies of the world's output is due in part to the fall off in production of beet sugar in the countries recently participating in the war, the indications are that Europe will be slow in returning to anything like pre-war production, and that therefore the enlarged demands upon Cuba will continue indefinitely. Germany, Russia, and Austria-Hungary were the chief producers of the European beet sugar crop. Russia is so completely disorganized that there seems little prospect of a return in the near future to anything like normal production; Austria-Hungary has been broken up into half a dozen new political divisions, few if any of them, having a frontage on tide-water, while the German press is bitterly complaining of the inability to obtain labor, soil, foods, or capital with which to re-establish the beet production which was reduced about 33% during the war despite an effort of the Government to maintain this important food supply.

With these conditions in Europe and the growing demand of the world for additional supplies of sugar, Cuba's prospect in this, the most important of her industries, seems good. The world's consumption of sugar practically doubled in the decade preceding the war, advancing from 21,310,000,000 pounds in 1905 to 41,972,000,-000 in 1914, and with the whole world hungry for sugar due to the governmental and other attempts at restriction of consumption during the war there seems good reason to expect a somewhat similar increase in consumption in the next decade.

Other facts as to the prospective conditions of the world's demands upon the sugar producers of Cuba are especially important to the United States in view of the fact that American capital forms nearly one-half of the total investments in sugar production in Cuba. While no exact figures can be cited as to the amount of American capital invested in sugar production in Cuba, especially since the ownership in many of the mills and plantations is divided between Americans, Europeans and Cubans, the opinion of those who have carefully studied the subject is that Americans own between 40% and 50% of the approximately $600,000,000 worth of sugar mills, plantations and other appurtenances of sugar production in Cuba.

The share of the mills nominally "American" has increased rapidly in very recent years, from approximately 15% in 1906 to about 35% in 1919. We are fond of saying that "trade follows the flag," but the real facts are that trade follows invested capital, and as nearly or quite one-half of the greatest industry of Cuba is controlled by American capital, and a large proportion of the remainder is held by Cubans who are disposed to be friendly to their nearest neighbor—an avowed protector of safe and sane governmental authority—it may be assumed that the capital of the island is friendly to American trade. This is evidenced by the fact that while merchandise from the United States formed but 43% of the imports of Cuba in 1905 it was 53% in 1913, and 76% in the greatly increased total of 1918.

This growing demand for American products, which growth has been coincidental with the increased investment of American capital in that island, is illustrated by the fact that our own exports to Cuba have grown from $69,000,000 in the fiscal year 1914, which immediately preceded the war, to $236,000,000 in 1918, and will approximate $250,000,000 in the fiscal year 1919, while our imports from that island have increased from $131,000,000 in 1914 to $264,000,000 in 1918, and seem likely to approximate $300,000,000 in the fiscal year 1919. The trade between the United States and Cuba which was $200,000,000 in 1914 will exceed $500,000,000 in 1919 and may total $550,000,000.

The above facts regarding Cuba as a sugar producer, present and prospective, are especially interesting in view of the fact that the chief growth in sugar production in the island in recent years

has occurred in the eastern section of the island in which section
The National City Bank has recently established several branches.

DOCUMENT 2.   Consolidation in the Cuban Sugar Industry,
1920. ("Many Changes in Ownership of Cuban Mills," *The
Cuba Review*, October, 1920. Pp. 32–33.)[1]

One of the most interesting developments in the Cuban sugar
industry during the present year has been the numerous changes
in the ownership of mill properties that have taken place.

Three notable tendencies are observable in these transactions
which in turn reflect the marked changes that are taking place in
the sugar industry of the world at large.

In Cuba these tendencies may be classified as follows: First,
the beginning of a movement, destined to grow, toward the acquisition of producing properties by American refineries; second, the
purchase by manufacturers of the United States of Cuban mills
and plantations in order to insure their supply of sugar; and,
third, a growing interest on the part of United States investors, not
directly connected with the industry, in sugar mill properties.

The first of the refining interests seeking to acquire a Cuban
mill this year was the Imperial Sugar Refining Company of Sugar
Land, Texas. This refiner secured an option on the Santa Lucia mill
and plantation in Oriente Province. This proposed purchase, however, finally fell through, and the project was abandoned.

The second important transaction of this character, which was
successfully carried out, was the purchase by the American Sugar
Refining Company of Central Cunagua.

The Warner Sugar Refining Company interests acquired this
year a controlling interest in Central Gomez Mena and Amistad.
These mills have a combined capacity of 625,000 bags.

The Revere refinery at Boston, owned by the United Fruit
Company, was the pioneer refiner to own Cuban production, having acquired Centrals Boston and Preston several years ago. There
have been repeated rumors, though unconfirmed, that this interest
intended enlarging its Cuban properties through the acquisition of
additional mills. The aggregate estimated source of supply for
Revere from its two mills runs close to 1,200,000 bags annually.

The Howell interests, which are identified with the National
Sugar Refining Company, are well known to be heavily interested
in Cuban producing companies, both wholly and partially owned
by American capital. The group is strengthening its position

through the new Cuba–Santo Domingo Sugar Development Syndicate, which plans to control the Island mills with an aggregate capacity of 425,000 bags. In Santo Domingo this syndicate will also have very extensive holdings.

MANUFACTURERS ALSO BUY

The general tendency today of American manufacturers, large users of sugar, to acquire Cuban sugar properties is as marked as that of the refiners, and is nearly as important. The difficulties of obtaining their supplies during the war, brought home to many of them the economic advantages accruing from ownership by a manufacturer of his source of supply.

The pioneer American manufacturer to enter this field was the Hershey Chocolate Company, of Pennsylvania, who built Central Hershey several years ago. This company continues to add to its Cuban holdings, having recently purchased Central Rosario.

Among the large manufacturers of this country who have acquired Cuban properties recently are the Hires Root Beer interests, who purchased Central Dos Rosas, with a capacity of 50,000 bags, and George W. Loft, the candy manufacturer, who has bought Central Dulce Nombre, now Central Loft.

• • •

The American intervention in 1917 did not end unrest in Cuba. A large strike in Havana, in 1919, resulted in a visit of units of the United States Navy to that city, and General Enoch Crowder was sent, in March 1919, to revise the Cuban electoral code. Agitation increased in 1920 as the political climate was heated by economic problems. Threats to American property were made, but Woodrow Wilson decided against either armed intervention or American supervision of the presidential election. Wilson did decide to send General Crowder back to Cuba as his "Personal Representative." Crowder's instructions directed him to use the loan negotiations between the Cuban government and J. P. Morgan and Company as a tool to force certain reforms. The State Department had decided to use this approach in November 1920, when the Morgan Company first informed the government of the Cuban loan request. Albert Rathbone—a former Treasury Department official—went to Cuba in December as "financial advisor" to the government, but his mission produced only a report and no financial reforms. Then the decision was made to send the "old Cuba hand," Crowder. The General was considered to be one of the few men with the necessary experience and prestige to reform Cuba peacefully, and thus to eliminate the problems which could cause revolution and armed intervention.

DOCUMENT 3. Boaz Long (Minister to Cuba) to the Secretary of State, September 25, 1920. (U. S. Department of State, *Foreign Relations of the United States: 1920*. 3 vols. Washington, 1936. II: 23.)

. . . Request for additional marines Camaguey based on necessity for protection sugar interest owned by Americans in four eastern provinces. It is estimated that a considerable percentage of total sugar production of 1920 crop controlled by American interests. English, Spanish and other foreign interests are also important. It is openly stated by partisans of both parties that in event of revolution or other disturbances American interests will be first to be destroyed.

DOCUMENT 4. Norman H. Davis (Acting Secretary of State) to General Enoch Crowder, December 31, 1920. (*Foreign Relations of the United States: 1920*. II: 41–43.)

By order of the President, you are hereby directed to proceed at once to Cuba as his Personal Representative on special mission. You will proceed to Havana on the U.S.S. *Minnesota*.

Upon your arrival in Havana, you are instructed to obtain at the earliest opportunity an interview with President Menocal and to inform him that the Government of the United States is most gravely concerned because of the very serious political and financial conditions now obtaining in Cuba. As you are aware, the Presidential elections were held two months ago and the result of those elections is as yet unknown. So far as the Department is informed, the provisional returns in all six provinces have been posted by the Provisional Electoral Boards. These returns show certain colleges in which no elections were held, others where the elections have been declared null and void, and a large number of colleges where the results have been protested by one or the other of the political parties to the courts. The total number of colleges protested and appealed to the courts is sufficient to place the result of the Presidential election in doubt, and from all reports received by the Department there has not only been shown no progress by the courts in deciding these appealed cases, but an indefinite delay in reaching a decision is indicated. . . .

You should not only advise President Menocal of the above, but you should likewise make it altogether clear that the unsettled Presidential election in Cuba has the most important bearing upon the flotation of the proposed Cuban loan in this country and that American bankers can naturally not be indifferent to the present disturbed conditions, particularly when there is no certainty who the successor to the Presidency will be and when the situation is such that the possibility of serious disturbances is by no means remote.

In conclusion, you may advise the President that the Government of the United States is unwilling to approve any increase in the national debt of Cuba until it is assured that the Presidential succession will be legally and peacefully determined, and finds itself, therefore, unable to take any further action in furthering the negotiations for the proposed loan or to devote any more assistance towards the settlement of the Cuban financial situation unless it has positive proof that the Cuban courts, with the cooperative assistance of the Government, will faithfully carry out the provisions of the Election Law and will resolve, with the utmost expedition, the contested election cases.

In confirmation of a conversation had with you and in accordance with instructions sent to the American legation at Havana for communication to the Government of Cuba, it is thought to be particularly desirable that emphasis be laid upon the fact that the present situation in Cuba is proving harmful to commercial intercourse between the United States and Cuba and to the general relations between the two countries and that the resultant detriment to the prosperity of Cuba cannot but be a matter of close concern to the United States.

●   ●   ●

Resident American investors in Cuba were generally quick to appeal to Washington for protection and support. In some cases the appeal would be a collective measure, usually voiced by the

American Chamber of Commerce of Cuba—which had been organized under State Department auspices in 1919. In other instances individuals would contact State Department officials and Congressmen, and plead their case by letter or even by personal contact. Documents 5 and 6 are examples of such appeals.

Marine detachments sent to Cuba in 1917 were still stationed on Cuban soil in 1921. These units were guarding American property and acting as strike preventers. The Cuban government demanded the removal of the Marines in 1921, and the Navy Department was willing to oblige since it would save departmental funds. Herbert C. Lakin, the President of the Cuba Railroad Company, protested the proposed withdrawal, and even made personal visits to Secretary of the Interior Albert B. Fall, Assistant Secretary of War J. Mayhew Wainwright, and Senator George B. Moses. The Marines were finally withdrawn in January 1922, when General Crowder decided that such a step would make his "moralization" program more palatable to the Cuban government.

Frank Robins was a prominent Havana merchant. The Cuban government owed money to his firm, and Robins wanted the United States to pursue a more aggressive policy in regard to the financial program of the Cuban government. This letter indicated the feeling of the resident investors, and the pressure which they applied to Crowder and the State Department.

DOCUMENT 5.   Herbert C. Lakin to Charles Evans Hughes (Secretary of State), August 18, 1921. (U. S. State Department, General Files: 837.00/2155.)

Probably there has been called to your attention the fact that the Cuban Government is getting uneasy over the presence of United States Marines at Camaguey. The matter was brought to a crisis by an attack which two Cubans made on our Assistant General Superintendent at Camaguey, who is a reserve officer in the U. S. Army. He was clubbed from behind and very seriously injured, his skull being fractured. These men had been leaders of the workmen in very serious labor disturbances which have been going on for a year or more but which have finally terminated in the defeat of the workmen. My information is that these men lost their positions with the Company.

The newspapers report that immediately after the assault an officer and two enlisted men of the Marines entered the house of the assaulting brothers in an attempt to arrest them, and the papers state that this has resulted in a protest by the Cuban Government against the presence of our Marines in Camaguey.[2]

The Marines were sent to Camaguey in July 1917, immediately after our railroad and constitutent companies had suffered a seven million dollar damage in the Cuban Revolution of Jose Miguel Gomez against President Menocal. Their camp is on our property, near our railroad shops. They have been of very material assistance to us at various times and their presence there has saved us from much more trouble than we have had, and from actual property damage. That section of Cuba is a hotbed of Bolshevism. The Bolshevists are inclined to destroy property. The presence of the Marines has prevented them. It would literally be a calamity for us to have the Marines withdrawn.

I do not pretend to make an argument as to the legality of the presence of the Marines in Camaguey, but I hope some arrangement can be made with the Cuban Government, under which they will be allowed to remain.

DOCUMENT 6. Frank Robins to General Enoch Crowder, January 21, 1922. (U. S. Department of State, General Files: 837.00P81/20.)

I am wondering if the commerce and industry of the Island or even if just myself as one lone merchant may not soon be fortified against further disaster by some intimation from either the Cuban or the American Government, or both, as to what may be expected for the relief of the workers of this Island thru constructive efforts of those governments.

During the twenty years thru which my house has existed in Cuba, we have sold American goods to the value of some twenty millions of dollars. . . . The owners of our enterprise have never withdrawn any profits from the business but on the contrary profits made in other countries have been invested by me here and constitute over one half of our entire capital. We have for years given the best of employment to more Cubans and more Americans than any other commercial concern in Cuba. Are we not entitled to some indication as to what may be the intention of those in public authority whose determinations have been awaited for some fifteen months? If there is to be any co-operation between the American and Cuban governments may we not know it, and if there is not to be may we not be told so?

⚹ ⚹ ⚹ ⚹ ⚹

Meanwhile how are we ever going to pay the $1,250,000 that our company alone owes American Manufacturers and banks if this thing keeps up? and it does keep up and grows apace, in spite of your presence and splendid effort of over twelve months.

God knows, General, that you have done and given your talented best to this situation. Also you are one of our greatest Americans, and keen with sympathy and knowledge of Cuba. Of all men you are the one to lead this work. But either our government at Washington should initiate a more aggressive program, or let us know there is no such hope. American business with Cuba has counted on Washington. We ourselves can carry on with sales of several millions of dollars a year of American manufactured articles and can pay our creditors in reasonable time, or we can die game. What we can scarcely be expected to do is to hang on in the dark much longer.

My letter to Mr. Hoover gives some of the figures. Attached also is copy of letter to Mr. Hughes. The boldness of sending these three letters is that of desperation.

May we not hope that you will influence for the life of Cuba and of us here who serve the business and investment of America in Cuba, a policy from Washington that may be definite and aggressive for good and efficient government in this Island.

• • •

General Crowder wanted the State Department to threaten Cuba with intervention under the Platt Amendment in order to convince the reluctant Cuban President to cooperate with the proposed reform program. Crowder believed that the threat to withhold approval for a loan was much too mild (Documents 7 and 8). Secretary Hughes, however, wanted to improve United States relations with Latin America, and was extremely reluctant to use threats of force. Hughes was generally following a policy of substituting "dollars for bullets" in the Caribbean and Central America, and Crowder's request for permission to use threats of intervention were denied.

The negotiations between President Zayas and the New York bankers produced no results until Zayas changed his request and asked for a short-term loan of five million dollars. Representatives

of the Morgan Company reached an agreement with the Cuban
President in October 1921, and then requested formal State Department approval (Document 9). Crowder still advised against
approval, but Secretary of Commerce Herbert Hoover, and others,
expressed the fear that Cuba would fall into chaos unless a stop-
gap loan were granted (Document 10). President Zayas made a
more concrete commitment to lower his budget and the loan was
made in January 1922. This probably saved the Cuban government from defaulting on its foreign debt.

DOCUMENT 7. General Enoch Crowder to Charles Evans
Hughes, September 7, 1921. (U. S. Department of State,
Foreign Relations of the United States: 1921. 2 vols. Wash-
ington, 1936. I: 728–29.)

If the problem of Governmental finance here were one for a
Government of American Intervention its solution would not present great difficulty. By putting into effect the economies listed
above and others which a closer investigation of the Government's
departments would certainly suggest, and the budgetary expenses
would easily [be] reduced to between 45 and 50 millions, with
ample provision for an efficient administration. By a comprehensive
revision of the revenue laws, (including the customs tariff) and
the honest administration of such laws, the receipts could be easily
made to exceed 80 millions. The budgetary surplus of more than
30 millions annually would permit the speedy liquidation of the
floating indebtedness and the prosecution of extensive public works
which could be made to take care of the existing contractual obligations as a part of a general scheme of internal improvement
and thus be made to furnish employment for the large army of
unemployed; and there would still be most ample revenues to meet
the service of any additional public debt that might be incurred
to dispel the industrial crisis and rehabilitate the country.

I fully appreciate that the Department is most anxious to avoid
intervention and desires most earnestly to accomplish the needed
reforms in Cuba through the administration of President Zayas.
The recitation, therefore, of what might be easily accomplished
under a Government of American Intervention can serve no useful purpose except to indicate some of the more essential reforms
which may properly be exacted of President Zayas. In his present
mood (created for him largely by a hungry political following)

it is certain that he will continue to obstruct many of the reforms outlined above, unless coerced into a more compliant attitude by pressure from Washington. Eventually Zayas must be told in unmistakable terms that his policy of a 65 million dollar budget, with a continuation of governmental extravagance and fraud, with insufficient resources for present and possible future needs, and with liquidation of the floating and contractual indebtedness protracted over a long period of years (this method of liquidation being objectionable and of doubtful efficacy for the reasons I have already stated) imperils the kind of stable government which we are pledged by treaty stipulation to maintain in Cuba and must yield to a policy of definite and specific reforms which, of course, will be outlined by the Department only after the gravest deliberation and which ought, I think, under the policy of utilizing the Cuban agencies to embody the minimum of essential reforms compatible with maintaining a solvent Government here. . . . I am quite ready, when assured by the Department that its deliberate [judgment] is that a firmer attitude must be adopted in our dealings with the Cuban Government to present its most insistent demands whatever they may be. My effort thus far has been to accord the fullest and fairest opportunity to the Cuban Government to bring about these reforms and to make its failure so to do, under all the circumstances, a demonstration of either incapacity or unwillingness and a logical basis and justification for the firmer and more insistent attitude on our part.

The sooner a decision is reached as to our future policy the better it will be for the success of my mission. I realize that the policy to be pursued here will be profoundly influenced by our general Latin American policy and that the Department, out of deference to that policy, may find it necessary to modify the more important recommendations that I have, from time to time, made or which I may make in the future.

DOCUMENT 8. General Enoch Crowder to Charles Evans Hughes, September 11, 1921. (*Foreign Relations of the United States: 1921.* I: 731.)

Unofficial but reliable reports reach me that Zayas is ready to cancel negotiations for any kind of loan, interior or exterior, believing that by that course he will be left free to adopt the kind of budget he desires. For this reason I think the Department should go as far as it feels it can go in basing our insistence for

a lower budget primarily upon our treaty obligation to maintain
stable financial government in Cuba with only secondary reference to the necessity for a lower budget as a condition precedent
to securing our sanction for a loan.

DOCUMENT 9. General Enoch Crowder to Charles Evans
Hughes, October 9, 1921. (U. S. Department of State, General Files: 837.51/610.)

J. P. Morgan and Company yesterday made following propo-
sitions to Cuban Government.

First. To purchase immediately five million dollars one year
seven per cent notes of Cuban Government at ninety-nine and
one-half guaranteed by pledge of seven million internal and other
bonds. Proceeds to be applied as follows: (A), Payment of amounts
due United States on postal order balances: (B), allocation of
amounts necessary to pay interest and sinking fund on all exterior
debts for next six months; (C), balance for payment outstanding
checks, estimated about one million, and other governmental
purposes.

Second. This loan shall be part of more comprehensive measures
which shall include: (A), budget for present year shall be fifty-
nine million plus additional appropriation of six million for contingencies: (B), budget for 1922, 1923 shall be fifty-five million
plus additional appropriation of five million for contingencies;
(C), revision of customs and revenue laws to provide income of
ten million in excess of government expenditure; (D), loan of
fifty million dollars described below.

Third. This fifty million dollar loan shall be contracted for following purposes; (A) repayment of five million dollars loan; (B)
liquidation of floating debt; (C) balance for public works. This
loan shall be repaid: twenty million dollars in one, two and three
years and thirty million dollars in twenty to thirty years. Guaranties and other conditions to be arranged in subsequent negotiations. There is nothing in the proposition which would oblige
Cuban Government to make this loan necessarily with Morgan and
Company.

Zayas in answer to Morgan approves proposition in general,
except refrains from definitely committing himself; (A) to budget
reductions indicated above; (B) to revision of customs and revenue
laws saying he will try to accomplish it but cannot answer for
action of Congress and, (C) to repayment of twenty million dol-

lars of fifty million dollars loan in brief period of one, two and three years, which both bankers and myself regard as a means of enforcing rigid economy.

Zayas has transmitted whole of this correspondence to me with letter in which he failed to give the definite commitment to budgetary reduction mentioned in your number 161, September 30, 1 P.M., paragraph two, respecting a budget for the year for current fiscal year and makes no commitments with regard to future budgets. Taking correspondence as a whole Zayas is not thereby committed to that constructive financial program which would justify the Department in sanctioning the loan. Have appointment with him Tuesday when I will discuss further the essentials of such a program and endeavor to secure from him more definite commitments.

Morgan bankers show every desire to conform to Department's policy and have done effective work. Weinberger of Blair and Company who arrived Friday and Bollard of Dillon, Read and Company, who arrived yesterday, had long conferences with me today and will see Zayas soon regarding loan.

DOCUMENT 10. Charles Evans Hughes to President Warren Harding, December 28, 1921. (U. S. Department of State, General Files: 837.51/672.)

Secretary Hoover has very kindly shown me the letter which he addressed to you on December 13th, in regard to the sugar situation in Cuba. I note that among his recommendations there is the following statement:

"(c) There should be an immediate settlement of the loan contract between the Cuban Government and Messrs. Morgan so as to relieve the trades of apprehension of Cuban Government bankruptcy and social chaos. This latter matter is so important that we would be well justified in at once instructing General Crowder to be more liberal in the requirements (no doubt very properly set up) as a condition of American government approval for this loan." In view of this statement, I feel that you may be interested in knowing just what is the present situation in regard to this loan.

This Department has endeavored in every way to expedite the conclusion of a loan by the Cuban Government by cooperating with that Government in measures aiming to place Cuba's finances in such a position that the United States could properly give its sanction to the loan without disregarding the obligations imposed upon us by our Treaty with Cuba.

Under present conditions, it is very evident that the ordinary revenues of Cuba are not adequate to provide for the service of an increased public debt after defraying the necessary expenses of the Government. For some months, there has been a steadily increasing governmental deficit. It has been felt that the further growth of this deficit must be stopped and a margin of receipts over expenditures adequate to provide for the service of the new loan must be created before the United States Government could properly give its consent to this new loan. For this reason, General Crowder has been discussing with the Cuban Government methods of increasing the public revenues by revising the tariff and the internal taxation system and methods of decreasing the expenditures by a downward revision of the budget. The consummation of the loan has thus far been delayed because President Zayas has as yet been unable to effect economies in the budget for the current year which would offer any hope of leaving a margin of receipts over expenditures.

I am glad to be able to inform you, however, that a Presidential Decree, making the desired revision of the current budget, will probably be issued within a very short time since President Zayas has confidentially informed General Crowder that such a Decree was being prepared. I hope, therefore, that this Department will be able to approve the loan in the very near future.

•   •   •

After the granting of the five-million-dollar loan early in 1922, Crowder's "moralization" program moved into high gear. In February, the General delivered the first of his famous "Fifteen Memoranda" dealing with political and financial reform. During the course of the year Crowder forced the Cuban government to institute various changes. Tax revision, budget reduction, and the formation of the "Honest Cabinet" were the most notable of these reforms. Concurrently the New York bankers were negotiating with the Cuban president in regard to the request for a fifty-million-dollar loan. On the basis of the three reforms noted previously, the State Department gave its formal approval, and the loan was granted in January 1923. The syndicate headed by J. P. Morgan and Company made the loan on the basis of its high bid of 96.77.[3]

After the loan had been granted, President Zayas began to pursue a more independent course. Crowder and the bankers were quite concerned over this return of Cuban politics to normal channels (Document 11). Zayas was able to preserve stability, however, as economic conditions began to improve. Thus, the State Department did little but lecture Zayas on the need for honesty and frugality (Document 12).

Evidence of anti-United States sentiment combined with a growing Cuban nationalism became more evident during this period, and resentment of the Crowder mission was a contributing factor (Document 13). Latin American criticism of the Monroe Doctrine and "Dollar Diplomacy" also became more intense. Various groups and individuals in the United States attacked the country's foreign policy, and the combined effect of these protests may have helped to influence the policy of the State Department. Sumner Welles was a major advocate of the new "Dollar Diplomacy," and his reply to Dr. Samuel Guy Inman was, in effect, a defense of the Crowder mission.

DOCUMENT 11. Elliot C. Bacon (J. P. Morgan and Company) to General Enoch Crowder, January 22, 1923. (U. S. Department of State, *Foreign Relations of the United States: 1923*. 2 vols. Washington, 1938. I: 840–41.)

The principal reasons that induced the group of bankers and banks to enter a bid for this new $50,000,000. loan were their belief that the improvement in the financial situation, which has taken place during the administration of President Zayas, might be permanent and their confidence that the services of a strong able cabinet could be depended upon. Throughout the negotiations conducted during the past year and one-half, this group has recognized its obligation definitely to determine, as far as possible, that the loan, if made, would really serve the best interests of the Cuban people and that its proceeds should, without possibility of a failure, be devoted to the needs of the hospitals and to the payment of wages, pensions, salaries and other obligations to the school teachers, soldiers, veterans and other public employees. Moreover it was also recognized that, as far as possible, the just and audited claims against the government for supplies and construction would be satisfied and that important and necessary improvements to roads, sanitary systems and other public works could be made. In the opinion of the group under no other condition would the loan have been justified.

As you know, my partner, Mr. Morrow,[4] discussed this situation, in all its aspects, with the Secretary of State of the United States, who gave his approval of the loan to Cuba with the understanding that a Cuban cabinet, holding the confidence of the public both in Cuba and abroad, would be retained in office. This was clearly and definitely understood by the group and largely influenced it in making a bid of 96.77, this price placing the credit of Cuba on a higher plane than ever before attained. With this in mind, therefore, it is a matter of very great concern to me that from the daily press in Havana I learn there is the threat of a crisis in the Cuban cabinet and that it is possible, in the near future, changes in the personnel of the cabinet may be expected.

            ✓   ✓   ✓   ✓   ✓

As you well know the Group of bankers has an important duty to the investors in the United States to whom it is offering these bonds. Anything that tends to weaken the guaranties is of vital concern to purchasers of these bonds. Furthermore our bid for the loan was upon our definite understanding that the acquiescence of the United States Government in the bond issue was in effect conditional upon the assurance of the Cuban Government that there would be stability in the announced policy and the existing personnel of the departments dealing with the finances and public works. We do not like to contemplate the ill effect upon the foreign credit of Cuba, nor in particular the future status of the present bond issue, legally or politically, if important changes in the government are presently to occur.

DOCUMENT 12. Memorandum of a Conversation Between Cosme de la Torriente (Cuban Ambassador to the United States) and Charles Evans Hughes, November 15, 1923. (*Foreign Relations of the United States: 1923*. I: 850–51.)

The Secretary then said that the situation of the United States vis-à-vis Cuba was a very simple one; that it was hardly necessary to speak of our friendship for the Cuban people and of our desire that they should enjoy the utmost prosperity and have a firm and stable government. The Secretary said that there was no thought among our people of intervention; that no responsible statesman desired intervention in Cuba; that that was the last thing that he thought of and that it would not occur unless Cuba herself made it necessary. . . . The Secretary said that this Government had been much disquieted at the conditions in Cuba; he referred to the fact that the loan of $50,000,000 had been put through on the distinct understanding that there should be a moralization program,—President Zayas himself had asserted this in unequivocal terms. The United States had no desire to get anything for themselves; they wished to see the Cuban Government on the soundest possible basis. The cancer which was eating into the prosperity and hopes of Cuba was corruption and extravagance, and he hoped that the administration would set itself resolutely to cure this. . . .

DOCUMENT 13. A Cuban Attack on the Platt Amendment and the Crowder Mission, 1922. (Emilio Roig de Leuchsenring, "The Platt Amendment: Its Early Interpretation and Its Later Application," Cuba Contemporánea. August, 1922. Pp. 335–36.)

From the time that Dr. Torriente resigned the office of Secretary of State and in the period that followed under General Menocal American meddling occurred in an unusual form and with appalling frequency: repeated notes, constant visits to the Presidential Palace by the North-American minister, appointment of supervisors, "experts," assessors, foreign advisors for different branches of the government, landing of troops of the Union which remained in several regions of the Island . . . and finally, the arrival of General Enoch Crowder in January 1921 after the general elections held in November 1920 which were protested by the Liberal Party in almost every respect.

From that date General Crowder remained in our midst as special envoy and personal representative of the President of the United States, Wilson at that time, now Harding. His official residence is no longer on a ship of the North-American fleet, as in the beginning, but at the legation of his country which for many months has not had an accredited minister to our Republic. He intervened and made decisions regarding our recent grave problems, the electoral and the economic; and made daily visits to the President and department secretaries, presenting them "notes" and "memoranda."

In several articles I propose to study thoroughly the form and special ways in which our relations with the United States have developed in these later times during the administrations of Menocal and Zayas. My purpose will be to state later, as a summary of the whole matter, detailed conclusions which will lead me to determine exactly the consequences which the application given to the Platt Amendment by the governments of North America has had for Cuba and continues to have. This application, as I said in the beginning of this study, is in disagreement with its spirit and purposes according to the interpretation which its own authors gave to it. Far from being beneficial to Cuba it is today a threat to our sovereignty and to our independence, and is leading us toward the destruction of nationality.

DOCUMENT 14. Sumner Welles Defends United States Policy, 1924. (Sumner Welles, "Is America Imperialistic?" *Atlantic Monthly*. September, 1924. Pp. 36–44.)[5]

The policy of the United States with regard to Cuba is necessarily a policy which applies to the other countries of the Caribbean. Our Government must be guided not only by its altruistic desire to help develop civilization and progress in general, but also by purely selfish motives; for what better protection can there be for the United States in the event of foreign menace than the presence throughout the continent of strong governments maintained in power by the consent of the governed, well disposed toward the United States? . . . . Such actual intervention in or occupation of Cuba as the United States has been obliged to undertake is, of course, at best, an artificial method of restoring outward tranquillity so that constitutional government may once more be established. Of far greater value is the friendly advice which may be offered to the Cuban Government and the Cuban people through our representatives.

•   •   •

Article VI of the Platt Amendment specified that the Isle of Pines be omitted from the constitutional boundaries of Cuba. The article also stated that the title to the island should be settled by a future treaty. This treaty was negotiated on March 2, 1904. The United States agreed to relinquish all claims to the island, but the Senate refused to approve it. In April 1907, the United States

Supreme Court ruled that the island was at least *"de facto"* Cuban territory. The Senate, however, again rejected the treaty in 1908.

The Cuban government continued to administer the affairs of the island, but its unsettled status caused much resentment among Cubans; especially since the American residents of the island continually demanded annexation by the United States. In 1922 Secretary Hughes and the Republican leaders in the Senate decided to push for approval. This move was part of Hughes's policy of improving relations with Latin America, and it represented a concession to growing Cuban nationalism. The treaty ran into serious opposition led by Senators William Borah and Royal S. Copeland. As a result, approval and ratification was delayed until March 1925. When news of the ratification was received in Cuba a national holiday was declared.

DOCUMENT 15. The Isle of Pines Treaty; Negotiated in 1904, Ratified in 1925. (U. S. Senate, *Papers Relating to the Adjustment of Title to the Ownership of the Isle of Pines.* Senate Document No. 166. 68th Cong., 2nd Sess. Washington, 1924. P. 232.)

ISLE OF PINES

The United States of America and the Republic of Cuba, being desirous to give full effect to the sixth article of the Provision in regard to the relations to exist between the United States and Cuba, contained in the Act of the Congress of the United States of America, approved March second, nineteen hundred and one, which sixth Article aforesaid is included in the Appendix to the Constitution of the Republic of Cuba, promulgated on the 20th day of May, nineteen hundred and two and provides that "The Island of Pines shall be omitted from the boundaries of Cuba specified in the Constitution, the title of ownership thereof being left to future adjustment by treaty;" have for that purpose appointed as their Plenipotentiaries to conclude a treaty to that end:

The President of the United States of America, John Hay, Secretary of State of the United States of America; and

The President of the Republic of Cuba, Gonzalo de Quesada,

Envoy Extraordinary and Minister Plenipotentiary of Cuba to the
United States of America:

Who, after communicating to each other their full powers,
found in good and due form, have agreed upon the following
articles:

Article I.

The United States of America relinquishes in favor of the
Republic of Cuba all claim of title to the Island of Pines situate in
the Caribbean Sea near the southwestern part of the Island of
Cuba, which has been or may be made in virtue of Articles I and
II of the Treaty of Peace between the United States and Spain,
signed at Paris on the tenth day of December eighteen hundred
and ninety-eight.

Article II.

This relinquishment, on the part of the United States of America, of claim of title to the said Island of Pines, is in consideration
of the grants of coaling and naval stations in the Island of Cuba
heretofore made to the United States of America by the Republic
of Cuba.[6]

Article III.

Citizens of the United States of America who, at the time of
the exchange of ratifications of this treaty, shall be residing or
holding property in the Island of Pines shall suffer no diminution
of the rights and privileges which they have acquired prior to the
date of exchange of ratifications of this treaty; they may remain
there or may remove therefrom, retaining in either event all their
rights of property, including the right to sell or dispose of such
property or of its proceeds; and they shall also have the right to
carry on their industry, commerce and professions being subject in
respect thereof to such laws as are applicable to other foreigners.

DOCUMENT 16.   Senator Medill McCormick Defends the Isle
of Pines Treaty, 1925. (*Congressional Record*, 68th Cong.,
2nd Sess., 1925. Vol. 66, Part 2. P. 2020.)

Mr. President, I have taxed the patience of Senators in order
thus to present to the Senate the historical fact that the Isle of
Pines has been an integral part of the territory of Cuba from
remote time until this very hour and was administered as such

even during the administration of Cuban affairs under Governor Wood prior to the adoption of the Cuban Constitution and later under Governor Magoon during the period of American intervention. I have laid before the Senate the evidence which has convinced me that in the Supreme Court decision Justice Day, who as Secretary of State negotiated the protocol and the treaty of peace, held with Secretary Root that the Isle of Pines was politically and geographically appurtenant to Cuba and not one of the "other islands" which, together with Porto Rico, Spain ceded to the United States.

Senators, we must bear in mind that the government in the Isle of Pines to-day is a Cuban government, as it was a Cuban government 20 years ago and five times 20 years ago. It is not enough to reject this treaty to bring the Isle of Pines under the Government of the United States. Another treaty, absolutely contrary to this in purpose, must be negotiated and ratified by the Presidents and Senates of two countries before that can be. . . .

Let us in common candor and simple honesty vote upon this treaty to ratify it or reject it. It has been pending before the Senate for over a score of years; four times it has been reported from the Committee on Foreign Relations; it is wellnigh 20 years since Senator Foraker, with incontrovertible fact and remorseless logic, answered the opponents of the treaty, and yet year after year we have failed to face the issue. . . . Policy, justice, honor, all call for the ratification of the treaty. The historical, legal, and moral title of Cuba to the island is so clear, that rejection of the treaty by the Senate will not be construed as a mere difference between the Senate and the Executive, but rather as a callous indifference on our part to the rights of a sister Republic unable to assert those rights against the mighty colossus of the North. The defeat of this treaty will not [only] impair the beneficent influence of the United States in Cuba, but it will injure us in all Latin America. It will make difficult the friendly exercise of those good offices through which by persuasion we have been able to contribute to internal and international peace in the other Republics to the south of us. At the very moment when American marines are withdrawing from Nicaragua, and almost at the hour when by treaty we are to confirm their wise withdrawal from the Dominican Republic, it will give color to the charges made against us, that we have little regard for the rights of the weaker States in the Caribbean; it will add greatly to the number of those in Latin

America who voice their distrust of us. The failure of the treaty must inevitably harm our credit and commerce in this hemisphere, but far worse impair our influence and challenge our honor in all the other Republics of the Americas.

• • •

President Gerardo Machado pledged during the campaign of 1924 to begin an extensive public works program. The revenues of the Cuban government were not sufficient for the type of program which Machado desired, so he quickly made overtures to American bankers. The bankers were eager to float bonds for the Cuban government, and the competition for the loans led the banks to adopt tactics which they hoped would make favorable impressions on Machado and his cabinet (Document 17). The Chase National Bank and the National City Bank were the most active in this competition.

General Crowder opposed these loan negotiations, and maintained that public works bond issues could not be sanctioned under Article II of the Platt Amendment. The bankers, however, worked out a legal maneuver to by-pass the article, and the State Department raised no objections to the various loan proposals. By the end of February 1930, the Cuban government had incurred an eighty-million-dollar indebtedness through the Chase Bank and its associates. How much of this went into the pockets of Machado and other officials is an interesting—but unsolved—question.

DOCUMENT 17.   Cuba—Memorandum: Mr. Graves (Vice-President of the Chase National Bank on detached service in Cuba) to Mr. Edward R. Tinker (President, Chase Securities Corporation), March 22, 1926. (U. S. Senate, *Stock Exchange Practices: Hearings Before the Committee on Banking and Currency*. 73rd Cong., 2nd Sess. Washington, 1933 and 1934. Part 5. Pp. 2608–2610.)

On Saturday, March 20, Mr. Benard suggested that I see Tarafa[7] promptly on Monday and point out the convenience to him, in an indirect way, of a prompt decision on the part of the Cuban Government as to this matter of financing. He called attention to the present unsatisfactory state of the security market and stated that whereas a substantial amount of securities could be absorbed at this time without difficulty, that a sudden change in market conditions is not improbable, in which case this financing might be rendered much more expensive, if not impossible. I stated that I would get in touch with Tarafa today.

On Sunday, March 21, about 3 o'clock in the afternoon, General Crowder approached Mrs. Graves at the Jockey Club, stating he was very anxious to see me at once. Upon learning that I was at the Country club, he immediately came there and sent for me on the golf links. He seemed to be much exercised. He stated that he had heard persistent rumors that Blair & Co. and the Chase Securities Corporation were attempting to negotiate a loan to the Cuban Government of 100 million dollars, and that in view of the fact that their indebtedness was already 98 million and the financial and economic condition of the country was in such a deplorable state, he found it very difficult to credit the above statement. He stated that the character of his information was such, however, that he could not disregard it and, as a matter of fact, Cespedes[8] was supposed to present to him the proposed project today, Monday, March 22; that, as he understood it, they were attempting to make a loan to the Government but under another name, and that we all knew if any difficulty arose, the United States Government would be appealed to, to make Cuba comply with her engagements.

General Crowder stated that he and I had been friends for a long time and he thought it was only fair to tell me of the situation because as he saw it, it placed upon him the responsibility of making an immediate protest to the State Department in Washington. He called my attention to article 2 of the Platt amendment and further said that he supposed these people had secured advice from American lawyers who really were insufficiently acquainted with the proper construction of the Constitution of Cuba of which the Platt amendment was a part.

I pointed out to him that I represented neither Blair & Co. nor the Chase Securities, although both organizations were friendly with the Chase Bank; that any financial plans or discussions they may have had with the Cuban Government, were matters which I was not in a position to discuss. I told him that I would assume, however, the first thing any group of bankers would be sure of was that any plans they had would not run counter to the provisions of the Cuban constitution or the Platt amendment, and that I would presume that any such groups would not only have the best legal advice from American lawyers but from the most outstanding legal talent in Cuba as well.

General Crowder said, you know, I believe in treating American interests alike, to which I replied that I was well aware of this. He said that 2 or 3 years ago, representatives of Blair & Co. came to Cuba in an attempt to loan the Cuban Government $40,000,000 but they did not call on him and they had not even had the courtesy of calling on him this time either.

I made no comment on these statements but told him that I would attempt to find out something about the situation that night and if I were successful, I would communicate with him as soon as I was in position to do so..

In view of the fact that General Crowder was to have the plans submitted to him today and he knows that Mr. Tinker and Mr. Benard had been here and that I had been with them, it would be foolish to pretend utter lack of knowledge of their interest in the public-works program, and in view of the fact that General Crowder expected to hear from me in some form, it was better I should communicate with him and tell him that Mr. Benard had not returned but I would get in touch with him immediately upon his arrival in Habana, so that he might explain to General Crowder any ideas they might have on the financing plan. Failing to do so, I expected to get into communication with Mr. Tinker during the course of the day and would let him know whatever Mr. Tinker wished to communicate to him.

Pursuant to my arrangement with Mr. Benard, I had an interview with Colonel Tarafa today and explained to him the attitude of General Crowder. Tarafa said at once that, in his opinion, Cespedes would not submit the matter to Crowder and Crowder had tried to deceive me in this respect; that Cespedes was the last man in the Cabinet to submit anything to the American Government and if he were obliged to do so, he would certainly have it done by some other member of the Cabinet.

When I suggested to Tarafa the possibility that Crowder had secured his information from Field, former secret-service agent of the United States, a friend of Cespedes and who now does secret-service errands for Crowder, he stated that he was sure this was what had happened when Field had learned from Cespedes, in a general way, of the plan, and that he had given Crowder his own digest of the matter.

I talked with Mr. Tinker about 3:15 p.m., setting forth the

above facts. He said that I should not communicate with Crowder again unless he called me, in which case I was to tell him that Mr. Tinker had left for Florida last Thursday, and I was not sufficiently informed of his plans to be able to discuss them—that I should get in touch with Mr. Benard as soon as possible and turn the whole matter over to him, giving Mr. Tinker's opinion that it was not necessary to communicate our plans at the present time to Crowder, but to say that when the proper moment arrived a discussion would be had.

✓   ✓   ✓   ✓   ✓

It is clear that the bank should preserve cordial relations with the United States Ambassador but, while not telling him anything that would damage our interests in Cuba, to be careful not to make any statements which, he might easily learn, were contrary to facts.

•   •   •

As an aspiring presidential candidate Gerardo Machado developed a reputation as a foe of the Platt Amendment. This appeal to Cuban nationalism was a good vote-getting device, but United States officials and businessmen understood the "official nationalism" of Machado. As president, Machado did make an effort to obtain at least a modification of the Platt Amendment (Document 18). Modification or abrogation of the Amendment would have increased the President's prestige in Cuba; especially when serious political opposition began to develop in 1927. A few American businessmen also tried to help Machado in this matter (Document 19). The State Department would not consider such a move, but the Department did not object when Machado did not include the Platt Amendment in the official publication of the Cuban Constitution in 1930.

DOCUMENT 18. Memorandum: Conversation Between Señor Don Orestes Ferrara (Cuban Ambassador to the United States) and Stokeley W. Morgan (Division of Latin American Affairs), February 21, 1927. (U. S. Department of State, General Files: 611.3731/234.)

The Ambassador then went on to speak of the Platt Amendment, saying that Cuba had no cause to complain of the Platt Amendment or the manner in which it had been interpreted, but it was very embarrassing to Cuba; that she was subjected to constant criticism from all parts of the world due to the fact that the Platt Amendment limited the sovereignty of Cuba and that Cuba was not therefore, entirely an independent sovereign state. This was very galling to the pride of the Cubans. I remarked that criticism levied at Cuba on that score seemed to come from the same antagonistic and irresponsible elements which were constantly criticizing the United States on the ground of imperialism. . . . The Ambassador said that was entirely true, but nevertheless there was a good deal of talk about Cuba's sovereignty being limited and they would very much like to see that criticism stilled. He said Cuba did not desire to avoid any of the responsibilities incurred under the Platt Amendment, but he did wish the form of the Amendment or the manner in which she recognized this responsibility could be altered. He hoped that some arrangement could be made by which the United States would still retain the same rights but they would not appear in the same form as the Platt Amendment. Possibly the Platt Amendment could be abrogated with some sort of a stipulation that in the event of certain emergencies it would automatically go into effect again. . . .

The Ambassador also spoke of the naval base at Guantanamo and asked me if we considered it of vital importance to the United States. I said that it was my impression that the Navy did so regard it. The Ambassador said there was some resentment in Cuba with regard to our occupation of Guantanamo and he had hoped that some arrangement could be worked out by which the United States would have the complete cooperation of Cuba in time of need—a cooperation greater than was provided for by the present relations, but which would alter the status of the Guantanamo base.

⚓   ⚓   ⚓   ⚓   ⚓

I think the impossibility of altering the form of the Platt Amendment without altering the substance should be pointed out and the Ambassador should be told frankly that the United States Government sees no imperative reason for any change.

I presume that the Navy Department would not consider for a moment any change in the status of the Guantanamo base. The suggestion for further Cuban cooperation in time of need is too vague for serious consideration at this time. There is little doubt that in the event of difficulties between the United States and a European or Asiatic power we should have the complete sympathy of Cuba and probably could count upon her as an ally if we needed her. In the event of difficulties with a Latin American country the best we could count on would be an unsympathetic neutrality, but we would have no particular need of active Cuban cooperation.

DOCUMENT 19. General E. H. Crowder (United States Ambassador to Cuba) to Frank B. Kellogg (Secretary of State), February 17, 1927. (U. S. Department of State, General Files: 711.27/126.)

In the last two days, Mr. Horatio Rubens, who is at present in Habana, brought me information that he was reliably informed that Mr. Henry C. Catlin would precede the President to New York and there organize a banquet in his honor. As you are aware, Mr. Catlin represents in Cuba the Electric Bond & Share Company and, prior to General Machado's induction into the office of President, had, as such representative, business dealings with him out of which there sprang a rather close friendship. The most important information given me was that at this banquet in New York, the proposition to abrogate the Platt Amendment would receive rather prominent attention.[9]

Later I saw Mr. Catlin and asked him the question as to whether a banquet of this character was being organized. He answered positively as to the banquet but rather equivocally at first as to the proposition to abrogate the Platt Amendment. I take it that he is not fully convinced himself that the occasion will be suitable for either the President or his New York hosts to announce a policy upon a question as fundamental in the relation between the two countries as the abrogation of the Platt Amendment. In the course of the conversation Mr. Catlin referred to the fact that his Company had one hundred million dollars (which I think is an exaggeration) invested in Cuba and asked if I questioned the right of such a large interest to carry out such a program as we were discussing if it thought it fitting to do so. I answered that we were not discussing any question of right; that it was rather a question of the opportuneness of any announcement of that kind during President Machado's visit in the United States. Further answering him I said,—"You speak for one hundred millions of invested capital. Do you know the attitude of the other fourteen hundred millions of invested capital in Cuba?"

My purpose in talking with Mr. Catlin was to ascertain if any incident of the kind referred to was likely to occur during the President's visit and to give you early information in order that if the matter comes up in any conference with the President, you will have ample opportunity to consider the reply which should be made.

Personally, I do not think that the Platt Amendment is a "straight jacket" in which Cuba must always live and develop her national life. I also know that practically all American interests in Cuba share my view that any agitation of abrogation of the Platt Amendment at the present time would cause a downward movement for outstanding bonds of Cuba and would seriously affect the credit of Cuba in financing the scheme of public works which she has undertaken.

•   •   •

The situation in Cuba degenerated rapidly during 1930. An armed uprising occurred in 1931, but Machado was able to suppress it without much difficulty. The United States did not proclaim a formal embargo on the sale of arms to other groups, but Ambassador Guggenheim assured the Cuban president that such shipments of arms were being prohibited.

Guggenheim and representatives of the Chase Bank repeatedly urged Machado to make concessions to the opposition groups in order to prevent a full-scale revolution (Document 21). Machado ignored this advice, and Guggenheim became convinced that the chief executive should be replaced. Secretary of State Stimson, however, maintained that the United States was following the "Root Interpretation" of the Platt Amendment and therefore would not meddle in Cuban politics. The opposition groups asked for armed intervention by the United States, and in 1933 Ambassador Guggenheim recommended that the Platt Amendment be modified so as to eliminate the intervention clause. He believed that opposition groups were trying to provoke trouble in order to obtain the ouster of Machado through intervention. In spite of his efforts, Guggenheim was identified with Machado in the eyes of the Cubans, and the negative policy of the United States was interpreted as support for Machado, which in one sense it was (Document 20).

The Chase Bank gave advice to Machado, and tried to avoid default on Cuba's foreign debt by extending credits to the government. Machado continued to make the payments on the debt, although he had to default on the salaries of governmental employees in order to do so. The bank's support for Machado paid dividends—both literally and figuratively.

DOCUMENT 20. The Cuban Opposition Attacks Machado and Guggenheim, 1931. (Cuban Information Bureau, *Ambassador Guggenheim and the Cuban Revolt*. Washington, 1931. Pp. 8, 19–20.)

The power of the American diplomatic representative and the epoch-making power of the great nation behind it, ruthlessly employed to crush its self-determination, taught the Cuban people a fateful lesson.

Thereafter every gesture of the American Ambassador has had a precise and definite import to the Cuban people; his slightest word, his faintest suggestions are filled with worlds of meaning and so interpreted by the public. His smile speaks volumes, his bearing, his home-life, his associations, his outings, his recreations, even his state of humor, all speak to the Cubans, watchfully scrutinizing to ascertain "on what side" is the American representative. And there appears to be no question as to their findings in the present instance.

It is not exaggerating to confirm the exactness of the head-line in "La Prensa" of New York on June 9th last stating: "The whole of Cuba pending from the interview between Machado and Guggenheim" and there is no clearer truth than that contained in the Scripps-Howard editorial of August 12, last: "No Cuban government can long survive without Washington's approval."

Could the Cuban people obtain any other impression but one of whole-hearted support and approval of Machado from every spoken and unspoken act of Ambassdaor Guggenheim? Would it be improper to assert that even the Cuban army's loyalty to Machado is tracable to the Ambassador?

One army Colonel, eager to join hands with the rebellion and thoroughly nauseated with the prevaling tyranny and despotism, was known to remark: "There is no chance. I know the Ambassador backs him to the limit and under the circumstances my sacrifice would be useless." He doubtless remembered how the previous revolt had been crushed by Minister Gonzalez' proclamations and that the many army officers who joined the rebels were left in the lurch, falling into disgrace and losing their career.

Cuba has been under martial law almost uninterruptedly for one year.

The University is still padlocked; the schools are closed.

There is no free press, no free speech, no free assembly. Papers have been suppressed wholesale; more editors have been killed.

Assassinations, mysterious disappearances and suppression by violence of all individual liberties has continued unabated. Nay; intensified. Torture is being inflicted in prisons. There are something like 2,000 political prisoners in jails and fortresses.

The anticipated Cuban revolt has come and subsided. Guggenheim has been powerless or unwilling to stop it. Latent revolution is still prevalent. Further armed strife is doubtless imminent.

Business is at a standstill. Governmental receipts at a low ebb. Default on external debt payments is in sight. Bankruptcy is general. Importations have decreased to an appalling figure.

The right of Habeas Corpus is consistently denied. The judiciary is powerless or else controlled by Machado.

Cuba's debt has been doubled in the last two years.

Various international complications have set in, with the British, Danish, Spanish, and Chinese governments.

There is an illegitimate government and congress in Cuba, acknowledged to be so by the Supreme Court, brazenly wringing an enormous lottery graft from a starving people. Taxes are unbearable and extortionate. Official expenses and extravagance amazing. The Cuban budget provides a daily appropriation of 38 cents for an Army horse and 9 cents per hospital patient. Ten millions for the army and less than one million for agriculture. The Director of the Leprosy Hospital threatens to send patients home, unable to keep and feed them. Hospitals are neglected; infant mortality enormously on the increase.

Ninety-five per cent of the people are against both Machado and Guggenheim.

What has Guggenheim done? What has he accomplished?

It may be that the Ambassador has merely played to his own policies.

In Cuba, however, he has become the "man of the hour" and the most unpopular individual in the Island, barring Machado. . . .

DOCUMENT 21. James Bruce (Vice-President, Chase National Bank) to Joseph Rovensky (Vice-President, Chase National Bank), February 23, 1931. (*Stock Exchange Prac-*

tices: Hearings Before the Committee on Banking and Currency. Part 5. Pp. 2630–33.)

First of all, one of the things we should do in Habana is to have a secretary there that we can write letters with; and my suspicions may be unfounded, but I think that any communications made from the office at the moment are known at the palace before they are known in New York.

ꙮ   ꙮ   ꙮ   ꙮ   ꙮ

3. The interests of the President: The President's personal loan is now $130,000. and he promises to pay it off within 30 days. I should doubt very much whether he does this.

The loan of Mistre Machado is now about $45,000 unsecured. We have a proposition from them stating that they would pay this off if we would loan them $145,000 on Cuban internal government bonds at market value without margin. We decided that we would rather take our chances on losing $45,000 than to put up an adidtional [*sic*] $100,000 in unmarketable securities, so this item remains the same.

With regard to the shoe factory belonging to the President, when Rosenthall took over the office this loan was altogether $89,000, and he has reduced the same to $9,000. Undoubtedly, in my opinion, if this had been allowed to run along for a year or two the same would have been a total loss. You are familiar, of course, with the transaction by which Sherrill and Rosenthall collected $200,000 from Cespedes, as I think this should have also been eventually a loss, and collection was really the best single thing that has been done for the bank this year.

ꙮ   ꙮ   ꙮ   ꙮ   ꙮ

To Touch for a Moment on Obregon.[10]

ꙮ   ꙮ   ꙮ   ꙮ   ꙮ

As we know, from any business standpoint he is perfectly useless—
[Laughter]
He has neither any ability for banking, nor has he the slightest ability in negotiating, which was something which we thought it might be possible to build him up to do. The only use that Joe has would be to do a certain amount of entertaining of our more important customers when they come to Habana in the winter, and also to do a certain amount of contact with regard to new business, etc. This latter of course can be much better done by Lopez. From what I could gather in listening to some of the

Cubans, talk is that Joe has very little standing with the President, and I think this is probably true. On the other hand, where the rub comes in is that if we did not pay him his salary the President would have to give him an allowance—
[Laughter]
and in times as hard as these this might be fairly difficult to do, so it would seem to me that the best thing to do at the moment would be to let things go on as they are.

First of all I saw the Ambassador and he thought that the re-newal should be for 60 days. I told him that we had thought that a renewal for 60 days would be undignified and that the same had better be for 6 months in accordance with the wishes of the President. He said that he was trying very hard to have the Presi-dent balance his budget, that the same had been reduced from 77 million to 67 million and that the President had promised him to further reduce it to 60 million. Furthermore, the President said that he would receive 10 million from the new taxes. The ques-tion was as to whether it was not in our interest to keep as tight a hold as we could on the fiscal policies of Cuba. With this in mind, I had a talk with the President along the following lines:

First, we agreed to renew the $20,000,000 for 90 days. I told him that it was most important from our standpoint that he car-ried out the reduction in the budget and put his house in order financially, and furthermore that it was most important, both from his standpoint and from ours, that he went right to work to re-establish the credit of Cuba on a better basis than it now was. This of course could only be done by making a compromise with his political enemies, and naturally the only way he could do this was to make some concessions, but the result of which would be that Cuba would present a uniform front rather than have the tourist trade disputed and the security holders made nervous by not know-ing when, if at all, the Government would be thrown out of power. The President admitted all this, and in fact went on to elongate on the same, stating what he was doing to bring it all about. He mentioned that in this last Congress there were one or two dissen-ting voices, but he said that in the Congress which would convene on April 1 there would not be one dissenting voice (I suppose the two dissenting voices are already in jail).

. . . Altogether the President was extremely satisfied with every-thing except one. He is very hard up for a million and a half dollars, and he wanted to know if we would loan him $1,300,000 of this amount. I told him it was a matter which I would have to take up with my associates on my return to New York, as I did not feel that it should be discussed on the telephone. Naturally I don't think that we should make the loan, but as it was brought up quite unexpectedly in the sense that we had already indicated our unwillingness to do this, and I did not think that the President would mention it, but I did, however, go so far as to find out what the best terms would be.

To explain: We have in the Habana branch approximately $240,000 of money advanced to various local contractors, which is not covered by bonds similar to the Warren Brothers bonds.[11] I think this money is in considerable jeopardy. I therefore asked the President if, in the event that this was favorably considered, whether he would pay off those particular contractors and substitute Warren Brothers bonds for the amount due us. He said that he would do that. I then asked him the length of time that he wanted, and he said that he would like to borrow the money until the public financing was done. I said that this was a matter that we could not even consider, but wondered if it would be possible for him to pay the same at the rate of $100,000 a month. He said that he could do this. I told him then that I would discuss the matter when I got back to New York. In the meantime, in turning it over in my mind and so that we can all consider it, it would seem to me that it might be a good trade to loan the Government $500,000 to be secured by Warren Brothers bonds on condition that they would secure our present loan to the contractors, also to make this re-paper at the rate of, say, $50,000 a month. In this way I think we would turn a bad loan into a good one without putting up any great amount of additional money. I think that at the moment the President is so hard up that he will jump at anything which looks like additional cash. In this regard, Henry Catlin[12] arrived on the scene just 2 days before I left, and although I have no particular objection to Henry personally, he would have complic ted my position very much had I remained, because he runs in and out of the palace every little while and is trying to get his own taxes reduced, and would be delighted to play Lady Bountiful with the funds of the Chase Bank. Another thing is that, although Henry is on our advisory committee, it is impossible to talk frankly with him, as you know what you say will be repeated in the palace.

He told me, which I think is entirely true, that the President is desperately in need of the money for the Government, and that

it was most important for us to put up $1,500,000. In fact, he had at
least 10 very good reasons why we should do this. He stated,
among other things, that the $30,000 which the President borrowed
from us in his private account he loaned to the Government.

In this connection a matter which is most important and which
I could not touch on over the telephone, except very slightly to
Mr. Eddy, is the fact that the President had practically gotten to
the bottom of the trust fund, which of course he had no business
in using. These funds are down in the neighborhood of approximately $3,000,000, and they should be around $12,000,000. This
money will have to be replaced at some time, as the chief trust
fund is a pension fund, although there are various others which I
have sent to you with other data. Naturally, the public do not
know about this, although why they should not get on to it I do
not know, but it is worrying both the President and our own State
Department very much. . . .

•   •   •

Beet sugar growers and refiners in the United States were quick
to join in the postwar clamor for higher tariffs. Several important
Congressional leaders of the Republican Party took a direct interest
in sugar duties since they represented states with important beet
sugar interests. Senator Reed Smoot of Utah, and Representative
Joseph Fordney of Michigan were two staunch advocates of a
higher sugar tariff, and both were chairmen of important committees. The Emergency Tariff Act was rushed through a special
session of Congress in 1921, and the duty on raw sugar from
Cuba was increased from 1.0048 cents a pound to 1.6 cents a
pound. The domestic producers were not satisfied with this increase, and the Fordney-McCumber Tariff Act of 1922 pushed the
rate up to 1.7648 cents a pound. Protests by exporters and investors
in Cuba may have helped to prevent a larger increase (Document
22).

In 1929 the sugar tariff battle erupted again. Several well-
financed lobby groups entered the fight on behalf of Cuban sugar.
One of the most active of these groups was the one sponsored by
the American Chamber of Commerce of Cuba and the United
States Sugar Association. Herbert C. Lakin—the President of the
Cuba Company—was put in charge of the lobby operations, and his
reports to President Machado (Document 24) provide an interesting insight into the activities of a lobbyist. The battle with the

protectionists was waged in committee hearings, hotel rooms, and even in the White House. Support was solicited from labor unions, religious bodies, and chambers of commerce.

Some large banks sided with the Cuban interests because of investment links. The National City Bank of New York had taken over a number of sugar properties after the crash of 1920, and these had been combined into the General Sugars Company. Thus, the bank became a leading exponent of low duty on Cuban sugar (Document 23).

When the shouting, tumult, and logrolling ended, the duty on Cuban raw sugar was 2.0 cents a pound. This was a compromise which pleased none of the interests concerned. Some of the Cuban interests were relieved that the rate of 3.0 cents a pound—as proposed by the Farm Bureau Federation—had not won approval, but this was a "negative blessing" as far as most of the Cuban interests were concerned. The ink was hardly dry on the Hawley-Smoot Tariff Act before organized attacks were launched against the sugar duty.

The Cuban government had experimented with production controls in the sugar industry, but American interests generally protested these moves. As the Depression deepened, however, some American businessmen became advocates of controlled competition. Thomas L. Chadbourne was one of the leaders in the movement to form an international production control system for the sugar industry. Chadbourne had invested in the Cuban sugar industry in 1920–21, and had become quite disillusioned in regard to free competition (Document 25). By 1930 he was convinced that stability depended upon controlled competition, but the plan he devised did not work. Producers in the United States had refused to participate, and the cooperation of the signatory nations was purely voluntary. By 1933, a number of businessmen with Cuban interests—such as Chadbourne—were convinced that stability in the sugar industry depended on the solution of these two problems.

DOCUMENT 22. Resolution: "Improving the Commercial Relations Between the United States and Cuba." American Manufacturers Export Association, October 11, 1921. (U.S. Department of State, General Files: 611.3731/115.)

Whereas Cuba is bound to the United States by ties of a special political and economic nature, as evidenced in the Treaty of Commercial Reciprocity of 1902 between the two countries, and

Whereas the trade of the United States with Cuba, which amounted in 1920 to over half a billion dollars, or more than the trade with all the Spanish speaking countries of South America, depends upon both the prosperity of Cuba and the ability of American exporters to meet foreign competition in the latter country, and

Whereas Cuba looks to the United States as the chief market for her products, and any economic handicap in the commercial relations with Cuba is bound to adversely affect the sales to the United States, and the prosperity of the Island, and

Whereas the differential in the tariffs of both countries as compared with the tariff arrangements with other countries, is 20% as provided in the Treaty of 1902, and this has been of enormous advantage to the United States in steadying competition and thereby increasing American exports to Cuba, and the growing severity of competition, especially from Germany, emphasizes the greater need for the preferential arrangements between the two countries,

Therefore, be it hereby resolved by the members of the American Manufacturers Export Association to recommend to Congress a most careful consideration of the effect that an undue increase in the tariff would have upon the trade between the two countries, the large American investments in Cuba, and the prosperity of the Island, and further recommends to the Secretary of State the advantages that would follow favorable consideration of the petition of the Cuban Commercial Mission now in the United States, for a rearrangement of the existing Treaty between the United States and Cuba, by which the present differential of 20% would be substantially increased. Resolution unanimously adopted.

DOCUMENT 23. National City Bank of New York Attacks the Tariff on Sugar, 1929. (*Monthly Bank Letter*. June, 1929. P. 160).

We have more intimate relations with Cuba than with any other member of the Pan-American Union. . . . In view of this natural community of interests, as well as the political ties existing, it would seem that if Pan-Americanism means anything in the trade policies of this country it should appear in our trade relations with Cuba. . . .

When the full measure is taken of what the ruin of the sugar industry would mean to the 3,500,000 inhabitants of Cuba, no parallel for the disaster can be found outside of the annals of war, and the injury done in this case would be far more lasting than the injuries of war. Devastated Belgium and France have been rebuilt and are more prosperous than before, but there would be no rebuilding of Cuba until a market was found for her products. The prosperity of Cuba depends upon her ability to utilize her soil and climate for the purpose to which they are supremely suited and to trade with a population which will take such products in exchange for their own. In all history there has been no such destruction of property values or displacement of an industrial population by legislative decree as would result from forcing the people of Cuba to abandon sugar production, or even to cut it one-half. Alternative employment for the population cannot be named. The people are unskilled and without experience in anything else, and the United States wants nothing else from Cuba any more than it wants sugar. Exclusion of its products from this country would mean the depression of Cuba to a distinctly lower level of social life.

It cannot be too forcibly stated that while the beet sugar industry is fighting for expansion—to capture the full United States market—Cuba is fighting for life, to hold the place she has long held in the only available market for her product, and for the only means of a decent livelihood for her people.

DOCUMENT 24. Herbert C. Lakin to President Gerardo Machado, August 21, 1929. (U. S. Senate, Subcommittee of the Committee on the Judiciary, *Hearings: The Lobby Investigation.* 71st Cong., 1st Sess. 1929 and 1930. Washington, 1930. Part 4. Pp. 1745–49.)

It is now two months since I have made a personal report to you. I have not written a report because I expected each week to be able to come to Cuba and report orally. I now find that it may be several weeks before I can come to Cuba and I think you ought to know how Mr. Shattuck[13] and I feel about the situation and what we have been doing.

Of course, Colonel Tarafa has kept you fully informed of any events in Washington and New York with which he was personally familiar. He and Crowder and Shattuck and myself have cooperated. We have not always agreed about policy, but we have had no

controversy among ourselves. All four have been trying to do what
was best for the Cuban interests.

✦   ✦   ✦   ✦   ✦

You, of course, know about the hearings which took place
before the Senate Finance Committee. In addition to the hearings,
Shattuck and I have seen many Senators and have corresponded
with many others. He also has been in constant touch with the
White House and Senator Smoot.

As you know, Colonel Tarafa, when he was first in Washington,
saw Senator Smoot and President Hoover. Although the arrangement to see the President was ostensibly made by Senator Smoot,
Mr. Shattuck had actually arranged it some weeks before Tarafa
came to Washington. Tarafa at that time approved our activities
before the Senate Finance Committee but was inclined to believe
that we had not shown sufficient willingness to cooperate with
Senator Smoot or the remolacheros.[14] As a matter of fact, Shattuck
had used every effort to cooperate with Senator Smoot, but found
that to be impossible because Senator Smoot was not willing to
cooperate, although Senator Smoot and Shattuck had been asked
by the President to cooperate. This request was made many months
ago. Shattuck obeyed the request, but Smoot did not do so. Shattuck and I informed Tarafa also that the remolacheros were not as
yet willing to negotiation [sic] with the Cuban interests because
they thought that they could obtain from Congress a duty of 2.4
cents against Cuban sugar. . . .

✦   ✦   ✦   ✦   ✦

. . . The sugar rate of 2.20 cents will be opposed by nearly all
the Democrats and most of the so-called insurgent Republicans. It
is a very close question whether a combination of the Democrats
and the insurgent Republicans will make a majority against the
2.20-cent rate. Undoubtedly a majority of the Senate will be against
the 2.20-cent rate, but each Senator has some constitutent who desires an increase in the tariff on some article which the constituent
manufactures. That constituent is probably the largest contributor
to the campaign fund of the Senator, and the Senator is bound to
obtain what his constituent desires. In order to do that the Senator
is often obliged to exchange a vote for his product in return for a
vote for the product of somebody else. This is what we call in this
country "log rolling." The danger to the Cuban interests is that in
this process of log rolling Senators who disbelieve in any increase
in the sugar tariff will be obliged to vote for it in order to obtain

votes for their own schedules. Senator Borah . . . is studying the question of a direct bounty to the remolacheros and the Louisiana cane producers. . . . Senator Harrison, of Mississippi, will have charge for the Democrats of the Senate debate on the sugar schedule. He has informed me that it is quite possible that he will propose an amendment to the project of law under which the duty would be reduced from 1.76 to 1.23 cents. The lower figure is the one which was arrived at by the United States Tariff Commission in 1924.[15] Such a proposal will result in still further debate.

Meantime, Mr. Shattuck and I must engage in the following activities:

(1) He must keep in constant touch with the White House and endeavor to persuade the advisers of President Hoover that it would be poor politics for Congress to pass any law increasing the sugar tariff and poor politics for him to approve such a law if passed.

(2) We must continue to stir up publicity on the subject throughout the United States, calling attention to the injustice to Cuba, the injustice to consumers, the injustice to exporters from the United States to Cuba, and the provable fact that an increase in the tariff will not eventually be of benefit to the remolacheros. This publicity work takes an enormous amount of time and effort.

(3) We must constantly importune the friends of Cuba and the consumers of the United States and the exporters to communicate with their Senators and Congressmen and with the newspapers in order to keep the sugar tariff subject widely agitated while the debate is taking place in the Senate.

✓   ✓   ✓   ✓   ✓

Please command Mr. Shattuck or myself for any further information or any action. It is only fair for me to say that our activities have thus far met with the unanimous approval of the New York sugar interests, who have cotributed [sic] to the expense of our campaign. I ought to say also that the campaign is proving to be very expensive, and the New York producers of Cuban sugar have responded handsomely to requests for contributions to the fund.[16] There never has been a time during the life of Cuba when these interests have cooperated so thoroughly and willingly. I feel in honor bound to inform you of this fact because I consider it especially important that everybody in Cuba should realize that the American producers of Cuban sugar are acting entirely from motives of the welfare of Cuba and the Cuban producers as well as for their own welfare. I know that you feel as I do, that without their cooperation it would have been impossible to accomplish anything whatever in Washington. The Congress of the United States in its present condition of mind resents any foreign intervention in matters of tariff, whether relating to sugar or any other article of import. This resentment would have manifest [sic] itself against any intervention by Cuba because Cuba is a foreign country. I consider that Cuba is very fortunate at the present time because a considerable part of Cuban sugar is produced by American interests, who are willing to support the fight which is now taking place in Congress. These Americans, as citizens of the United States and taxpayers of the United States, have a legal right to present their claims to Congress, and they are exercising that right to the fullest extent, not only for their own good but for the welfare of Cuba.

DOUMENT 25. Thomas L. Chadbourne Proposes Controlled Competition, 1931. (*Cuba and Sugar Stabilization:* A privately printed pamphlet reproduction of his speech before the Institute of Public Affairs of the University of Virginia, July 7, 1931. Pp. 3–6, 13–18, 27–28.)

The law of supply and demand, the law of the survival of the fittest, the fine old business maxim, "Competition is the life of trade," all of blessed memory—these three old comrades have had a stormy road to travel since the end of the World War.

Many of us are now wondering when the demand will come to absorb the surplus supply the world is staggering under. We are wondering whether it would not have been better to have looked forward to the demand more carefully before we leaped forward with the supply.

     ✦   ✦   ✦   ✦   ✦

. . . Production is no longer trying to keep up with consumption. Production has overshot consumption in practically every important commodity in the world. Competition has been unrestrained and unenlightened, with the result that production has now to be curtailed, and this in turn has caused unemployment on a scale hitherto unknown. This unemployment may in time taper off the consumption through the inability of the unemployed to buy, but such a process is at the expense of human lives, human health and finally, of necessity, at the expense of orderly government.

"Survival of the fittest" must have descended to us from the "missing link," because it is the law of the jungle. It was and is the law of the strong to kill off the weak, in order that the strong may enjoy more of the good things of the world. Its unrestrained processes may be tolerated by soulless animals, but cannot and will not be by human beings.

There is no unhappier illustration of what I have just been saying than the island and the industry in whose behalf I am here to address you tonight. Cuba's present pitiable position is due primarily to the tariff barriers erected against its principal industry, which constitutes eighty per cent of all its industry, by its self-appointed guardian, the United States. This guardian denies its ward that free competition which is said to be the life of trade and denies it the benefits of the adage of the jungle, "the survival of the fittest," for, on even terms and without the handicap of a tariff barrier, Cuba could compete with the sugar producers of the United States and its insular possessions, and Cuba would prosper.

Secondarily, but secondarily only, Cuba and her chief industry are suffering from unrestrained and unenlightened competition in production.

OUR POLICY TOWARD CUBA

I am presenting to you a strange and not too pleasing spectacle tonight, entitled "What Price Liberty." Our country, through her war with Spain, took to her bosom, as an integral part of herself, Porto Rico and adopted the Philippine Islands. We did not give them their liberty, but we gave them everything else. Through that same war we gave Cuba her liberty, but gave her little else.

From a brief survey of the balance sheet as it exists today, I suggest that America constitute herself Cuba's ward, not Cuba's guardian, because the United States enriched herself last year at Cuba's expense to the tune of $95,000,000 by collecting that amount of tariff on Cuban sugar alone, while the total receipts of the Cuban Government from customs upon American and all other goods during the past year were only $26,000,000.

A fine guardianship that, where the guardian profits four times as much as the ward!

There is pathos in thinking that little Cuba has become great America's godfather instead of great America being little Cuba's godfather.

A $750,000,000 INVESTMENT

The hope and expectation of that parental benediction promised by Presidents McKinley and Roosevelt and advocated by Secretary Root materializing, together with the encouragement given Cuba by the United States during the World War when our country needed Cuban sugar, induced a huge amount of American capital to be invested in Cuba's sugar industry. From my knowledge of the situation, I estimate the total of that investment to be not less than $750,000,000. The failure of the parental benediction has caused a shrinkage of 95 per cent in the value of that investment, as the securities representing the whole investment are now selling for about $37,000,000.

But this it not all. That American investment so increased the Cuban production of sugar that for the past three years it has overshot its consuming markets by hundreds upon hundreds of thousands of tons.

OUR LOSS IN CUBAN TRADE

And even that is not all. Our producers, through this process of Cuban emasculation, have lost a great outlet for their exports. Cuba's purchase of American goods (and she buys eighty per cent of all she buys anywhere from the United States) has declined approximately $400,000,000 from the peak to the present.

PRESIDENT MACHADO'S EFFORTS

It was because of this pathetic situation in Cuba that President Machado, who saw the situation in its largest sense and saw it earlier and more clearly than any one else, began three years ago to attempt its cure. His first two experiments for an international accord upon sugar failed, although he had in charge of them able and devoted public servants, Jose M. Tarafa in the first experiment and Viriato Gutierrez in the second. These representatives failed not through lack of ability or industry on his or their part, but because the tariff-protected sugar-producing and sugar-exporting nations of the world had not yet sufficiently felt, because so protected, the crushing disaster of low prices.

CUBA WAS FIRST TO BE AFFECTED

"The survival of the fittest" had not yet pursued its ugly career to the same point in these countries that it had in Cuba. Capital had not endured the losses nor labor suffered the privations which appear to be necessary to bring an industry in a world-wide sense to an appreciation that unrestrained and unenlightened competition may be the life of trade when production is trying to overtake consumption, but is more likely to be the destruction of society once production has overshot consumption.

✓   ✓   ✓   ✓   ✓

THE SUGAR-GROWING NATIONS UNITE

The people of Cuba were and still are suffering from the soothing business antidotes, "Competition is the life of trade" and "Survival of the fittest," when the competition and the fittest are protected by tariff walls.

But a year ago, when I became the leader in Cuba's third great experiment to cure the ills of her people, she knew and I knew the sugar-producing world as a whole, goaded and bleeding under the spur of necessity, would be more amenable to reason than it had been before, and out of this conviction upon our part grew the so-called Chadbourne Plan, which crystallized two months ago into the international agreement between the seven great sugar-exporting nations of the world.

✓   ✓   ✓   ✓   ✓

There are but three possibilities before us—chaos, collective leadership or collective control—and the last means governmental control of industry, such as exists in Russia, which is no more or less than State Socialism. The advocates of unrestrained and unenlightened competition as it exists today being the life of trade and the advocates of the survival of the fittest are, as little as they may think it, the best friends of the Russian Bolshevik theory, while the advocates of collective leadership in each industry are the worst enemies of the bolshevists.

Self-interest is the greatest and best fulcrum the human level can rest upon, but if it continues to be a planless, greedy, selfish, stupid self-interest, another fulcrum is certain to be tried.

●   ●   ●

CHAPTER IV

NEW DEAL DIPLOMACY AND
THE CUBAN SETTLEMENT
(1933–45)

Roosevelt is expected to put new stress on Latin American trade.
Intervention by the United States in the affairs of any Latin American country is tremendously unpopular. Roosevelt has evidently chosen to attack the problem from another angle.

Business Week (1933)

FRANKLIN D. ROOSEVELT took office in 1933 amidst domestic and international depression. These economic conditions were producing severe political problems in the world, and unrest in Cuba was viewed by the new administration as one of the most important of these foreign problems affecting American interests. Cuba provided the first real test of Roosevelt's "Good Neighbor" Policy, and in meeting this problem the administration was to develop techniques which would combine the revival of domestic prosperity with the stabilization of foreign countries. These new techniques— and some of the old ones—would still be designed to provide stable, friendly governments in Latin America which would protect the interests of the United States.

Roosevelt began to work on the Cuban situation prior to his inauguration. Charles W. Taussig and Adolph A. Berle, Jr. went to Cuba in December, 1932, to study the situation, and after reporting to Roosevelt, both men began working on sugar stabilization plans. Later, the "old Caribbean hand," Sumner Welles, was selected by the administration to be the new Ambassador to Cuba. Welles's immediate assignment was to effect a political settlement which would save the Machado Administration and to negotiate a trade agreement which would bolster the Cuban economy and stimulate the flow of American exports. The former task proved to be impossible, and this caused a delay in the economic settlement.

In August, 1933, Machado was ousted by the ranking officers of the Cuban Army, but the new administration held power for only a short time. Early in September a group of army noncommissioned officers joined forces with other groups to seize control of Cuba. Ramón Grau San Martín became the head of this reform-minded administration, but the new government was unable to obtain recognition from the United States. Faced with a more radical government in Cuba, the Roosevelt Administration sent a number of warships to Cuban waters, mobilized Marine units in the United States, and authorized the use of landing parties to protect American properties near the coast. President Roosevelt and Secretary of State Cordell Hull did not want to revive armed intervention because of the impact this would have on the other countries of Latin America. Thus, Roosevelt and Hull relied on the behind-the-scenes diplomacy of Welles and Jefferson Caffery.

Out of this turmoil, however, there emerged a settlement which lasted for over twenty-five years. Fulgencio Batista, the Cinderella Colonel, ousted Grau San Martín in January, 1934, and installed the conservative faction which Welles had been backing. Batista, with his control of the army, remained the real man of power. From 1934 to 1940 he exercised his power as Chief of Staff of the Army, and then served as President from 1940 to 1944. Under his leadership Cuba was one of the first Latin American nations to declare war on the Axis powers, and during the war Cuba provided the United States with bases and training sites.

The economic aspects of the New Deal settlement were embodied in the Export-Import Bank silver loans, the Reciprocal Trade Agreement, and the sugar marketing allotment system. As a result of these arrangements the Cuban sugar economy became an integral part of the United States sugar market, and exports from the United States steadily increased. Thus, a new dimension was added to "Dollar Diplomacy." The United States government now began to play a more active role in reconciling the international economic interests of the country with its domestic interests. The sugar marketing allotment system combined with the new reciprocal trade agreement to provide stability for the sugar industry, and through the Export-Import Bank the government loaned money to Cuba to stabilize its finances.

Between 1929 and 1946, American direct investments in Cuba declined in value from $919 million to $553 million. Part of this decline was the result of the revaluation of overcapitalized sugar properties. As a result of the deflation in values stemming from the Depression, and the prosperity of World War II, the Cubans were able to regain control of a portion of the island's sugar industry. The flow of private investment funds from the United States dropped after 1929, but did not completely stop. Investments in Cuban public utilities increased in value between 1929 and 1940, in contrast to investments in other fields.

By 1945 United States-Cuban relations seemed to be entering a new era of tranquillity. Cuban stability was demonstrated when Fulgencio Batista peacefully handed over the presidency to the victorious candidate in the 1944 election, Ramón Grau San Martín. The Cuban economy appeared to be in good condition. American tourists returned to Sloppy Joe's in Havana, the potent rum from Señor Bacardí's distillery flowed across the Florida Straits, and all seemed tranquil in the Caribbean.

Sumner Welles worked for several months to try to arrange a compromise settlement between President Machado and the conservative opposition groups. At first, Welles was hopeful that administration plans for stabilizing the sugar industry—including a reciprocity treaty—could be used to induce Machado to compromise, and to distract the attention of the Cuban people from political affairs (Document 1).

Early in August, 1933, however, Welles became convinced that Machado was the major obstacle to the restoration of political calm. When Machado rejected the Ambassador's plan for a peaceful transfer of power to another president, Welles recommended to the State Department that recognition of Machado be withdrawn (Document 3). Roosevelt and Hull were willing to back Welles's plan to transfer the presidency of Cuba, but they hoped to persuade Machado to abdicate by less harsh means than withdrawal of recognition (Documents 2 and 4).

The ranking officers of the Cuban Army removed Machado on the night of August 11, and adopted virtually all of Welles's plan. Dr. Carlos Manuel de Céspedes became the new president, and the Ambassador believed that the crisis was over (Document 5).

American businessmen in Cuba had supported Machado to the last. He was still the symbol of stability to many Americans in Cuba, and reports concerning the brutality of his policies were written off as "newspaper propaganda" (Document 6). Machado's sudden departure was undoubtedly a shock to many, but the Céspedes Administration promised to be a continuation of conservative control which posed no threat to American business interests.

DOCUMENT 1. Sumner Welles to Cordell Hull, May 13, 1933. (U. S. Department of State, *Foreign Relations of the United States: 1933.* 5 vols. Washington, 1952. V: 287–90).

At the outset of my conversation with the President I indicated in general terms the policy of the Government of the United States towards Cuba. I stated that my Government reiterated the interpretation of its responsibilities under the Platt Amendment in the sense laid down by Secretary Root in 1901, namely that the right of intervention was not construed as being synonymous with intermeddling in the domestic or political concerns of Cuba. I further stated that my Government believed that the prime requisite to insure the permanent welfare of Cuba was the maintenance of constitutional government and the fortification of the tradition of orderly procedure in constitutional government; and that to secure those ends the Government of Cuba could count on the friendly cooperation of the United States in every appropriate manner.

I stated that my Government had been caused very grave disquiet by the long-continued political agitation which had existed in Cuba and the public opinion in the United States had been very frequently shocked by acts of terrorism committed by the opponents of the administration of President Machado and as deeply shocked by acts of cruelty and oppression on the part of the military authorities of the Cuban Government. I said that it was our desire to offer our unofficial good offices for the purpose of putting an end as soon as possible to this state of political agitation with all of its inherent evils both because of our abiding interest in and sympathy with the people of Cuba as well as because of our well-founded belief that steps toward any permanent basic economic improvement in the Republic of Cuba could not be taken with complete success until political quiet once more existed.

I continued by saying that it was my hope that President Machado would find it possible to carry out a program of conciliation leading towards the holding of absolutely fair and uncontrolled national elections in the autumn of 1934 and that for this reason it seemed to me highly desirable that the Cuban Government adopt, at as early a moment as the President deemed appropriate, certain measures providing for the gradual return to the Cuban people of their constitutional guarantees. . . .

I seized the opportunity of discussing in some detail the various plans which had been under consideration in Washington before my own departure providing for an improvement of our commercial relations with Cuba. I stated that at the present time it was impossible to give any definite assurances as to what form these plans would eventually take but that I felt able to say that my Government would be prepared to consider a fixed allotment for Cuban sugars; an increase in the existing preferential [tariff?] covering such allotment; and that it held the belief that under such conditions the anticipated stabilization of the price of sugar in the American market at a fair figure would be of the utmost benefit to the Cuban people as a whole. I was given the positive assurances that were the United States to negotiate on such a basis a reciprocal trade agreement with the Cuban Government, the Cuban Government in turn would grant us a practical monopoly of the Cuban market for American imports, the sole reservation being that in view of the fact that Great Britain was Cuba's chief customer for that portion of sugar exports which did not go to the United States the Cuban Government would desire to concede certain advantages to a limited category of imports from Great Britain. The Secretary of State was particularly emphatic in amplifying this statement by declaring that the Government would be willing to agree to abolish, as regards American imports, those consumption and other taxes which have in so many instances seriously restricted American importations during the past few years.

I hold the very strong belief that the policy to be pursued in Cuba under present conditions should be as follows:

The economic benefits to be derived from a fair commercial

agreement between the United States and Cuba and even the negotiations leading towards such an agreement will assist in part in distracting public attention from politics;

By acting through and with the present Cuban Government, which is well aware of the fact that it could not for long remain in power were the support of the United States to be even negatively withdrawn from it, it may be possible to carry out a program of constitutional and electoral reform which will make it possible for fair national elections to be held in 1934;

⸻ ⸻ ⸻ ⸻ ⸻

. . . President Machado is able to preserve order joined with unquestioned loyalty and discipline of the Cuban Army. If some other individual replaced him the loyalty of the Army would be questionable; the Opposition would be as it is now, divided into factions which have absolutely no common ground other than that of desiring the removal of the President. Under such conditions general chaos might well result during the course of which the first objective on the part of malcontents would be the desire to bring about intervention by the United States through the destruction of American property.

I am hopeful that by a series of concessions which the President may make to public opinion and by the continuance of negotiations for commercial agreement agitation may be kept relatively quiet until such time as the Cuban Congress can make essential amendments to the electoral code and approve the needed reforms to the existing constitution, which would be later voted by a freely elected constituent assembly.

Finally, the negotiation at this time of a reciprocal trade agreement with Cuba along the lines above-indicated, will not only revivify Cuba but will give us practical control of a market we have been steadily losing for the past 10 years not only for our manufactured products but for our agricultural exports as well notably in such categories as wheat, animal fats, meat products, rice and potatoes.

DOCUMENT 2.   Sumner Welles to Cordell Hull, August 8, 1933. (*Foreign Relations of the United States: 1933.* V: 339–40.)

To be delivered immediately to the President at Hyde Park. President Machado has this afternoon informed the Senators and Representatives that my statement to him that the solution presented by me was offered with your full approval and was presented with your authorization is false and that no such approval has been given me by you. I am informed that Cintas has cabled him to that effect. I understand that you are seeing Cintas at noon tomorrow. I beg that you inform him that I am acting in every detail with your fullest authorization and approval. I also beg to request that you inform Cintas that while the purpose of my mission here is to avoid the existence of a situation which would give rise to intervention by the United States if a situation of anarchy exists and there is no government in Cuba capable of protecting "life, property and individual liberty" as provided in the third article of the permanent treaty the United States will not evade its obligations under that provision. Both Cintas and President Machado have repeatedly given important leaders here the belief that I am not authorized by you to act and that the attitude I have adopted is one of bluff. I feel that it is essential if I am to succeed in procuring a solution of this grave situation that Cintas be told by you to inform President Machado immediately that absolutely no act of mine has been taken except with your full approval and authorization.

DOCUMENT 3. Sumner Welles to Cordell Hull, August 9, 1933. (*Foreign Relations of the United States: 1933.* V: 344.)

1. There is absolutely no hope of a return to normal conditions in Cuba as long as President Machado remains in office. No one other than the exceedingly small clique of officeholders surrounding him has any trust or confidence in him and he represents in his person to every other Cuban the cause of economic distress and personal suffering which has existed during the past 3 years.

2. So long as this condition continues there is no possible chance of improving economic conditions in Cuba, and there will be immense loss to the Cuban people themselves and as a natural corollary to all of the American interests doing business in or with Cuba.

3. The solution proposed by me as mediator represents a compromise framed by the representatives of all Cuban factions both of the opposition and of those which have in the past been cooperating with the Government and if such solution could be car-

ried into effect I have the utmost confidence that peace and tranquility would be restored to Cuba within a week.

4. If my recommendations are adopted and recognition is withdrawn from the Machado Government I believe that the President would be forced to resign his office within a very limited period and that a stable government could be installed in strict accordance with the provisions of the existing constitution within a period of hours thereafter provided arrangements to that end are made by me before recognition is withdrawn.

5. If recognition is withdrawn there will in all likelihood be for a brief period disturbances in the city of Habana. If my recommendations are adopted and this eventuality takes place I feel that two American warships should be in Habana harbor with instructions not to land a man except in the gravest emergency the terms of which should be precisely defined beforehand.

DOCUMENT 4. Cordell Hull to Sumner Welles, August 9, 1933. (*Foreign Relations of the United States: 1933.* V: 348.)

The President appealed to President Machado, through Ambassador Cintas, to prove to the world his high purpose in this crisis.

The President informed Ambassador Cintas that you are and had been acting at Habana with his fullest authorization and approval. He added that he had no desire to intervene but that it was our duty to do what we could so that there should be no starvation and chaos among the Cuban people.

Ambassador Cintas then pointed out the difficulties surrounding President Machado's position and that he could not allow himself to be forced out of the presidency. The Ambassador agreed that, if means could be found by which President Machado could act as of his own initiative, there was still hope that he could be persuaded to do so. He agreed that a face-saving device was necessary. The President suggested that the economic situation should be utilized for this purpose rather than the political crisis, that if President Machado could step out in order to save the Cuban people from starvation, he would not only be saving his "face," but would be performing a noble act. The President suggested that, in this event, a shipload of food supplies could be sent from this country to Habana for the benefit of the Cuban people.

DOCUMENT 5.   Sumner Welles to Cordell Hull, August 19,
1933. (*Foreign Relations of the United States: 1933.* V:
368–69.)

My personal situation is becoming increasingly difficult. Owing
to my intimate personal friendship with President Céspedes and
the very close relationship which I have formed during these past
months with all of the members of this Cabinet I am now daily
being requested for decisions on all matters affecting the Government of Cuba. These decisions range from questions of domestic
policy and matters affecting the discipline of the Army to questions involving appointments in all branches of the Government.
This situation is bad for Cuba and bad for the United States. . . .

  ✔   ✔   ✔   ✔   ✔

In my judgment the policy which this Embassy should from
now on pursue is a policy which should have no connection whatever except in the event of urgent necessity with the political picture and which should limit itself to cooperating in the elaboration
of constructive measures in benefit of the economic prosperity of
Cuba and in benefit of American exports to the Cuban market.

  ✔   ✔   ✔   ✔   ✔

. . . It is unwise not only from the point of view of our relations with Cuba but with the whole of Latin America as well for
the American Embassy here to possess the measure of control over
the Government which it now does possess owing to the peculiar
developments of the past 2 months. Caffery unquestionably will obtain all of the needed influence immediately after his arrival but
it will be an influence exerted behind the scenes and not apparent
to the public.

DOCUMENT 6.   American Businessmen and the End of the
Machado Era; Observations of a Newspaper Correspondent's
Wife, August 14, 1933. (R. Hart Phillips, *Cuba: Island of
Paradox.* New York, 1959. Pp. 45–46.)[1]

Now begins the amusing and embarrassing period in which
Americans here about-face. I mean the managers of branches of
American companies. Americans in Cuba are divided into two
classes, employees of big American companies, and the few who

settled in Cuba and established their own businesses. Managers of the American companies usually gather at the American Club. As a whole they have supported Machado. They refused to believe that he had committed murders, terming it newspaper propaganda. They complained the Cuban revolutions have been "fought on the front pages of the American newspapers." Lots of them used to call Phil up and want to know why we sent in such stories. They were afraid business would be damaged. They haven't had any business for the past three years, so I can't see their reasoning. The manager of one of the largest companies has called Phil many times, angry over some dispatch. Saturday night this manager called Consul-General Dumont and said he had received threats that his home would be burned. He demanded protection. Dumont, knowing Phil has contacts among the army officers, asked him to get in touch with Camp Columbia. Phil telephoned Captain Torres Menier and a detail of soldiers was sent immediately to protect the home of the American.

Even harder to understand is the attitude of the American Chamber of Commerce. Machado consistently favored European exports, to the detriment of American trade, and practically nullified the tariff preferential, giving special privileges to European nations. His customs department deals out favors with a lavish hand where it will do the most harm to American exporters. Yet the only time the American Chamber of Commerce protested, very feebly, was over the Emergency Tax Law. When Machado decided to register all foreigners and fingerprint them, the Chamber of Commerce remained silent, while both the British Minister and the Spanish Ambassador protested vigorously.

•　•　•

The situation in Cuba changed abruptly on September 5, 1933. The new regime was composed of faculty and students from the University of Havana, noncommissioned army officers, and various reform-minded individuals. Sumner Welles branded the regime as "ultra-radical," and United States warships were promptly dispatched to Cuban ports. The Ambassador advocated intervention at first, but Hull and Roosevelt vetoed the suggestion (Document 8). With armed intervention virtually ruled out, Welles went to work to try to effect a change in the Cuban government. Welles and Hull frankly recognized that the key element in Cuban politics was the Army, and that Fulgencio Batista would be a factor in any governmental shift (Document 7). Early in September Batista —now Chief of Staff of the Army—indicated that he was willing to talk terms with other political groups, and Welles began a campaign to persuade Batista to desert the Grau San Martín government (Document 10).

The big problem was how to formulate a working agreement between Batista and such conservative political leaders as Carlos Mendieta, Miguel Mariano Gómez, and Mario Menocal. Batista was a wily politician and kept a foot in both camps. In January, 1934, he decided that the Grau San Martín government was in trouble, and engineered the coup which placed Mendieta in the presidency. The refusal of the United States government to grant recognition to Grau San Martín was a definite factor in this development. The United States promptly recognized Mendieta, and American businessmen breathed a sigh of relief (Document 11).

DOCUMENT 7. Memorandum: Telephone Conversation Between Cordell Hull and Sumner Welles, September 6, 1933. (*Foreign Relations of the United States: 1933.* V: 389–90.)

Secretary: How is everything looking?
Ambassador: I had four hours of sleep last night and I feel somewhat better.
Secretary: How are conditions?
Ambassador: There was some trouble in the city last night, but not as bad as might have been expected. I think the presence of the destroyer did a great deal to prevent more disturbance. The situation in the interior seems to be becoming very serious and while Santiago during the early night was quiet, there is no word as to what happened after midnight.

✓   ✓   ✓   ✓   ✓

Secretary: We have been discussing this last evening and this morning as best we could. It seems to us that the whole thing down there revolves around the army, and the question comes up with us as to whether the landing of men before we are absolutely compelled to do so—if we should land a thousand men there—it would in all probability mean intervention, and while we will not hesitate to go in if compelled to, we do not want to unless compelled. Because if we have to go in there again, we will never be able to come out and we will have on our hands the trouble of thirty years ago. . . . Now if in the meantime some of our American friends should get unduly alarmed, we might consider dropping submarine destroyers in at such ports as Guantanamo, Santiago and Cienfuegos for the time being. Everything is revolving around the army now and if they were to receive some cooperation from the different leaders, whether they are immediately a part of the army or not but had liberal ideas, that would be very helpful. . . .

¶   ¶   ¶   ¶   ¶

Ambassador: I am in full accord with what you say.

Secretary: I am just getting these facts before you for what they may be worth, because we have implicit confidence in your judgment and in your ability to keep yourself ingratiated with all groups while we are giving Cuba and the dominant forces in it an opportunity to work out of the snarl or to take such steps as would make intervention by us unnecessary. I do not know whether I have said anything at all which would fit in there according to your judgment, but I wanted to get these things before you.

Ambassador: I agree absolutely with everything you have said. One or two members of the present group in power I know and one was here with me for an hour and a half last night. I will be in touch with them constantly, but for the time being we ought not even to consider recognizing any government of this character, in my opinion.

Secretary: Until it has shown its ability to preserve law and order.

Ambassador: What they want is an expression of opinion from me and I have refused to give any opinion whatever except to insist on the maintenance of order.

Secretary: It is natural that from their viewpoint they would be urging us, just like our Chamber of Commerce friend last night, to rush in and intervene. But of course you and I are keeping our eyes on the other side of the thing as well and we can only hope that those people will be patient and give such cooperation as the dominant forces are willing to receive. . . .

DOCUMENT 8. Sumner Welles to Cordell Hull, September 7, 1933. (*Foreign Relations of the United States: 1933.* V: 396–97.)

Late last night Dr. Horacio Ferrer, Secretary of War in the Céspedes Cabinet, called to see me. He told me that he had spent the preceding 24 hours in continuous conferences with political leaders of all the groups which had supported the Céspedes Government and that the plan which he would outline to me met with the approval and support of all of them. He told me that he had been in touch with the sergeants in control of the Fortress Cabaña; that they realized that they had been deceived in participating in the mutiny and that they were prepared to make any reparation for their action. . . . He stated that he had already been in touch with the officers of the military forces of Matanzas and Piñar del Río as well as in other portions of the Republic and that as soon as the proclamation from Cabaña has been issued the loyal troops and officers throughout the country would make a simultaneous proclamation. He was confident that within a very brief period the present regime would be overthrown.

He inquired whether, should this action be taken, and should the Céspedes Government make such request the Government of the United States would be willing to land troops from the battleships now due to arrive at Cojimar, immediately to the east of Cabaña Fortress, in order to assist the Céspedes Government in maintaining order. He stated of his own initiative that he fully understood my position and that of my Government and that he wished merely to inform me of the plans which he had made without expecting or desiring any assurances of any character from me, and that he would follow through the plan he had in mind no matter what action the United States Government might take.

* * * * *

If the plan formulated by Dr. Ferrer were carried out successfully I desire to lay the following considerations before the President and yourself. The Céspedes Government came into power through constitutional procedure and was immediately recognized by all of the nations having diplomatic relations with Cuba including the Latin American Republics as the legitimate Government of Cuba. The President and his Cabinet have not voluntarily resigned but have had to give in in the face of a mutiny in the Army. If the legitimate and recognized Government of Cuba can make an effective demonstration of its intention to reestablish itself, it would most decidedly appear to me to be in the best interest of the United States Government to afford them immediate support. Any solution of this character is more advantageous to our interests and to our policy than full intervention and the possible necessity of an American Military Government. What I propose would be a strictly limited intervention of the following nature:

The Céspedes Government should be permitted to function

freely in exactly the same manner as it did until the time of its overthrow, having full control of every branch of the Government. It is obvious, of course, that with a great portion of the Army in mutiny it could not maintain itself in power in any satisfactory manner unless the United States Government were willing, should it so request, to lend its assistance in the maintenance of public order until the Cuban Government had been afforded the time sufficient, through utilizing the services of the loyal officers of the Cuban Army, to form a new Army for which it would possess a nucleus in the troops which are still loyal and detachments of the rural guard, most of whom have not come out in support of the present regime. Such policy on our part would presumably entail the landing of a considerable force at Habana and lesser forces in certain of the more important ports of the Republic.

DOCUMENT 9. Sumner Welles to Cordell Hull, September 18, 1933. (*Foreign Relations of the United States: 1933*. V: 447–48.)

. . . I am more than ever confident that the wisest policy for us to pursue is to keep our hands off except insofar as the protection of American lives is involved. If the solution is long postponed it will be difficult to lift Cuba from the economic and financial prostration towards which it is rapidly headed. It is also within the bounds of possibility that the social revolution which is under way cannot be checked. American properties and interests are being gravely prejudiced and the material damage to such properties will in all probability be very great. All of these contingencies seem to me preferable to intervention. By intervention we not only would seriously jeopardize our continental interests but we also would once more give the Cuban people and particularly the Cuban leaders to understand that they do not have to assume the responsibility for their own lack of patriotism or lack of vision, and that the United States Government stands always ready to repair the damage which they themselves cause their own country. It is my sincere belief that Cuba can never become a self-governing republic so long as this feeling persists.

DOCUMENT 10. Sumner Welles to Cordell Hull, October 7, 1933. (*Foreign Relations of the United States: 1933*. V: 477–78.)

I had a conference with Batista this afternoon. He advised me that he realized now fully that the present regime was a complete failure and that a concentration government in which the political groups and the commercial interests of the country could have confidence was an absolute necessity. He also stated that he appreciated the fact that recognition by the United States was essential before any improvement in conditions here could be expected.

He was deeply impressed by the fact that delegates of all of the important business and financial groups in Cuba had visited him this afternoon before I saw him to insist upon the creation of a government in which the public could have confidence.

He also assured me of his intention to proceed immediately with a firm hand in all of the American sugar plantations where labor troubles still existed, by arresting and removing all Communist leaders and by using the troops to restore order whenever it was necessary.

DOCUMENT 11. The National City Bank Praises the Administration of Mendieta, February 1934. (*Monthly Bank Letter*, February, 1934. P. 19.)

The Cuban situation has taken a sudden and most gratifying turn for the better, by the accession of Dr. Carlos Mendieta to the presidency of the provisional government, with the support of representative groups apparently strong enough to accomplish the restoration of order and constitutional government. He is a man of strong personality, high intelligence and character, himself representative of the best type of Cubans. His devotion to Cuba cannot be questioned, but it will not take the mistaken form of antagonism to the legitimate business activities and interests of foreigners in the island. Among the purposes which he has publicly disclosed in taking office is that of "strengthening the relations with our great northern neighbor and best customer," which he made more emphatic by adding that "the future of Cuba lies in her going hand in hand with the United States." This declaration should reawaken the generous sentiments which the people of the United States have felt and manifested toward Cuba in the past. Unfortunately for both countries, through a misguided economic policy, the United States has been mainly responsible for the troubles of Cuba in recent years. After fostering the development of sugar as the chief industry, it suddenly reversed its policy, with the result that the economic life of the island was paralyzed. The United States has the power to restore prosperity to Cuba by means which will also promote the prosperity of this country and be in harmony with the policy of trade expansion with Latin America. President Roosevelt has handled our relations with Cuba through the crisis of recent months with great good judgment, including the prompt recognition of the Mendieta Government, and there is reason to be hopeful that the relations between the two countries are entering upon a new era, more intimate and mutually helpful than that of any period in the past.

• • •

For a number of years pressure had been building up in Cuba for the abrogation of the Platt Amendment and the complete revision of the old commercial arrangements. The policies followed by the United States during the latter part of the Machado era and during the brief tenure of Grau San Martín, provoked even more hostility toward the Platt Amendment. Many Cubans were convinced that under this amendment the United States denied them the right to institute reforms or to overthrow dictatorial governments. The high tariff policy followed by the United States since 1921 had added to this discontent, since the privileged position of Cuban sugar in the American market had been the *quid pro quo* given for Cuban acceptance of the hegemony of the United States.

A most perceptive and intelligent analysis of United States-Cuban relations was presented in July, 1933, by Dr. Juan Andres Lliteras of Havana (Document 12). Part of his argument, however, was about thirty years ahead of understanding in the United States. The State Department could understand the arguments for abrogating the Platt Amendment, but the plea for American consideration for socio-economic problems, and the need for extensive reforms, was ignored by some and misinterpreted by others. Most United States officials viewed Latin America through the lenses of North American conditions and attitudes, which contributed to the glorification of external forms of political and economic stability. This view ignored the deeper social and economic maladjustments cited by Lliteras; these would produce a bitter harvest three decades later.

One of the changes demanded by Dr. Lliteras was effected in May, 1934, when most of the Platt Amendment was abrogated by a new treaty (Document 13). Various United States officials were convinced that the amendment was a cause of political instability in Cuba, and a hindrance to improving the image of the United States in Latin America. The obstinacy of Machado and the subsequent upheaval postponed the abrogation until the prestige of effecting such a change could be conferred upon a friendly administration which protected American interests. In addition, the events leading to the fall of Grau San Martín had shown that these interests could be protected by more subtle tactics.

DOCUMENT 12. Dr. Juan Andres Lliteras, "Relations Between Cuba and the United States," July, 1933. (*International Conciliation.* Carnegie Endowment for International Peace, Document No. 296. Worcester, Mass., January, 1934. Pp. 9–12, 18–23.)[2]

Thirty years ago Cuba and the United States were engaged in the negotiation of two treaties. One was a political covenant, the Permanent Treaty of May 22, 1903, embodying the Platt Amendment; the other an economic agreement, the Reciprocity Treaty, which became effective on December 27 of the same year. These treaties were intended to regulate the relations between the two countries, and statesmen in Cuba as well as in the United States were deeply concerned over them. They were of basic importance to Cuba. Her whole future depended upon them. But they were of no less importance to the United States.

Cuba had just entered into a new historical epoch. After four centuries of colonial isolation and exploitation under the rule of Spain she had become an independent republic. She had paid dearly for her independence. It had required the efforts of three generations, and had cost her the flower of her youth, and the destruction of her agricultural and industrial wealth. Yet withal independence had come in the manner of a gift. The donor was the United States. It had intervened near the end of the struggle, declared war on Spain, and dictated the conditions of the peace. Thus Cuba received her freedom from the hands of an American military governor, by the good grace and thanks to the sense of honor of the President and of the Congress of the United States.

And the terms of the treaties were naturally colored by these circumstances.

Geographic and economic determinism had compelled an interest in Cuba on the part of the United States during the better part of a century. Annexation had seemed desirable to the peoples of both countries at different periods, and the United States had tried more than once to purchase Cuba from Spain, for a price greater than that paid for any other territory. When Spain obstinately refused to sell she had been allowed to keep Cuba only on condition that she should not part with her, and had been given the assurance of the military assistance of the United States in case of attack.

But by the '90's, it had become increasingly apparent that Cuba either had to be free or become a part of the Union. Spain's commercial policy was erratic as well as stupid and had become obnoxious to the United States; and her colonial policy on the Island inevitably drove its inhabitants from increasing restlessness to open rebellion. The struggle for freedom and the Spanish-American War were thus a matter of historic fatality.

Cuba and the United States are bound by ties stronger than those of friendship. Their mutual interests are, because of their very nature, of vital character to both countries. Cuba commands the outlet of the Mississippi basin to the sea and the main shipping lanes between North and South America. She stands in the way of communication between the Pacific and the Atlantic, through the Panama Canal, and her shores are a potential point of departure for attack on the eastern seaboard of the United States. On the other hand, a tropical climate enables her to produce raw materials and food, that the United States needs and cannot obtain either at all or in sufficient quantities from its continental territory.

The United States has become a thoroughly industrialized country, while Cuba is still in the agricultural stage of economic development. Cuba lacks fuels, but has an abundance of minerals. Cuba needs machinery and steel and textiles and flour; and the United States needs sugar and vegetables and fruit, tobacco, coffee, manganese and copper.

Such are the interests; strategic and political interests; economic, geographical and commercial interests that the treaties of 1903 attempted to regulate.

The men who conceived and drafted them no doubt believed that in a measure they had succeeded in their purpose. But it is difficult for us to share their optimism today. Three decades of bitter experience of friction and intervention, of dictatorship and revolution, and the final collapse of Cuban economy and destruction of a once prosperous trade with the United States, have taught us that the task of regulating in a harmonious and mutually profitable manner the relations between the two countries still lies ahead.

THE PERMANENT TREATY

The Permanent Treaty, embodying the Platt Amendment, was intended to furnish the United States with adequate naval bases on the coast of Cuba, to improve the sanitary conditions on the Island, and to preserve a solvent government in Cuba, adequate for the protection of life, property, and individual liberty. In its two first objectives it has met with success, in the third it has failed lamentably.

The right of intervention granted to the United States by Article III of the Platt Amendment, originally conceived as an instrument for emergencies, to be used only in case of a veritable state of anarchy within the Republic, has been construed to permit the intervention of the United States in the government of Cuba. And the right of intervention thus interpreted and applied has not served to increase the prestige of the United States in Latin America generally or in Cuba particularly. It has given rise, on the contrary, to many complications and problems that the Department of State has frequently been unwilling to face, and has attracted toward the United States criticisms and accusations oftentimes unmerited and unjust.

The United States has only intervened in Cuba in the manner contemplated by the Platt Amendment on one occasion—in 1906; and the government then set up left a bad memory, as one of the worst and most corrupt that Cuba has ever had.

Since then the Department of State has bent its efforts to avoid intervention and adopted a policy of secrecy and mystery, or insinuations, of memoranda and personal representatives, which has been still more damaging to Cuba, because it has had to rest on the principle of non-revolution. In other words, the United States has sought in every way to prevent the Cuban people from making use of the right of rebellion against despotism, but has not assumed the responsibility of avoiding their oppression, or of terminating it in the cases when it has occurred.

On two occasions, in 1917 and 1921, the United States publicly declared that it would maintain the constitutional government of Cuba, and would not countenance armed revolt as a means of substituting the orderly functions of government. And, in both cases, official correspondence reveals that the suffrage had been emasculated and the elections held under conditions of violence and oppression, and that the so-called constitutional government had proceeded with the purpose either of remaining in power or installing its candidates in office against the will of a majority of the people.

Thus the Platt Amendment has tended to increase and make more intolerable the evils that it proposed to avoid. Far from avoiding Cuban Governments incapable of preserving life, property, and liberty, it has become an instrument of despots and tyrants, and a means of oppression of the people of Cuba, whose liberty the people of the United States have always generously desired. As a result the Cuban people have come to regard all efforts towards self-determination as futile, and to look upon politics with distrust and despair, as a game in which they are but the pawns, not the players. The Platt Amendment, therefore, while serving no useful purpose to the United States, has been a cause of damage and an unmerited stigma of incapacity for the people of Cuba.

ɤ   ɤ   ɤ   ɤ   ɤ

Cubans and Americans both are faced with the duty of bending their efforts to remedy the damage done to our peoples through ignorance or greed. But the size and power of the United States, when contrasted with the relative smallness and weakness of Cuba, seems to impose upon Americans the greater part of the burden and the responsibility in this respect.

It will be Cuba's part to put her case before the United States as clearly and intelligently as possible, and it will be the part of the United States to strive to know Cuba and to understand her. Cuba's problem is a complex one, and it lies in the hands of the United States to aid or impede her in solving it.

There is room for optimism, however. The opportunity for approaching these matters is today perhaps the most favorable that may ever present itself. Revolutions have taken place in both countries, and in both the tendency is to place the general welfare of the nation above the welfare of special interests.

In the United States the Democratic administration and in Cuba the ABC[3] advocate substantially the same means and pursue an identical purpose,— the adequate distribution of wealth. In both countries we have come to realize that the distribution of wealth is economically and socially as important as its production.

But whereas in the United States, this is purely an internal or class problem, for Cuba it is a matter of life or death, of sovereignty or dependency.

The history of Cuba during the past century is a story of destruction; and during this century it has been a story of exploitation. First the agricultural and industrial wealth of the Cubans was demolished. Later they lost their land.

Under the rule of Spain the Cubans were the owners of the soil and the Spaniards had control of political office. As a consequence of the war for independence they secured political office but lost their land.

Every war implies destruction for some and enrichment for others.

During the war for freedom, the mills, the tobacco and coffee plantations, the orchards and the cattle of the Cubans were destroyed. The whole island was at times a field of battle and a torch. But in the cities Spanish and foreign merchants waxed rich, and profiteered from the sale of supplies to the armies in conflict.

When peace was made there were no reparations for the Cubans because it was the United States who negotiated and dictated its terms. They came back from the struggle with empty hands; the continuity of their lives had been severed, they were without resources or means to make a living and quite naturally they were compelled to take refuge in politics and administrative office, for these were the only spoils that fell to their lot.

Then came the displacement in the ownership of land. Those that still possessed a ruined estate here and there, lacking the credit wherewith to rebuild it, were compelled to sell out for a ridiculous price. And the great sugar industries devoured the landed wealth of Cuba bit by bit.

Cuba today is an immense cane field. Forty per cent of the total surface of the Island and surely 60 per cent of her arable lands are in the hands of foreign companies. A system of land tenure consisting of great estates is always bad; when under absentee ownership it is still worse. But when, as in Cuba, the owners of the land are foreign stock companies, it inevitably leads to social degeneration and political deterioration.

And this process of alienation and concentration of wealth has not been limited to the land. It has repeated itself in the fields of transportation, mining, public utilities and lastly, in finance.

The directors of a few banks and of a few companies have come to be the dictators of Cuban economy. And these banks and these companies have no interest in community life or social conditions in Cuba other than that which may be inspired by their balance sheets or by their dividends.

A recent instance may serve as an example. The government decided to restrict the sugar crop. A company possessing several mills was assigned a production quota for each. Experts decided that a saving in overhead might be effected by grinding the cane of the several mills in one and closing the others down. This was done, and no doubt it proved profitable to the company, but the people of these communities where the mills had been closed were left without employment and subjected to terrible suffering, which of course did not appear on the balance sheets.

Political liberty and economic vassalage are not compatible. Cuba today is bent on reconquering her independence. A new generation of Cubans has arisen against these economic and political evils, and their efforts have culminated in a formidable movement of youth, the ABC. Its program envisages redistribution of land, agricultural cooperation, and an adequate financial system which will serve to extend credit to those who need it and are today helpless. It is a vast program of national reconstruction and political reform which embodies the present needs and highest ideals of the Cuban people. And the future relations between Cuba and the United States cannot be properly determined without taking into account these needs and these ideals.

A NEW INTERNATIONAL POLICY

Our relations face a crisis. The political and economic problems which confront us are of no mean scope, and we must approach them with the purpose of finding definite solutions, for this is no time for palliatives or temporary measures. But the work to be done is one which requires knowledge and study; it admits of no delay, but neither does it allow for haste.

If we are to arrive at an adequate regulation of the relations between Cuba and the United States, it is necessary first to adopt a policy and an attitude radically different from that of the past. We must accept the fact that the interests of the people of the United States and those of the people of Cuba are substantially identical, and direct our efforts to the service of those interests in so far as they are common to both nations and for their general good. We must consequently set aside all private considerations envisaging the interests of certain classes or producers. We must not only weigh the immediate advantages of an increment in commerce or the raising of the price level, but take into account as well the social consequences of the measures to be adopted. And we must, above all, deny the spirit of barter and reject the notion that our's is a business which requires that one of the peoples benefit at the expense of the other.

It seems evident that both the Permanent Treaty and the Treaty of Reciprocity have outlived their usefulness, and that in the future more harm than good can come of their existence. Both should consequently be abrogated, and the first superseded by a Perpetual Treaty of Friendship and Alliance, and the second by a Customs Union.

There is no basis for maintaining the right of intervention or any reason that can justify the continuance of the tutorship that the United States has assumed over the people of Cuba. Interventions have invariably proved fruitless. They may produce certain momentary advantages, such as better sanitation, efficiency in public services, or other material benefits like public works and railroads. But instead of teaching peoples to govern themselves they appear to delay their political and cultural advancement. For nations have to build themselves, they cannot be built from without.

It is true that the abrogation of the Platt Amendment gives rise to certain doubts; but if analyzed it may be seen that they are all produced by the problem of the protection of property.

What if, in the case of a revolution, the properties of Americans or other foreign citizens are damaged? What if Cuba should refuse to pay an external debt, or its tribunals render a questionable decision? These and similar questions may be asked, but there is no valid reason for answering them in a different manner in the case of Cuba than in that of any other nation, Spain or Denmark for instance. Should such unfortunate events occur the question of damage should be adjusted through usual diplomatic channels, and any differences settled by conciliation or arbitration.

Cuba is not and should not be treated as a "backward" country. Her people are acknowledged by foreigners to be industrious, intelligent and progressive; and ethnically they are in the vast majority of pure Hispanic stock. In fact more than half a dozen States in the Union have a colored population proportionately larger than that of Cuba. She has further shown a love of liberty and an unwillingness to tolerate oppression and despotism, and has made such heroic efforts for her freedom, as to command the respect of all nations. And the United States should be the last to withhold from her such consideration as it would be willing to show to other countries more remote from its shores.

It is to be hoped that the United States will abandon the rôle of continental policeman and debt-collector that it has felt obliged to assume in the past as a consequence of the Monroe Doctrine, and that the principle proclaimed by Drago and accepted by the Second Hague Conference against the use of force for economic redress shall receive factual recognition.[4]

Cuba's position in respect to the United States is a peculiar one, because while economically she is a part of the mechanism of the North American continent, ethnically, socially, and even romantically she belongs to the peoples of South America. And this obstacle precludes the possibility of her incorporation into the political system of the United States.

But in determining future relations, it would be unreasonable to refuse to accept, with all its consequences, the economic affinity which exists between the two nations.

A free exchange of products, under a special Customs Union, would be the logical solution. Undoubtedly certain vested interests would, in the circumstances, have to be taken into account. But there are ways of caring for them, at least temporarily. A system of bounties, to be progressively reduced and, in time, disappear altogether, would serve the purpose. And such a system could be employed as well for the protection of industries which, for political reasons, it might seem advisable to preserve permanently within the national boundaries of either country.

It would have obvious advantages over the tariff system. Firstly, it would be an exceptional instead of a general treatment, in so far as the favored producers are concerned. And secondly, the amount of the bounties, the exact beneficiaries, and the total cost to the nation would be a matter of common knowledge. And from the point of view of public revenue the loss in customs duties might well be compensated by internal consumption taxes and income derived from increased commercial activity due to lower prices and the stimulation of consumption.

It would not be too much to say that under such a system, Cuba would in less than a decade import in the vicinity of half a billion dollars worth of American goods per year.

If this plan should not prove feasible, then the alternative would be a readjustment of the present reciprocity Treaty which would bring the rate on Cuban sugar down to where it was in 1913, that is in the vicinity of one per cent per pound, by increasing the differential margin in favor of Cuban exports, and likewise revising the schedule on imports to Cuba from the United States with a view to facilitating the exchange of goods between the two countries.

There are two other points that cannot be disregarded in

connection with future economic policy. One concrens production
and the other the investment of foreign capital in Cuba.

Cuba has to take [*sic*] a decision on the issue of economic
nationalism. In the past her best efforts have been dedicated to
the production of sugar. But she learned a bitter lesson the day
that the doors of her markets were closed in her face. She cannot
run the risk that this may happen again. She must either receive
the assurance of a permanent outlet for her basic products, or turn
to the satisfaction of the internal needs of her population. In other
words, either her future economic relations with the United States
are to be such that she can rely on their being as permanent in
character as her political relations, or she must resign herself to
improving her present condition of economic isolation.

As far as investments are concerned, Cuba is naturally interested in attracting foreign capital for the development of her
resources, because she has not yet attained economic maturity.
But such investments should be welcome only when they are
tendered as loans or in the manner of a partnership whereby the
investor and the native may mutually profit. Not when they take
the form of an outright purchase of basic wealth, as in the past,
and tend to reduce the indigenous population to a condition of
miserable proletarianism.

Finally we must not forget that the work of arranging the relations between two countries does not end with the signing of a
Treaty, but rather begins; and that if there is any future need it
shall be that of providing proper channels through which to exchange the mutual knowledge that a permanent understanding
requires between nations as well as individuals.

It is clear that on traditional diplomacy we cannot rely. En-
folded in the vain pomp of cordial words it has seen the world
crumble before it without scarcely becoming aware of the fact.

Oftentimes, besides, statesmen and diplomats represent governments which have lost the confidence of their people, nay, are
even detested by them as their oppressors! And, under such circumstances, friendly gestures rather than good will arouse public
odium and execration.

The mutual understanding and sympathy that must always
exist between Cuba and the United States is too precious a gift
to be exposed to such risks, and we cherish the hope that such
acts as this Conference shall be encouraged and repeated by the
private initiative of our universities and cultural institutions, and
serve to bring together, for our happiness and our weal the statesmen of tomorrow: our thinkers, our writers, and our artists.

DOCUMENT 13. Treaty of Relations With Cuba Abrogating the Platt Amendment: Signed May 29, 1934. (*U. S. Statutes at Large.* XLVIII: 1682).

Article I.

The Treaty of Relations which was concluded between the two contracting parties on May 22, 1903, shall cease to be in force, and is abrogated, from the date on which the present Treaty goes into effect.

Article II.

All the acts effected in Cuba by the United States of America during its military occupation of the island, up to May 20, 1902, the date on which the Republic of Cuba was established, have been ratified and held as valid; and all the rights legally acquired by virtue of those acts shall be maintained and protected.

Article III.

Until the two contracting parties agree to the modification or abrogation of the stipulations of the agreement in regard to the lease to the United States of America of lands in Cuba for coaling and naval stations signed by the President of the Republic of Cuba on February 16, 1903, and by the President of the United States of America on the 23rd day of the same month and year, the stipulations of that agreement with regard to the naval station of Guantánamo shall continue in effect. The supplementary agreement in regard to naval or coaling stations signed between the two Governments on July 2, 1903, also shall continue in effect in the same form and on the same conditions with respect to the naval station at Guantánamo. So long as the United States of America shall not abandon the said naval station of Guantánamo or the two governments shall not agree to a modification of its present limits, the station shall continue to have the territorial area that it now has, with the limits that it has on the date of the signature of the present treaty.

Article IV.

If at any time in the future a situation should arise that appears to point to an outbreak of contagious disease in the territory of either of the contracting parties, either of the two Governments shall, for its own protection, and without its act being considered unfriendly, exercise freely and at its discretion the right to suspend communications between those of its ports that it may designate and all or part of the territory of the other party, and for the period that it may consider to be advisable. . . .

•   •   •

After the recognition of the Mendieta government, the Roosevelt Administration started to work on the economic portion of the Cuban solution. Lower duties and market stabilization were commonly regarded as the basic ingredients needed to increase American exports, revive the value of investments, stabilize Cuba, and aid the sugar refiners using Cuban raw sugar. At the same time a compromise would be offered to placate the domestic and insular sugar producers.[5]

The Jones-Costigan Act became law in May 1934. This act created a "closed sugar area," and authorized the Secretary of Agriculture to set yearly quotas for the sugar producing areas included in the act (Document 14). A processing tax was levied on all sugar consumed in the United States, and the receipts were used to pay subsidies to domestic producers of sugar. In 1937 the terms "excise tax" and "conditional payments" were substituted to meet the objections raised by the Supreme Court. President Roosevelt lowered the duty on Cuban raw sugar to 1.5 cents a pound in June 1934, and the Reciprocal Trade Agreement—signed on August 24, 1934—further reduced this duty to .9 cents a pound. This agreement also provided numerous concessions for United States exports to Cuba.

Taken together, the Jones-Costigan Act and the Reciprocal Trade Agreement provided a compromise solution for competing economic interests combined with a system for stabilizing Cuba within the framework of expanding American economic interests. Like all compromises, this one produced some objections. Congressman Everett Dirksen of Illinois accused the Roosevelt Administration of subsidizing "Wall Street" at the expense of domestic producers (Document 15). The American Sugar Refining Company liked most of the arrangement, but complained that the Walsh Amendment to the Jones-Costigan Act did not go far enough in keeping out Cuban refined sugar (Document 17). The compromise was highly praised by such groups as the National Foreign Trade Council and the National City Bank (Document 16).

The Second Export-Import Bank was established in March 1934 as a subsidiary of the Reconstruction Finance Corporation. This agency was designed to meet several related problems. The Cuban government needed funds to pay its bills and American exporters wanted government loans and long-term credits to stimulate foreign trade. Two loans were made to Cuba in 1934: the first in March for approximately $3,774,724, and the second in December for approximately $4,359,095. With these loans the Cuban government purchased silver from the United States. These transactions not only pumped money into Cuba's economy—for the purchase of American goods—but they also subsidized the exportation of a surplus commodity.

DOCUMENT 14. President Franklin D. Roosevelt Requests the Passage of the Jones-Costigan Act, February 8, 1934. (U. S. House of Representatives, Committee on Agriculture, *Hearing on H.R. 7907, to Include Sugar Beets and Sugarcane as Basic Commodities Under the Agricultural Adjustment Act.* 73rd Cong., 2nd Sess., 1934 Pp. 1–2.)

To The Congress:

Steadily increasing sugar production in the continental United States and in insular regions has created a price and marketing situation prejudicial to virtually everyone interested. Farmers in many areas are threatened with low prices for their beets and cane, and Cuban purchases of our goods have dwindled steadily as her shipments of sugar to this country have declined.

There is a school of thought which believes that sugar ought to be on the free list. This belief is based on the high cost of sugar to the American consuming public.

The annual gross value of the sugar crop to American beet and cane growers is approximately $60,000,000. Those who believe in the free importation of sugar say that the 2 cents a pound tariff is levied mostly to protect this $60,000,000 crop and that it costs our consuming public every year more than $200,000,000 to afford this protection.

I do not at this time recommend placing sugar on the free list. I feel that we ought first to try out a system of quotas with the three-fold object of keeping down the price of sugar to consumers, of providing for the retention of beet and cane farming within our continental limits, and also to provide against further expansion of this necessarily expensive industry.

Consumers have not benefited from the disorganized state of sugar production here and in the insular regions. Both the import tariff and cost of distribution, which together account for the major portion of the consumers' price for sugar, have remained relatively constant during the past 3 years.

This situation clearly calls for remedial action. I believe that we can increase the returns to our own farmers, contribute to the economic rehabilitation of Cuba, provide adequate quotas for the Philippines, Hawaii, Puerto Rico, and the Virgin Islands, and at the same time prevent higher prices to our own consumers.

The problem is difficult but can be solved if it is met squarely and if small temporary gains are sacrificed to ultimate general advantage.

The objective may be attained most readily through amendment of existing legislation. The Agricultural Adjustment Act should be amended to make sugar beets and sugarcane basic agricultural commodities. It then will be possible to collect a processing tax on sugar, the proceeds of which will be used to compensate farmers for holding their production to the quota level. A tax of less than one half cent per pound would provide sufficient funds.

Consumers need not and should not bear this tax. It is already within the Executive power to reduce the sugar tariff by an amount equal to the tax. In order to make certain that American consumers shall not bear an increased price due to this tax, Congress should provide that the rate of the processing tax shall in no event exceed the amount by which the tariff on sugar is reduced below the present rate of import duty.

By further amendment to the Agricultural Adjustment Act, the Secretary of Agriculture should be given authority to license refiners, importers, and handlers to buy and sell sugar from the various producing areas only in the proportion which recent mar-ketings of such areas bear to total United States consumption. The average marketings of the past 3 years provide on the whole an equitable base, but the base period should be flexible enough to allow slight adjustments as between certain producing areas.

The use of such a base would allow approximately the following preliminary and temporary quotas:

Short tons

Continental beets	1,450,000
Louisiana and Florida	260,000
Hawaii	935,000
Puerto Rico	821,000
Philippine Islands	1,037,000
Cuba	1,944,000
Virgin Islands	5,000
TOTAL	6,452,000

The application of such quotas would immediately adjust market supplies to consumption and would provide a basis for reduction of production to the needs of the United States market.

Furthermore, in the negotiations for a new treaty between the United States and Cuba to replace the existing Commercial Convention, which negotiations are to be resumed immediately, favorable consideration will be given to an increase in the existing preferential on Cuban sugars, to an extent compatible with the joint interests of the two countries.

In addition to action made possible by such legislative and treaty changes, the Secretary of Agriculture already has authority to enter into codes and marketing agreements with manufacturers which would permit savings in manufacturing and distributing costs. If any agreements or codes are entered into, they should be in such form as to assure that producers and consumers share in the resulting savings.

DOCUMENT 15. Congressman Dirksen Attacks the Administration's Cuban Policy, June 1934. (*Congressional Record.* 73rd Cong., 2nd Sess., 1934. Vol. 78, Part 11. Pp. 11552, 11556–57.)

But recently I have been getting suspicious that there is something wrong in Washington. These suspicions were aggravated when I noticed the speed with which the United States Senate recently confirmed the treaty with Cuba. . . . The ink was scarcely dry on that treaty down in the State Department at the other end of Pennsylvania Avenue until it was rushed to the Senate by special messenger and passed by that body. Ordinarily the Senate does not do business that way. . . . This treaty business therefore seemed very strange indeed. Senators, too, were suspicious and the word went around that they were getting ready to break the gentle

news to Cuba about how much or how little sugar she could send
to the United States next year and perhaps the year after that.
They figured that Cuba would get mad. They were afraid of open
hostilities and of the need for taking the fleet right away from the
imposing review in New York Harbor and dispatching it to Cuba to
comfort and assuage the anger of Cubans. . . . Bullets have been
breaking the window lights in the home of Jefferson Caffery, the
American Ambassador down there, and his chauffeur was informed
that if he and his boss did not move out of Cuba, they might have
an informal engagement with the undertaker. Anyway, a lot of
reasons, real and fancied, were advocated for the immediate adoption of the treaty and so it was adopted and ratified.

Mr. Chairman, may I suggest to the gentlemen that a great
deal of the Cuban industry, particularly sugar, blackstrap molasses,
and the alcohol which is made from blackstrap molasses at the
expense of the grain farmers' market, is owned by the Chase
National, the National City Bank, and in which Mr. Chadbourne,
Mr. Astor, Mr. Rockefeller, Mr. Woodin, and many others have a
heavy interest, and that a great deal of the sugar and blackstrap
molasses which we are purchasing from Cuba constitutes or at least
is income or profit to Americans, citizens such as Mr. Astor, Mr.
Chadbourne, Mr. Rockefeller, Mr. Morgan, and all the others who
are linked with them directly or indirectly.[6]

To the farmer of the Midwestern States I say: Take a look at
this set-up which seems to have an unusual interest in sugar and
in the protection of those wild-cat investments in Cuba; take a
look at the names of those whose interest in sugar denotes an
interest in the blackstrap molasses . . . which is converted into
alcohol and thereby steals away your market for grain; take a look
at the high and responsible key positions held by those who have
heretofore been identified with the protection of sugar and its
byproducts, and you can readily understand why little heed has
been given to the demand for a limitation on importations of blackstrap.

It becames easier to understand why this cry of "brain truster"
and "radical" and "Socialist" went up to frighten the people. To me
it appears to have been a mere smoke-screen to cloak the activities
of the sugar-and-blackstrap-molasses-alcohol interests. My own notion is that in some respects Mr. Tugwell is about as radical as
last year's hat; Mr. Ezekiel is about as radical as J. P. Morgan; Mr.

Behrle [sic] is about as much of a "brain truster" and "left winger" as Percy Rockefeller; if these gentlemen are radical "brain trusters," then J. P. Morgan is a younger brother of Stalin and J. D. Rockefeller is a first cousin of Mussolini.[7]

I am afraid that both the American people and the President are being fooled by this group, and before long there will be an awakening.

DOCUMENT 16. The National City Bank Praises the Sugar Compromise, September 1934. (*Monthly Bank Letter.* September 1934. Pp. 136–37.)

The conclusion of the new trade pact between the United States and Cuba, reducing the tariff on Cuban sugar from 1½ cents a pound to 9/10ths of a cent, against 1.875 cents on other foreign sugar, and granting additional concessions on Cuban rum, tobacco, fruits and vegetables, should mark a real turn for the better in that distressed country.

That the people of the United States have a large responsibility for the conditions existing in Cuba must be clear to anyone familiar with the development of trade relations between the two countries. As early as 1903, the United States, recognizing Cuba as a natural source of sugar for this market, concluded with that country a reciprocity treaty granting Cuban sugar a preferential rate of 20 per cent against all other foreign sugar in return for satisfactory concessions on our products entering Cuba. On the strength of this treaty, which seemed to put the economic relations between the countries on a safe and assured basis, capital flowed freely into Cuba and the sugar industry underwent a broad development.

The treaty which has just been signed represents a further step in a program inaugurated early this year for dealing with the sugar situation as a whole and for restoring trade relations between Cuba and this country. At the last session of Congress legislation was enacted which provided for production control and the allocation of quotas among the various areas supplying the American market. Under this Act quotas were set for 1934 at 1,700,000 long tons for Cuba, 1,620,000 tons for domestic beet and 2,440,000 for the insular possessions. Inasmuch as the Cuban quota is less than the actual imports of any years save 1932 and 1933, it is evident that the new trade agreement, together with the quota assigned, falls considerably short of a full solution of Cuba's economic difficulties. Nevertheless, the steps that have been taken are the most constructive by far that have been initiated, and for this both parties are deserving of commendation. On the basis of the treaty it is predicated that the gain in Cuban exports during the first year of the agreement might amount to as much as $50,000,000.

All of which has a definite significance to the United States, for Cuba was formerly one of our best customers, ranking sixth in the year 1924. In that year Cuba took $199,800,000 worth of merchandise from us, including $5,000,000 agricultural products, $20,880,-000 cotton manufactures, $37,400,000 iron and steel, including machinery, and $9,560,000 vehicles, mostly automobiles. By 1933 the over-all total of our exports to Cuba had shrunk to $25,100,000. It will be seen therefore that the United States is vitally interested in anything calculated to increase Cuban buying power.

DOCUMENT 17. The American Sugar Refining Company Analyses the Sugar Compromise, 1934. (*Annual Report of The American Sugar Refining Company for the Forty-Fourth Year, Ending December 31, 1934.* New York, 1935. Pp. 4–7, 9, 11.)

(a) Acting under the Agricultural Adjustment Act, as amended by the Jones-Costigan Act, the Secretary of Agriculture has fixed quotas of sugar which domestic beet sugar producers and cane sugar producers in Louisiana and Florida, the Philippines, Hawaii, Puerto Rico, the Virgin Islands, and Cuba and other foreign countries may market in the United States. During the life of the plan, these quotas are expected to check the tendency of domestic beet sugar and of raw cane sugar from the Philippines, Hawaii and Puerto Rico to increase to such an extent that the excess of sugar produced for this market would result in ruinous prices for all producers within the United States tariff wall, and to such an extent that Cuban sugar, which must pay a duty here, would be practically excluded from the United States. (b) Under the same Act as so amended, the Secretary of Agriculture imposed a processing tax equal to 53½¢ per 100 pounds, or somewhat over ½¢ per pound, with respect to all *refined* sugar from any source marketed in the United States. The proceeds of this tax are to be used for benefit payments to domestic growers of sugar beets and of sugar cane, also for benefit payments to growers of sugar cane, and for agriculture in general, in the respective Insular areas, not including Cuba. (c) Coincident with the imposition of this processing tax, June 8, 1934, the President, under the flexible tariff provisions of the Tariff Act, reduced the duty on 96° Cuban raw sugar to 1½¢ per pound. It had been 2¢ per pound. (d) Under a new Reciprocal Trade Agreement with Cuba, which became effective September 3, 1934, the duty on 96° Cuban raw sugar was further reduced to 9/10¢ per pound. During the life of the agreement Cuba is assured that the duty on her sugar will be at least 20% lower than on sugar from any other country, and that when quotas end, this rate will not exceed the previous 1½¢ rate. (e) Aside from the centralized control in the Department of Agriculture, separate controls in the form of marketing agreements have been set up in the several sugar areas for: (1) domestic beet; (2) domestic cane; (3) the Philippines; (4) Hawaii; (5) Puerto Rico; (6) Virgin Islands. Cuba already has sugar control under her Five-Year Plan, handled by the Cuban Sugar Institute and National Sugar Export Corporation, under an elaborate system of quotas, licenses and permits. Unless Congress grants further authorization, the above-mentioned United States quotas and processing taxes will terminate not later than May 9, 1937.

The following table shows, in long tons, refined sugar value, the 1925–1933 averaged United States consumption from different sources, that of 1933 and 1934 and the quotas fixed for 1934 and 1935. Noteworthy are the increases in domestic beet sugar, Puerto Rican sugar and Philippine sugar and the decrease in Cuban sugar until helped by quotas which, however, leaves Cuba's share far below its average.

✓ ✓ ✓ ✓ ✓

The benefit payments from the proceeds of the processing tax are in fact a subsidy, payable to growers of sugar beets and of sugar cane within the United States tariff wall, to reimburse them for refraining from producing beyond their respective quotas, and to compensate for the possible lowering of prices for their products, caused by the reduction in duty on sugar coming here from Cuba. United States consumers of sugar will, of course, pay this subsidy, which amounts to some $60,000,000 annually, or perhaps to $180,000,000 for the three-year period. However, consumers will benefit to the indeterminable extent that the two reductions in duty may lower the price of sugar below what it would be otherwise. The heart of the plan is the restriction of sugar production marketable in this country.

✓ ✓ ✓ ✓ ✓

In its Sugar Plan, our Government had an excellent opportunity to provide belated relief for domestic sugar refiners. Quotas could have been fixed under which *refined* sugar from tropical sources would have been excluded from this country. Duties on sugar refined in Cuba could have been adjusted so as to afford protection for United States *refiners*. Tariff protection could have been granted as against *refined* sugar from Puerto Rico and the Philippines.

The Sugar Plan extended liberal treatment to the domestic beet and domestic cane sugar industries, whose quotas were fixed at figures far in excess of average production, and who also continue to enjoy tariff protection. Correspondingly favorable treatment could also have been accorded to domestic cane sugar refiners. These refiners, in wages paid, cost of materials used and value of output at their refineries in Massachusetts, New York, New Jersey, Pennsylvania, Maryland, Georgia, Louisiana, Texas and California, constitute by far the most important factor in the sugar industry in the United States. They were deserving of consideration because, due largely to high tariff protection for domestic beet and cane sugar, and failure to furnish any protection for domestic cane refiners, their production had declined almost one-third, or from over 5,100,000 tons in 1925 to less than 3,700,000 tons in 1933, or from 83% to 64% of the country's sugar consumption.

The Government did not take advantage of this opportunity to aid United States sugar refiners. The program finally approved again discriminated against them, as contrasted with the treatment accorded to the domestic beet and domestic cane sugar industries, and even with that accorded to tropical raw and refined sugar interests. The quotas fixed by law permit Cuba to send more *refined* sugar here than the average sent here by her during the five years, 1929–1933, both inclusive, and permit Puerto Rico and the Philippines to send as much as they ever sent. While these quotas check increases in tropical refined sugar entering this country, they maintain sales of this sugar here not far below their highest output, which automatically reduces the output of domestic refiners. If there was to be solicitude about not impairing the volume of any sugar refining industry, it might well have been exercised in favor of the domestic cane sugar refining industry, which for some 200 years has furnished a dependable supply of refined sugar for this country, rather than in favor of the tropical sugar refining industry, which commenced scarcely 10 years ago to duplicate the domestic industry and to invade this country.

Nor, in establishing the new tariffs on sugar, was any protection whatever provided for the United States sugar refining industry. No duties were placed on refined sugar coming here from Puerto Rico or the Philippines. The new tariff on Cuban sugars not only affords no protection for domestic refiners, but continues to place a premium on the refining of sugar in Cuba. The Cuban refiner gets his *refined* sugar into this country at a duty of .954¢ per pound, while the domestic refiner must pay a duty of .963¢ on enough Cuban *raw* sugar to make a pound of refined sugar here.

United States cane refiners, long lacking relief, still look forward to protection against tropical refined sugar. They are plainly entitled to this relief. There can be no justification for continuing the existing arrangement, which takes away from domestic refiners a volume equivalent to the consumption of over 13,500,000 people in this country and hands this volume over to recently built refineries in Cuba, Puerto Rico and the Philippines.

✓ ✓ ✓ ✓ ✓

The Recovery Program has accentuated the domestic refiners' need for protection. Since the summer of 1933 the United States cane sugar refining industry has operated under the President's Re-employment Agreements. N. R. A. and A. A. A. have raised the average cost of domestic refining by some 13¢ per hundred pounds of output.

United States refiners, in asking for relief, are seeking to regain their lost volume, and not higher prices. Refined sugar prices in this country are determined by domestic competition, which is always severe. If tropical *refined* sugar were excluded, domestic refiners' volume would increase and their unit costs would go down.

Restoring domestic refiners' volume would increase employment for American labor. This would reverse the present situation, where, with millions of Americans out of work, and billions of dollars being appropriated to provide relief for them at the expense of American taxpayers, including the domestic sugar refiners, the United States in effect subsidizes Cuban, Puerto Rican and Philippine refiners, and permits their tropical labor to take away the jobs of American citizens heretofore normally employed in sugar refineries in this country.

Providing protection for domestic sugar refiners will also aid general business recovery in this country. Normally United States cane refiners, besides paying salaries and wages in excess of $27,-000,000 per year, expend even more annually for cotton, oil, coal, paper, other supplies and power, the production and distribution of which furnish business for numerous industries and employment for many thousands of American workmen.

It is earnestly hoped that our Government will afford early relief to domestic cane sugar refiners, so that this essential American industry will not be crippled irreparably, to the disadvantage of the national sugar supply, and of American labor, and of American supply firms, and of the many thousands of persons who have invested their savings in founding and in developing this industry, one of the oldest and most efficient in the country.

✓   ✓   ✓   ✓   ✓

The U. S. Sugar Plan is particularly significant in that it represents a step in the direction of a sound Colonial Policy, under which Insular manufacturing industries would be prevented from displacing those long established in this country. The imposition of duties on *refined* sugar from Insular areas would be a further logical step in carrying out such a policy. No other policy can be depended upon to safeguard the national sugar supply, as is recognized by all other important countries in the World.

The plan also marks a forward step toward recognizing the obligation of this country to Cuba and to the Cuban *raw* sugar industry. The steadily increasing tariff duties here, and throughout the World, and the never-ending and constantly varying and always futile sugar controls in Cuba, had brought the Cuban sugar industry to the brink of complete ruin. During a comparatively recent period, Cuba had declined from 21% to 8% of the world production and from 58% to 25% of the United States consumption, and the trend was rapidly toward further decline. The new plan definitely halts this tendency and provides a respite.

•   •   •

The intimate connection between domestic economic factors and the "Good Neighbor" Policy was illustrated by Sumner Welles's analysis of the Cuban policy of the Roosevelt Administration (Document 18). This pattern of United States-Cuban relations, established by the end of 1934, was to last for twenty-five years. Some modifications were made in the economic arrangements, but the basic programs remained the same.

United States officials were generally well pleased with the solution in Cuba. This view was not shared by all the people of

Cuba, but the State Department characterized this opposition as "communist inspired." Strikes and turmoil continued in Cuba until March of 1935 when the general strike called by the students of the University of Havana was ruthlessly crushed. Batista once more displayed his ability to guarantee order and insure conservative rule in Cuba.

DOCUMENT 18. Sumner Welles, "Good Neighbor Policy in the Caribbean," July 1935. (U. S. Department of State, Latin American Series, No. 12. Washington, 1935. Pp. 7–10.)

The policy of your Government toward Cuba has been for the past 2 years, in the best sense of the word, the policy of the "good neighbor." . . . Cuba had fallen into a vicious circle. There was no hope for economic improvement without business confidence, which could not be reestablished until and unless some solution of the political problem was arrived at. There was no possibility of a permanent solution of the political problem so long as the Cuban people were starving and the social unrest resulting therefrom threatened to break into the flames of anarchy. . . .

The acute hostility to the Machado dictatorship was heightened by the prolonged depression in the sugar industry, the mainstay of the Cuban economy. About 80 percent of Cuba's national income is derived from the sale in foreign markets of sugar, and when, in 1924, these markets began to dwindle and the price of sugar began its steady decline, all Cuba felt the deflationary effects. With Cuba already reeling from the effects of the world depression, the passage of the Smoot-Hawley Tariff Act, by which Cuban sugar would have been rapidly excluded from the American market and through which her other exports to the United States were likewise in great part shut out, condemned Cuba to economic ruin.

The longer the depression continued, the more it became evident that the Cuban people would not long endure the standard of living that did not permit them sufficient food or clothing or adequate shelter. This state of affairs was also of concern to American exporters, who were faced with the loss of the Cuban market. Cuba, which in 1924 was the sixth best customer of the United States, had, largely because of the Smoot-Hawley tariff, by 1933 fallen to sixteenth.

The most important feature of the policy of cooperation tendered by this Government to Cuba in the summer of 1933 was the offer to replace the earlier commercial agreement by a new one adapted to present needs. Owing to the political turmoil which characterized Cuban political developments during the latter part of 1933, it was not possible to complete the negotiations until the summer of 1934. The new commercial agreement is based upon the double premise that economic rehabilitation in Cuba and recovery of the onetime attractive Cuban market for our exporters depend in the last analysis upon increase in Cuban purchasing power. This end was accomplished by reductions in duties by both countries that have permitted an expanded volume of goods to move between them. With the proceeds from the sale of her goods in the United States, and because of the larger tariff preferences and decreased duties accorded to American products, Cuba has expanded enormously her purchases from this country.

Concomitant with the negotiation of the trade agreement was the passage by the Congress of the Costigan-Jones sugar legislation, under which there has been established for sugar a balance between the consumptive requirements and the amount to be permitted entry to the market. In other words, the supply of sugar has been equated to the demand. Quotas were established for the several supply areas, including Cuba, based upon previous marketings in this country.

The statesmanship of these two measures—that is, the trade agreement and the Costigan-Jones legislation—has been fully borne out by developments during the last year. During the first 9 months that the trade agreement has been in effect, American exports to Cuba increased by over 15 million dollars, which is an expansion of 73 percent over the similar period for the previous year. This has meant a very substantial increase in the volume of sales of all types of American products in Cuba. Although in the United States the farm and the factory have benefited primarily, there have also been important secondary benefits. Railroads and shipping companies are carrying freight instead of ballast; all those who perform services in connection with the movement of goods, such as insurance companies and warehouses, are enjoying increased business; and persons who have invested capital in Cuba are beginning to look forward to the resumption of return on their investments.

•   •   •

In 1933 and 1934 Cuba defaulted on the public works bonds which had been issued by Machado. In 1934 a Cuban commission ruled that the bonds had been illegally issued, but this ruling was later reversed by the Supreme Court of Cuba. The United States government did not press for an immediate settlement of these debts due to financial conditions in Cuba. In December 1937 a plan for the resumption of payments on most of these defaulted bonds was negotiated by the Cuban government and the Foreign Bondholders Protective Council. The bonds held by Warren Brothers Company and the Purdy and Henderson Company were not included in this settlement.

The Cuban government in 1938 wanted to negotiate a revised reciprocity treaty and to obtain another loan from the Export-Import Bank. The State Department, however, stipulated that both of these actions hinged on a settlement with the remaining bondholders and the revision of certain fiscal policies (Documents 19 and 20). On July 20, 1939 the State Department issued an economic ultimatum to Cuba. The Cuban government was told that negotiations on the supplemental trade agreement would be "indefinitely suspended" unless Cuba settled the problems involved. A postponement of the suspension announcement was arranged, but on September 12, the United States suspended all sugar quotas. This action automatically raised the tariff on Cuban raw sugar to 1.5 cents a pound. The Cuban government interpreted this as a move to force payment of the bonds, although there is no evidence that Roosevelt had this in mind. State Department officials, however, were not averse to using this to prod the Cubans.

Ambassador J. Butler Wright realized that war in Europe would raise sugar prices, and improve Cuba's bargaining power (Documents 21 and 22). Thus, the State Department negotiated a stop-gap agreement with Cuba which would reduce the tariff on raw sugar to the 1934 rate when quotas were reimposed. This was effected late in December 1939, and the tariff was restored to 0.9 cents per pound

During 1940 the Cuban government arranged a settlement with the remaining bondholders, and the credit moratorium was lifted. During the next two years the United States granted the concessions promised in 1939. The supplementary trade agreement, signed in January 1942, reduced the raw sugar duty to .75 cents per pound. A few months earlier the Export-Import Bank had loaned $25 million to Cuba.

DOCUMENT 19. Williard Beaulac (Chargé in Cuba) to
Cordell Hull, October 6, 1938. (U. S. Department of State,
Foreign Relations of the United States: 1938. 5 vols. Wash-
ington, 1956. V: 481.)

I saw Colonel Batista this afternoon and urged upon him in
similar terms to those used in previous conversations with Cuban
officials Cuba's need of immediately arriving at a settlement with
its remaining public works creditors. . . . When I asked Colonel
Batista if I might tell the Department that he fully understood
the difficulties Cuba might face particularly with the American
Congress if its credit were not restored promptly but that the
internal difficulties in the way of prompt settlement by Cuba were
so great that they could not be overcome, Colonel Batista replied
that I might say that he doubted that Cuba could make prompt
payment to these creditors but that he would speak to President
Laredo[8] and to members of the Debt Commission and urge that
an early study be made of the means of reaching agreements with
those creditors.

DOCUMENT 20. Sumner Welles to J. Butler Wright (Am-
bassador to Cuba), July 19, 1939. (U. S. Department of
State, *Foreign Relations of the United States: 1939.* 5 vols.
Washington, 1957. V: 530–31.)

You will indicate to the Cuban Government that this Government considers as prerequisite to any resumption of conversations
leading to increased economic cooperation between the two countries the settlement of the admitted claims of Warren Brothers and
Company and Purdy and Henderson Company, and of the so-called
Morris claim.[9]
    The Government of the United States considers, further, that
the circumstances surrounding the discussions of November 1938,[10]
at which time this Government expressed its willingness to enter
upon a program of economic cooperation with Cuba, have been
materially altered by the credit moratorium situation and the recent
enactment of monetary legislation referred to in the attached note.
This Government believes that the enactment of a satisfactory
measure to liquidate the Cuban credit moratorium and the amendment of the recently enacted monetary law[11] to eliminate certain

undesirable features and ambiguities are essential to the reestablishment of normal commercial and financial relations between the two countries, and it is prepared, at the request of the Cuban Government, to furnish competent technical experts to advise the appropriate authorities of the Cuban Government in the determination of the provisions of such legislation.

In view of the close relationship of the fiscal situation to an economic atmosphere in Cuba favorable to the carrying out of a program of economic cooperation, the Government of the United States considers that the enactment of suitable tax legislation embodying the recommendations of the Magill report, which was prepared at the request and expense of the Cuban Government, would be most helpful.

You will further indicate that this Government is prepared, if the Cuban Government takes action settling the claims of Warren Brothers and Company and Purdy and Henderson Company, and the so-called Morris claim, and disposing satisfactorily of the credit moratorium and monetary legislation matters referred to above, to extend immediately to the Cuban Government the benefits of a broad program of economic cooperation including:

1. The speedy conclusion of a supplementary trade agreement on mutually advantageous terms, and the simultaneous signature of a Treaty of Establishment and Navigation;

2. The immediate consideration by the Government of the United States of the extension of financial assistance for the carrying out of a reasonable program of public works in Cuba;

3. Assistance by experts of the United States Department of Agriculture in developing and diversifying agricultural production;

4. Technical aid by the United States Treasury, if requested, in putting into effect the recommendations of the Magill report; and

5. The active cooperation of experts of this Government in studying methods of improving the existing monetary, banking and exchange systems of Cuba.

DOCUMENT 21. Memorandum: Conversations Between J. Butler Wright, Miguel Angel Campa (Cuban Secretary of State), and Federico Laredo Bru (President of Cuba), August 31, 1939. (*Foreign Relations of the United States: 1939*. V: 552–55.)

The Secretary asked me whether I was not perturbed by the situation which was about to be created: I inquired whether he

meant the European situation. He replied that that was bad
enough, but he thought that our proposal to announce tomorrow
the suspension of negotiations for the supplementary trade agreement was fraught with very serious consequences not only for
Cuba but for relations between our countries: I said that, with all
consideration for his views, I did not share his opinion, for our
action was intended to put an end to indefinite and repeated delays
and postponements and that I felt constrained to observe that his
Government had had ample opportunity for the consideration of
this matter since the delivery of my first Note on July 20th last. . . .

✓   ✓   ✓   ✓   ✓

The secretary then said that he requested in the name of the
President of the Republic that this decision be postponed until
Saturday the 9th of September, and he added that if it were necessary he (the Secretary) would appear before Congress and explain
to the members the situation. I replied that in view of the fact that
this request came through him from the Chief of State my only
alternative was to transmit it immediately to my Government,
which I undertook to do.

At 11 o'clock (Habana time) I informed Mr. Welles thereof
and I stated, in order to aid him in any position he might make,
that I believed that at last this Government was thoroughly
frightened and had become aware of the effect upon Cuba's
economical and financial position which would inevitably arise
from continued disinclination to meet this recognized obligation
and the resultant necessity that we should announce the suspension
of the aforementioned negotiations: therefore we were in a much
stronger position than before and, furthermore, the efficacy of
subsequent representations on our part would depend largely
upon the consistency with which we maintained our position in
this matter. I said that on the other hand, however, we should have
to face the probability that, in case of a European war which
seemed so imminent, Cuba would obtain a higher and practically
limitless market for her sugar which might change certain aspects
of the situation entirely. I said further that a friendly Cuba—perhaps achieved by reasonable elasticity in this matter, might be of
greater value to us than an antipathetic Cuba—possibly brought
about by insistence upon the letter of the agreement. Mr. Welles
stated that he would think it over and call me later.

✓   ✓   ✓   ✓   ✓

At 2 o'clock (1 o'clock Washington time), Mr. Welles called
me and stated that in view of the source of this latest request and

of his high regard for the President, he could not do otherwise than accede thereto, with the understanding, however, that the postponement of the date of the announcement of our intention to suspend negotiations would be extended until September 9th, and that my Government would find it impossible to agree to a further postponement. . . .

At that hour I saw the President who was very cordial and seemingly unconcerned. I delivered the message orally as above described: he requested me to inform Mr. Welles not only of his high regard, but also of his appreciation of the attitude which he had assumed. He said nothing about the latent dangers of the situation, but he stated unequivocally that his Government would do everything in its power to secure the passage of this legislation by both Houses on the 7th.[12]

I improved the opportunity to remind him that, although such action would be a great step forward, there were certain other points contained in my note of July 20th upon which the fulfillment of the entire program of assistance and cooperation were dependent. I asked whether I might again bring them to his recollection in order that there may be no misunderstanding: he replied that he would be glad to hear any observations that I had to offer.

I first cited the Morris Claim. The President replied that this was, of course, an acknowledged debt of the Cuban Government based upon a ruling of the Supreme Court, but that the determination of the final amount must depend upon the examination which Dr. Cataya was conducting and the results of his conferences with the representatives of the claimants. Our ground as to the final amount of this claim is so uncertain and we have so little information as to what the claimants would actually accept that I deemed it wiser to pursue this subject no further. . . .

I recalled to his attention the understanding that he had given me that the Regulations under the Monetary Law would be embodied in that Law. The President replied that a provision to that effect was included in the Tax Bill. I did not discuss with him the point as to whether such was the proper place for it to appear, but I infer that this expedient is intended to overcome the necessity of remedial legislation directed to this point alone.

I then referred to the Tax Bill—improving the reference which the President had made thereto and I said that, although I had understood that many of the features of the bill which had been deemed objectionable by certain interests, both Cuban and American, had been eliminated, there still remained provisions which were in conflict with the Reciprocal Trade Treaty. . . .[13]

I then referred to the Revaluation Bill[14] and said, quite frankly, that Ambassador Martínez Fraga had acquainted me with the general program to be followed: i.e. that the matter would be discussed in the House as a result of which amendments would undoubtedly be suggested which would necessitate discussion by the Joint Committee of the House and Senate; that the President will then view the situation in the light of all the existing circumstances and may be able to indicate his opinions either by suggested compromise or, in the last analysis, by veto. The President said that that was exactly his intention and that he was reserving his decision until that time—when he would give the matter his close attention and would decide matters according to his best judgment. I asked him whether he recalled the observations which the Chamber of Commerce had had the honor to present to him with regard to the Tax Bill: he said that he did and that he thought it was an admirable document. I asked him whether there had been brought to his attention the observations by the American Chamber of Commerce and other sources and individuals, concerning the Revaluation Bill: he replied in the affirmative. I asked him whether he had seen the memorandum which our Department of State had informally communicated to Ambassador Martínez Fraga on the date of the latter's departure from Washington and which Martínez Fraga had translated for Colonel Batista: he replied that he had not. I said that I would either request Ambassador Martínez Fraga to supply him with a copy of the translation or, if it might be understood that I would do so unofficially, I would undertake to do so myself: he replied that he would give it immediate attention.

DOCUMENT 22.   Miguel Angel Campa to J. Butler Wright, September 13, 1939. (*Foreign Relations of the United States: 1939.* V: 568–69.)

The personal communication which Your Excellency made to me yesterday concerning the decision of the Government of the United States to declare abolished the system of quotas which governed the sugar market, on which was specifically based the only important advantage which the Reciprocal Trade Agreement of 1934 offered the people of Cuba following the suspension of the advantages to our tobacco, has caused a painful impression to my Government which it would be both insincere and useless on my part not to hasten to make known to the Government which Your

Excellency so worthily represents. In fact, the disorder which this unexpected measure causes in our national economy is so complete and arouses such deep anxiety in the Cuban people that my Government does not hesitate to request, in a friendly manner, that the Government of the United States consider emergency action with a view to the immediate remedying of this seriously unbalanced situation which, without a doubt causes, with respect to Cuba, a condition of obvious inequality in the field of our reciprocal relations. Fortunately, I cherish the hope that within the instructions received from your Government—which I had the privilege of learning yesterday through the medium of Your Excellency, and which leave open the door for carrying on the negotiations with a view to broadening the Treaty of 1934—it may be possible to find a provisional formula which will permit the Government of Cuba—inclined perhaps to reduce the benefits accorded the United States to the limits fixed by the Treaty of 1902—to maintain those commercial relations from which both countries have derived positive advantages within the brilliant scope which they have attained to their mutual convenience, and to the extent made necessary by the seriousness of the present time.

In that regard I do not consider it inopportune to suggest to Your Excellency that if it is the purpose of the Government of the United States in destroying the quota barriers to promote a just balance in prices—a commendable policy which all governments may perhaps have to pursue during this war in order to retain undue speculation in products of prime necessity—the reestablishment of the current tax of 90 cents imposed on Cuban sugars would further that end.

In such a case Cuba would be prepared to sacrifice the unquestioned privilege which the system of quotas represents to her, the reestablishment of which might be considered later when the disagreeable circumstances of the moment will have changed. . . .

•   •   •

During World War II, United States-Cuban relations were characterized by close cooperation. The shortage of shipping plagued the Cuban economy, but this situation was alleviated as the war progressed. The need for sugar in the United States provided an increased market for Cuba's basic export which helped to relieve some of the monetary problems of the island. All sugar quotas were suspended in April 1942, and were not reimposed until December 1947.

In January 1942, Cuba subscribed to the Joint Declaration of the United Nations, and in September 1942 the United States and Cuba signed a treaty of military and naval cooperation. The United States obtained sites in Cuba and constructed air bases for training and patrol purposes. After the termination of the war these were turned over intact to the Cuban government.

DOCUMENT 23. A *New York Times* Correspondent Describes U.S.-Cuban Relations During World War II. (Phillips, *Cuba: Island of Paradox.* Pp. 207–8, 211, 214–16, 218–20, 227, 230–31.)

On January 29, 1941, Batista ordered suppression of all totalitarian propaganda in Cuba. The Communist Party, which had supported Batista for President, was exempt from this order, so that the measure really referred to propaganda by the Germans, Italians or Spanish Fascists. Propaganda agents were ordered arrested and legal machinery created for the deportation of foreigners convicted of such activities.

The Cuban tourist season opened but with the war in Europe, which was already causing great uneasiness in the United States, tourist traffic began to decline. This was to be the last tourist season for several years.

✓   ✓   ✓   ✓   ✓

The Cuban Congress on December 9th approved a declaration of war against Japan. Three thousand university students demonstrated outside the Capitolio, demanding organization of armed forces and deportation of fifth columnists or their imprisonment in concentration camps. . . .

The authorities appealed for calm. Soldiers and rural guards were ordered to protect foreigners and their property throughout Cuba. On December 10th Cuba forbade the entry of European nationals with exception of those of the British Empire into Cuba. The measure was directed at European refugees, who were continuing to arrive in droves from Spain and Portugal. On December 11th President Batista signed a declaration of war against Germany and Italy. He ordered immediate confiscation of Italian, German and Japanese holdings and the internment of Axis nationals on the Isle of Pines, located south of Havana Province.

✓   ✓   ✓   ✓   ✓

On May 4th a Nazi broadcast from Berlin warned President Batista that the palace might be shelled by Axis war craft. Berlin was annoyed with Batista for cooperating with President Roosevelt. "President Batista of Cuba, close friend of War Promoter Roosevelt, said we Germans were vile animals that must be attacked in our dens. Friend Batista, remember you live only a few meters from the waterfront."

Shipping difficulties increased, handicapping foreign trade. Economic conditions in Cuba grew steadily worse. Fruit and vegetable growers were able to export only about two-thirds of their customary tonnage to the United States, owing to the lack of vessels. Raw material supplies of industries began to run low. The United States system of priorities made it almost impossible to obtain materials. Stocks of merchandise were being depleted and prices rose beyond the purchasing power of the average Cuban. Lack of steel and iron threatened to paralyze the construction industry, with resulting unemployment. Cuba had no war industries to take up the slack in labor.

✔   ✔   ✔   ✔   ✔

Cuba granted bases to the United States armed forces, on a temporary basis, since the agreement stated, "after termination of the emergency it is understood that the facilities will become a training center of the Cuban Air Force." The agreement of military cooperation between Cuba and the United States was signed on June 19th at the Cuban Ministry of State. Dr. José Manuel Cortina, Minister of State, signed for Cuba and American Ambassador Spruille Braden for the United States. The first base was built at San Antonio de los Baños, twenty-five miles from Havana. At San Julian, in Pinar del Rio Province, a smaller base was constructed, strategically located at the western tip of the island. From there, bombers could patrol the waters of the Gulf of Mexico and the Caribbean between Cuba and Mexico.

In August, 1942, Cuba lost two ships between Key West and Havana. The two ships, moving in a large convoy, were torpedoed. They were small freighters, the *Santiago de Cuba* and the *Manzanillo*. The bodies of the crew were recovered and brought to Havana by a United States destroyer on August 19, 1942. Thousands crowded the docks and lined the streets as the coffins were unloaded and borne to the Capitolio where they lay in state until the burial next day in Colon cemetery. President Batista decreed a state of mourning. . . .

✔   ✔   ✔   ✔   ✔

On November 16th some fifteen hundred Cubans crowded into
the Ministry of National Defense to volunteer for foreign military
service against the Axis. The Ministry ordered 127 registration
centers opened in the island and the number expected to volunteer
at that time was between ten thousand and fifty thousand. Nothing
ever came of this because the United States did not ask Cuba for
soldiers.

On March 6th President Fulgencio Batista appointed several
new cabinet members. For the first time he gave the Communists
representation. Dr. Juan Marinello, Communist leader and member
of the House of Representatives, was appointed Minister without
Portfolio. Then on April 7th Cuba recognized the Soviet Republic.
Maxim M. Litvinoff, Soviet Ambassador to Washington, came to
Havana and presented his credentials on April 9th. The same
day President Batista gave the Communist controlled Confederation of Cuban Workers, which dominated all island labor, official
status, thus tightening the hold of the Communists on labor.

In June the Cuban navy bagged its only German submarine,
after a battle which took place off the north coast. The United
States had transferred to Cuba ten submarine chasers. It was one
of those which sunk the submarine.

On July 4th Cuba for the first time celebrated the United States
Fourth of July. Some eighty thousand Cubans from all walks of life
paraded. President Batista attended ceremonies held at the Maine
Monument. Four Havana newspapers published special editions.
Eight radio stations broadcast special programs in honor of the
United States. The Rotary Club sent American troops on Guadal-
canal ten tons of candy.

American Ambassador Spruille Braden sternly and publicly
warned the Americans in Cuba that they should take no part in
political affairs of the island. "I am sure that I express the sentiment of every patriotic citizen of the United States when I declare
that no single American should participate in any way directly or
indirectly in the domestic political affairs of Cuba," Ambassador
Braden said. Many Americans and Cubans stored away this statement for future use.

In November Cuba rejoiced over the reelection of President
Franklin D. Roosevelt for the fourth time. Headlines in newspapers
declared it was a great democratic victory. "Roosevelt's victory is
our victory," *El Pais* declared. "He is the best guarantee of the

permanency of the postulates of the Atlantic Charter." The House of Representatives approved a motion to send congratulations to President Roosevelt in the name of the Cuban people.

    ✓   ✓   ✓   ✓   ✓

In April the death of President Roosevelt shocked and saddened Cuba. Dr. Raul Menocal, Mayor of Havana, ordered all public spectacles closed. The Minister of Education, Luis Perez Espinos, suspended classes in schools. Flags throughout the island were lowered as a tribute to the late American President.

    ✓   ✓   ✓   ✓   ✓

The surrender of Germany on May 7, 1945, caused no celebration in Cuba. The island had no soldiers fighting, except the small number with the United States forces. On May 16th the Cabinet decided to release the Germans in concentration camps.

On August 14th the Cubans rejoiced over the news of the surrender of Japan. Celebrating crowds gathered in Central Park. Firecrackers exploded and flags and banners were in profusion. Buildings were floodlighted and the searchlights in the Capitolio and Cabañas Fortress were turned on. On September 3, 1945, President Grau San Martin declared a two-day official holiday in celebration of V-J day. . . .

•   •   •

CHAPTER V

POSTWAR DRIFT AND THE
CASTRO REVOLUTION
(1946–62)

Senator, let me explain to you that the United States, until the
advent of Castro, was so overwhelmingly influential in Cuba that
. . . the American Ambassador was the second most important
man in Cuba; sometimes even more important than the President.
That is because of the reason of the position that the United
States played in Cuba. Now, today, his importance is not very great.
                                        —EARL E. T. SMITH (1960)

AFTER THE END of World War II the United States government
devoted most of its attention to the Cold War with Soviet Russia.
Latin America received less emphasis than Europe and Asia, since
the continent seemed to be fairly well insulated behind the Monroe
Doctrine and the Good Neighbor Policy. As insurance against
Communist infiltration the United States proposed a series of inter-
American agreements during the period 1946 to 1960. These were
generally statements by the nations of the hemisphere declaring
their opposition to Communism, and pledging their cooperative
efforts against Communist activities. In addition, the United States
sent arms, equipment, and military missions to a number of Latin
American countries.

The Cold War did not change the basic goals of the Latin
American policy of the United States. The descriptive term "anti-
Communist" was added to the vocabulary describing these goals,
but this was synonymous with the meaning attached to the words
"order" and "stability." The Cold War did have some serious effects
on the tactics employed by the United States to help maintain
stability. American aid of a military nature was increasingly
extended to leaders expressing anti-Communist views, and this
tended to hallow certain kinds of stability in an era when pressure

was building up for economic and social changes. As a result, United States policy became even more identified with the old status quo in Latin America, and various protectors of the status quo learned how to obtain military aid by voicing the correct slogans. In the process, dictators such as Fulgencio Batista, Pérez Jiménez, and Rafael Trujillo were decorated, embraced—both literally and figuratively—, and praised as "bulwarks against communism" by the United States government.

Thus, concentration on the Cold War resulted in American officials following the path of least resistance. Traditional definitions and formulas were applied to Latin American problems at a time when many people in this area were defining stability in completely different terms. Social and economic justice were basic elements in this new outlook, but many Americans continued to view stability in terms of external factors. Thus, economic statistics were often taken at face value when in reality these indicated only the prosperity of the upper classes. A relative absence of political unrest was often interpreted as national contentment, when in reality it only indicated a temporary stifling of opposition groups. By failing to look beneath the surface, American officials continued to view Latin America in terms of the past generation.

Storm warnings appeared in the 1950's in Bolivia and Guatemala, and some officials began to see the new realities in Latin America. In 1954, John Moors Cabot—the Assistant Secretary for Latin American Affairs—stated:

Social reform is coming. It may come by evolution or revolution. There are reactionary elements in every country in the hemisphere which do not want social reform. They are willing to tie down the safety valve and wait for the boiler to burst. . . . To my mind there is nothing more dangerous from the viewpoint of long-range American policy than to let the Communists, with their phony slogans, seize the leadership of social reform. We simply cannot afford to identify ourselves with the elements which would tie down the social safety valve.[1]

Such warnings were not heeded until 1958. Vice-President Richard Nixon's spit-covered reception in several countries opened many eyes to the fact that the United States was identified with the old order. The major shock, however, came in 1959–60 when Fidel

Castro implemented sweeping changes in Cuba, and completely reoriented the foreign relations of the island.

After 1958, the United States government began to take the problems of Latin America more seriously. Increased economic aid and the Inter-American Development Bank were the first fruits of this new concern. These were in the old tradition of the Good Neighbor Policy of the 1930's, and reflected the "trickle down" theory of economics. A new program was launched in 1961 by President John F. Kennedy. His "Alliance for Progress" stressed the need for internal social and economic reform as a concomitant to American aid. The hemispheric conference held at Punta del Este, Uruguay in August 1961 indicated the dilemmas posed by this policy. Most of the Latin American leaders were enthusiastic about increased economic cooperation, but the delegations from several key nations forced a modification of the proposed supervisory role of the United States. Whether these nations will undertake the necessary reforms, and whether the program will be too late to prevent revolutionary changes, are still unanswered questions.

Between 1946 and 1959, United States-Cuban relations were generally characterized by friendly cooperation, and growing economic ties. By 1956 the United States Department of Commerce could report: "This intimate economic relationship is so much the outgrowth of mutually helpful association that many of the problems that have plagued less close relationships in other areas have largely been avoided in Cuba."[2]

The island was also a vigorous participant in the hemispheric aspects of the Cold War. Cuba was one of the first countries in Latin America to sign a Mutual Defense Assistance Agreement with the United States in 1952. In March 1952 Fulgencio Batista ousted President Carlos Prío Socarrás, and announced that Cuba fully supported the United States in the Cold War. Batista's anti-Communism was more vocal than real, however. The Communists in Cuba had lost power and prestige between 1947 and 1952, but under Batista they were able to revive. The Soviet Union broke off diplomatic relations with Cuba in April 1952, but this did not prevent Batista from utilizing the services of Cuban Communists in his government.

Batista was regarded by many American officials as a rock of stability in the Caribbean. Cuba was one of the major Caribbean recipients of military aid in the 1950's, and military advisors from the United States helped to train the Cuban Army. Cuba was far from stable, however. Batista was faced with sporadic riots and uprisings which were symbolic of the growing dissatisfaction of large segments of the Cuban populace. Much of this opposition to Batista was unorganized, but during 1957 the 26th of July Movement—led by Fidel Castro—became the major nucleus of anti-Batista activities. In reaction to the guerilla tactics of Castro's rebels, the Batista government became even more dictatorial. By late 1958 Batista's army began to disintegrate as the Castro rebels moved out of the Sierra Maestra Mountains and the rebels of the *Directorio Revolucionario* advanced from the Escambray Mountains. On New Year's Eve 1958, Batista and various ranking colleagues hastily departed from Cuba, and the bearded militia of Fidel Castro took control of the island.

January 1, 1959 marked the beginning of one of the most chaotic periods in the history of United States-Cuban relations. On the one hand Fidel Castro, a messianic idealist, came to power with visions of radical economic reforms, and with a strong distrust for the United States government. The power of American businessmen in Cuba, United States aid to Batista, and the long history of American predominance in the Caribbean provided part of the background for this distrust. On the other hand, the United States government pursued an ambivalent policy toward the revolution, both before and after Castro's victory. American military aid to Batista had been terminated early in 1958, but American military advisors remained in Cuba until Castro sent them home. In November 1957 the United States Air Force bestowed the Legion of Merit on the commander of Batista's Air Force, and Marine General Lemuel C. Shepherd toasted Batista as a "great general" and a "great president."[3]

The United States government quickly recognized the new government of Cuba, and then proceeded to adopt a wait-and-see policy. The United States, however, was not prepared to accept radical social and economic reforms of a socialistic nature. Phillip Bonsal—who had been instrumental in moderating the Bolivian Revolution—became the new Ambassador to Cuba. Castro visited the United States in April, and was given a cautious reception

marked by President Dwight Eisenhower's golfing expedition and
an interview with Secretary of State Christian Herter in a hotel
room. In May 1959 Castro announced his agrarian reform program, and Ambassador Bonsal moved to moderate it. From this
point on relations between Cuba and the United States steadily
deteriorated. Frustrated by the ambivalence of the United States
and desperately seeking the economic means to continue his
grandiose reform program, Castro began to turn to the pro-Soviet
members of the 26th of July Movement. In the process the Cuban
Communist Party—the only organized political force—began to
move into positions of power. Beginning in late 1959, this gradual
movement caught the anti-Communist officials of the Cuban government by surprise, and they lacked both the organization and
the personal prestige which was needed to take the revolution
away from the new *caudillo*.

During 1960 the Cuban government seized most of the property
owned by Americans. The unfilled portion of the 1960 Cuban
sugar quota was drastically cut in July by the United States government. In October an embargo was placed on a wide variety of
exports to Cuba. The United States broke off diplomatic relations
with Cuba in January 1961 after Castro demanded an immediate
and drastic cut in United States Embassy personnel.

In April 1961 a varied group of Cuban exiles attempted an
invasion of the island. This expedition was sponsored by the Central Intelligence Agency, but it turned into a monumental failure.
After this abortive attempt at direct action, the new administration of John F. Kennedy began to lay the foundation for a renewed
effort to obtain inter-American backing for an anti-Castro policy.
During 1961 Castro strengthened his ties with the Soviet bloc, and
on July 26, 1961 he announced the merger of the 26th of July
Movement and the Communist Party. The White Paper issued by
the United States government in December 1961 declared that
Cuba was irrevocably bound to the Soviet bloc.

In three years Castro had instituted several reforms, and created
a thorough police state. Fidel Castro had found what appeared to
be a short cut to utopia, but the path led directly into the Communist empire. The full implications of this connection will probably not be apparent to the Cuban people for some time. The dis-

tance between Soviet Russia and Cuba provides the latter with more freedom of action than the states of eastern Europe, and the Soviet bloc will probably continue to subsidize the Cuban economy for display purposes. In time, however, the present supporters of Castro—with the exception of the hard-core Communists—may see the tragedy involved in their revolution; a tragedy involving a jump from the frying-pan of the old Cuba into the fire of totalitarianism without seeking a workable alternative.

Perhaps it has taken the Cuban experience to shock the United States into a realization that ignorance about conditions in Latin America, complacent support for the crumbling status quo, slogans about "Good Neighbors," and military aid alone can add up to a situation which opens a Pandora's box of complications. A new generation of impatient, ambitious, and messianic *caudillos* stand ready to follow Soviet leadership in reconstructing the old social and economic order. If the United States is to preserve its claims to leadership in the hemisphere, it must develop an intelligent policy which will help the nations of Latin America to overcome their problems, and to make social justice a living reality. There is still a chance that this can be done without resorting to totalitarian methods, if the present leaders of the hemisphere—north and south—will make a reasonable effort to substitute the Christian ethic of responsibility for one's brother, for the laissez-faire materialism which still conditions too much of the thinking of both Latin Americans and North Americans.

What of the future of United States-Cuban relations? Only a reckless prophet would advance a dogmatic estimate at this time. This much is clear. Whatever happens in Cuba must be the work of Cubans. The United States may be able to help, but in the end the solution to the Cuban problem can only be made by Cubans who are dedicated to the welfare of all the Cuban people. Nonintervention is a myth, but the intervention of the United States can only end in fiasco if it does not have the support of substantial numbers of Cubans. The old order cannot be reimposed on Cuba, and utopia cannot be built by firing squads. It will require intelligence and patience for the United States to help Cuba— and other Latin American countries—find a course between these extremes.

The value of American .investments in Cuba began to increase
after 1946. By the late 1950's direct investments amounted to approximately $850 million, and portfolio investments totaled ap-
proximately $210.9 million. These were the only foreign invest-
ments of any importance and they have been reduced to practically
nothing by the Castro Government. Prior to 1959, however, the
United States Department of Commerce considered Cuba an excellent investment risk as indicated in Document 1.

The sugar marketing system was renewed by Congress in 1948,
1952, and 1956. Some modifications were made, but the general
structure of the system remained the same. The domestic and
insular sugar producers fought for higher quotas during each
renewal debate. The State Department was the major defender
of the Cuban sugar quota until 1960. The one-year extension of
the sugar marketing system was rushed through Congress in late
June and early July 1960. This act eliminated the remainder of the
Cuban quota for 1960, and the quota for the Dominican Republic
was practically quadrupled. The act passed in 1961 excluded Cuba,
increased the domestic producer's quota, and left an uncommitted
quota to be assigned to Cuba in the event that a government
friendly to the United States would replace the Castro regime.

DOCUMENT 1.   United States Investments and the Cuban
Economy, 1956. (U. S. Department of Commerce, *Investment in Cuba: Basic Information for United States Businessmen.* Washington, 1956. Pp. 4–5, 10–11, 32, 159.)

The final major item on the asset side of the development
ledger is the general attitude of the Cuban Government and people
toward private initiative and toward foreign participation in the
country's economic development. These attitudes are reflected in
the nature of Government intervention in economic activities, the
rights and privileges of foreigners, the establishment of business
organizations, and the general incidence of taxation.

While the Government does intervene in economic activities,
particularly in sugar and a few other basic commodities, intervention has been largely regulatory rather than operational in nature.
Further, it has resulted primarily from efforts to meet the social
and economic problems which plagued the country from the middle
1920's down to the outbreak of World War II rather than from

any particular ideological tendencies on the part of the Government or people of Cuba.

No better illustration of the foregoing has arisen than in sugar and banking. Domestic control of both of these all-important sectors of the economy was lost in the crash of 1921 and was not regained until the late 1940's, yet Cuba refrained from recourse to the confiscatory legislation which has marred the records of many of the underdeveloped countries.

A high degree of equality prevails in the treatment of foreigners and Cubans. Thus, the Constitution of 1940 provides that aliens have the same status as Cubans in the protection of their persons and property and the enjoyment of rights, except as the latter may be specifically modified by law. Such exceptions are principally in the field of employment, although the Constitution of 1940 contemplates that the acquisition and possession of land by foreigners will at some time be restricted by law.

✦ ✦ ✦ ✦ ✦

Another major obstacle to development is the attitude of labor. This is a human problem and one that can be more easily understood than remedied. Briefly stated, Cuba suffers from both chronic unemployment and chronic underemployment induced by the highly seasonal nature of its major agricultural pursuits and the lack of complementary employment opportunities. At the height of the sugar season in 1953, for example, when employment reached a maximum, 8.4 percent of the labor force was unemployed. Thereafter, unemployment rose to an estimated 20 percent in the rainy or dead season. In contrast, the unemployment in the United States in 1953 was 2.4 percent.

The fear of being left without a job pervades the thinking of labor and has led to strong support of union organization, rigid seniority rules, featherbedding, almost insurmountable obstacles to the dismissal of unsatisfactory workers, and opposition to mechanization and to the adoption of more efficient production methods. A distinct improvement has occurred in recent years, however, in the atmosphere of labor-management relations. This has resulted primarily from a more balanced Government emphasis on the rights and interests of labor, management, and the public. Declining economic activities have also had an influence in moderating excessive demands.

Labor relations continue to require understanding and expert handling. The dismissal of unsatisfactory employees and the adoption of improved production methods are among the most difficult problems faced by management. In practice, indemnified dismis-

sals are frequently arranged. Also, new industries, particularly
those in new fields of activity, frequently install the latest in modern equipment and adopt the most advanced industrial practices
with the cooperation rather than the opposition of labor organizations.

    ✓   ✓   ✓   ✓   ✓

The only foreign investments of importance are those of the
United States. American participation exceeds 90 percent in the
telephone and electric services, about 50 percent in public service
railways, and roughly 40 percent in raw sugar production. The
Cuban branches of United States banks are entrusted with almost
one-fourth of all bank deposits. This intimate economic relationship is so much the outgrowth of mutually helpful association that
many of the problems that have plagued less close relationships in
other areas have largely been avoided in Cuba.

Cuba ranked third in Latin America in the value of United
States direct investments in 1953, outranked only by Venezuela and
Brazil. However, in 1929, Cuba had ranked first in Latin America.
United States investments declined 25.4 percent in value between
1929 and 1953, in the face of an overall increase of 74.3 percent
in total United States investments in the Latin American area
during that period. Further, after the trend of investment in Cuba
began moving upward subsequent to 1946, the rate of increase
has been the lowest of any of the major Latin American countries.

    ✓   ✓   ✓   ✓   ✓

The very substantial decline in the value of United States investments during the depression was largely due to financial read-
justments resulting from the crash of 1929, which heavily affected
the value of almost all United States holdings in Cuba.

    ✓   ✓   ✓   ✓   ✓

The explanation for the slow growth of United States investments in Cuba in the post-World War II period is a fairly simple
one in view of the fact that, of the $3 billion added to direct
United States investments in all of Latin America since 1946, the
most important were about $1 billion for petroleum projects, $750
million for manufacturing, and $500 million for mining. No petro-
leum resources have as yet been found in Cuba warranting other
than exploratory expenditures; metallurgical difficulties hindered
the development of the extremely important nickel deposits until
recently and still prevent exploration of the potentially valuable
iron ore reserves, investment in sugar has reached an apparent
saturation point; and conditions for manufacturing investments
have not been too favorable until quite recently.

In the field of public utilities, heavy investments have been made in power, but an important telephone expansion program has been held up for 6 years by an antiquated rate structure. Additional investments in railways are unlikely, given the financial outlook in Cuba for this mode of transportation.

The foregoing does not warrant the conclusion, however, that the decade ahead will be barren of new United States investments. Projects announced through 1955 assure United States investments of $205 million during the period 1955–60 in electric power, refining, mining, and manufacturing.

The outlook for additional investments is also good. Public demand for an increase in telephone service will almost certainly facilitate a solution of the present impasse which has been delaying a much-needed expansion program. Metallurgical advances may bring additional foreign capital into mining ventures; large sums are scheduled to be risked in the next 3 years in petroleum exploration; and increasing protectionist sentiment suggests growing interest from abroad in Cuban industrial opportunities.

꜡ ꜡ ꜡ ꜡ ꜡

Large landholdings, such as those of the sugar companies, have given rise to considerable agitation in the past few decades. The problem has never reached critical proportions, however, even though demands for land reform gathered such momentum in the thirties as to lead to the inclusion of provisions in the Constitution of 1940 proscribing large landholdings and providing for the fixing by law of the maximum amount of land to be held by a person or entity. The Constitution also provides that the acquisition and possession of land by foreigners may be restricted by law. The only legislation implementing any of the foregoing provisions was that passed in 1948 affecting the rental of rural property by foreigners.

꜡ ꜡ ꜡ ꜡ ꜡

Sole proprietors subject to the profits tax and all companies, whether civil or mercantile, domestic or foreign, are required to pay an annual tax of 5 pesos for each 1,000 pesos, or fraction, of declared capital. The declared capital need have no relation to the capital with which the taxpayer is actually operating in Cuba. Taxpayers may freely determine the amount of the capital they wish to report and may change the amount from year to year.

꜡ ꜡ ꜡ ꜡ ꜡

The tax on excess profits is a tax of 25 percent on all profits exceeding 10 percent of the capital declared each year for the purpose of the 5 pesos per 1,000 pesos tax on declared capital. This tax is therefore related to the tax on capital since taxpayers declaring a small capital and showing large profits are required to pay a heavier excess profits tax. The taxpayer, therefore, eliminates his expected profits of the year and declares a capital at least 10 times greater than the anticipated profits.

DOCUMENT 2. Statement by Henry F. Holland (Assistant Secretary of State for Inter-American Affairs) Concerning the Cuban Sugar Quota, 1956. (U. S. Senate, Committee on Finance, *Hearings on Sugar Act Extension.* 84th Cong., 2nd Sess., 1956. Washington, 1956. Pp. 19–21.)

It is the view of the Department that it would be unwise to allocate to the full-duty countries more than 40 percent of the foreign share of increases in consumption during the period of the bill. The Department is opposed to any larger increase, expecially [*sic*] in view of our normal dependence on Cuba for emergency supplies of sugar and the current depressed economic situation of the Cuban sugar industry, and also the fact that Cuba is the country which is most directly affected by the increase in the domestic share.

I should like to call your special attention to the fact that to adopt legislation less favorable to Cuba than that recommended by the executive branch would mean a further worsening of economic conditions in Cuba. Cuba's sugar production has already been reduced from 8 million tons in 1952 to 5 million in 1955. Cuba, a small country with a population of about 6 million is financing a surplus of sugar well in excess of 1 million tons in addition to necessary carry-over. The Cuban Government estimates that, because of the cutback already made in its sugar production, salaries in the industry have had to be reduced by approximately 13 percent. The take-home pay of workers has been reduced by a further 27 percent cut during the "dead season" which is, of course, now of longer duration because of the cutback in production. Care is obviously required to avoid action which would materially worsen Cuba's present economic position particularly since Cuba has always been our largest source of sugar as well as our most readily expansible source of additional sugar in event of emergency.

And I might add, Mr. Chairman, that it is probably known to you and to the members of the Committee that Cuba is our sixth best customer in the world for United States exports. It is, I believe, the major customer for a number of our agricultural products, including beans, ham, lard, bacon, rice, and certain others that don't come to my mind at this time.

✶   ✶   ✶   ✶   ✶

I believe that the recommendations of the executive branch regarding sugar legislation reflect one of the finest bipartisan aspects of United States policy in this hemisphere, that is, our desire by every practical means to expand and strengthen inter-American trade. As you know, the major part of our sugar imports come from Latin America. The enormous trade now being carried on between the nations of this hemisphere is one of the principal factors which account for the amazing economic progress that is going on in Latin America. It is also an important factor in our own prosperity. Twenty-seven percent of all our exports are sold in Latin America, more than in any other comparable area of the world. Thirty-four percent of all our imports come from the Latin American Republics. About 37 percent of all United States direct investment abroad is in this area. The benefits to all of us of protecting and increasing this great volume of trade are obvious.

•   •   •

On July 26, 1953, a small group of Cubans under the leadership of Fidel Castro attacked the Moncada Barracks in Santiago de Cuba. Castro and a few others survived this bloody fiasco, but were captured and brought to trial. Acting as his own attorney, Castro delivered a lengthy oration to the court. No official transcript was made at the trial, but a few reporters took down the speech stenographically. One reporter gave a copy to a group of Cubans who published it in June 1954. The speech in its entirety is a magnificent defense of the rights of man, and a blueprint for economic reform. Miss Teresa Casuso—a former official in the Castro government—has charged that the versions of the speech published after 1959 contain "statements which describe subsequent events, but which Fidel never made at the trial."[4] According to Miss Casuso, these additions were made in the part of the speech concerning the economic and political plans of the revolutionary movement (Document 3). It is difficult to prove or disprove this charge, but certain sentences in the presentation of the proposed "five revolutionary laws" sound like ex post facto descriptions rather than the Fidel Castro of 1953.

Castro was released from prison in 1955, and went to Mexico

to organize an invasion of Cuba. On December 2, 1956, the poorly organized landing took place, but only Castro and eleven others managed to escape into the Sierra Maestra Mountains. For the next two years a handful of American newsmen provided the major link between the rebels and the outside world. The first American reporter to locate Fidel Castro and to write about the revolution was Herbert Matthews of *The New York Times*. In February 1957 Mr. Matthews and a small group of Cubans made a secret trip into the Sierra Maestra Mountains. After an interview with Castro, Matthews brought to the outside world the first real news about the revolution in Cuba. The Batista government had been declaring that Castro and his followers were dead, but Matthews' report demolished this fabrication. In addition, Matthews' analysis of the Castro movement proved to be quite accurate. Some Americans, however, have ignored this aspect of the report.

DOCUMENT 3.   Fidel Castro's Speech Before the Emergency Session of the Court of Santiago de Cuba, October 16, 1953. (Fidel Castro, *History Will Absolve Me*, New York, 1961. Pp. 33–39.)[5]

I stated that the second consideration on which we based our chances for success was one of social order because we were assured of the people's support. When we speak of the people we do not mean the comfortable ones, the conservative elements of the nation, who welcome any regime of oppression, any dictatorship, any despotism, prostrating themselves before the master of the moment until they grind their foreheads into the ground. When we speak of struggle, the *people* means the vast unredeemed masses, to whom all make promises and whom all deceive; we mean the people who yearn for a better, more dignified and more just nation; who are moved by ancestral aspirations of justice, for they have suffered injustice and mockery, generation after generation; who long for great and wise changes in all aspects of their life; people, who, to attain these changes, are ready to give even the very last breath of their lives—when they believe in something or in someone, especially when they believe in themselves. In stating a purpose, the first condition of sincerity and good faith, is to do precisely what nobody else ever does, that is, to speak with absolute clarity, without fear. The demagogues and professional politicians who manage to perform the miracle of being right in everything and in pleasing everyone, are, of necessity, deceiving everyone about everything. The revolutionaries must proclaim their ideas courageously, define their principles and express their intentions so that no one is deceived, neither friend nor foe.

✓   ✓   ✓   ✓   ✓

In the brief of this cause there must be recorded the five revolutionary laws that would have been proclaimed immediately after the capture of the Moncada barracks and would have been broadcast to the nation by radio. It is possible that Colonel Chaviano[6] may deliberately have destroyed these documents, but even if he has done so, I conserve them in my memory.

The First Revolutionary Law would have returned power to the people and proclaimed the Constitution of 1940 the supreme Law of the land, until such time as the people should decide to modify or change it. And, in order to effect its implementation and punish those who had violated it—there being no organization for holding elections to accomplish this—the revolutionary movement, as the momentous incarnation of this sovereignty, the only source of legitimate power, would have assumed all the facilities inherent to it, except that of modifying the Constitution itself: In other words it would have assumed the legislative, executive and judicial powers.

✓   ✓   ✓   ✓   ✓

The Second Revolutionary Law would have granted property, not mortgageable and not transferable, to all planters, sub-planters, lessees, partners and squatters who hold parcels of five or less "caballerias"[7] of land, and the state would indemnify the former owners on the basis of the rental which they would have received for these parcels over a period of ten years.

The Third Revolutionary Law would have granted workers and employees the right to share 30% of the profits of all the large industrial, mercantile and mining enterprises, including the sugar mills. The strictly agricultural enterprises would be exempt in consideration of other agrarian laws which would have been implemented.

The Fourth Revolutionary Law would have granted all planters the right to share 55% of the sugar production and a minimum quota of forty thousand "arrobas"[8] for all small planters who have been established for three or more years.

The Fifth Revolutionary Law would have ordered the confiscation of all holdings and ill-gotten gains of those who had com-

mitted frauds during previous regimes, as well as the holdings and
ill-gotten gains of all their legatees and heirs. To implement this,
special courts with full powers would gain access to all records
of all corporations registered or operating in this country [in order]
to investigate concealed funds of illegal origin, and to request that
foreign governments extradite persons and attach holdings [right-
fully belonging to the Cuban people]. Half of the property recovered would be used to subsidize retirement funds for workers and
the other half would be used for hospitals, asylums and charitable
organizations.

Furthermore, it was to be declared that the Cuban policy in the
Americas would be one of close solidarity with the democratic
people of this continent, and that those politically persecuted by
bloody tyrants oppressing our sister nations would find generous
asylum, brotherhood, and bread in the land of Marti. Not the
persecution, hunger and treason that they find today. Cuba should
be the bulwark of liberty and not a shameful link in the chain of
despotism.

These laws would have been proclaimed immediately, as soon
as the upheaval were ended and prior to a detailed and far-reaching study, they would have been followed by another series of laws
and fundamental measures, such as, the Agrarian Reform, Integral
Reform of Education, nationalization of the Utilities Trust and the
Telephone Trust, refund to the people of the illegal excessive rates
this company has charged, and payment to the Treasury of all
taxes brazenly evaded in the past.

All these laws and others would be inspired in the exact fulfillment of two essential articles of our Constitution. One of these
orders the outlawing of feudal estates by indicating the maximum
area of land any person or entity can possess for each type of
agricultural enterprise, by adopting measures which would tend
to revert the land to the Cubans. The other categorically orders
the State to use all means at its disposal to provide employment
to all those who lack it and to insure a decent livelihood to each
manual laborer or intellectual.

None of these articles may be called unconstitutional. The
first popularly elected government would have to respect these
laws, not only because of moral obligation to the nation, but because when people achieve something they have yearned for
throughout generations, no force in the world is capable of taking
it away again.

The problems concerning land, the problem of industrialization,
the problem of housing, the problem of unemployment, the prob-

lem of education and the problem of the health of the people; these are the six problems we would take immediate steps to resolve, along with the restoration of public liberties and political democracy.

Perhaps this exposition appears cold and theoretical if one does not know the shocking and tragic conditions of the country with regard to these six problems, to say nothing of the most humiliating political oppression.

85% of the small farmers in Cuba pay rent and live under the constant threat of being dispossessed from the land that they cultivate. More than half the best cultivated land belongs to foreigners. In *Oriente,* the largest province, the lands of the United Fruit Company and West India Company join the north coast to the southern one. There are two hundred thousand peasant families who do not have a single acre of land to cultivate to provide food for their starving children. On the other hand, nearly three hundred thousand "caballerias" of productive land owned by powerful interests remains uncultivated.

Cuba is above all an agricultural state. Its population is largely rural. The city depends on these rural areas. The rural people won the Independence. The greatness and prosperity of our country depends on a healthy and vigorous rural population that loves the land and knows how to cultivate it, within the framework of a state that protects and guides them. Considering all this, how can the present state of affairs be tolerated any longer?

XIV

With the exception of a few food, lumber and textile industries, Cuba continues to be a producer of raw materials. We export sugar to import candy, we export hides to import shoes, we export iron to import plows. Everybody agrees that the need to industrialize the country is urgent, that we need steel industries, paper and chemical industries; that we must improve cattle and grain products, the technique and the processing in our food industry, in order to balance the ruinous competition of the Europeans in cheese products, condensed milk, liquors and oil, and that of the Americans in canned goods; that we need merchant ships; that tourism should be an enormous source of revenue. But the capitalists insist that the workers remain under a Claudian yoke; the State folds its arms and industrialization can wait for the Greek calends.

Just as serious or even worse is the housing problem. There are two hundred thousand huts and hovels in Cuba; four hundred thousand families in the country and in the cities live cramped into barracks and tenements without even the minimum sanitary requirements; two million two hundred thousand of our urban population pay rents which absorb between one fifth and one third of their income; and two million eight hundred thousand of our rural and suburban population lack electricity. If the State proposes lowering rents, landlords threaten to freeze all construction; if the State does not interfere, construction goes on so long as the landlords get high rents, otherwise, they would not lay a single brick even though the rest of the population should have to live exposed to the elements. The utilities monopoly is no better: they extend lines as far as it is profitable and beyond that point, they don't care if the people have to live in darkness for the rest of their lives. The State folds its arms and the people have neither homes nor electricity.

Our educational system is perfectly compatible with the rest of our national situation. Where the *guajiro* is not the owner of his land, what need is there for agricultural schools? Where there are no industries what need is there for technical or industrial schools? Everything falls within the same absurd logic: there is neither one thing nor the other. In any small European country there are more than 200 technical and industrial arts schools; in Cuba, there are only six such schools, and the boys graduate without having anywhere to use their skills. The little rural schools are attended by only half the school-age children—barefoot, half-naked and undernourished—and frequently the teacher must buy necessary materials from his own salary. Is this the way to make a nation great?

XV

Only death can liberate one from such misery. In this, however—early death—the state is most helpful. 90% of the rural children are consumed by parasites which filter through their bare feet from the earth. Society is moved to compassion upon hearing of the kidnapping or murder of one child, but they are criminally indifferent to the mass murder of so many thousands of children who die every year from lack of facilities, agonizing with pain. Their innocent eyes—death already shining in them—seem to look into infinity as if entreating forgiveness for human selfishness, as if asking God to stay his wrath. When the head of a family works only four months a year, with what can he purchase clothing and medicine for his children? They will grow up with rickets, with not a single good tooth in their mouths by the time they reach thirty; they will have heard ten million speeches and will finally die of misery and deception. Public hospitals, which are always full, accept only patients recommended by some powerful politician who, in turn demands the electoral votes of the unfortunate one and his family so that Cuba may continue forever the same or worse.

DOCUMENT 4. Herbert Matthews Documents the Existence of a Revolution in Cuba, and Provides the First Analysis of the Castro Movement. (The New York Times, February 24, 1957).[9]

Fidel Castro, the rebel leader of Cuba's youth, is alive and fighting hard and successfully in the rugged, almost impenetrable fastnesses of the Sierra Maestra, at the southern tip of the island.

President Fulgencio Batista has the cream of his Army around the area, but the Army men are fighting a thus-far losing battle to destroy the most dangerous enemy General Batista has yet faced in a long and adventurous career as a Cuban leader and dictator.

This is the first sure news that Fidel Castro is still alive and still in Cuba. No one connected with the outside world, let alone with the press, has seen Señor Castro except this writer. No one in Havana, not even at the United States Embassy with all its resources for getting information, will know until this report is published that Fidel Castro is really in the Sierra Maestra.

This account, among other things, will break the tightest censorship in the history of the Cuban Republic. The Province of Oriente, with its 2,000,000 inhabitants, its flourishing cities such as Santiago, Holguin and Manzanillo, is shut off from Havana as surely as if it were another country. Havana does not and cannot know that thousands of men and women are heart and soul with Fidel Castro and the new deal for which they think he stands. It does not know that hundreds of highly respected citizens are helping Señor Castro, that bombs and sabotage are constant (eighteen bombs were exploded in Santiago on February 15), that a fierce Government counterterrorism has aroused the people even more against President Batista.

Throughout Cuba a formidable movement of opposition to General Batista has been developing. It has by no means reached an explosive point. The rebels in the Sierra Maestra cannot move out. The economic situation is good. President Batista has the high officers of the Army and the police behind him and he ought to be able to hang on for the nearly two years of his present term that are still left.

However, there are bad spots in the economy, especially on the fiscal side. Unemployment is heavy; corruption is rife. No one can predict anything with safety except that Cuba seems in a very troubled period.

Fidel Castro and his 26th of July Movement are the flaming symbol of the opposition to the regime. The organization, which is apart from the university students' opposition, is formed of youths of all kinds. It is a revolutionary movement that calls itself socialistic. It is also nationalistic, which generally in Latin America means anti-Yankee.

The program is vague and couched in generalities, but it amounts to a new deal for Cuba, radical, democratic and therefore anti-Communist. The real core of its strength is that it is fighting against the military dictatorship of President Batista.

✸   ✸   ✸   ✸   ✸

Raul Castro, Fidel's younger brother, slight and pleasant, came into the camp with others of the staff, and a few minutes later Fidel himself strode in. Taking him, as one would at first, by physique and personality, this was quite a man—a powerful six-footer, olive-skinned, full-faced, with a straggly beard. He was dressed in an olive grey fatigue uniform and carried a rifle with a telescopic sight, of which he was very proud. It seems his men have something more than fifty of these and he said the soldiers feared them.

"We can pick them off at a thousand yards with these guns," he said.

After some general conversation we went to my blanket and sat down. Someone brought tomato juice, ham sandwiches made with crackers and tins of coffee. In honor of the occasion, Señor Castro broke open a box of good Havana cigars and for the next three hours we sat there while he talked.

No one could talk above a whisper at any time. There were columns of Government troops all around us, Señor Castro said, and their one hope was to catch him and his band.

The personality of the man is overpowering. It was easy to see that his men adored him and also to see why he has caught the imagination of the youth of Cuba all over the island. Here was an educated, dedicated fanatic, a man of ideals, of courage and of remarkable qualities of leadership.

As the story unfolded of how he had at first gathered the few remnants of the Eighty-two around him; kept the Government troops at bay while youths came in from other parts of Oriente as General Batista's counter-terrorism aroused them; got arms and supplies and then began the series of raids and counter-attacks of guerrilla warfare, one got a feeling that he is now invincible. Perhaps he isn't, but that is the faith he inspires in his followers.

✔   ✔   ✔   ✔   ✔

I asked him about the report that he was going to declare a revolutionary government in the Sierra.

"Not yet," he replied. "The time is not ripe. I will make myself known at the opportune moment. It will have all the more effect for the delay, for now everybody is talking about us. We are sure of ourselves.

"There is no hurry. Cuba is in a state of war but Batista is hiding it. A dictatorship must show that it is omnipotent or it will fall; we are showing that it is impotent."

The Government, he said with some bitterness, is using arms furnished by the United States, not only against him but "against all the Cuban people."

"They have bazookas, mortars, machine guns, planes and bombs," he said, "but we are safe in here in the Sierra; they must come and get us and they cannot."

Señor Castro speaks some English, but he preferred to speak in Spanish, which he did with extraordinary eloquence. His is a political mind rather than a military one. He has strong ideas of liberty, democracy, social justice, the need to restore the Constitution, to hold elections. He has strong ideas on economy too, but an economist would consider them weak.

The 26th of July Movement talks of nationalism, anti-colonialism, anti-imperialism. I asked Señor Castro about that. He answered, "You can be sure we have no animosity toward the United States and the American people."

"Above all," he said, "we are fighting for a democratic Cuba and an end to the dictatorship. We are not anti-military; that is why we let the soldier prisoners go. There is no hatred of the Army as such, for we know the men are good and so are many of the officers.

"Batista has 3,000 men in the field against us. I will not tell you how many we have, for obvious reasons. He works in columns of 200; we in groups of ten to forty, and we are winning. It is a battle against time and time is on our side."

To show that he deals fairly with the guajiros he asked someone to bring "the cash." A soldier brought a bundle wrapped in dark brown cloth, which Señor Castro unrolled. There was a stack of peso bills at least a foot high—about $4,000 he said, adding that he had all the money he needed and could get more.

"Why should soldiers die for Batista for $72 a month?" he asked. "When we win we will give them $100 a month, and they will serve a free, democratic Cuba."

"I am always in the front line," he said; and others confirmed this fact. Such being the case, the Army might yet get him, but in present circumstances he seems almost invulnerable.

"They never know where we are," he said as the group arose to say good-by, "but we always know where they are. You have taken quite a risk in coming here, but we have the whole area covered, and we will get you out safely."

They did. We ploughed our way back through the muddy undergrowth in broad daylight, but always keeping under cover. The scout went like a homing pigeon through woods and across fields where there were no paths straight to a farmer's house on the edge of the Sierra. There we hid in a back room while someone borrowed a horse and went for the jeep, which had been under cover all night.

There was one road block to get through with an Army guard so suspicious our hearts sank, but he let us through.

After that, washed, shaved, and looking once more like an American tourist, with my wife as "camouflage," we had no trouble driving back through the road blocks to safety and then on to Havana. So far as anyone knew, we had been away fishing for the week-end, and no one bothered us as we took the plane to New York.

• • •

Document 5 is an eye-witness account of the last days of the Batista regime. Mrs. Phillips also describes the attitudes of Americans in Cuba toward Batista and the revolution. This presentation helps to explain the background for anti-American feeling in Cuba.

Document 6 presents the views of two men who served as Ambassadors to Cuba in the 1950's. Arthur Gardner and Earl E. T. Smith were asked to testify before the Senate Internal Security Subcommittee in 1960, and their statements reveal the close ties that existed between the United States Embassy and the Batista dictatorship. This hearing was an attempt to prove that a few conspirators in the State Department and Herbert Matthews of *The New York Times* sold Cuba to the Communists. This is a monumental distortion of history, and one that ignores the complexity of human activities. The testimony produced does reveal, however, a major reason for anti-American feeling in Latin America: United States officials who associate and sympathize with the small ruling cliques in many of these countries. An important reason for the ambivalent policy pursued by the United States is also disclosed in these pages. Sharp division of opinion among State Department officials in regard to Batista and Castro helped to produce a policy which more or less drifted with events.

Both Gardner and Smith were devoted to American business interests in Cuba. Gardner served as Ambassador from 1953 to 1957, and was so friendly to Batista that the dictator was embarrassed. With Gardner's aid the Cuban Telephone Company obtained a big rate increase. Batista received a solid gold telephone and stand as a token of appreciation. Ambassador Smith served in Cuba from 1957 to 1959. John Hay Whitney, a large stockholder in the Freeport Sulphur Company, helped Smith to obtain this appointment, and the Ambassador negotiated a tax reduction for Freeport's Cuban subsidiary, the Moa Bay Mining Company. Smith was more objective in dealing with Batista than Gardner had been, but the activities of both men provided reasons for the people who would sing, "*Cuba sí, Yankee no.*"

DOCUMENT 5. Americans in Cuba During the Last Days of the Batista Era, 1957–1958. (R. Hart Phillips, *Cuba: Island of Paradox*. New York, 1959. Pp. 324–28, 335–36, 338–39).[10]

The new American Ambassador, Earl E. T. Smith, arrived and presented his credentials. He was replacing Mr. Arthur Gardner, who had been so pro-Batista that he had actually embarrassed the President. On one occasion Batista said, "I'm glad Ambassador Gardner approves of my government but I wish he wouldn't talk about it so much." With the arrival of Ambassador Smith, the opposition hoped for the best. The Ambassador gave a press conference and said he would be glad to hear about the political situation from all factions. However, most of the opposition representatives were afraid to go near the embassy. I arranged for some of

them to get in contact with the political officers of the embassy.
I thought someone should hear their story.

Ambassador Smith decided to go down to Santiago de Cuba.
Ted Scott and I were at a cocktail party the night before he left.
We told one of the officers of the embassy that undoubtedly the
rebel sympathizers would stage a demonstration, but he didn't
seem to agree with us. When the Ambassador arrived in Santiago
de Cuba on July 31, 1957, he went to the City Hall to receive the
keys of the city. As the ceremony ended a group of about one
hundred women dressed in black gathered in front of City Hall
shouting, "Libertad! Libertad!" and carrying placards protesting
the "reign of terror" in the city. The police broke up the demonstration with fire hose and roughed up the women, dragging thirty
of them off to jail. Several thousand spectators gathered to see
the demonstration which had been of course planned. The Ambassador, annoyed over the police methods which he saw there, issued
a statement: "I deplore the excessive action of the police."

That afternoon Santiago de Cuba buried Frank Pais and a
companion who had been killed "in a gun battle." Later however
it was revealed they had been captured and tortured to death.
Frank Pais was the son of a Presbyterian minister and a leader of
the "26th of July" revolutionary movement in Santiago. Almost
every person in Santiago de Cuba turned out for the funeral.
Thousands marched to the cemetery. Youths hauled down the
Cuban flag on the cemetery flagpole and ran up the black and red
rebel flag. The army had been withdrawn from the streets by the
military authorities, who feared a massacre, especially with Mr.
Smith present to witness it.

Ambassador Smith's statement about excessive police action
caused a furor in Havana. The press headlined the intention of the
Cuban government to ask for the Ambassador's recall. Senator José
Gonzalez Puente issued a statement that "The Republic of Cuba
rejects and repudiates interference in matters of Cuban sover-
eignty . . ." The United States State Department hastily assured
Batista that the United States "had no intention of interfering in
Cuba's internal affairs." A motion was presented in the United
States Congress asking for the immediate withdrawal of Ambassa-
dor Smith. Congress is never informed on what goes on in Latin
American countries. Congress, time after time, has undermined the
authority of our best diplomats.

President Batista suspended constitutional guarantees for the
fourth time since Fidel Castro landed. Censorship was imposed.

Foreign publications were censored also. *The New York Times* arrived at my office with a gaping hole on the front page. I usually obtained a copy uncensored since a minor government employee, who had to cut out the articles indicated by the secret police, always saved me an uncut copy which I claimed, to people who saw it in the office, had been brought to me from Miami.

    ❀   ❀   ❀   ❀   ❀

In Havana, Christmas was gay, but the prisons were full and the armed forces prowled the streets like big cats looking for someone to pounce on. Money was flowing freely in the western provinces. The sugar workers had been given a bonus, seventeen million dollars, which they promptly spent for Christmas. There were many tourists in the capital city and night life was lavish. Christmas trees, adopted by the Cubans during the past several years, appeared everywhere. In every house, from mansion to hovel, there was a Christmas tree and the stores were filled with shoppers. The new Havana Riviera opened with a gala fiesta. Tourists arriving in Havana asked where the revolution was and were told it was only a minor disturbance seven hundred miles away. American businessmen told me that I was contributing to the ruin of the economy by stories of the rebellion. Both American and Cuban businessmen were annoyed. With Cuba so prosperous and money so plentiful, they couldn't understand why anyone would support a revolution. They wanted Batista to crush the Fidel Castro rebellion so they could "get on with business."

    ❀   ❀   ❀   ❀   ❀

The English-speaking colony in Havana is made up of Americans, British and Canadians, usually referred to as the "ABC" colony. Owing to the stringent labor laws, designed to prevent foreigners from working in Cuba, most of this colony are executives of companies. This gives the lower classes in Havana the impression that all English-speaking people are wealthy. Also, since the Americans, British and Canadians have similar business and social interests, they tend to group together, admitting into their affairs only Cubans of similar interests and cultural standing. They live comfortably in beautiful houses, for which they pay high rent of course, employ one to three servants, and belong to one or two clubs, such as the American Club, the Rovers Club, the Country Club, Habana Yacht Club and Miramar Club. The number of clubs a man belongs to does not reflect his personal wealth as much as it does his company's expense accounts. There is of course a small group who settled in Cuba many years ago and built up industries or business firms. This group has a different interest in and attitude toward the Cubans, since their fate is tied to that of the island. But the average executive lives here a few years and is then transferred to some other Latin-American, European or Asian country. Conversely, it is easy to find someone who has lived in India, China, Lebanon, Egypt or France. This also applies to the diplomatic corps. It is easy to understand why the "ABC" colony favored Batista, who represented a degree of security for business and industry. They had little interest in the activities of the Castro rebels, except as a possible threat to the stability of their lives.

DOCUMENT 6. Arthur Gardner and Earl E. T. Smith Discuss the Castro Revolution, August 1960. (U.S. Senate, Sub-committee to Investigate the Administration of the Internal Security Act, *Communist Threat to the United States Through the Caribbean*. Washington, 1960. Part IX, Pp. 665–67, 686–87, 692–93, 700, 706–10).

Senator Dodd. Mr. Gardner, you have said in a newspaper interview that the United States was "just 2 years late" in acknowledging that Cuba under Castro is more of a police state than it was under Batista. Will you explain this for us, and perhaps expand on it, if you can?

Mr. Gardner. Well, during the time that I was there, the last year, Castro had landed, and was hiding in the hills. And there had been an endless number of shipments of arms and other things to Castro, which could only come from the United States. Every once in a while we were able to catch such a shipment, and stop it. But we were not very active about it. And one factor which I think was one of the most serious was that the former President, named Prio, was living in Miami. I don't know whether you know it or not, but he was arrested, convicted, and paid a fine of $5,000 for gunrunning. And he was also indicted a second time. And yet no action was ever taken on it. My personal reason for thinking it was serious was that many times Batista would send for me and ask me why this was. I don't know whether I have gotten off the track here, but that is my answer. The 2 years were 2 years of gradually making Batista feel we were pulling the rug out from under him.

Senator Dodd. Yes.

Mr. Gardner, when did you first have doubt about Castro, do you remember?

Mr. Gardner. Well, I saw a manifesto that he had printed in Mexico, which stated his principles, what he was going to do. He was going to take over the American industries, he was going to nationalize everything. I mean I don't remember the words of this particular manifesto. I have a copy of it in Washington. That, to me, meant only one thing, that this man was a radical. I couldn't tell you how much of a radical.

Senator Dodd. Mr. Gardner, you have been quoted as saying that Washington, "pulled the rug out" from under Batista. Is this a correct quote, and, if so, what did you mean by that?

Mr. Gardner. Yes, I think it is a correct quote, I mean that Batista had always leaned toward the United States. I don't think we ever had a better friend. It was regrettable, like all South Americans, that he was known—although I had no absolute knowledge of it—to be getting a cut, I think is the word for it, in almost all the things that were done. But, on the other hand, he was doing an amazing job, and I will give you a specific example.

Former presidents had built roads, and they put cement on the sand, and he made them put rock ballast in. The other people were doing it because each year they could build a new road, and get their cut. But everything we did, from the time I went there, I think encouraged Batista. Then just at the end he began to get extremely worried about this development. He had made rather insignificant efforts to send troops down to get Castro, but fighting in the mountains was not what the Cuban troops were ever taught. So that when we talk about pulling out the rug, I mean there are a number of factors that occurred repeatedly which showed that the State Department did not want to have anything to do with Batista.

Senator Dodd. Well, would you say that these things that occurred also showed that the State Department was anxious to replace Batista with Castro?

Mr. Gardner. I think they were.

Senator Dodd. Mr. Gardner, you have been quoted as saying that while you were Ambassador to Cuba in 1953 to 1957, you fought all the time with the State Department over whether Castro merited the support or friendship of the United States. Would you explain this for us, and then perhaps more fully develop it, if you can?

Mr. Gardner. Well, it wasn't a question of my officially writing letters, but in my conversations, in my everyday contact with the State Department, I always stressed this point—that I felt that

Batista had proved a great friend to this country, and his administration had proved a great ability to develop the country itself, and develop the friendship with us. And I feel it very strongly, that the State Department was influenced, first, by those stories by Herbert Matthews, and then it became kind of a fetish with them. I mean I don't care about it myself, although most ambassadors are asked to come and be debriefed, but they never asked me. So the only time I ever was able to get into the State Department was making special appointments, and that was only done after—maybe a year after I had actually resigned.

✓   ✓   ✓   ✓   ✓

Mr. Gardner. I had one conversation with Christian Herter, in which I recommended that in order to help him, and help the Cuban picture, and also help the Latin American desk, as they call it, that he should get somebody with the practical know-how, somebody with experience. I mentioned three or four men. One of them was the vice-president of the American Foreign Power. He spent his whole life in countries in Latin America. I mean I mentioned the names of people. And he said, "Well, that sounds very interesting." But he never called me in to do anything about it.

✓   ✓   ✓   ✓   ✓

Mr. Smith. I have been asked many times what part if any the United States played in Castro and Communist rise to power in Cuba. The U. S. Government agencies and the U. S. press played a major role in bringing Castro to power.

Three front-page articles in the *New York Times* in early 1957, written by the editorialist Herbert Matthews, served to inflate Castro to world stature and world recognition. Until that time, Castro had been just another bandit in the Oriente Mountains of Cuba, with a handful of followers who had terrorized the campesinos, that is the peasants, throughout the countryside.

✓   ✓   ✓   ✓   ✓

After the Matthews articles which followed an exclusive interview by the *Times* editorial writer in Castro's mountain hideout and which likened him to Abraham Lincoln, he was able to get followers and funds in Cuba and in the United States. From that time on arms, money, and soldiers of fortune abounded. Much of the American press began to picture Castro as a political Robin Hood.

Also because Batista was the dictator who unlawfully seized power, American people assumed Castro must on the other hand, represent liberty and democracy. The crusader role which the press and radio bestowed on the bearded rebel blinded the people to the leftwing political philosophy with which even at that time he was already on record.

＊　　　＊　　　＊　　　＊　　　＊

From there, to get back to your question, there were a number of times, number of occasions when I was asked as the Ambassador if we would help the church in its efforts to establish a bridge between Castro and Batista, or if we, in any way, would support a national unity government. Such government would act as a provisional government in Cuba to maintain law and order while elections were being held.

The United States would never agree to support or would never permit me to negotiate, because it would be considered as intervening in the internal affairs of Cuba.

Batista made three big mistakes. The last big mistake he made was when he did not hold honest elections, which he had promised me on numerous and many occasions that he would have. Rivero Aguero, the former Prime Minister of Cuba, was elected, I believe it was November 8, 1958, to succeed Batista. It is true, in reply to your question, Senator, that the U.S. Government instructed me through the State Department to say that we would not give aid and support to the Rivero Aguero government when installed because we did not feel that he could maintain effective control of the country. As far as the disintegration of the armed forces around the Batista government, the answer to your last question is that this negative action helped shatter the morale of the existing government. The responsibility for the deterioration in the morale of the army, navy, and Cuban Air Force dates back to many other forms of direct and indirect—I use the word "intervention" advisedly.

Primarily I would say that when we refused to sell arms to the Cuban Government and also by what I termed intervening by innuendo (which was persuading other friendly governments not to sell arms to Cuba) that these actions had a moral, psychological effect upon the Cuban armed forces which was demoralizing to the nth degree.

＊　　　＊　　　＊　　　＊　　　＊

Mr. Smith. I repeat, Senator, I said that nothing specific was said, but I clearly received the impression from my briefings when I was in Washington that we were too close to the Batista government, and when I went to Cuba, I felt that I had three missions.

Two of the missions I planned on arrival in Cuba. The third I
assumed after I got over there. Mission No. 1 was to have the
United States Embassy assume an impartial stand, have it generally understood that the U.S. Embassy took an impartial view
in the political affairs of Cuba.

No. 2, to assist and do everything that I could to see that the
press censorship was lifted and that constitutional guarantees
were again restored. And, No. 3, was to do everything that I could—
without intervening in any way in the internal affairs of Cuba—to
bring about, through Batista, free and open elections.

I was successful in step 1. I was successful in step 2. However,
the revolutionaries stepped up their terroristic activities and forced
Batista to again clamp on the press censorship and to again suspend constitutional guarantees.

Then I concentrated on trying to persuade Batista to hold
free and open elections. On numerous occasions, Batista gave me
his solemn word he would hold honest elections. He not only said
he would hold free and open elections, but he also promised me
that he would ask the world press to witness these elections, that
he would ask the United Nations to send representatives to witness
these elections, that he would ask the Organization of American
States to send representatives to witness these elections. He failed
in that promise.

I have reviewed the answers to these questions a little bit, sir,
because if I answer them yes or no, I am afraid it may give the
wrong interpretation.

Senator Hruska. Mr. Smith, in that same field you have made
several references to pressure on Roy Rubottom. Could you tell
us the source or the nature of this pressure?

Mr. Smith. The pressure on Roy Rubottom came from Members of Congress who it is not necessary for me to name because
you gentlemen know them.

Pressures on Roy Rubottom came from some sections of the
press in the United States. Pressure on Roy Rubottom came from
the representatives and sympathizers of the 26th of July Movement in the United States and particularly those in Washington.

Senator Eastland. What is the name that you named as one
of them who is now President of ——?

Mr. Smith. No, he is not. He has the same name. It is not
the same man. His name was Betancourt. He was the legal official
representative, registered and legally accepted of the Cuban revolutionaries in Washington.

Many of these people, who later became members of the first

Cabinet of Castro were asylees in the United States. They had close contacts with members of the State Department.

To name a few: Urrutia, the first President of Cuba, Agramonte, the first Foreign Minister of Cuba, the first Prime Minister of Cuba, Miro Cardona. . . .

Senator Hruska. Mr. Smith, moving into another area, what was the attitude and what were the manifestations on the part of American investors in Cuba in regard to Batista and Castro prior to the time that Castro actually took charge?

Mr. Smith. I would say that American business was for the Government of Cuba, because the Government of Cuba gave normal protection to American business.

Senator Hruska. What truth is there to some representations that some of the big business investments there, investors there, paid a part of their taxes to Castro and a part of their taxes to Batista in the latter time of Batista's administration?

Mr. Smith. All right, sir; I am glad you brought that question up.

The revolutionaries under Fidel Castro demanded tribute throughout Cuba. By the fall or the late summer of 1958, they decided to also demand tribute from American business and American property holders.

As soon as I heard this, I wrote a letter to every American business in Cuba in which I clearly stated that Americans should not pay tribute, and I asked them not to give any money to the revolutionaries, that we were still doing business with a friendly government, and that as Americans we had no right to pay money to active revolutionaries who were trying to overthrow a friendly government by force.

This letter was approved by the State Department before it was sent out. Every week I regularly had a meeting in my Embassy, of some of the leading businessmen in Havana, and they assured me that the Americans were not paying money.

However, toward the closing days of the Batista regime, I believe some Americans did pay protection money. They were paying taxes to the Batista government and were also paying taxes to the Castro people. I couldn't prove it. They wouldn't let me know.

It was unofficially reported that the revolutionaries demanded $500,000 from a large oil company. Otherwise, the rebels said, they would blow up the refinery of this oil company. The American officials of the company refused to pay tribute. I give you this as an example of what took place.

Senator Hruska. To the extent that it might have gone on,

that would be testimony to the idea that Batista's hold and conrol
and ability to protect property was dissipating?
   Mr. Smith. That is true.

       ✓   ✓   ✓   ✓   ✓

   Senator Eastland. Who were those individuals in the State
Department?
   Mr. Smith. That were doing what, sir?
   Senator Eastland. That were slanting the news that way; that
were telling falsehoods; that were pro-Castro.
   Mr. Smith. There were quite a few, Senator.
   Senator Eastland. Who were they?
   Mr. Smith. I repeat again. Do I have to mention names?
   Senator Eastland. Yes. We have reasons, Mr. Smith.
   Mr. Smith. Yes, sir. You see my point: I do not want to get
people in trouble, either.
   Senator Eastland. Well, I know that.
   Mr. Smith. Because I do not believe that they are dangerous.
If I thought they were dangerous, I would not hesitate.
   Senator Eastland. I am not certain about that.
   Mr. Smith. All right, sir.
   Senator Eastland. We have sources of information.
   Mr. Smith. Yes.
   I believe Wieland, William Wieland, and that is as far as I
would like to go in the State Department. I had my own troubles
in the Embassy, but I corrected it in the Embassy by never allow-
ing one single cable to go out that did not have my signature.
   I wrote practically every political cable that went out.
   Senator Eastland. Who is William Wieland?
   Mr Smith. He is Director of the Caribbean Division and Di-
rector of Mexican Affairs in charge of San Domingo, Cuba, Haiti,
Mexico.
   At that time he had all of Central America in addition to these.
   In an embassy where I served as Ambassador at that time,
when I first went there, I saw the difference. Those in the eco-
nomic field were pro-Batista because they were dealing with
American business. Those in the political section and the intelligence section were pro-revolutionary. We could say for humanitarian reasons, or whatever the reasons may be.

       ✓   ✓   ✓   ✓   ✓

   Senator Eastland. As a matter of fact, now, wasn't it the impartiality of the U. S. Government that brought Castro to power?

Mr. Smith. Wasn't it the impartiality?

Senator Eastland. Yes.

Mr. Smith. Senator, we are responsible for bringing Castro in power. I do not care how you want to word it.

Senator Dodd. Wouldn't you want to say the partiality?

Senator Eastland. I mean the partiality, certainly.

Mr. Smith. Senator, let me explain to you that the United States, until the advent of Castro, was so overwhelmingly influential in Cuba that, as I said here a little while ago, the American Ambassador was the second most important man in Cuba; sometimes even more important than the President.

That is because of the reason of the position that the United States played in Cuba. Now, today, his importance is not very great. . . .

⸙ ⸙ ⸙ ⸙ ⸙

Mr. Sourwine. Former Ambassador Gardner told us there was no question—in his words—"that Mr. Roy Rubottom, while he was in charge of Latin American Affairs for the State Department, favored Castro."

Do you agree with this?

Mr. Smith. Once I had made up my mind, which was obvious, that if Castro succeeded to power, that it was not in the best interests of the United States, and also not in the best interests of Cuba, I used every power within my means to try to have the State Department cooperate with the existing government and to adhere strictly to a nonintervention policy.

I believe that Roy Rubottom, when I first went down to Cuba, would like to have cooperated with the existing regime.

He was, I repeat, under terrific pressure by Members of Congress, I repeat. He was called before a subcommittee such as this on a number of occasions, by the press, by all these various sources that I mentioned. He told me once over the telephone that it was perfectly evident to him now that as far as the sympathy of the United States was concerned, it was no longer with Batista.

I think that is the best answer I can give you to the question.

Senator Eastland. Yet, he yielded to the pressure?

Mr. Smith. He sure yielded, yes sir; he said he did.

Mr. Sourwine. Mr. Smith, did you have, or do you have, any reason to believe that the State Department or State Department officials knew in December 1958 that Castro was coming into power at the end of the year?

Mr. Smith. The State Department knew that Batista was

through in December 1958, and as soon as Batista was through, it was obvious that only one person was going to come into power, and that was Fidel Castro.

*   *   *   *   *

Mr. Sourwine. Mr. Smith, former Ambassador Gardner expressed the view that Castro was a Communist tool rather than being himself an active Communist.

Do you agree with that?

Mr. Smith. Castro was a revolutionary and a terrorist.

From the time that he was a university student, he was a guntoter. I was informed by a diplomat that he had killed one nun and two priests in Bogota during the uprisings in 1948.

I checked very carefully into Mr. Castro's background shortly after I was there and talked to people in Cuba who were anti-Batista but who knew Castro well; I would rather not mention their names because I do not want to get them into trouble. There were many.

There is no question that Castro was a revolutionary and a terrorist but whether he started out as a Communist or not, I doubt. I believe that the beginning of his 26th of July Movement was a leftist revolutionary movement. There are many that exist in the world. But his brother Raul was different; "Che" Guevara was different. Guevara was and is a Marxist.

I do not think there is any question or doubt about their Marxist theories.

But Fidel Castro did make a number of statements at Costa Rica and out of Mexico which clearly showed his Marxist line of thinking. He was also an active member as a student, of the FEU (a radical group).

I brought that to the attention on numerous occasions of various newspaper people when they came down and asked them, when they visited Castro in the hills, whether they would get Castro to repudiate any of these statements. To the best of my knowledge, he never did.

Mr. Sourwine. Is there any doubt in your mind that the Cuban Government, under Castro, is a Communist government?

Mr. Smith. Now?

Mr. Sourwine. Yes.

Mr. Smith. I would go further. I believe it is becoming a satellite.

*   *   *   *   *

Mr. Sourwine. I have just one or two more questions, sir.

Do you, or did you, know General Tabernilla, the former chief of staff of the Cuban Army?

Mr. Smith. Yes, sir.

Mr. Sourwine. General Tabernilla has told this committee that just before he resigned his post, he conferred with you.

Mr. Smith. That is correct.

Mr. Sourwine. Do you remember this? Can you give us briefly the gist of that conference?

Mr. Smith. I believe it was the day after Christmas, December 26, 1958. I received word from the military attaché that General Tabernilla, who was in charge of all the Armed Forces of Cuba, and his son, Gen. Carlos Tabernilla, who was in charge of the Air Force, and Gen. Del Rio Chaviano, who had formerly been in charge of the forces in Oriente Province, wanted to have an interview.

So it was arranged at the American Embassy.

They arrived in their police cars and they came into the Embassy residence.

General Tabernilla said he wished to talk with me alone and his son and the other general went into the adjoining room.

At the time General Tabernilla said that the Cuban soldiers would not fight any longer and that the Cuban Government, per se, would not be able to last.

He stated that the purpose of his visit to me was to save Cuba from chaos, Castro, and communism.

He said he wanted to form a military junta comprised of himself, I believe the names were General Cantillo, General Soa Quensada, Colonel Casores, and an officer of the navy.

He said that they wanted to give Batista safe convoy out of the country, wanted to know whether I would support such a junta.

I said that I would report the conversation to the State Department, but that I was sure they would not give me a direct reply to give to him, and I said that would be correct, because I added:

"If we answer you directly, it would be undermining General Batista, and I can only do business with Batista because I am accredited to him."

General Tabernilla asked me what suggestions I had to make.

I said, "Have you mentioned this visit to me to Batista?"

And he said, "No, I have not." He said, "I have not told him I was coming to see you, but I have discussed in general our future possibilities with Batista."

I asked him what Batista said, and he replied, "He told me to come up with a plan."

I told Tabernilla he should go back and talk it over with Batista and that any suggestion coming from Batista, I would relate to the State Department. Then we could continue our exchange of views.

If you wish me to go into more detail on this meeting, I would be glad to do it. That is generally in capsule form what took place.

Mr. Sourwine. Was this after you had seen Batista and advised him that the American Government felt that his Government could not persist and he had to get out?

Mr. Smith. I saw Batista on December 17, 1958, and this conference you are talking about took place December 26, 1958.

Mr. Sourwine. So when you saw Tabernilla, you already had told Batista he ought to get out?

Mr. Smith. I did not tell Batista he ought to get out. I would not put it so bluntly as that. I spent 2 hours and 25 minutes trying to tactfully explain that the Department believed he had lost effective control. To avoid further bloodshed, did he not think it might be in the best interests of all concerned if he retired. This had to be done without giving the impression that I was intervening.

•   •   •

During the first half of 1960 the Cuban government steadily increased its seizures of property belonging to Americans. The Eisenhower Administration asked Congress to include quota cutting powers in the 1960 extension of the sugar marketing system. Cuba was not mentioned directly in the request, but there was no doubt that the State Department wanted the power to curtail the United States market for Cuban sugar. The hearings on the extension act developed into a battle between groups which did not want to seriously upset the market system, and groups which saw the Cuban situation as an opportunity to break into the closed system. The House Agriculture Committee reported a bill which would have extended the program for one year with no changes. This bill was sent back to committee, and on June 27 another bill was sent to the House. Prolonged debates in both houses, pressure from the administration, and extensive lobbying characterized the remaining days of the Congressional session. The issue of Castro became involved with the competing elements in the sugar industry, and the controversy, to a certain extent, cut across party lines. Finally, after a hectic twenty-three hour session during the Fourth of July weekend a compromise bill was passed extending the program only to March 1961. The President received the power to cut quotas, and three days later he used this weapon (Document 7).

In August 1960 the United States took its fight against Castro to the Conference of Foreign Ministers of the Organization of American States. Secretary Herter hoped to obtain a condemnation of the growing ties between Cuba and the Soviet bloc, but several of the leading Latin American countries refused to support a strong stand against Cuba. Herter was able to obtain only a general disapproval of intervention by an "extra-continental power." The Cuban representative, Raúl Roa, refused to repudiate the Soviet offer of military assistance in case of an attack on Cuba. This repudiation had been cited by Herter as a *sine qua non* for improved relations between the United States and Cuba.

In October 1960 the State Department issued a ban on all exports to Cuba, with the exception of food and medicine. Exports to Cuba had already been drastically restricted by the refusal of the Cuban government to release funds for payment (Document 9). The final break in diplomatic relations came on January 3, 1961, after a calculated move by Castro which was probably designed to provoke such a step (Document 10).

DOCUMENT 7. Statement by President Eisenhower on Signing the Cuban Sugar Quota Bill, July 6, 1960. (*The New York Times*, July 7, 1960. P. 8.)

I have today approved legislation enacted by the Congress which authorizes the President to determine Cuba's sugar quota for the balance of calendar year 1960 and for the three-month period ending March 31, 1961. In conformity with this legislation I have signed a proclamation, which in the national interest, establishes the Cuban sugar quota for the balance of 1960 at 39,752 short tons, plus the sugar certified for entry prior to July 3, 1960. This represents a reduction of 700,000 short tons from the original 1960 Cuban quota of 3,119,655 short tons.

. . . Despite every effort on our part to maintain traditionally friendly relations, the Government of Cuba is now following a course which raises serious questions as to whether the United States can, in the long run, continue to rely upon that country for such large quantities of sugar. I believe that we would fail in our obligation to our people if we did not take steps to reduce our reliance for a major food product upon a nation which has embarked upon a deliberate policy of hostility toward the United States.

The Government of Cuba has committed itself to purchase substantial quantities of goods from the Soviet Union under barter arrangements.[11] It has chosen to undertake to pay for these goods with sugar—traded at prices well below those which it has obtained in the United States. The inescapable conclusion is that Cuba has embarked on a course of action to commit steadily increasing amounts of its sugar crop to trade with the Communist bloc, thus making its future ability to fill the sugar needs of the United States ever more uncertain.

It has been with the most genuine regret that this Government has been compelled to alter the theretofore mutually beneficial sugar trade between the United States and Cuba. Under the system which has existed up to this time, the people of Cuba, particularly those who labor in the cane fields and in the mills, have benefited from the maintenance of an assured market in the United States, where Cuban sugar commands a price well above that which could be obtained in the world market. These benefits also reached many others whose livelihood was related to the sugar industry on the island.

The American people will always maintain their friendly feelings for the people of Cuba. We look forward to the day when the Cuban Government will once again allow this friendship to be fully expressed in the relations between our two countries.

DOCUMENT 8. The Declaration of San Jose, adopted at San Jose, Costa Rica on August 28, 1960. (A. G. Mezerik, ed., *Cuba and the United States.* International Review Service, Vol. VI, No. 60. New York, 1960. Pp. 47–48.)[12]

The Seventh Meeting of Consultation of Ministers of Foreign Affairs.

1. Condemns emphatically intervention or the threat of intervention, even when conditional, from an extra-continental power

in the affairs of the American republics and declares that the acceptance of a threat of extra-continental intervention by any American state jeopardizes American solidarity and security, wherefore the Organization of American States is under obligation to disapprove it and reject it with equal vigor.

2. Rejects, also, the attempt of the Sino-Soviet powers to make use of the political, economic or social situation of any American state, inasmuch as that attempt is capable of destroying hemispheric unity and jeopardizing the peace and the security of the hemisphere.

3. Reaffirms the principles of nonintervention by any American state in the internal or external affairs of the other American states, and it reiterates that each state has the right to develop its culture, political, and economic life freely and naturally, respecting the rights of the individual and the principles of universal morality, and, as a consequence, no American state may intervene for the purpose of imposing upon another American state its ideology or political, economic, or social principles.

4. Reaffirms that the Inter-American system is incompatible with any form of totalitarianism and that democracy will achieve the full scope of its objectives in the hemisphere only when all the American republics conduct themselves in accordance with the principles stated in the Declaration of Santiago, Chile, which was approved at the Fifth Meeting of Consultation of Ministers of Foreign Affairs, the observance of which it recommends as soon as possible.

5. Proclaims that all member states of the regional organization are under obligation to submit to the discipline of the Inter-American system, voluntarily and freely agreed upon, and that the soundest guarantee of their sovereignty and their political independence stems from compliance with the provisions of the Charter of the Organization of American States.

6. Declares that all controversies between member states should be resolved by the measures for peaceful solution that are contemplated in the Inter-American system.

7. Reaffirms its faith in the regional system and its confidence in the Organization of American States, created to achieve an order of peace and justice that excludes any possible aggression, to promote solidarity among its members, to strengthen their collaboration, and to defend their sovereignty, their territorial integrity, and their political independence, since it is in this organization that the members find the best guarantee for their evolution and development.

8. Resolves that this declaration shall be known as the "Declaration of San Jose, Costa Rica."

DOCUMENT 9. United States Embargo on Exports to Cuba, October 19, 1960. (Mezerik, *Cuba and the United States.* Pp. 43–44.)

Over the course of the past twenty-one months the United States has been subjected by the Castro regime to an increasing campaign of hostility and slander. Accompanying its words with actions, the Government of Cuba has instituted a series of arbitrary, illegal and discriminatory economic measures which have injured thousands of American citizens and have drastically altered the hitherto mutually beneficial pattern of trade between the United States and Cuba. Illustrative of what has happened is the fact that the movement of United States exports to Cuba has been reduced to less than 50 per cent of the figure in 1958 and that payment has never been received for about a fourth of the goods shipped since Castro came to power. Meanwhile, Cuban exports to the United States remained normal until July of this year, when it became necessary to reduce the Cuban sugar quota in order that the United States Government might comply with its duty to make proper provision for the future sugar needs of the American consumer.

The principal measure taken by the Government of Cuba aimed at reducing the movement of goods and services from the United States to Cuba are listed below. None of these measures can be justified by a need to conserve foreign exchange reserves, which, according to Cuban Government officials, are adequate. Rather they are the result of a deliberate political policy to divert trade away from the United States:

1. In the first months of the Castro regime a variety of taxes and other restrictions were levied against United States flour, potatoes, rice, drugs, cigarettes, shoes, automobile components and other products. For example, with regard to rice, a commodity in which the United States has long had a principal trade interest, the government of Cuba, without providing a hearing for the interested parties, demanded a special "contribution" of $2.75 per hundred pounds from Cuban importers of this American product, and made the American quota for rice almost meaningless by not releasing dollar exchange for its importation, while importing large quantities of rice duty free from another supplier country.

PAYMENT WAS RESTRICTED

2. Over the course of the year 1959, during which American exporters continued to ship in good faith under the generous credit terms which had long been customary in trading with Cuba, the Government of Cuba made it difficult for Cuban importers to pay for United States goods. Surcharges ranging from 30 per cent to 100 per cent were imposed in September, 1959, on remittances of foreign exchange for certain additional categories of imports. Regulations governing the disposition of dollar exchange were gradually tightened until on Nov. 3, 1959, an order was issued which stipulated that all exporters of Cuban products, as well as all persons receiving dollar exchange for services rendered in Cuba, must surrender their dollars to the National Bank of Cuba. Foreign exchange required to pay for imported goods had to be requested from an agency of this bank and approval of applications for legitimate payments of all sorts became subject to long and indefinite delay. At the end of June, 1960, the commercial backlog owed to American business men had reached over $150 million.

3. Some American exporters have been pressured to continue shipments of their products on a ninety-day open account under the threat that only under this condition would dollars be released to pay for earlier shipments. United States-owned financial institutions were refused rediscount facilities with the aim of forcing them to bring their own funds from abroad and American firms operating factories in Cuba were threatened with intervention unless they continued to ship in raw materials in a normal manner, despite the fact that dollars had not been released to pay for earlier shipments of raw materials or for remittance of normal earnings.

DISCRIMINATED AGAINST U.S.

4. The Castro regime discriminated against the United States in the administration of its trade regulations. It has used import licensing, state trading and threats of intervention to force the diversion of trade away from the United States. Traditional customers of the United States in Cuba are under continuous official pressure to divert orders. It is well known that refineries of the Texaco and Standard Oil Companies in Cuba, which had been supplied from Venezuela and other Western Hemisphere sources, were presented with demands to refine Soviet petroleum and were seized when they declined to do so. At the time of seizure over $50 million was owed to these companies by Cuba for petroleum

products, which for over a year they had continued to supply without reimbursement in order to meet Cuba's needs.

5. The Castro regime's seizure of private American factories, mills, lands, retail establishments, service organization, technical commercial files and other properties has also served to distort further the traditional pattern of trade between Cuba and the United States.

6. All efforts on the part of the United States to reach a fair and equitable solution on these trade problems have been rebuffed by the Castro regime. United States interests which have suffered injury have found no recourse in the Cuban courts.

For these reasons and under the authority of the Export Control Act, the United States Government is today placing into effect general controls, to prohibit American exports to Cuba except for non-subsidized foodstuffs, machines and medical supplies. This step has been reluctantly taken by the United States in the exercise of its sovereignty and in order to carry out the responsibility of this Government to defend the legitimate economic interests of the people of this country against the discriminatory, aggressive and injurious economic policies of the Castro regime.

The Department of Commerce is issuing the necessary implementing regulations and copies will be obtainable from that department.

DOCUMENT 10. President Eisenhower's Statement Announcing the Break in Diplomatic Relations With Cuba, January 3, 1961. (*The New York Times,* January 4, 1961. P. 3.)

Between 1 and 2 o'clock this morning, the Government of Cuba delivered to the United States Chargé d'Affaires ad interim of the United States Embassy in Havana a note stating that the Government of Cuba had decided to limit the personnel of our embassy and consulate in Havana to eleven persons. Forty-eight hours was granted for the departure of our entire staff with the exception of eleven. This unusual action on the part of the Castro Government can have no other purpose than to render impossible the conduct of normal diplomatic relations with that Government.

Accordingly, I have instructed the Secretary of State to deliver a note to the Chargé d'Affaires ad interim of Cuba in Washington which refers to the demand of his Government and states that the

Government of the United States is hereby formally terminating diplomatic relations with the Government of Cuba. . . .

This calculated action on the part of the Castro Government is only the latest of a long series of harassments, baseless accusations, and vilifications. There is a limit to what the United States in self-respect can endure. That limit has now been reached. Our friendship for the Cuban people is not affected. It is my hope and my conviction that in the not-too-distant future it will be possible for the historic friendship between us once again to find its reflection in normal relations of every sort. Meanwhile, our sympathy goes out to the people of Cuba now suffering under the yoke of a dictator.

• • •

In September 1960 Fidel Castro brought his anti-United States campaign to the United Nations. Backed by pledges of armed support from Soviet Russia, the bearded Cuban put on a grandstand performance designed to smear the United States. The first act was a dramatic move from one hotel to another located in Harlem, on the pretext that the first hotel had deliberately overcharged the Cuban delegation. The Cubans actually paid higher rates at the Harlem hotel. This was followed by Castro's five-hour tirade before the UN General Assembly in which he voiced almost every charge against the United States which had ever been voiced by the Soviets.

In addition, Castro's speech is his official history of the causes of the revolution and the reasons for hostility between the United States and Cuba. In spite of the distortions and misrepresentations, this speech does reveal how some of the past actions of the United States have led many people to accept the Marxist view of history and international relations. This view is a vastly oversimplified one which paints everything in black and white. Nonetheless it is appealing to those who feel frustrated by the slow tide of reform, and turn with revolutionary impatience to the quick creation of a supposed utopia.

The final act was Castro's departure from New York in Nikita Khrushchev's personal plane. Although the plane could have carried all of the Cuban delegation, Castro left fifteen members standing in the rain and blamed this on the United States.

DOCUMENT 11. Speech by Fidel Castro to the General Assembly of the United Nations, September 26, 1960. (Fair Play for Cuba Committee Print. New York, 1960. Pp. 1–2, 3–5, 8–10, 13–14, 16–23, 29–30.)

Although it has been said of us that we speak at great length, you may rest assured that we shall endeavor to be brief and to put before you what we consider it our duty to say. We shall also speak slowly in order to co-operate with the interpreters.

Some people may think that we are very annoyed and upset by the treatment that the Cuban delegation has received. This is not the case. We understand full well the reason for the state of things. That is why we are not irritated. Nor need anyone concern himself that Cuba will spare any effort to bring about an understanding in the world. But of this you may be sure, we shall speak frankly.

It is extremely expensive to send a delegation to the United Nations. We of the underdeveloped countries do not have too many resources to squander, and when we do spend money in this fashion it is because we wish to speak frankly in this meeting of the representatives of practically all the countries of the world.

Perhaps none of you, gentlemen delegates, who bring, not the individual representation of anyone, but rather that of your respective countries and for which reason, the matters which refer to each of you should concern you for what each of you represent; perhaps none of you, I say, upon your arrival in this City of New York has had to suffer the personal mistreatment, the physically humiliating treatment, as that which was meted out to the President of the Cuban delegation.

I am not trying to arouse anyone in this Assembly. I am merely stating the truth. It was time for us to take the floor and to speak. Much has been said about us. For many days we have been a bone of contention. The newspapers have referred to us, but we have held our peace. We cannot defend ouselves against attacks in this country, but our day to tell the truth has dawned and, therefore, we will speak the truth.

I have said, we had to undergo degrading and humiliating treatment including eviction from the hotel in which we were living and efforts at extortion. We headed towards another hotel, without any upset on our part, and we did all in our power to avoid difficulties. We refrained from leaving our hotel rooms and we went nowhere except to this assembly hall of the United Nations on the few times that we have come to the General Assembly. We also accepted an invitation to a reception at the Soviet Embassy, but we have curtailed our movements in order to avoid difficulties and problems. Yet, this did not suffice, this did not mean that we were left in peace.

Were we of the caliber of men that we are described as, then imperialism would not have lost hope, as it has lost hope long ago, of buying us or of seducing us in some way. But, since for a long time imperialism has lost its hope of getting us back and it never had a right to hope so—after affirming that the Cuban delegation had taken rooms in a brothel they should recognize the fact that imperialist finance capital is a prostitute that cannot seduce us—and it is not necessarily the "respectful prostitute" of Jean Paul Sartre.

The problem of Cuba. Perhaps some of you may be well aware of the facts; others, perhaps, may not—it all depends on the sources of information—but, as far as the world is concerned the problem of Cuba has come to a head, it has appeared in the last two years, and as such it is a new problem. The world had not had many reasons to know that Cuba existed. For many it was an offshoot of the United States. And this is the case of many citizens of this very country—Cuba was virtually a colony of the United States. As far as the map was concerned, the map said something different. Cuba was colored differently from the color that was used for the United States, but in reality Cuba was a colony of the United States.

How did our country become a colony of the United States? It was not so by origin; it was not the same men who colonized the United States and who colonized Cuba. The ethnic roots and the cultural roots of Cuba are very different, and for centuries this root grew stronger.

Cuba was the last country of America to shake off Spanish colonial rule, to cast off, with all due respect to the representative of Spain, the Spanish colonial yoke; and because it was the last, Cuba had to struggle because Spain had one last foothold in America and Spain defended it with tooth and nail. Our people, small in numbers, scarcely a million inhabitants at that time, had to stand alone for nearly thirty years confronting an army that was considered to be one of the strongest in Europe. Against the small national population of Cuba the Spanish Government mobilized such an enormous number that it compared favorably with the

armies it had mobilized to combat all the efforts of all Latin
American countries to achieve independence. Half a million Spanish soldiers fought against the heroic and indomitable desire of
our people to be free. For thirty years the Cubans fought alone for
their independence; thirty years which are also part of the strength
with which we love independence and freedom.

But, according to the opinion of John Adams, one of the Presidents of the United States of the beginning of the last century,
Cuba was like a fruit, like a ripe apple on the Spanish tree that
had to fall, as soon as its ripeness had reached the right point,
into the hands of the United States.

The Spanish power had worn itself out in Cuba. Spain had
neither the men nor the economic resources left with which to
continue the fight in Cuba. Spain had been routed. Apparently
the apple was ripe—and the United States Government held out its
open hands. It was not only one apple that fell. A number of apples
fell into the open hands of the United States. Puerto Rico fell—the
heroic Puerto Rico which had begun its struggle for independence
at the same time as Cuba. The Philippine Islands fell. A number of
other possessions fell.

But the measures used to dominate our country had to be different. Our country had struggled for independence and world
opinion was in our favor. Therefore our country had to be taken
in a different way. The Cubans who had fought for our independence, the Cubans who at that very moment were giving their
blood and their lives believed in all good faith in the joint resolution of the United States Congress of April 20, 1898 which declared
that "Cuba is, and by right ought to be, free and independent."
The people of the United States were with the Cubans in their
struggle for independence. That joint declaration was a law
adopted by the Congress of the United States by virtue of which
war was declared on Spain.

But that illusion was ended by a cruel deception. After two
years of military occupation of our country, the unexpected happened. At the very moment when the people of Cuba, through
their Constituent Assembly, were drafting the Constitution of the
Republic, a new law was passed by the United States Congress,
a law proposed by Senator Platt, of such unhappy memories for the
Cubans. That law stated that the Constitution of Cuba must have
a rider under which the United States would be granted the right
to intervene in Cuba's political affairs and to lease certain parts of
Cuba for naval bases or coaling stations. In other words, under a
law passed by the legislative body of a foreign country Cuba's

Constitution had to contain a rider with those provisions, and the drafters of our constitution were clearly told that if they did not accept the rider the occupation forces would not be withdrawn. That is to say, the legislative body of a foreign country imposed upon our country, imposed by force, its right to intervene and its right to defend bases or naval stations.

It is well, I think, for countries just entering this Organization, countries just beginning their independent life, to bear in mind our history for the similarities which they may find waiting for them along their own road and if not they, then those who may come after them, or their children, or their grandchildren, although it seems to us that we shall not get that far.

The colonization of our country then began: the acquisition of the best agricultural land by United States firms, concessions of Cuban natural resources and mines, concessions of public services for purposes of exploitation, commercial concessions, concessions of all types, which when linked with the constitutional right of intervention in our country, turned our country from a Spanish colony into a North American colony.

Colonies do not speak. Colonies are not recognized in the world. Colonies are not allowed to express their opinions until they are granted permission to do so. That is why our colony and its problems were unknown to the rest of the world. In geography books there appeared one more flag, one more coat of arms. There was an [sic] another color on the maps. But there was no independent republic on the maps where the word "Cuba" appeared. Let everyone realize that by allowing ourselves to be mistaken in this respect we only played the parts of fools. Let no one be mistaken. There was no independent republic. It was a colony where orders were given by the Ambassador of the United States of America. We are not ashamed of proclaiming this from the rooftops. On the contrary: we are proud that we can say that today no embassy rules our people; our people are goverened by Cuba's people.

Once again, the Cuban people had to turn and fight to achieve independence and that independence was finally attained after seven bloody years of tyranny. What tyranny? The tyranny of those who in our country were nothing but the cat's-paws of those who dominated our country economically.

How can any unpopular system, inimical to the interests of the people, stay in power unless it be by force? Will we have to explain to the representatives of our sister republics in Latin America what military tyrannies are? Will we have to outline to them how these tyrannies have kept themselves in power? Will we have to draw a blueprint of the history of many of those tyrannies that are already classical? Will we have to show them what kept them in power? Will we have to say what national and international interests kept them at the helm?

The military group that tyrannized over our country was built upon the most reactionary sectors of the nation and, over and above all, was based upon the foreign interests that dominated the economy of our country. Everybody here knows, and we understand that even the Government of the United States recognizes, that that was the type of government that was preferred by the monopolies. Why? Because, with power, you can repress any claims upon the part of the people. With power, you repress strikes that seek better conditions of work and of life. With power, you quell all movements on the part of the peasants to own the land. With power, you can quash the most deeply felt aspirations of the nation.

That is why the governments of force were the governments that the guiding circles of the United States policy preferred. That is why governments of force were able to stay in the saddle for so long. And that is why governments of force still rule in America.

Naturally, everything depends on the circumstances in order to receive or not to receive the support of the United States Government. For example, it is now said that the United States Government opposes one of these governments of force, the government of Trujillo. But they do not say that they are against another one of these governments of force—that of Nicaragua or that of Paraguay, for example. In Nicaragua there is no longer a government of force; it is a monarchy that is as constitutional almost as that of the United Kingdom, where the reins are handed down from fathers to sons.

The same would have occurred in our own country. It was the type of government of force—that of Fulgencio Batista—that was most appropriate for the United States monopolies in Cuba, but that was not the type of government that was appropriate for the Cuban people. Therefore, the Cuban people, squandering life, rose up and threw that government out. And, when the revolution was successful in Cuba, what did it uncover? What did it find? What marvels lay spread out before the eyes of the victorious revolutionaries of Cuba? First of all, the revolution found that 600,000 Cubans, able and ready to work, were unemployed—as many, proportionately, as were unemployed in the United States at the time of the great depression which shook this country, and which almost produced a catastrophe in the United States. This is what we met with—permanent unemployment in my country. Three million out of a population of somewhat over six million had no electric light and none of the advantages and comforts of electricity. Three and a half million out of a total population of more than six million lived in huts, in slums, without the slightest sanitary facilities. In the cities, rents took almost one-third of family incomes. Electricity rates and rents were among the highest in the world.

Thirty-seven and one-half per cent of our population were illiterate; 70 per cent of the rural children lacked teachers; 2 per cent of our population suffered from tuberculosis, that is to say, one hundred thousand persons, out of a total population of a little over six million, were suffering from the ravishes of tuberculosis. Ninety-five per cent of the children in rural areas were suffering from parasites. Infant mortality was astronomical. The standard of living was the opposite. On the other hand, 85 per cent of the small farmers were paying rent on their land to the extent of almost 30 per cent of their gross income, whilst 1½ per cent of the total landowners controlled 46 per cent of the total area of the country. Of course, the proportion of hospital beds to the number of inhabitants of the country was ludicrous when compared with countries that have even half-way decent medical services. Public services, electricity and telephone services, all belonging to United States monopolies. A major portion of the banking business, of importing business and the oil refineries, a greater part of the sugar production, the lion's share of the arable land of Cuba and the most important industries in all fields in Cuba belonged to North American companies.

The balance of payments in the last ten years, from 1950 to 1960, has been favorable for the United States vis-a-vis Cuba to the extent of one billion dollars. This is without taking into account the hundreds of millions of dollars that were extracted from the treasury of the country by the corrupt officials of the tyranny and were later deposited in United States or European banks. One billion dollars in ten years! The poor and underdeveloped country in the Caribbean, with 600,000 unemployed, was contributing to the economic development of the most highly industrialized country in the world!

This was the situation that confronted us. Yet it should not surprise many of the countries represented in this Assembly, because, when all is said and done, what we have said about Cuba is, one may say, an X-ray that could be superimposed and applied to many of the countries here represented in the Assembly.

✦　　　✦　　　✦　　　✦　　　✦

. . . Naturally, in theory everybody agrees with agrarian reform
—in theory. Nobody would dare to deny it; nobody except an igno-
ramus would deny that agrarian reform in the under-developed
countries of the world is one of the essential conditions for economic
development. In Cuba, even the landowners agreed about agrarian
reform—only they wanted their own kind of reform, like the
agrarian reform defended by many theorists: an agrarian reform
which neither in their way nor in any other way is ever put into
effect, as long as it can be avoided. Agrarian reform is something
that is recognized by the economic bodies of the United Nations.
It is something over which nobody argues.

In our country such reform was inevitable. More than 200,000
peasant families lived in the country without land upon which to
plant the essential foodstuffs. Without agrarian reform our country
could not have taken its first tottering step towards development,
but we were able finally to take that step. We instituted an
agrarian reform. Was it radical? It was a radical reform. Was it
very radical? It was not very radical. We instituted an agrarian
reform adjusted to the needs of our development, adjusted to the
possibilities of agricultural development, that is, an agrarian reform that would solve the problems of the landless peasants, that
would solve the problem of the lack of basic foodstuffs, that would
solve the great unemployment problem on the land, that would
end, once and for all, the ghastly misery which existed in the rural
areas of our country.

And that is where the first major difficulty arose. In the neighboring Republic of Guatemala a similar case had occurred. When
the agrarian reform was agreed to in Guatemala, problems mush-
roomed. And I notify my colleagues of the Latin American Republics and of Africa and of Asia with complete honesty, that when
they plan a just and fair agrarian reform they must be ready to
confront situations similar to that which confronted us, especially
if the best and largest lands are in the hands of the monopolists
of the United States, as was the situation in Cuba.

It may well be that we may be accused of giving bad advice
in this Assembly. It is not our intention to keep anybody from his
just sleep. We are merely desirous of expressing facts—though
facts are enough to keep anybody awake.

Then the question of payments and of indemnities came up.
Notes from the State Department rained on Cuba. They never
asked us about our problems, not even out of a desire to express
condolence or commiseration, or because of the hand that they
had had in creating the problems. They never asked us how many

died of starvation in our country, how many were suffering from tuberculosis, how many were unemployed. No, they did not ask about that. The feeling of solidarity regarding our needs was never expressed. The conversations of the representative of the United States Government were concerned with the telephone company and with the problem of the lands owned by American companies. How were we going to pay?

Naturally, the first thing that should have been asked was "What with?", not "How?"

Can you gentlemen conceive of a poor, under-developed country carrying the onus of 600,000 unemployed, with such a high number of sick and illiterate, whose reserves have been sapped, that has contributed to the economy of a powerful country to the tune of one billion dollars in ten years, can have the wherewithal to pay for the lands that are going to be affected by the agrarian reform, or at least pay for them on the conditions on which the North American State Department wanted [sic] be paid in compensation for their affected interests?

They demanded three things: speedy, efficient and just payment. Do you understand that language? Speedy, efficient and just payment? That means, "Pay right now, in dollars and whatever we may ask for our lands."

We were not 150 per cent communits [sic] at that time. We just appeared slightly pink. We were not confiscating lands. We simply proposed to pay for them in twenty years, and the only way in which we could pay for them was by bonds—bonds which would mature in twenty years—at 4½ per cent interest, which would be amortized yearly. How were we to be able to pay for these lands in dollars? How were we going to pay cash, on the spot, and how could we pay for them what they asked? It was ludicrous.

It is obvious that under those circumstances, we had to choose between carrying through an agrarian reform and nothing. If we chose nothing then there would be a perpetuation of the economic misery of our country, and if we did carry out the agrarian reform then we were exposing ourselves to incurring the hatred of the Government of the powerful neighbor of the north.

 ✓   ✓   ✓   ✓   ✓

The attitude of the Revolutionary Government already had been too bold. It had clashed with the interests of the international electric trust; it had clashed with the interests of the international telephone trust; it had clashed with the interests of the international mining trusts; it had clashed with the interests of the United Fruit Company and it had clashed, virtually, with the most powerful

interests of the United States, which, as you know, are very closely
linked one with the other. And that was more than the Government
of the United States could tolerate—that is, the representatives of
the United States monopolies.

Then there began a new stage of punishment meted out to our
revolution. Can anyone who objectively analyses the facts, who is
ready to think honestly and not as the UPI and the AP tell him, to
think with his head and to draw conclusions from the logic of his
own thinking, to see the facts without prejudice, sincerely and
honestly—can anyone who does this consider that the things which
the Revolutionary Government did were such as to decree the
destruction of the Cuban Revolution? No.

But the interests which were affected by the Cuban Revolution
were not concerned over the case of Cuba; they were not being
ruined by the measures of the Cuban Revolutionary Government.
That was not the problem. The problem lay in the fact that those
same interests owned the natural wealth and resources of the
greater part of the peoples of the world.

So then the attitude of the Cuban Revolution had to receive
its punishment. Punitive actions of every type—even the destruction of those foolhardy people—had to be carried out against the
audacity of the Revolutionary Government. On our honor we
swear that up to that time we had not had the opportunity even
to exchange letters with the distinguished Prime Minister of the
Soviet Union, Nikita Khrushchev. That is to say that, when for
the North American press and the international news agencies who
supply information to the world Cuba was already a Communist
Government, a Red peril ninety miles from the United States,
with a Government dominated by Communists, the Revolutionary
Government had not even had the opportunity of establishing
diplomatic or commercial relations with the Soviet Union. But
hysteria can go to any length; hysteria is capable of making the
most unlikely and absurd claims. But of course, let no one for one
moment think that we are going to intone here a *mea culpa*. There
will be no *mea culpa*. We do not have to ask anyone's pardon.
What we have done we have done with our eyes wide open and,
above all, fully convinced of our right to do it.

Then the threats began against our sugar quota. The cheap
philosophy of imperialism began to show its nobility, its egotistical
and exploiting nobility; began to show its kindness to Cuba, declaring that they were paying us a preferential price for sugar
which amounted to a subsidy to Cuban sugar—a sugar which was
not so sweet for Cubans since we were not the owners of the best

sugar-producing lands or of the greatest sugar plants. Furthermore, in that claim there lay hidden the true history of Cuban sugar, of the sacrifices which had been imposed on my country, of the periods when it was economically attacked.

✓ ✓ ✓ ✓ ✓

When the supplies of sugar began to diminish in our favor, then we received the hard blow. By a request of the executive power of the United States, the Congress approved an act according to which the President or the executive power of the United States was empowered to reduce to what limits he deemed appropriate the import quotas of sugar from Cuba. The economic weapon was wielded against our revolution. The justification for this stand had already been prepared in advance by the public relations people. A campaign had been carried on for a long time, because you know perfectly well that here monopoly and public relations are completely identified.

The economic weapon is wielded. At one fell swoop our sugar quota was cut down by about one million tons—sugar that was already produced, that had been prepared for the North American market, and thus to deprive our country of the resources it needed for development—to reduce our country to impotence in order to obtain political advantages.

That measure had been prohibited expressly by the regional international law. As all representatives of Latin America know, economic aggression is expressly condemned by regional international law. Yet the Government of the United States violated that right, wielded the economic weapon and cut our sugar quota to about almost a million tons, and that was that. They could do it. What could Cuba do when confronted by the fact? Turn to the United Nations. Go to the United Nations. Denounce the political and economic aggression. Denounce the incursions, the overflights. Denounce the economic aggression, aside from the constant interference of the United States Government in the policy and politics of our country; the subversive campaigns carried out by the United States Government against the revolutionary Government of Cuba.

So we turn to the United Nations. The United Nations has power to deal with these matters. The United Nations in the hierarchy of international organizations stands at the head; it is the greatest international authority. It has authority over and above the Organization of American States. Besides which we wanted the problem aired in the United Nations because we

understand full well the condition of dependency on the United
States in which the economy of Latin America finds itself.

The United Nations was seized of the question. It seeks an
investigation to be carried out by the Organization of American
States. The Organization of American States meets. Fine. And
what was to be expected? That the Organization of American
States would protect the country attacked; that the Organization
of American States condemn the political aggression against Cuba
and especially the Organization of American States condemn the
economic aggression of which we were the victims. We expected
this. We had a right to expect it. . . .

But what happens in Costa Rica? Lo and behold, by an
ingenious production a miracle happened in Costa Rica. What
resulted from Costa Rica was not a condemnation of the United
States, or the Government of the United States. I do wish to avoid
any misunderstanding about our feelings: we regard the Government of the United States and the people of the United States as
two completely different entities. The Government of the United
States was not condemned in Costa Rica for the sixty overflights
by pirate aircraft. The Government of the United States was not
condemned for the economic and other aggression of which we
had been the victim. No, the Soviet Union was condemned. That
was really bizarre. We had not been attacked by the Soviet Union.
We had not been the victims of aggression by the Soviet Union.
No Soviet aircraft had flown over our territory. Yet in Costa Rica
there was a finding against the Soviet Union for interference.

The Soviet Union only said that, figuratively speaking, if there
was military aggression against our country the Soviet Union
could support the victim with rockets. Since when is support for a
weak country, support conditioned on an attack by a powerful
country, regarded as interference? In law there is something called
an impossible condition. If a country considers that it is incapable
of committing a certain crime, well then, it is enough to say that
there is no possibility that the Soviet Union will support Cuba,
because there is no possibility that they will attack the little
country. The principle was established that the intervention of the
Soviet Union had to be condemned. About the bombing of Cuba
nothing was said. Of the aggression against Cuba, nothing.

The correct investment of this wealth and of these resources
is allowing the Revolutionary Government at the same time to
carry out a plan of industrialization and of increase in agriculture,

to build houses, build schools, send teachers to the fartherest corners of the country, and give medical assistance to everybody in other words, carry out a true program of social development.

And precisely now, at the Bogota meeting, as you know, the Government of the United States proposed a plan. But, was it a plan for economic development? No, it proposed a plan for social development. Now, what does this mean? What is understood by this? Well, it was a plan for building houses, building schools and building roads. But does this settle the problem? Does this solve it all? How can there be a solution to the social problems without a plan for economic development? Is it that they want to hoodwink the other people of Latin America? What are the families going to live on when they inhabit those houses, if those houses are actually built? What shoes, what clothes, are they going to wear, and what food are they going to eat, when they go to those schools, if those schools are actually built? Or perhaps is it not known that, when a family does not have clothes or shoes for the children, the children are not sent to school? With what resources are they going to pay the teachers? With what resources are they going to pay the doctors? With what resources are they going to pay for the medicines? Do you want a good way of saving on medicines? Increase the nutrition of the people for what is spent in feeding the people will not have to be spent on hospitals.

In view of the tremendous reality of underdevelopment, the Government of the United States now comes out with a plan for social development. Naturally it is something that it is concerning itself with some of the problems of Latin America. Thus far it has not cared very much. Is it not a coincidence that now, at this juncture, it is worried about these problems? And any similarity with the fact that that concern has arisen after the Cuban revolution, well, possibly they'll say that it's purely coincidental.

Thus far the monopolies have certainly not cared very much except for exploiting the underdeveloped countries, but suddenly the Cuban revolution rears its head and the monopolies start worrying. While our economy is attacked and they try to squash us, with the other hand the United States Government offers charity to the peoples of Latin America, not the resources for development which is what Latin America wants but resources for social development, for houses for people to live in who have no work, for schools to which children cannot go, and for hospitals that would not be necessary if there were enough food to eat in Latin America.

Thus far we have referred to the problems of our country. Why

haven't those problems been solved? Is it because we did not
want them solved? Hardly. The Government of Cuba has always
been ready to discuss its problems with the Government of the
United States, but the Government of the United States has not
been ready to discuss the Cuban problems with Cuba. It must
have its reasons for not wanting to discuss these problems with
Cuba.

      ✓   ✓   ✓   ✓   ✓

In other words, the Government of the United States does not
deign to discuss matters with the small country of Cuba on the
Cuban problems. What hope can the people of Cuba nurture for
the solution of these problems?

All the facts that we ourselves have noted conspire against
the solution of such problems, and it is good for the United Nations
to take this very much into account, because the Government of
Cuba, and the people of Cuba too, are, most justifiably, concerned
at the aggressive turn in the American policy regarding Cuba,
and it is appropriate and good that we should be up-to-date and
well informed.

First of all, the Government of the United States considers it
has the right to promote and encourage subversion in our country.
The Government of the United States of America is promoting the
organization of subversive movements against the Revolutionary
Government of Cuba, and we here denounce it in the General
Assembly. Concretely we wish to denounce, for example, that in
a Caribbean Island, a territory which belongs to Honduras and
which is known as the Swan Islands, the Government of the
United States has taken over this Island in a military manner.

There are now North American infantrymen there, despite the
fact that this is Honduran territory. And there, in violation of
international law, despoiling a neighbor country of its territory,
in violation of the international conventions which govern radio
broadcasting, it has set up a powerful transmitter, which it has put
at the disposal of war criminals and of the subversive groups
which are sheltered in this country. And there, in addition, military
training is being given to promote subversion and to promote the
landing of armed forces in our Island.

      ✓   ✓   ✓   ✓   ✓

A naval base in the territory of any country is surely reason
for just preoccupation and concern. First of all, there is the concern and the fear that a country which has followed an aggressive
and warlike policy possesses a base in the very heart of our Island,

that turns our Island into a possible victim of any international conflict, that forces us to run the risk of any atomic conflict without our having even the slightest intervention in the problem—because we have nothing to do with the problems of the United States Government, or the crises that the Government of the United States produces and provokes. And yet, there is a base in the heart of our Island that is a dire risk for us in the case of any conflict breaking out.

But is that the only danger? Far from it. There is a fear and a danger that is even greater, since it is closer to home. The Revolutionary Government of Cuba has repeatedly expressed its concern at the fact that the imperialist government of the United States of America takes that base in th [sic] heart of our national territory as a means of promoting self-aggression, to justify an attack on our country. And I repeat: the Revolutionary Government of Cuba is seriously concerned, and makes known this concern, at the fact that the imperialist government of the United States of America may take as a pretext a self-aggression in order to try to justify its attack and its assault on our country.

✓   ✓   ✓   ✓   ✓

In the entire history of bases set up anywhere in the world the most tragic case is that of Cuba—a base thrust upon us by force, in a territory that is unmistakably ours, that is a good many miles from the coast of Cuba [United States?], a base against the Government of Cuba, imposed by force and a constant threat and a constant cause for concern.

That is why we must say here that all this talk of attacks is intended, in the first place, to create hysteria in preparation of an atmosphere of aggression against our country and that we have never spoken one single, solitary word of aggression, or any word that might be taken as implying any type of attack on the Guantanamo base, because we are the first in not wanting to give imperialism a pretext to attack us.

We state this categorically and positively, but at the same time we also declare that from the moment when that country has become a threat to the security and tranquility of our people, a threat to our people itself, the Revolutionary Government of Cuba is seriously considering requesting, within the framework of international law, that the naval and military forces of the United States be withdrawn from the Guantanamo base, from that portion of the national territory, and there will be no option for the imperialist Government of the United States but to withdraw its forces, because how will it be able to justify before the world its right to install an atomic base or a base which is dangerous to our people in a bit of our national territory, in an unmistakable island which is the portion of the world where the Cuban nation is situated?

How will they be able to justify to the world any right to maintain and to hold sovereignty over a part of our territory? How will they be able to stand before the world and justify such an arbitrary procedure? And since it will be unable to justify itself to the world when our Government requests it, within the framework of international law, the Government of the United States will have no option but to abide by the canons of international law.

But this Assembly has to be up to date and informed regarding the problems of Cuba, because we must be alert against confusion and against misrepresentation. We have to explain these problems very clearly because with them go the security and the fate of our country. That is why we want very clear note to be taken of the words I have spoken—especially if note is taken of the fact that there seems to be no chance of correcting the erroneous impression that the politicians of this country have regarding the question of Cuba.

Here, for example, I have declarations of Mr. Kennedy that are enough to surprise anybody. On Cuba he says: "We must use all the power of the Organization of American States to avoid Castro's interfering in other Latin American countries and force him to return Cuba to freedom." They are going to give freedom back to Cuba!

"We must state our intention," he says, "of not allowing the Soviet Union to turn Cuba into its Caribbean base, and apply the Monroe Doctrine." More than half-way through the twentieth century and this candidate speaks of the Monroe Doctrine! "We must force Prime Minister Castro to understand that we propose to defend our right to the naval base of Guantanamo." This is the third person who speaks of this problem. "And we must show the Cuban people that we agree with its legitimate economic aspirations,"—why did they not do this before—"that we know full well their love for freedom, and that we shall never be satisfied until democracy returns to Cuba." What democracy? The democracy made by the monopolists of the United States of America?

So that we may understand why airplanes fly from United States territory to Cuba, attention should be given to what this gentleman says:

"The forces that are struggling for freedom in exile and in the mountains of Cuba must be supplied and assisted, and in other countries of Latin America communism must be confined without allowing it to expand or spread."

If Kennedy were not an illiterate and ignorant millionaire he would understand that it is not possible to carry out a revolution against the peasants in the mountains with the aid of the landowners and that every time that imperialism has tried to stir up counter-revolutionary groups the peasant militia has put them out of combat in the course of a few days. But it seems he has been reading some novels or seeing various Hollywood films—some story about guerrilla warfare—and believes it possible, socially speaking, to carry on guerrilla warfare in Cuba.

In any case, this is discouraging. And let nobody think, nevertheless, that these opinions on Kennedy's statements indicate that we feel any sympathy for the other one, for Mr. Nixon, who has made similar statements. As far as we are concerned, both of them lack political brains.

The President. I am sorry to have to interrupt the Prime Minister of Cuba, but I am sure that I am faithfully reflecting the feelings of the Assembly as a whole when I ask him to consider whether it is right and proper that the candidates in the current election in this country be discussed at the rostrum of the Assembly of the United Nations.

I am sure that in this matter the distinguished Prime Minister of Cuba will, on reflection, see my point of view, and I feel that I can rely with confidence on his good-will and co-operation. On that basis I would ask him kindly to continue with his remarks.

Mr. Castro. It is not our intention in the least to infringe upon the rules which determine our behavior in the United Nations, and the President can depend fully on my co-operation to avoid having my words misunderstood. I have no intention of offending anyone. It is somewhat a question of style and, above all, a question of trust in the Assembly. In any case, I will try to avoid wrong interpretations.

Up to this point we have been dealing with the problems of our country, the fundamental reason for our attending this session of the United Nations. But we understand perfectly that it would be somewhat selfish on our part if our concern were to be limited to our specific case alone. It is also true that we have used up the greater part of our time informing the Assembly on the case of Cuba, and that there is not much time left for us to deal with the remaining questions, to which we wish briefly to refer.

Still, the case of Cuba is not an isolated case. It would be an

error to think of it only as the case of Cuba. The case of Cuba is
the case of all underdeveloped peoples. It is, as it were, the case
of the Congo; it is like the case of Egypt, of Algeria, of West Irian;
it is like that of Panama, which wishes to have its Canal; it is like
that of Puerto Rico, whose national spirit they are destroying; like
that of Honduras, a portion of whose territory has been taken
away. In short, although we have not made reference specifically
to other countries, the case of Cuba is the case of all the under-
developed colonial countries.

✶   ✶   ✶   ✶   ✶

The world has been divided among the monopolistic interests.
Who would dare deny this historic truth? The monopolistic interests do not want to see the development of peoples. What they
want is to exploit the natural resources of the countries and to
exploit the people in the bargain, and the sooner they amortize
their investments or get them back, the better it is for them.

The problem that the Cuban people have suffered from the
imperialist Government of the United States are the same problems that Saudi Arabia would have if it decided to nationalize
its oil fields, or if Iran or Iraq decided to do so; the same problems
that Egypt had when it quite justifiably and correctly nationalized
the Suez Canal; the very same problems that Indonesia had when
it wanted to become independent; the same surprise attack that
was made against Egypt and on the Congo. Has there ever been
a lack of pretext for the colonialists or imperialists when they
wanted to invade a country? They have never lacked pretexts;
somehow they have always managed to pull out of the hat the
pretext that they wanted. Which are the colonialist countries?
Which are the imperialist countries? There are not four or five
countries but four or five groups of monopolies which possess the
world's wealth.

If a person from outer space were to come to this Assembly,
someone who had read neither the Communist Manifesto of Karl
Marx nor the cables of the UP or the AP or the other publications
of a monopolistic character, and if he were to ask how the world
was divided and if he saw on a map of the world that its riches
were divided among the monopolies of four or five countries, he
would say: "The world has been badly divided up, the world has
been exploited." Here in this Assembly, where there is a majority
of the under-developed countries, he would say that the great
majority of the people you represent are being exploited, that they
have been exploited for a long time; the forms of exploitation may

have varied, but they are still being exploited. That would be the verdict.

In the statement made by Premier Khrushchev there is a statement that attracted our attention because of the value that it holds, and that was when he said that the Soviet Union did not have colonies and that the Soviet Union has no investments in any country. How great would our world be today, our world which today is threatened with catastrophe, if all the representatives of all countries could make the same statement: Our country has no colonies and no investments in any foreign country.

We shall trust in the reason and in the honesty of all. There are aspects of these world problems with regard to which we should like to sum up our views, on which there can be no doubt whatever. We have made known the problem of Cuba, which is part of the world problems. Those who attack us today are those who assist in attacking others elsewhere in the world. The Government of the United States cannot be on the side of the people of Algeria, because the United States is an ally of France; it cannot be with the Congolese people, because the United States is an ally of Belgium; it cannot be with the Spanish people, because it is an ally of Franco. It cannot be in favor of the Puerto Rican people, whose nationality it has for fifty years been destroying; it cannot be with the Panamanians, who are claiming their canal. It cannot allow the growth of civilian power in Latin America, Germany or Japan. It cannot be on the side of the peasants who want their own lands because it is an ally of the land-owners. It cannot be with the workers who seek better living conditions in any part of the world, because it is an ally of the monopolies. It cannot be with the colonies that wish for liberation, because it is an ally of the colonizing Powers. In other words, it is with Franco, with the colonizers of Algeria, with the colonizers of the Congo. It is in favor of perpetuating its interests over the Panama Canal; it is in favor of colonialism all over the world.

World public opinion, including North American public opinion, has to be taught to understand the problems from another point of view, from the other person's point of view. The under-developed countries cannot always be presented as aggressors; the revolutionaries cannot always be presented as aggressors, as enemies of the North American people.

We cannot be enemies of the American people, because we have seen Americans, such as Carleton Beals or Waldo Frank, illustrious and distinguished intellectuals, who weep at the thought of the errors that are committed, at the lack of hospitality which was committed particularly against us.

There are many Americans, those humane Americans, those intellectuals, the progressive writers, the most valuable writers, and it is in them that I see the nobility of the true, first pioneers of the Washingtons, Jeffersons and Lincolns of this country.

I am not using demagogy; I am speaking with the sincere admiration that we feel for those who one day knew how to free their people, destroy colonialism and fight; but not for this country to become today the ally of all the reactionaries of the world, the ally of all the gangsters in the world, the ally of the landowners, the monopolists, the militarists and the fascists of the world, the ally of the most retrograde and reactionary groups of the world.

✔   ✔   ✔   ✔   ✔

In conclusion, fulfilling what we consider to be our duty, we bring to this Assembly the essential part of the Havana Declaration. You know that the Havana Declaration was a reply of the Cuban people to the Declaration of Costa Rica. It was not ten, nor one hundred, nor 100,000; there were more than a million Cubans—and those who doubt it can go and count them at the next concentration, or the general assembly that we hold in Cuba, and you will see a spectacle of a fervent and conscious people that I think you will scarcely have seen elsewhere; a sight that you can only see when the people are truly, fervently defending the most sacred interests.

At that assembly, in answer to the Declaration of Costa Rica in full consultation with the people, and by acclamation of the people, these principles were proclaimed as the principles of the Cuban revolution:

"THE NATIONAL GENERAL ASSEMBLY OF THE PEOPLE:

"Condemns the latifundium, a source of poverty for the peasants and a backward and inhuman agricultural system; condemns starvation wages and the iniquitous exploitation of human labor by immoral and privileged interests; condemns illiteracy, the lack of teachers, of schools, of doctors and hospitals, the lack of protection of old age that prevails in Latin America; condemns the inequality and exploitation of women; condemns the discrimination against the Negro and the India [sic?]; condemns the military and political oligarchies that keep our peoples in utter poverty and block their democratic development and the full exercise of their sovereignty; condemns the handing over of our countries' natural resources to the foreign monopolies as a submissive policy that betrays the interests of the peoples; condemns the governments that ignore the feelings of their people and yield to the directives of Washington; condemns the systematic deception of the people by the information media that serve the interests of the oligarchies and the policies of oppressive imperialism; condemns the news monopoly of the Yankee agencies, instruments of the North American trusts and agents of Washington; condemns the repressive laws that prevent workers, peasants, students and intellectuals, which form the great majority of each country, from organizing themselves and fighting for the realization of their social and patriotic aspirations; condemns the monopolies and imperialistic organizations that continuously loot our wealth, exploit our workers and peasants, bleed and keep in backwardness our economies, and submit the political life of Latin America to the sway of their own designs and interests.

In short, the National General Assembly of the People of Cuba condemns both the exploitation of man by man and the exploitation of under-developed countries by imperialistic finance capital.

Therefore, the National General Assembly of the People of Cuba proclaims before America:

The right of the peasants to the land; the right of the workers to the fruit of their labor, the right of children to education; the right of the ill to medical and hospital attention; the right of youth to work; the right of students to free, experimental, and scientific education; the right of Negroes and Indians to "the full dignity of man," the right of women to civil, social and political equality; the right of the aged to a secure old age; the right of intellectuals, artists, and scientists to fight, with their works, for a better world; the right of nations to their full sovereignty; the right of nations to turn fortresses into schools, and to arm their workers, their peasants, their students, their intellectuals, the Negro, the Indian, the women, the young and old, the oppressed and exploited people, so that they may themselves defend their rights and their destinies."

Some wanted to know the line followed by the Revolutionary Government of Cuba. There you have our line.

•   •   •

Interpretations of the Castro Revolution have flooded the news media since 1958. Two views from opposite extremes have already been presented in this chapter (Documents 6 and 11), but historical understanding can only be approached by an examination of various interpretations.

Senator John F. Kennedy analyzed the events in Cuba against the background of Latin American history and the role of the United States in a revolutionary world (Document 12). The views expressed in this document also provide an insight into President Kennedy's "Alliance for Progress."

James N. Wallace, the Havana correspondent for *The Wall Street Journal,* wrote a speculative analysis of the future of Cuba which displays moderation and understanding (Document 13). The honest evaluation of the problems and needs of the Cuban economy also provides a significant insight into a segment of business opinion in the United States. Document 14 is an example of the publishing activities of some of the Cuban exiles. This booklet by Professor Fermín Peinado—former dean of the Law School of the University of Oriente in Cuba—was particularly designed to answer *Listen Yankee,* by C. Wright Mills. It was probably published by the *Frente Revolucionario Democratico* (FRD) in Coral Gables, Florida. The *Frente* was organized in June 1960 by five groups of exiles. According to Theodore Draper, "the FRD represented the Center of the exile world at a time when the Right was still unduly prominent and the Left had not yet arrived in large numbers."[13]

Document 15 is an interesting report of the views of the Manati Sugar Company. The company president seemed to be quite optimistic concerning the recovery of the company's property in Cuba. The president may have been in contact with the groups which were planning the April 1961 invasion of Cuba. Other sugar companies expressed similar views early in 1961.

DOCUMENT 12.   Senator John F. Kennedy Analyzes Cuba and Latin America, 1960. (John F. Kennedy, *The Strategy of Peace.* Allen Nevins, ed. Popular Library Edition. New York, 1961. Pp. 167–69.)[14]

The wild, angry, passionate course of the revolution in Cuba demonstrates that the shores of the American Hemisphere and the Caribbean islands are not immune to the ideas and forces causing similar storms on other continents. Just as we must recall our own revolutionary past in order to understand the spirit and the significance of the anticolonial uprisings in Asia and Africa, we should now reread the life of Simón Bolívar, the great "Liberator" and sometimes "Dictator" of South America, in order to comprehend the new contagion for liberty and reform now spreading south of our borders. On an earlier trip throughout Latin America, I became familiar with the hopes and burdens which characterize this tide of Latin nationalism.

Fidel Castro is part of the legacy of Bolívar, who led his men over the Andes Mountains, vowing "war to the death" against Spanish rule, saying, "Where a goat can pass, so can an army." Castro is also part of the frustration of that earlier revolution which won its war against Spain but left largely untouched the indigenous feudal order. "To serve a revolution is to plow the sea," Bolívar said in despair as he lived to see failure of his efforts at social reform.

Whether Castro would have taken a more rational course after his victory had the United States Government not backed the dictator Batista so long and so uncritically, and had it given the fiery young rebel a warmer welcome in his hour of triumph, especially on his trip to this country, we cannot be sure.

But Cuba is not an isolated case. We can still show our concern for liberty and our opposition to the *status quo* in our relations with the other Latin-American dictators who now, or in the future, try to suppress their people's aspirations. And we can take the long-delayed positive measures that are required to enable the revolutionary wave sweeping Latin America to move through relatively peaceful channels and to be harnessed to the great constructive tasks at hand.

Unfortunately, in no other area has the work of anti-American agitators been made more easy by inconsistent, inconsiderate, and inadequate U.S. economic and diplomatic policies. As a member of the Senate Foreign Relations Committee's Special Subcommittee on Latin American Affairs, I have studied our recent sorry performance firsthand. The Inter-American Capital Development Bank that I urged in the 1958 talk below has come into existence, but this is only one of many steps necessary.

Fortunately, the Commonwealth of Puerto Rico, an island that is in full association with us, and that has taken an enlightened course of democratic economic development, is available to help us bridge the gap between North America and the revolutionary Latin South.

DOCUMENT 13. James N. Wallace, "Castro Seems Secure, But if He Should Fall Many of His Changes Would Remain," February 1961. (*The Wall Street Journal*, February 16, 1961.)[15]

Granting Fidel's present firm control, it is nonetheless possible that his regime will one day topple—most Cuban revolutions have in time collapsed from their own internal sins. One aspect of what would come next is whether U. S. business, long so important to the Cuban economy, would regain its old place.

This naturally concerns hard core Castroites not at all. But the present temper of Cubans it does concern—people ranging all the way from active oppositionists through the simply disenchanted to mild backers of the revolution—makes it evident the answer is a highly qualified yes. American-controlled public utilities and transportation companies have the least chance of setting up shop on the island again. There's widespread belief in Cuba, as in a great many other underdeveloped lands, that such businesses should be publicly owned. It's an article of faith that won't be shaken by any amount of figures purporting to show that private foreign owners can do a better and cheaper job than a government ministry.

Nor will all of Cuba's agrarian reform ever be undone. Restrictions on the size of holdings and nationality of landowners very likely will stay, and it's probably a good idea. The need for crop diversification, broader-based land ownership and rural development in pre-Castro Cuba was very real. The effort to achieve these things has often been mismanaged but turning back the clock would simply provide some future rebel leader with a powerful cause. The companies with the best chance of going back on something like old terms probably will be food processors, manufacturers, importers and financial institutions. Castro's nationalizers have pictured the takeover of these businesses as great victories for "the people" but the claims haven't stirred any great enthusiasm except among Fidel's most rabid supporters.

Even if Castro's ouster appears highly unlikely now the question of American business's future in Cuba isn't at all academic.

There's an understandable temptation in the U. S. both among businessmen and government officials, to listen most sympathetically to Castro opponents who promise that for American business things someday will be restored pretty much as they were. But this element of the opposition doesn't command any great following inside Cuba, particularly among the people who stand the best chance of making a successful counter-revolution. In several important ways America's current troubles with Cuba began long before Castro took over. Many stem from too close an economic identification with forces—Batista was only their symbol—that a great many Cubans sincerely believed were repressing their country's development. These people, who made one revolution and ultimately can make another, didn't get what they wanted in Castro, but that doesn't mean they've shucked all their old ideas.

It's more likely than not that post-Castro Cuba will see a nationalist, non-Communist though at least mildly Socialist government in Havana. American diplomacy and American business both will be able to operate profitably there, but not if the main goal is recreating "the good old days." Another Batista could be imposed, for a while. But the reaction would be another Castro, or worse.

Actually, saying that things never will be the same after Fidel is one of the safest assertions about Cuba. The revolution, no matter how far it has strayed from its original aims, has gone too wide and too deep for that.

DOCUMENT 14.   A Cuban Exile's View of the Castro Revolution, December 1960. (Fermín Peinado, *Beware Yankee: The Revolution in Cuba*. Miami, Florida, 1961. Pp. 35, 36–37, 39–40, 43–44.)

The anti-American campaign of Castro's communist regime has not been a reaction against the hostile conduct of President Eisenhower's Administration. That statement is erroneous. From the outset, since January 1959, that campaign, carefully prepared beforehand, became clearly evident. In my Province of Oriente anti-American indoctrination began as early as January 1959 with mimeographed publications that the author of this article then had the opportunity to read, in which the history of relations between Cuba and the United States was distorted to foment anti-Yankeeism. A residue of that falsified history can be read in

Professor C. Wright Mills' chapter, conveying the message of the Cuban revolutionaries.

✓   ✓   ✓   ✓   ✓

The picture of a poverty-stricken, illiterate and dirty pre-Castro Cuba is erroneous. Until a short time ago, and Professor Wright Mills could have verified this in his intense study, Cuba had the highest standard of living of any country in the tropics. Fidel Castro himself, in numerous speeches that the Columbia professor should have read, has boasted of his feat of creating a revolution under conditions of economic prosperity in Cuba, as contrasted to the usual thesis that poverty generates revolutions. Life, of course, is change and movement and it is evident that any "status quo" presents many aspects that ought to be altered. In Cuba, like everywhere else, such was the case. But the communist or communistic reforms that Fidel is implanting by force were never desired by the Cuban people. Prior to Batista, the two big Cuban parties were the Cuban Revolutionary Party (Auténtico), which was in power, and the Cuban People's Party (Ortodoxo), which was in the opposition. The Cuban proletariat and peasantry were almost entirely in the ranks of those two political organizations. The most ardent revolutionary desire was for administrative integrity. It is not that people did not want greater economic progress, better distribution of wealth, more social justice and fuller realization of the dignity of man, a concept so dear the heart of our José Martí, but all of that was sought and it was understood by almost everyone that it could be attained within the constitutional channels that had been freely laid out by the people of Cuba. It is by no means true, as we have so often read from pens ignorant of Cuban events, that the economic and social situation in pre-Castro Cuba is the *raison d'être* of the present communistic regime. It was the armed will of steel and cunning of the group directing the revolution, a Leninist-trained group, which caused the Cuban revolution against Batista to follow the Communist path evident today. Blas Roca, the old and experienced general secretary of the Popular Socialist Party of Cuba (Communist), was therefore able to state at the closing session of the plenary assembly of his party held in July 1960 and to which we have already referred that communist objectives were being carried out under different names and that constituted "the astuteness of history, the astuteness of the people, the astuteness of the revolution." Indeed a cynical statement, but very Leninist.

✓   ✓   ✓   ✓   ✓

As for our sovereignty, Cuba has never been less sovereign than it is at present. When the United States purchased our sugar at prices well above world market prices, we were paid in dollars which we could spend anywhere. The reason why we Cubans preferred to buy in the United States is simply, as even the Russians admit, that this country is the world's leading industrial power and producer of goods in quantity and variety. And an elementary knowledge of geography teaches us that Cuban [sic] is only 90 miles off the coast of Florida. But in the present commercial dealings with Russia, our sugar is bought at a much lower price, only 20% being paid for in foreign exchange and the rest being received in Russian products not quoted on the world market, of poor quality and which we shall have to accept at the price they set. It is extraordinary that it should be claimed, even by professors, that Russian trade makes us independent, while American trade enslaved us. All of that does not take into account the obligation to cooperate in international affairs in fabrication and dissemination of the rosy picture of "peaceful coexistence." Although in the last twenty years our balance of trade with the United States has ben [sic] unfavorable to us, in the previous forty it was favorable. This means that if the fact that the balance is favorable to the United States is a sign of imperialism, the United States was not imperialistic from 1900 to 1940. A curious conclusion.

It is good for Americans to be well informed and always to know the truth. But it is very harmful, under the pretext of telling them the truth, to try to convince them of facts that do not exist. When one reads books and articles in specialized periodicals in which previous American foreign policy is described, not with a historical criterion but with contemporary appraisals, one gets the impression that that policy has been guided by a perverse and calculating will and that the United States is a monster. And that is false. To describe an event of 1898 in terms of 1960 is rather unscientific. The fact that the United States granted independence to Cuba in 1902, but added the Platt Amendment, makes it possible to stigmatize the United States in 1960 as "imperialistic." On the other hand, the recent subjugation of millions of people by Soviet force, occurring at the same time as and in sharp contrast to the gradual liquidation of western colonialism, does not serve to describe Russia as "imperialistic."

We, the democrats of Latin-America are very well aware of the fact that the guarantee of continuing to remain free and to think and speak without hypocracy (as our José Martí defined freedom) is afforded us by the power of the United States. We know that everything tending to weaken the United States weakens freedom throughout the world. We believe that the most dangerous foes of this great nation are to be found from within. It is necessary to be very alert. Communism does not fight face to face, but infiltrates and creeps in through its numerous fifth columns. The case of Cuba, communized against the will of its people through the treason of a small group controlling the arms and the propaganda is, we repeat, an example. It is necessary to regain freedom and democracy for the world. And it is necessary to begin with Cuba. That is why we are in full accord with the concluding sentences of Professor C. Wright Mills: What does Cuba Mean? It means another chance for you. Beware, Yankee!

DOCUMENT 15. The Manati Sugar Company Plans $50 Million Cuban Claim for Property Seizures, February 1961. (*The Wall Street Journal*, February 16, 1961.)

Manati Sugar Co. is preparing a formal claim of about $50 million against the Cuban government for properties seized there last August. The claim will be submitted to the U. S. State Department for prosecution.

George A. Braga, president, also told the annual meeting that because of confiscation of its holdings in Cuba, including 142,000 acres of land, the company is not in a position to furnish a year-end statement on operations.

The company's present assets in this country amount to $700,000, he said, but at the end of 1960, Manati had 6% collateral trust bonds due April 30, 1965, in the principal amount of $1,653,400. Mr. Braga said interest on these bonds runs about $100,000 and is paid to date.

Mr. Braga said the company has sufficient funds to meet future interest payments. He said company offers to purchase bonds have not been accepted by bondholders.

Mr. Braga said reports received last week indicate the present operators of Manati's Cuban ranch holdings have been doing no pasture maintenance and have been slaughtering good breeding cattle. "When we return . . . we will find our property in a horrible condition," he stated.

To conserve the sugar company's supply of cash, Mr. Braga

said, office expenses in New York have been cut 85% from a year ago and directors are receiving no compensation. Czarnikow-Rionda, which owns 25.68% of the outstanding common of Manati, is paying the salaries of key Manati employes.

"This is being done," Mr. Braga said, "because we believe Cuba will be liberated. We believe it could happen this year and we think it's important to have our people available to resume operations."

He estimated that in the 46 years of operation the company put about $300 million into the Cuban economy and took out 3% to 4% of that amount in dividends. Alfred Webber, manager of the Manati sugar operation in Cuba, said plans were being drawn up to determine "what we will do when we get back."

One of the 25 shareholders attending the meeting offered a solution for the company's problems in Cuba. Hyman B. Cantor suggested, "Why doesn't the U. S. propose a merger with Cuba. Then Cubans would get the same advantages enjoyed by Puerto Rico and maybe it would help our stock."

•   •   •

In April 1961 the State Department released a White Paper which formally accused the Castro regime of betraying the revolution. Largely written by Harvard historian Arthur M. Schlesinger, Jr., the White Paper was an attempt to condemn the Castro movement, and place the United States on the side of social and economic reform. The major theme of the document is the insistence that the United States does not oppose change—or even revolution—and that Castro is being opposed because he has betrayed the revolution and delivered it into Soviet hands. A portion of the paper consists of a long recital of former Castro supporters who have fled from Cuba.

This White Paper was the prelude to invasion. On April 17, 1961 a group of Cuban exiles landed at Cochinos Bay in Cuba. This group had been organized, equipped, and trained by the Central Intelligence Agency of the United States at bases in Florida, Texas, and Guatemala. In two days this group of 1,500 Cubans had been defeated by Castro's militia. The invasion and its failure has produced many questions and heated debates. Should the United States have supplied air-cover—as in the original plan—or even troops? Should American officials have repeatedly

denied the fact that the CIA was deeply involved in organizing
an invasion? Why did the invasion fail? Some of these questions
are analyzed by the astute reporter Stewart Alsop in Document
18. Alsop has uncovered some of the behind-the-scenes struggles
which hit the Kennedy Administration during the first months of
power, and some of the implications of the fiasco for United States
policy.

The last word has not been said on this subject, but the failure
seems to have been compounded by several factors. Extreme
dissension among the exiles was certainly one. This was sharpened
by the fact that the CIA backed the right-wing exile groups, and
gave the leadership of the operation to these groups. Operational
confusion, and faulty information regarding the fighting ability
of the militia were other factors. Another interesting interpretation is that the invasion failed only in that the exiles were not
able to hold the beachhead long enough for the exile government
to arrive and call for armed help from the United States.[16]

DOCUMENT 16. The State Department's White Paper on
Cuba, April 1961. (U. S. Department of State, *Cuba*. Inter-
American Series No. 66. Washington, 1961. Pp. 1–20, 22–26.)

The present situation in Cuba confronts the Western Hemisphere and the inter-American system with a grave and urgent
challenge.

This challenge does not result from the fact that the Castro
government in Cuba was established by revolution. The hemisphere rejoiced at the overthrow of the Batista tyranny, looked
with sympathy on the new regime, and welcomed its promises
of political freedom and social justice for the Cuban people. The
challenge results from the fact that the leaders of the revolutionary
regime betrayed their own revolution, delivered that revolution
into the hands of powers alien to the hemisphere, and transformed
it into an instrument employed with calculated effect to suppress
the rekindled hopes of the Cuban people for democracy and to
intervene in the internal affairs of other American Republics.

What began as a movement to enlarge Cuban democracy and
freedom has been perverted, in short, into a mechanism for the
destruction of free institutions in Cuba, for the seizure by inter-

national communism of a base and bridgehead in the Americas, and for the disruption of the inter-American system.

It is the considered judgment of the Government of the United States of America that the Castro regime in Cuba offers a clear and present danger to the authentic and autonomous revolution of the Americas—to the whole hope of spreading political liberty, economic development, and social progress through all the republics of the hemisphere.

I. THE BETRAYAL OF THE CUBAN REVOLUTION

The character of the Batista regime in Cuba made a violent popular reaction almost inevitable. The rapacity of the leadership, the corruption of the government, the brutality of the police, the regime's indifference to the needs of the people for education, medical care, housing, for social justice and economic opportunity —all these, in Cuba as elsewhere, constituted an open invitation to revolution.

When word arrived from the Sierra Maestra of the revolutionary movement headed by Dr. Fidel Castro Ruz, the people of the hemisphere watched its progress with feeling and with hope. The Cuban Revolution could not, however, have succeeded on the basis of guerrilla action alone. It succeeded because of the rejection of the regime by thousands of civilians behind the lines—a rejection which undermined the morale of the superior military forces of Batista and caused them to collapse from within. This response of the Cuban people was not just to the cruelty and oppression of the Batista government but to the clear and moving declarations repeatedly made by Dr. Castro concerning his plans and purposes for post-revolutionary Cuba.

As early as 1953 Dr. Castro promised that the first revolutionary law would proclaim the Constitution of 1940 as "the supreme law of the land." In this and subsequent statements Dr. Castro promised "absolute guarantee of freedom of information, both of newspapers and radio, and of all the individual and political rights guaranteed by the Constitution," and a provisional government that "will hold general elections . . . at the end of one year under the norms of the Constitution of 1940 and the Electoral Code of 1943 and will deliver the power immediately to the candidate elected." Dr. Castro, in short, promised a free and democratic Cuba dedicated to social and economic justice. It was to assure these goals that the Rebel Army maintained itself in the hills, that the Cuban people turned against Batista, and that all elements of the revolution in the end supported the 26th of July Movement. It was because of the belief in the honesty of Dr. Castro's purposes that the accession of his regime to power on January 1, 1959, was followed within a single week by its acceptance in the hemisphere—a recognition freely accorded by nearly all the American Republics, including the United States.

For a moment the Castro regime seemed determined to make good on at least its social promises. The positive programs initiated in the first months of the Castro regime—the schools built, the medical clinics established, the new housing, the early projects of land reform, the opening up of beaches and resorts to the people, the elimination of graft in government—were impressive in their conception; no future Cuban government can expect to turn its back on such objectives. But so far as the expressed political aims of the revolution were concerned, the record of the Castro regime has been a record of the steady and consistent betrayal of Dr. Castro's prerevolutionary promises; and the result has been to corrupt the social achievements and make them the means, not of liberation, but of bondage.

The history of the Castro Revolution has been the history of the calculated destruction of the freespirited Rebel Army and its supersession as the main military instrumentality of the regime by the new state militia. It has been the history of the calculated destruction of the 26th of July Movement and its supersession as the main political instrumentality of the regime by the Communist Party *(Partido Socialista Popular)*. It has been the history of the disillusion, persecution, imprisonment, exile, and execution of men and women who supported Dr. Castro—in many cases fought by his side—and thereafter doomed themselves by trying to make his regime live up to his own promises.

✓   ✓   ✓   ✓   ✓

Not only the first Prime Minister and the first President of the Revolutionary Government but a large portion of the Revolution's original political and military leaders now reject Dr. Castro and his course of betrayal. Of the 19 members of the first cabinet of the Revolutionary Government, nearly two-thirds are today in prison, in exile, or in opposition. Manuel Ray Rivero, who organized the anti-Batista underground in Habana and served as Castro's Minister of Public Works, is now a member of the Revolutionary Council. Huberto Sori Marín, who as Castro's first Minister of Agriculture called for agrarian reform in the spirit of the 1940 Constitution, returned to Cuba early this year to resume his fight for the freedom of his people; according to recent reports, he has been shot and captured by the forces of Castro.

Men who fought with Dr. Castro in the hills are today the hunted victims of his revolutionary regime. Major Huber Matos Benítez, revolutionary *comandante* of Camagüey Province, was a hero of the Sierra Maestra. When Major Matos challenged the spread of Communist influence and requested permission to resign from the Army, he was put on trial for conspiracy, sedition, and treason and sentenced to 20 years' imprisonment. Major Matos is only one of the many foes of Batista who now protest Dr. Castro's perversion of the revolution. There are many, many others: Manuel Artime and Nino Díaz who fought valiantly in the Sierra Maestra; Justo Carrillo, a leader of the Montecristi opposition in Habana and Castro's first choice for President of the National Development Bank; Raúl Chibas, who raised much of the funds for the revolution and fought with Castro in the hills; Felipe Pazos, who represented the 26th of July Movement on the Junta of Liberation and was subsequently appointed by Castro as President of the National Bank of Cuba; Major Pedro Díaz Lanz, chief of the Cuban Air Force and Castro's personal pilot; Ricardo Lorie Vals, chief of arms supply for the Rebel Army; Dr. Manuel Antonio de Varona, leader of the *Organización Auténtica*, which was formed to oppose Batista and which supported its own revolutionary group in the Escambray Mountains; Evelio Duque and Osvaldo Ramírez, fighters in the Sierra Escambray first against Batista and today against Castro.

David Salvador, the labor leader, went to jail under Batista because of his work for Castro. After the revolution he became the military pro-Castro and "anti-Yanqui" secretary general of the Cuban trade union federation. In November 1959, the 26th of July Movement swept the national congress of the trade unions, defeated the Communist slate, and confirmed David Salvador as secretary general. But Dr. Castro, appearing in person at the congress, demanded acceptance of the Communist program of "unity." Salvador continued his fight for a free labor movement. A year later he was arrested as he tried to escape from Cuba. Today David Salvador is back again in a Cuban jail—this time not Batista's but Castro's.

Editors and commentators who had fought all their lives for freedom of expression found less of it under Castro even than under Batista. Miguel Angel Quevedo, as editor of *Bohemia*, had freely attacked Batista and backed Castro; the January 1959 issue of *Bohemia* hailing the new regime sold nearly a million copies.

But a year and a half later Quevedo concluded that it was impossible to put out an honest magazine in the new Cuba. When he fled the country in July 1960, Castro described it as "one of the hard blows which the Revolution has received." Today *Bohemia Libre's* dateline is Caracas. Luis Conte Agüero, the radio and television commentator, wrote the preface to Dr. Castro's revolutionary exhortation *History Will Absolve Me*. When Conte dared criticize Communist infiltration into the regime, Castro turned on him, angry crowds mobbed him, and he was forced to seek refuge in the Argentine Embassy. Today he is in exile. Even José Pardo Llada, notorious for his vitriolic daily attacks on the United States over the Habana radio, recently fled to Mexico City; he declared, "I am breaking with Fidel Castro upon reaching the conviction that in Cuba it is no longer possible to maintain a position that is not in accord with the line of the Popular Socialist [Communist] Party and that any expression of independence, even in defense of the social program of the Revolution, is considered as deviation, divisive, or counterrevolutionary."

Never in history has any revolution so rapidly devoured its children. The roster of Castro's victims is the litany of the Cuban Revolution. The Rebel Army and the 26th of July Movement expressed the profound and passionate desire of the Cuban people for democracy and freedom, a desire sanctified in the comradeship and sacrifice of the revolutionary struggle. When Dr. Castro decided to betray the promises of the revolution, he had to liquidate the instrumentalities which embodied those promises and to destroy men who took the promises seriously.

II. THE ESTABLISHMENT OF THE COMMUNIST BRIDGEHEAD

In place of the democratic spontaneity of the Cuban Revolution, Dr. Castro placed his confidence in the ruthless discipline of the Cuban Communist Party. Today that party is the *only* political party permitted to operate in Cuba. Today its members and those responsive to its influence dominate the government of Cuba, the commissions of economic planning, the labor front, the press, the educational system, and all the agencies of national power.

The Cuban Communist Party has had a long and intricate history. For years it had a working arrangement with the Batista government; indeed, Batista in 1943 appointed to his cabinet the first avowed Communist ever to serve in any cabinet of any American Republic. Later Batista and the Communists fell out. But the Communists were at first slow to grasp the potentialities of the

Castro movement. When Castro first went to the hills, the Cuban Communist Party dismissed him as "bourgeois" and "putschist." Only when they saw that he had a chance of winning did they try to take over his movement.

Their initial opposition was quickly forgiven. Dr. Castro's brother, Major Raúl Castro, had himself been active in the international Communist student movement and had made his pilgrimage to the Communist world. Moreover, Major Ernesto (Ché) Guevara, a dominating influence on Dr. Castro, was a professional revolutionary from Argentina who had worked with Communists in Guatemala and Mexico. Through Raúl Castro and Guevara, the Communists, though unable to gain control either of the 26th of July Movement or of the Rebel Army, won ready access to Dr. Castro himself. What was perhaps even more important, the Communist Party could promise Castro not only a clear-cut program but a tough organization to put that program into execution.

The period since has seen a steady expansion of Communist power within the regime. Dr. Osvaldo Dorticós Torrado, the present President of Cuba, was regional organization secretary of the Communist Party in Cienfuegos as a law student and has never publicly explained or repudiated his past party membership. Aníbal Escalante, secretary general of the Cuban Communist Party, is a member of the informal group which, under the chairmanship of Raúl Castro, makes policy for the Cuban Government. Raúl Castro himself runs the Ministry for the Revolutionary Armed Forces; and his friend, Major Ramiro Valdés Menéndez, who accompanied him on a tour of the Soviet bloc in 1960, is chief of military intelligence. Major Guevara is Minister of Industry and chief economic planner. The National Agrarian Reform Institute (INRA), with its vast power over the rural life of Cuba, is headed by Major Antonio Núñez Jiménez, a longtime coworker in Communist-front groups and another frequent pilgrim behind the Iron Curtain. The Bank for Foreign Commerce, which until recently controlled all exports and imports, had as its director Jacinto Torras, an oldtime Communist, who served for many years as economic editor of the Communist daily newspaper *Noticias de Hoy*. All centers of economic power have been taken over by the state and to a considerable degree delivered to the Cuban Communist Party.

This process of consolidation has been extended inexorably to every phase of Cuban national life. Political opposition has been extinguished, and all political parties, save the Communist, are effectively denied political activity. In recent months the regime, by completing its purge of the judiciary, has perfected its control over all organized institutions of political power. Justice is now the instrument of tyranny. Laws have been redefined in such a way that any manifestation of disagreement can be branded as "counterrevolutionary" and the accused hailed before military tribunals and sentenced to long prison terms or to the firing squad.

Professional groups and civic institutions have lost their autonomy and are systematically integrated into the "revolutionary" discipline of the regime. The remaining vestiges of opposition in the trade unions, represented by union leaders from the 26th of July Movement, have been destroyed. Recently the hand of the dictatorship has been reaching out beyond the middle class to strike down elements in organized labor. When the electrical workers of Habana marched last December from union headquarters to the Presidential Palace to protest against reductions in their standard of living, Dr. Castro himself took an early occasion to denounce them. A power failure in Habana led to the arrest of three workers as suspected saboteurs; on January 18, 1961, these men were executed by the regime as "traitors." Protest demonstrations by workers' wives against the executions were broken up by civilian strong-arm squads while police and militiamen looked on.

In characteristic Communist manner the regime has seized control of the nation's educational system, introduced Communist propaganda into the schools, destroyed academic freedom, and ended the traditional autonomy of the universities. The director of primary education in the Ministry of Education is Dulce María Escalona Almeida, a Communist. Secondary education is in the hands of Pedro Cañas Abril, long associated with pro-Communist groups. The director of the Department of Culture in the Ministry of Education is a veteran Communist, Vicentina Antuña. Well-known Communists served on the committee named by the Ministry of Education to rewrite the textbooks for the public school system. Two-thirds of the faculty of the University of Habana is today in exile. . . .

✓   ✓   ✓   ✓   ✓

In similar fashion the Castro regime has seized control of the agencies of public communication—the newspapers, the publishing houses, the radio and television networks, the film industry. No Cuban today, whether in field or factory, in school or cafe or home by the radio, can hope to escape the monotonous and implacable din of Communist propaganda.

The Cuba of Castro, in short, offers the Western Hemisphere a new experience—the experience of a modern totalitarian state. Castro's power touches the daily lives of the people of Cuba at every point; governs their access to jobs, houses, farms, schools, all the necessities of life; and subjects opposition to quick and harsh reprisal. The Castro regime is far more drastic and comprehensive in its control than even the most ruthless of the oldtime military dictatorships which have too long disfigured the hemisphere. On January 27, last, Major Núñez Jiménez, the head of INRA, summed up the inner logic of the Castro course. The Cuban Government, Major Núñez threatened, might have to replace its intended slogan for 1961, "Year of Education," with a new slogan, "Año del Paredón"—"Year of the Execution Wall" or, in effect, "Year of the Firing Squad."

By every criterion, it is evident that the permeation and penetration of political and intellectual life by Communist influences and personalities have reached the point of virtual domination. The North American journalist I. F. Stone, initially sympathetic with the Castro regime, reported after a recent trip to Cuba: "For the first time, in talking with the Fidelista intellectuals, I felt that Cuba was on its way to becoming a Soviet-style Popular Democracy."

It is for this reason that some of the most devoted and authentic fighters for social and economic democracy in Latin America— men who themselves spent years in prison or in exile and who have hailed the Castro uprising for its promises of deliverance for the Cuban people—have united in rejecting the Communist conquest of Cuba. Victor Raúl Haya de la Torre of Peru may stand as a symbol of this whole tradition of the democratic left.[17] "In the history of Latin America," Haya de la Torre recently said, "there has been a series of sell-outs. Sell-outs are not new to our America. What is new are sell-outs towards the left. Up until now they were only to the political right. We cannot confuse that which was idealistic, authentic and just in the beginning of the Cuban Revolution with the surrender, submission, and homage to something which is anti-American and totalitarian and which is opposed to the traditional sense of our ideal of bread with freedom."

Meeting in Lima at the end of February 1961, representatives of APRA of Peru, Acción Democrática of Venezuela, and similar political groups in other Latin American Republics summed up the situation when they said of Cuba that its "revolutionary process, justified in the beginning, has been deflected by its present agents, converting a brother country into an instrument of the cold war, separating it, with suicidal premeditation, from the community of interests of the Latin American people."

III. THE DELIVERY OF THE REVOLUTION TO THE SINO-SOVIET BLOC

The official declarations of the Cuban Government amply document the Lima resolution and make clear the subservience of the Castro regime to the world Communist bloc. The joint communique issued in Moscow on December 19, 1960, by Anastas Mikoyan, Deputy Chairman of the Council of Ministers of the U.S.S.R., and Major Guevara, as chief of the Economic Mission of the Revolutionary Government of Cuba, outline the terms of surrender. After announcing a series of trade, technical assistance, and cultural agreements, the communique noted, "During the talks, the two parties discussed problems relating to the present international situation, and they reaffirmed their agreement in attitude toward the principal problems of mankind today." The Cubans agreed that the Soviet Union is "the most powerful nation on earth" and that every Soviet proposal and policy represented a magnificent contribution to world peace. In return for a total acceptance of Soviet leadership, Cuba received pledges of Soviet economic assistance and of "the Soviet Union's willingness to lend Cuba full assistance in maintaining its independence against unprovoked aggression." The joint communique amounts in effect to an alliance between Cuba and the Soviet Union.

Officials of the Castro government have repeatedly made clear their fidelity to this alliance. Major Guevara, endorsing the conclusions of the Moscow Congress of world Communist parties, said "Cuba wants to tread the way of the Soviet Union" and praised the "militant solidarity of the Cuban and Soviet people." In the presence of Dr. Castro, Faure Chomón, the Cuban Ambassador to Moscow, told an audience on March 13, 1961, "We Communists together will continue forward with our truth . . . and the students of today and the students of tomorrow will be greatly interested in seeing how a whole people made itself Communist, how even the children, deceived by religious schools, have become Communists, and how this is to follow that truth which unites the Cuban people. Very soon we shall see all the peoples of Latin America become Communists."

It is important to understand the detail and the magnitude of this process of takeover. Since the middle of 1960, more than 30,000 tons of arms with an estimated value of $50 million have poured from beyond the Iron Curtain into Cuba in an ever-rising flood. The 8-hour military parade through Habana and the military maneuvers in January 1961 displayed Soviet JS-2 51-ton tanks,

Soviet SU-100 assault guns, Soviet T-34 35-ton tanks, Soviet 76 mm. field guns, Soviet 85 mm. field guns, Soviet 122 mm. field guns. Except for motorized equipment, the Cuban armed forces have been reequipped by the Soviet bloc and are now dependent on the bloc for maintenance of their armed power. Soviet and Czech military advisers and technicians have accompanied the flow of arms. And the Castro regime has sent Cubans to Czechoslovakia and the Soviet Union for training as jet pilots, ground maintenance crews, and artillerymen.

As a consequence of Soviet military aid, Cuba has today, except for the United States, the largest ground forces in the hemisphere —at least ten times as large as the military forces maintained by previous Cuban Governments, including that of Batista. Estimates of the size of the Cuban military establishment range from 250,000 to 400,000. On the basis of the lower figure, one out of every 30 Cubans is today in the armed forces against one out of every 50 in the Soviet Union and one out of 60 in the United States.

Soviet domination of economic relations has proceeded with similar speed and comprehensiveness. A series of trade and financial agreements has integrated the Cuban economy with that of the Communist world. The extent of Cuban economic dependence on the Communist world is shown by the fact that approximately 75 percent of its trade is now tied up in barter arrangements with Iron Curtain countries. The artificiality of this development is suggested by the fact that at the beginning of 1960 only 2 percent of Cuba's total foreign trade was with the Communist bloc. The Soviet Union, East Germany, Czechoslovakia, and Poland have permanent technical assistance missions in Cuba; and a Communist Chinese delegation will soon arrive in pursuance of the Cuban-Chinese agreement of December 1960. According to Major Guevara, 2,700 Cubans will be receiving technical training in bloc countries in 1961.

ꜰ   ꜰ   ꜰ   ꜰ   ꜰ

In every area, the action of the Castro regime is steadily and purposefully directed toward a single goal—the transformation of Cuba into a Soviet satellite state.

IV. THE ASSAULT ON THE HEMISPHERE

The transformation of Cuba into a Soviet satellite is, from the viewpoint of the Cuban leaders, not an end but a beginning. Dr. Castro's fondest dream is a continent-wide upheaval which would reconstruct all Latin America on the model of Cuba. "We promise,"

he said on July 26, 1960, "to continue making the nation the example that can convert the Cordillera of the Andes into the Sierra
Maestra of the hemisphere." "If they want to accuse us of wanting
a revolution in all America," he added later, "let them accuse us."

Under Castro, Cuba has already become a base and staging
area for revolutionary activity throughout the continent. In prose-
cuting the war against the hemisphere, Cuban embassies in Latin
American countries work in close collaboration with Iron Curtain
diplomatic missions and with the Soviet intelligence services. In
addition, Cuban expressions of fealty to the Communist world have
provided the Soviet Government a long-sought pretext for threats
of direct interventions of its own in the Western Hemisphere. "We
shall do everything to support Cuba in her struggle," Prime
Minister Khrushchev said on July 9, 1960, ". . . Speaking figuratively, in case of necessity, Soviet artillerymen can support with
rocket fire the Cuban people if aggressive forces in the Pentagon
dare to start intervention against Cuba."

As Dr. Castro's alliance with international communism has
grown closer, his determination to export revolution to other
American Republics—a determination now affirmed, now denied—
has become more fervent. The Declaration of Habana of September
2, 1960, was an open attack on the Organization of American
States. Cuban intervention, though couched in terms designed to
appeal to Latin American aspirations for freedom and justice, has
shown its readiness to do anything necessary to extend the power
of *Fidelismo*. Indeed, Dr. Castro has plainly reached the conclusion
that his main enemy in Latin America is not dictatorship but
democracy—that he must, above all, strive to discredit and destroy
governments seeking peaceful solutions to social and economic
problems. Thus in recent months the Cuban Government has abandoned its aggressive campaign against the Trujillo dictatorship in
the Dominican Republic and has accelerated its attacks on the
progressive democratic government of Rómulo Betancourt in
Venezuela.

Cuban interventionism has taken a variety of forms. During
1959 the Castro government aided or supported armed invasions
of Panama, Nicaragua, the Dominican Republic, and Haiti. These
projects all failed and all invited action by the Organization of
American States. In consequence, after 1959 the Castro regime
began increasingly to resort to indirect methods. The present
strategy of *Fidelismo* is to provoke revolutionary situations in other
republics through the indoctrination of select individuals from
other countries, through assistance to revolutionary exiles, through

incitement to mass agitation, and through the political and propaganda operations of Cuban embassies. Cuban diplomats have encouraged local opposition groups, harangued political rallies, distributed inflammatory propaganda, and indulged in a multitude of political assignments beyond the usual call of diplomatic duty. Papers seized in a raid on the Cuban Embassy in Lima in November 1960 display, for example, the extent and variety of clandestine *Fidelista* activities within Peru. Documents made public by the Government of El Salvador on March 12, 1961, appear to establish that large sums of money have been coming into El Salvador through the Cuban Embassy for the purpose of financing pro-Communist student groups plotting the overthrow of the government. The regime is now completing construction of a 100,000-watt radio transmitter to facilitate its propaganda assault on the hemisphere.

Most instances of serious civil disturbance in Latin America in recent months exhibit Cuban influence, if not direct intervention. At the time of the November riots in Venezuela, the government announced the discovery of high-powered transmitting and receiving sets in the possession of Cubans in Caracas. In the following weeks about 50 Cubans were expelled from the country. Similar patterns appear to have existed in troubles in El Salvador, Nicaragua, Panama, Colombia, Bolivia, and Paraguay.

To such covert activities have been joined open and direct attacks on the duly elected leaders of the American states. Thus the Cuban Foreign Minister has applied unprintable language to President Frondizi of Argentina. Government broadcasts have denounced President Lópes Mateos as "the betrayer of the Mexican Revolution," President Alessandri as "the corrupter of the faith of the Chilean people," President Lleras Camargo of Colombia as "the intimate friend of exploiting imperialism," President Betancourt of Venezuela as the "revolutionary of Mercurochrome Bandaids," President Eisenhower of the United States as "decrepit" and "bottle-fed," and so on.

In consequence of Dr. Castro's campaign against the hemisphere, seven American states no longer have diplomatic relations with Cuba. Of the states which retain formal relations, several have found it necessary to ask that Cuban Ambassadors and other official representatives be recalled because of their flagrant intervention into domestic affairs. A number of governments have withdrawn their own ambassadors from Habana.

The nations of the hemisphere, including the United States, have made repeated attempts to dissuade Cuba from thus turning its back on its brother Republics. Though the Cuban Government has tried to portray the United States as the sworn and unrelenting enemy of the Cuban Revolution, Dr. Castro was in fact cordially received when he visited the United States in the spring of 1959. American officials made clear to him the willingness of the United States Government to discuss his country's economic needs. For many months thereafter, the United States sought direct consultations with the Castro government. The United States took the initiative in suggesting negotiations as early as the summer of 1959. That offer and many others made subsequently were not accepted. For a long time the United States Ambassador in Habana was unable even to obtain an audience with Dr. Castro.

Dr. Castro had already made clear his contempt for the Organization of American States and for the entire inter-American system. Early in his regime he declared, "I have no faith in the OAS . . . it decides nothing, the whole thing is a lie." Though Cuba signed the Santiago Declaration of August 1959, with its enunciation of free elections, human rights, due process, freedom of information and expression, and hemisphere economic collaboration, it has systematically disregarded and violated each item in the Declaration. In March 1960 Castro publicly stated that the Cuban Government did not regard itself as obligated by the Rio Treaty, the keystone of hemispheric cooperation for defense, because "the revolution" did not sign the document.

In August 1960 the Foreign Ministers of the hemisphere, meeting at San José, Costa Rica, adopted a declaration condemning the threat of extracontinental intervention in the affairs of the hemisphere and condemning also the acceptance of any such threat by an American Republic; rejecting the attempt of the Sino-Soviet powers to exploit the political, economic, or social situation of any American State; and declaring that the inter-American system was incompatible with any form of totalitarianism and that democracy would achieve its full scope only as all American Republics lived up to the Santiago Declaration.

After the San José Declaration the Cuban regime, identifying itself as the object of these pronouncements, launched an all-out attack on the inter-American system. The Declaration of Habana condemned the Declaration of San José. The United States twice proposed that fact-finding and good-offices procedures created by the OAS be used as an approach to resolving differences; these proposals were ignored by Cuba. Cuba refused to join with the other American Republics in the effort to bring about economic and social advance through the continent in the spirit of the Bogotá economic meeting of 1960. It refused to support the recommendations made by the November 1960 Special Meeting of Senior Representatives to strengthen the Inter-American Economic and Social Council. It has hurled insults on the whole conception of *Alianza para el Progreso*. It stands today in defiance not only of the Declarations of Santiago and San José and the Treaty of Rio but also of the Charter of the Organization of American States.

No one contends that the Organization of American States is a perfect institution. But it does represent the collective purpose of the American Republics to work together for democracy, economic development, and peace. The OAS has established the machinery to guarantee the safety and integrity of every American Republic, to preserve the principle of nonintervention by any American State in the internal or external affairs of the other American States, and to assure each nation the right to develop its cultural, political, and economic life freely and naturally, respecting the rights of the individual and the principles of universal morality.

The Organization of American States is the expression of the moral and political unity of the Western Hemisphere. In rejecting the OAS, the Castro regime has rejected the hemisphere and has established itself as the outpost in the Americas for forces determined to wreck the inter-American system. Under Castro, Cuba has become the agency to destroy the Bolivarian vision of the Americas as the greatest region in the world, "greater not so much by virtue of her area and wealth, as by her freedom and glory."

V. CONCLUSION

It is not clear whether Dr. Castro intended from the start to betray his pledges of a free and democratic Cuba, to deliver his country to the Sino-Soviet bloc, and to mount an attack on the inter-American system; or whether he made his original pledges in all sincerity but, on assuming his new responsibilities, found himself increasingly dependent on ruthless men around him with clear ideas and the disciplined organization to carry those ideas into action. What is important is not the motive but the result.

The first result has been the institution of a repressive dictatorship in Cuba.

The existence of a regime dedicated to so calculated an attack on human decencies would by itself be sufficient occasion for intense concern within the hemisphere. In recent years the American family of nations has moved steadily toward the conclusion that the safety and welfare of all the American Republics will be best protected by the establishment and guarantee within each republic of what the OAS Charter calls "the essential rights of man."

But Dr. Castro has done more than establish a dictatorship in Cuba; he has committed that dictatorship to a totalitarian movement outside the hemisphere.

Just as the American Republics over 20 years ago, in conferences beginning at Lima in 1938 and culminating at Rio de Janeiro in 1942, proclaimed that they could not tolerate the invasion of the hemisphere and the seizure of the American States by Nazi movements, serving the interests of the German Reich, so today they reject such invasion and seizure by Communist movements serving the interests of the Sino-Soviet bloc.

The people of Cuba remain our brothers. We acknowledge past omissions and errors in our relationship to them. The United States, along with the other nations of the hemisphere, express a profound determination to assure future democratic governments in Cuba full and positive support in their efforts to help the Cuban people achieve freedom, democracy, and social justice.

We call once again on the Castro regime to sever its links with the international Communist movement, to return to the original purposes which brought so many gallant men together in the Sierra Maestra, and to restore the integrity of the Cuban Revolution.

If this call is unheeded, we are confident that the Cuban people, with their passion for liberty, will continue to strive for a free Cuba; that they will return to the splendid vision of inter-American unity and progress; and that in the spirit of José Martí they will join hands with the other republics in the hemisphere in the struggle to win freedom.

Because the Castro regime has become the spearhead of attack on the inter-American system, that regime represents a fateful challenge to the inter-American system. For freedom is the common destiny of our hemisphere—freedom *from* domestic tyranny and foreign intervention, *from* hunger and poverty and illiteracy, freedom *for* each person and nation in the Americas to realize the high potentialities of life in the twentieth century.

DOCUMENT 17. Fidel Castro Proclaims a Socialist Cuba and Attacks the April Invasion Attempt, May 2, 1961. (Fair Play for Cuba Committee print of Fidel Castro's May Day Speech. New York, 1961. Pp. 7–8, 10–12.)

We can tell the people right here that at the same instant that three of our airports were being bombed, the Yankee agencies were telling the world that our airports had been attacked by planes from our own airforce. They coldbloodedly bombed our nation and told the world that the bombing was done by Cuban pilots with Cuban planes. This was done with planes on which they painted our insignia.

If nothing else, this deed should be enough to demonstrate how miserable are the actions of imperialism. It should be enough for us to realize what Yankee imperialism really is and what its press and its government is. It is possible that millions have heard only the report that Cuban planes piloted by defectors had attacked our airports. This was planned, because the imperialist studied the plan to bomb and the way to deceive the entire world. This should serve to keep us alert and to understand that the imperialist are capable of the most monstrous lies to cover the most monsterous deeds.

U. S. leaders publicly confessed their participation—without any explanation which they owe the world for the statements made by Kennedy that they would never would [sic] participate in aggression—and saved us the effort of finding proof. Who were those who fought against those workers and peasants? We will explain.

PRIVILEGED CLASS MERCENARIES

Of the first mercenaries captured, we can say that, without counting ships' crews, there are nearly 1,000 prisoners. Among that thousand we have the following: About 800 came from well-to-do families. They had a total of 27,556 caballerias of land, 9,666 houses, 70 industries, 10 sugar centrals, 2 banks, and 5 mines. So 800 out of 1,000 had all that. Moreover, many belonged to exclusive clubs and many were former soldiers for Batista.

Remember, during the prisoner interrogation that I asked who was a cane cutter and only one said that he had cut cane once. That is the social composition of the invaders.

We are sure that if we ask all those here how many owned sugar centrals, there would not be even one. If we asked the combatants who died, members of the militia or soldiers of the revolutionary army, if we compared the wealth of those who fell, surely there would be no land, no banks, no sugar centrals, or the like listed. And some of the shameless invaders said that they came to fight for ideals!

The invaders came to fight for free enterprise! Imagine, at this time for an idiot to come here to say that he fought for free enterprise! As if this people did not know what free enterprise is! It was slums, unemployment, begging. One hundred thousand families working the land to turn over 25 percent of their production to shareholders who never say [sic] that land. . . .

✔   ✔   ✔   ✔   ✔

How can one of those who never knew labor say that he came to shed the people's blood to defend free enterprise? (Chanting, applause) And they did not stop at their fathers' mention of free enterprise; they included United Fruit and the electrical company. Those were not free enterprises; they were monopolies. So when they came here they were not fighting for free enterprise; they came for the monopolies, for monopolies do not want free enterprise. They were defending the monopolistic interests of the Yankees here and abroad. How can they tell the Cuban people that they were coming to defend free enterprise?

✔   ✔   ✔   ✔   ✔

The recent invasion shows how right we were to arm. At Playa Giron, they came to kill peasants and workers. Imperialism forced us to arm for defense. We have been forced to put energy and material and resources into that, although we would prefer to put them into more schools, so that in future parades there can be more athletes and school children. If our people were not armed, they could not crush mercenaries coming with modern equipment.

The imperialists would have hurled themselves on us long ago if we had not been armed. But we prefer to die rather than surrender the country we have now. They know that. They know they will meet resistance, and so the aggressive circles of imperialism have to stop and think.

✔   ✔   ✔   ✔   ✔

To those who talk to us about the 1940 constitution, we say that the 1940 constitution is already too outdated and old for us. We have advanced too far for that short section of the 1940 constitution that was good for its time but which was never carried out. That constitution has been left behind by this revolution, which, as we have said, is a socialist revolution. We must talk of a new constitution, yes, a new constitution, but not a bourgeois constitution, not a constitution corresponding to the domination of certain classes by exploiting classes, but a constitution corresponding to a new social system without the exploitation of man by man. That new social system is called socialism, and this constitution will therefore be a socialist constitution.

If Mr. Kennedy does not like socialism, well we do not like imperialism! We do not like capitalism! We have as much right to protest over the existence of an imperialist-capitalist regime 90 miles from our coast as he feels he has to protest over the existence of a socialist regime 90 miles from his coast. Now then, we would not think of protesting over that, because that is the business of the people of the United States. It would be absurd for us to try to tell the people of the United States what system of government they must have, for in that case we would be considering that the United States is not a sovereign nation and that we have rights over the domestic life of the United States.

DOCUMENT 18. Stewart Alsop, "Lessons of the Cuban Disaster," June 1961. (*Saturday Evening Post,* June 24, 1961. Pp. 68–70.)[18]

Almost a year before the landings, President Eisenhower had given the go-ahead signal for the training of a landing force of anti-Castro shock troops, from the men of military age among the more than 100,000 Cubans who had fled the Castro terror. Throughout that year the day-and-night preoccupation of Bissell[19] and his subordinates had been the planning of the Cuban landings. Inevitably, being human, they had become infected with something of the fervor, the courage and the false optimism of the Cuban refugees, who were willing to bet their lives—or in the case of three members of the Revolutionary Council, the lives of their sons—on the proposition that the hated Castro could be brought down. Is it any wonder that the CIA men became, instead of coolly skeptical judges of the chances of success of the operation, its passionate partisans?

That, in any case, is what they did become. "Allen and Dick didn't just brief us on the Cuban operation," says one of President Kennedy's White House advisers. "They sold us on it." It is always difficult to distinguish between fact and self-exoneration when an official is employing twenty-twenty hindsight. But in this case there is no doubt that the CIA men responsible for mounting the Cuban operation did become its eloquent advocates.

Moreover, although the machinery for examining the operation with that much-needed coldly critical eye did exist within the CIA itself, in the board of "national estimates," the machinery was never used. Official knowledge of the operation was limited to its sponsors, on a "need-to-know" basis. The net effect was that the operational CIA men sat in judgment of their own much-loved offspring.

By the same token, the military men who were responsible for the detailed planning of the landing also sat in judgment on their own handiwork. The CIA employs many military men, and others were assigned by the Pentagon to help plan the Cuban invasion. The plans they evolved were reviewed in detail by the Joint Staff, top planning board under the august Joint Chiefs of Staff, and then by two of the chiefs, Gen. Lyman Lemnitzer, Chairman of the Joint Chiefs, and Adm. Arleigh Burke, Chief of Naval Operations.

Lemnitzer and Burke strongly endorsed the plans, in writing, to the President, on two conditions—that the CIA's political estimate was correct, and that the anti-Castro forces would control the air over the battlefield. As in the case of the CIA, the enthusiasm of the military for their own plans was at least understandable. A military man, asked to devise a plan to achieve a given objective, naturally becomes a partisan of the plan he has evolved. The military have in any case a natural proclivity for action as against inaction—excessive caution ill becomes a soldier.

But again, among the military there were none to assay the operation's chances of success with that much-needed cold and fishy eye. On the contrary, President Kennedy was assured by the Joint Chiefs as well as by the CIA that the Cuban adventure had a better chance of success than the successful anti-Communist operation in Guatemala.

Now consider President Kennedy's position, when, after his election, he found on his desk the Top Secret plan for a Cuban landing operation evolved under the Administration of his predecessor. Here is a new President, more experienced in the matter of winning primaries than judging the likelihood of success of a covert operation. He finds that all the professionals in this secret business, *without a single exception*, favor an operation which, if it succeeds, will greatly alter the situation in the Western Hemisphere in favor of the United States. He finds that nearly 3000 Cubans have been trained by the U. S. Government, with at least an implicit assurance that they will be helped by that Government to liberate their homeland from a Communist tyrant.

The President is told, moreover, that time is running out. Soviet jet fighters are arriving in crates in Cuba, Czech-trained Cuban pilots are due there soon, and the Guatemalan Government had given notice that the Cuban training camps in Guatemala must soon be evacuated. Suppose the President cancels the operation. Won't the Cubans—and a lot of other people, including Republicans—say then that the new President chickened out, that he lost the last chance to knock off Castro? And what is more, Kennedy must have asked himself, *Might they not be right?*

On one point all witnesses agree. From the start Kennedy's instinct was to kill the operation. "It never did smell right to the President," one of his aides says. After the disaster Kennedy took full responsibility for what had happened. Under our system that is precisely where the final responsibility belongs. But with all the old pros favoring the operation, it is not hard to understand why Kennedy did not follow his own instincts and cancel the operation.

What actually happened, when the President weighed the views of the new boys against those of the old pros, was that a peculiar, progressive watering-down process occurred. In the end, as a result of this process, the Cuban plan that was put into operation was different in essential ways from the plan Kennedy had inherited from Eisenhower.

That plan, like the final Kennedy plan, was based on the assumption that there would be widespread anti-Castro uprisings and defections. It was hoped that these would make any overt American military intervention unnecessary. But the Eisenhower plan also envisaged American intervention on a "contingency basis." American aircraft would intervene, either openly or in unmarked planes, if necessary to maintain control over the beachhead and prevent destruction of the anti-Castro forces.

From the very first this was the aspect of the Cuban plan which Kennedy and most of his new boys disliked most heartily. By early March, on Kennedy's insistence, an alternative plan had been devised. This plan called for air strikes against Castro's air force. The air strikes were to be billed for world consumption as the work of defectors from the Castro air force, but were actually to be mounted from Guatemalan bases and piloted by Cuban refugee pilots. These air strikes were to knock out the Castro air force, pathetically small by Pentagon standards, and thus obviate any need for American intervention. The new plan had been vetted and approved by the Pentagon and the CIA. But the final decisions were taken at two crucial meetings, on April fourth and April fifth.

The April fourth meeting, which must have been a rather dramatic occasion, took place in a crowded conference room in the vast new wing of the State Department Building. The President presided, and those present included Rusk, Secretary of

Defense Robert McNamara, Secretary of the Treasury Douglas
Dillon, Allen Dulles, General Lemnitzer, former Assistant Secretary of State Thomas Mann, Assistant Secretary of Defense Paul
Nitze, South American expert Adolf Berle, Bundy, Schlesinger[20]
and Bissell. And there was a new face, that of Sen. William Fulbright of Arkansas, who had been invited in his capacity as
Chairman of the Senate Foreign Relations Committee.

Bissell outlined the proposed operation, being careful to point
out that he strongly favored the plan and that his arguments
ought to be weighed accordingly. Dulles commented briefly on
the operation's purposes and chances of success. Then Fulbright
spoke, launching into an eloquent and obviously deeply felt denunciation of the whole operation. This sort of oblique attack on
another government, however abhorrent that government, was
inherently immoral, Fulbright argued. It was not the sort of thing
the United States did well, and therefore it was not the sort of
thing the United States ought to try to do at all.

Kennedy then went round the table, pointing his finger in a
typical gesture, and asking those present in turn whether they
favored or opposed the operation. He never did get all the way
around the table, and thus Schlesinger and one or two others—
doubtless to their relief—were nexer exposed to the pointing finger.
But all those Kennedy asked—including Rusk—gave explicit approval of the scheme, reluctant or enthusiastic as the case might
be. "Let 'er rip," one man said, and another, more pompously,
remarked that "a powerful confrontation with Communism in this
hemisphere" was ultimately inevitable, and that it might as well
come immediately.

Despite this unanimity—Schlesinger did not volunteer his views
—the President was visibly shaken by Fulbright's argument. A
number of those present felt sure that Fulbright had won the day,
and that the President would jettison the operation. But the President was also swayed by the counterargument that the United
States Government had to honor its implicit commitment to give
the Cubans a chance to liberate their homeland.

Presumably the President slept on the whole matter that night.
The next day he called a smaller meeting in his office, attended by
Rusk, McNamara and Allen Dulles. At this meeting Kennedy made
his final decision to go ahead with the operation. But, he ruled,
under no circumstances whatever would American forces become
involved. Moreover, the Cuban leaders must be categorically
warned in advance of this decision. Berle and Schlesinger were
accordingly sent to New York to inform the Cuban leaders, who

unanimously opted to go ahead with the plan regardless. And thus the disaster drew closer.

Clearly the President's ruling against American armed intervention under any circumstances—short of a Castro attack on the Guantanamo base—constituted a basic change in the whole nature of the operation. To an extent, the change was recognized, and taken into account. For example, an alternative landing area was chosen, in the light of the Kennedy decision. Moreover, the planners realized that, with American air support ruled out, there was as least a possibility that the beachhead could not be held. In that case, the Joint Chiefs ruled, the anti-Castro forces would have a "fall-back position" in the Escambray Mountains, where anti-Castro guerrillas were already operating.

     ✓   ✓   ✓   ✓   ✓

No doubt the chances are high that the eventual outcome would have been the same if the President had not announced his decision to bar all American intervention, and then canceled the second strike against the Castro air force. But the lesson remains clear. You cannot mount a covert operation designed to destroy a foreign regime you dislike and at the same time maintain that air of virginal innocence which American officials, especially our spokesman at the UN, so love to wear. "The trouble was," one cynical participant remarked rather brutally after the event, "that we were acting like an old whore and trying to pretend that we were just the sweet young girl we used to be."

This raises the basic question that Senator Fulbright raised when he denounced the whole operation on essentially moral grounds. Should we now try to go back to being the sweet young girl we were only a generation ago, when the American intelligence service largely consisted of a gaggle of old ladies with pincenez, who ran a sort of clipping service in the War Department?

The best answer to that question was given by implication by President Kennedy's brother, Attorney General Robert Kennedy, in a sad White House postmortem on the Cuban disaster. By the evening of April eighteenth it was clear that the invasion would be crushed, short of American intervention to regain control of the air over the beachhead. The President, summoned from a white-tie party, stayed up until the small hours of the morning of April nineteenth, arguing the pros and cons of intervention with Bundy, Bissell, Walt Rostow and other aides. Still undecided, he called a meeting of all his key advisers for the next day.

The meeting must have been an agonizing one, for almost all those present had a measure of personal responsibility for the bloody tragedy then being acted out in the Bay of Pigs. In the end, partly because he had already tied his own hands and partly because it was by then too late, the President decided to do nothing.

That decision marked the first great Kennedy failure. Bobby Kennedy, who hates failure more even than most Kennedys, was present. He remarked, as the sad meeting ended, that what worried him most was that now nobody in the Government would be willing to stick his neck out, to take a chance, to plan bold and aggressive action against the Communists.

Surely the President's brother was essentially right. If the Communists are permitted indefinitely to retain their present monopoly of the techniques of the oblique thrust, the invasion by proxy, they will win in the end all over the world, as they are winning now in Southeast Asia. Moreover, the hatred of Communist oppression within the Communist states—Cuba included—is surely the West's essential asset in the long struggle in which we are now engaged. Ways must be found to exploit that asset.

In Cuba we tried to use Communist ways, not American ways, to exploit the asset. In this sense Senator Fulbright's denunciation of the operation was entirely valid. Our kind of society, with a free people and a free press, simply does not permit the iron discipline and total secrecy required for a Communist-type exercise in subversion. But does this mean that our hands are forever tied?

One wise participant in the Cuban disaster, who has given much thought to its meaning, does not think so. "The trouble was," he says, "that we were trying to operate like Russians, not Americans. Suppose we'd done the whole thing in a typical American way, with a maximum of noise, publicity and confusion. Competing committees. Big ads for arms to free Cuba. Stories in the papers about the brave Cuban refugees training to free their country. Subscription drives to buy jets for the Cuban freedom fighters. Editorials pro and con, mostly pro, of course. The operation itself would have had to be secret enough to maintain tactical surprise— but that's all we maintained anyway. And, of course, there would have had to be some pretty firm direction behind the scenes. But I really think by hindsight the thing would have worked that way."

It might well have. There are precedents, after all, for "operating like Americans"—remember, for example, the "means short of war," such as Claire Chennault's Flying Tigers, which we used against the Axis in pre-Pearl Harbor days. The fourth lesson of Cuba seems to be something like this:

We cannot permit the Communist bloc to enjoy a monopoly of the techniques of the oblique thrust. But we must find our own ways, deriving from our own past and our own kind of society, for carrying the battle to the Communists.

•   •   •

Senator J. W. Fulbright of Arkansas was one of the few officials who spoke out vigorously against the April 1961 invasion of Cuba. It is well to note in this documentary survey the astute call for a dynamic and idealistic Latin American policy which the Senator made during the debate on the Inter-American Social and Economic Cooperation Program. In this speech Fulbright challenges the American people to combine ideals and actions into a policy which will offer the Latin Americans a workable alternative to Communism. This challenge can be ignored, perverted, or accepted. The future of the hemisphere depends on the answer of the people of the United States and Latin America.

DOCUMENT 19.   Senator J. W. Fulbright Calls for a New Approach to the Latin American Policy of the United States, May 9, 1961. (*Congressional Record*, 87th Cong., 1st Sess., 1961, Vol. 107, No. 77. Pp. 7117–19.)

Latin Americans have felt the domination of the United States. They have been on the receiving end of preachments of the advantages of capitalism and free enterprise. But these words have been at best meaningless to most of them, and at worst in their countries a source of exploitation. During the last century most Latin Americans have seen their neighbor to the north growing richer; they have seen the elite elements in their own societies growing richer—but the man in the street or on the land in Latin America today still lives the hand-to-mouth existence of his great, great grandfather.

In vast numbers Latin Americans are becoming increasingly dissatisfied with their traditional social structure. They are less and less happy with situations in which, to cite one example, 40 percent of the land is owned by 1 percent of the people, and in which, typically, a very thin upper crust lives in grandeur while most others live in squalor.

Continuation of situations of this kind can only lead to social explosions. The radios and the airplanes of the 20th century are bringing news of the outside world to the haciendas of the 17th century.

⸙   ⸙   ⸙   ⸙   ⸙

We have now an opportunity—and it may be our last—to put our relationships with Latin America in order. We have now an opportunity to begin a program that will provide things for the people, not for the governments—not for the upper crust.

The problem of the United States in its relations with Latin America is not with governments; it is with the people, particularly with workers, peasants, and students. And this is part of the dilemma we face—a dilemma that this bill will, I hope, help to overcome.

Although Latin America now has the best group of governments it has ever had, most of them are still heavily influenced by the traditional elite classes who give only lipservice, if that, to social reform. They do not really have it in their hearts to promote land reform and to revise tax structures. We must, of course, continue to deal with these governments. We must attempt, however, to make the conservative groups see that their survival . . . depends upon their willingness to come to grips with the needs and demands of their own people. We must make clear to them that the time for their conversion is short. If they are not soon converted and follow words with deeds, they will be overthrown. We must make clear to these governments that if they are converted to the cause of genuine social reform, we will help them; but if they are not, we do not propose to be swept away with them.

⸙   ⸙   ⸙   ⸙   ⸙

The real question concerning the effect of the Castro regime on Latin America and our policies, however, is whether Castro can in fact succeed in providing a better life for the Cuban people. Can he make Cuba into a little paradise, a real pearl in the Antilles? Can he, with the help of the Communist bloc, do a better job in this respect in Cuba than the United States and its friends can do in Latin America?

We have talked for years of the advantages of the American way; of the advantages of free enterprise; of the power of individual freedom. Now we have the challenge on our doorstep.

It would be a fatal confession of lack of faith in our values if we decreed—as we could—that Castro must go because he might succeed. I, for one, have confidence that our faith in human values, if supported by vigorous and intelligent action of the kind proposed in this bill, will be more than adequate to meet the competition of Castro and his partners in Moscow or Peking.

I think the time will not be long delayed until Moscow will find the Castro government a running abscess in the Caribbean. Already Moscow has loaned Cuba over $245 million. That island so long dependent on sugar exports to the United States and on U. S. tourists may soon become an albatross around Khrushchev's neck.

But our concern in this program, Mr. President, is not with Cuba. Our job is to help bring into being a new world. The North American Nation must devote more attention to helping our fellow Americans in the hemisphere move into the 20th century of sanitation, housing, communications, and production.

✓ ✓ ✓ ✓ ✓

I foresee an America that could put all other societies to shame. Between the nations of North and South America we have natural and human resources as great as, and perhaps, greater than those in any other relatively contiguous area in the world. . . .

✓ ✓ ✓ ✓ ✓

I would say in conclusion, Mr. President, that Latin America is not up for auction; it is not ours to exploit. The friendship of the people and representative governments in Latin America is certainly as important to us, as is our friendship for them. We are as interested in their rapid and democratic growth, as they are in our continued economic health.

Together and with mutual cooperation and sacrifice we can produce in the Americas a society in which our cultural, political, and economic values may flourish.

• • •

After the failure of the April, 1961, experiment with the use of military force by proxy, the Kennedy administration turned to the development of a two-pronged policy. One aspect of this policy has been the attempt to isolate Cuba both economically and politically, and to utilize the Organization of American States as an instrument in achieving this policy in the Western Hemisphere. The other aspect has been the development of the Alliance for Progress as a method of trying to bring about gradual socio-economic reform in Latin America (to blunt the appeal of *Fidelismo*), and as a device for wooing the support of the Latin American governments for an anti-Castro policy.

In January, 1962, at the Eighth Meeting of Consultation of Foreign Ministers of the Organization of American States held at

Punta del Este, Uruguay, the United States government tried to culminate its policy of isolating Cuba. Secretary of State Rusk circulated a proposal calling for automatic sanctions against Cuba if it did not break its ties with the Communist countries, but such a proposal was opposed by several of the larger countries in Latin America. The ministers did vote to expel Cuba from the OAS and the Inter-American Defense Board. Six nations abstained from the vote to expel Cuba from the OAS, and these six together contain seventy percent of the population of Latin America.

On February 3, 1962, the United States government proclaimed an extension of the embargo upon trade between the United States and Cuba. This action terminated the sale of Cuban tobacco to the United States, but the export to Cuba of certain foodstuffs and medicines was not affected. The formal expulsion of Cuba from the OAS was effected on February 14, 1962. Subsequently, the United States tried to obtain the cooperation of its Western allies in restricting trade with Cuba and eliminating their ships in the carrying trade between the Soviet bloc and Cuba. These suggestions were generally rebuffed by the nations concerned.

During the summer of 1962, Soviet Russia increased its shipments of military equipment to Cuba. In September the Congress passed a joint resolution on Cuba and the Monroe Doctrine which reflected the more cautious administration policy rather than the "big stick" position pushed by various political leaders and segments of the press. The Republican Party took up the cudgels for a militant Cuban policy during the fall elections, but President Kennedy firmly upheld the position that the United States would not attack Cuba so long as its military preparations were defensive in nature.

On the evening of October 22 the President electrified the world with his television announcement that he had definite proof of the construction of offensive missile bases in Cuba. The President demanded that the Soviets dismantle these bases, and remove the missiles and medium-range bombers from Cuba. As a first step, Mr. Kennedy ordered a "quarantine" (a polite term for a blockade) of Cuba until the Soviets complied. The world seemed to hang on the abyss as the two major powers confronted each other in the Caribbean.

The crisis cooled rapidly, however, after a number of Soviet ships turned back before reaching the American picket lines, and Premier Khrushchev agreed to dismantle the bases and remove the offensive weapons from Cuba. The United States won a unanimous vote in support of its position from the special meeting of OAS, but the Brazilian Government sent a mission to Cuba with the object of mediating between Cuba and the United States on a neutralist basis.

During the waning days of 1962, the Cuban government freed the prisoners captured in April, 1961, and also allowed about one thousand of their immediate relatives to leave Cuba. In exchange for these actions the Cuban government received a quantity of drugs and special food items.

These actions, however, did not presage any improvement in United States-Cuban relations. President Kennedy "assured" the repatriated members of the Bay of Pigs invasion force that their flag would be returned to their brigade in a "free Havana," and on January 2, 1963, Fidel Castro attacked President Kennedy in a lengthy and heated oration.

The *Overland Monthly* of October, 1890, contained the observation that, "Our history has seldom been without a Cuban question." This statement is still a valid summary of relations between the United States and Cuba.

DOCUMENT 20. Joint Congressional Resolution on Cuba; September, 1962. (*The New York Times*, September 20, 1962.)

Whereas President James Monroe, announcing the Monroe Doctrine in 1823, declared that the United States would consider any attempt on the part of European powers "to extend their system to any portion of this hemisphere as dangerous to our peace and safety"; and

Whereas in the Rio Treaty of 1947 the parties agreed that "an armed attack by any state against an American state shall be considered as an attack against all the American states, and, consequently, each one of the said contracting parties undertakes to assist in meeting the attack in the exercise of the inherent right of individual or collective self-defense recognized by Article 51 of the Charter of the United Nations"; and

Whereas the foreign ministers of the Organization of American

States at Punta del Este in January, 1962, declared: "The present Government of Cuba has identified itself with the principles of Marxist-Leninist ideology, has established a political, economic, and social system based on that doctrine, and accepts military assistance from extra-continental Communist powers, including even the threat of military intervention in America on the part of the Soviet Union"; and

Whereas the international Communist movement has increasingly extended into Cuba its political, economic, and military sphere of influence: now, therefore, be it

Resolved by the Senate and House of Representatives of the United States of America in Congress assembled, that the United States is determined—

(a) To prevent by whatever means may be necessary, including the use of arms, the Marxist-Leninist regime in Cuba from extending by force or threat of force its aggressive or subversive activities to any part of this hemisphere;

(b) To prevent in Cuba the creation or use of an externally supported military capability endangering the security of the United States; and

(c) To work with the Organization of American States and with freedom-loving Cubans to support the aspirations of the Cuban people for self-determination.

DOCUMENT 21. President Kennedy Demands the Withdrawal of Offensive Weapons from Cuba. October 22, 1962. (U.S. Department of State, *The U.S. Response to Soviet Military Buildup in Cuba,* Washington, D.C., 1962.)

This Government, as promised, has maintained the closest surveillance of the Soviet military build-up on the island of Cuba.

Within the past week, unmistakable evidence has established the fact that a series of offensive missile sites is now in preparation on that imprisoned island.

The purpose of these bases can be none other than to provide a nuclear strike capability against the Western Hemisphere.

Upon receiving the first preliminary hard information of this nature last Tuesday morning at 9 A.M., I directed that our surveillance be stepped up. And having now confirmed and completed our evaluation of the evidence and our decision on a course of action, this Government feels obliged to report this new crisis to you in full detail.

The characteristics of these new missile sites indicate two distinct types of installations. Several of them include medium range ballistic missiles, capable of carrying a nuclear warhead for a distance of more than 1,000 nautical miles. Each of these missiles, in short, is capable of striking Washington, D. C., the Panama Canal, Cape Canaveral, Mexico City, or any other city in the southeastern part of the United States, in Central-America or in the Caribbean area.

Additional sites not yet completed appear to be designed for intermediate range ballistic missiles—capable of traveling more than twice as far—and thus capable of striking most of the major cities in the western hemisphere, ranging as far north as Hudson's Bay, Canada, and as far south as Lima, Peru. In addition, jet bombers, capable of carrying nuclear weapons, are now being uncrated and assembled in Cuba, while the necessary air bases are being prepared.

This urgent transformation of Cuba into an important strategic base—by the presence of these large, long-range and clearly offensive weapons of sudden mass destruction—constitutes an explicit threat to the peace and security of all the Americas, in flagrant and deliberate defiance of the Rio pact of 1947, the traditions of this nation and hemisphere, the joint resolution of the 87th Congress, the Charter of the United Nations, and my own public warnings to the Soviets on Sept. 4 and 13.

This action also contradicts the repeated assurances of Soviet spokesmen, both publicly and privately delivered, that the arms build-up in Cuba would retain its original defensive character, and that the Soviet Union had no need or desire to station strategic missiles on the territory of any other nation.

The size of this undertaking makes clear that it had been planned some months ago. Yet only last month, after I had made clear the distinction between any introduction of ground-to-ground missiles and the existence of defensive antiaircraft missiles, the Soviet Government publicly stated on Sept. 11 that the "armaments and military equipment sent to Cuba are designed exclusively for defensive purposes," that "there is no need for the Soviet Union to shift its weapons . . . for a retaliatory blow to any other country, for instance Cuba," and that "the Soviet Union has so powerful rockets to carry these nuclear warheads that there is no need to search for sites for them beyond the boundaries of the Soviet Union."

That statement was false.

Only last Thursday, as evidence of this rapid offensive build-up was already in my hand, Soviet Foreign Minister Gromyko told me in my office that he was instructed to make it clear once again, as he said his Government had already done, the Soviet assistance to Cuba "pursued solely the purpose of contributing to the defense capabilities of Cuba," that "training by Soviet specialists of Cuban nationals in handling defensive armaments was by no means offensive," and that "if it were otherwise, the Soviet Government would never become involved in rendering such assistance."

That statement also was false.

Our policy has been one of patience and restraint, as befits a peaceful and powerful nation, which leads a worldwide alliance. We have been determined not to be diverted from our central concerns by mere irritants and fanatics.

But now further action is required—and it is under way; and these actions may only be the beginning. We will not prematurely or unnecessarily risk the costs of worldwide nuclear war in which even the fruits of victory would be ashes in our mouth—but neither will we shrink from that risk at any time it must be faced.

Acting, therefore, in the defense of our own security and that of the entire Western Hemisphere, and under the authority entrusted to me by the Constitution as endorsed by the resolution of the Congress, I have directed that the following initial steps be taken immediately:

First: To halt this offensive build-up, a strict quarantine on all offensive military equipment under shipment to Cuba is being initiated. All ships of any kind bound for Cuba, from whatever nation or port, will, if found to contain cargoes of offensive weapons, be turned back. This quarantine will be extended, if needed, to other types of cargo and carriers. We are not at this time, however, denying the necessities of life as the Soviet attempted to do in their Berlin blockade of 1948.

Second: I have directed the continued and increased surveillance of Cuba and its military build-up. The Foreign Ministers of the OAS in their communiqué of Oct. 6 rejected secrecy on such matters in this hemisphere. Should these offensive military preparations continue, thus increasing the threat to the hemisphere, further action will be justified. I have directed the armed forces to prepare for any eventualities; and I trust that, in the interest of both the Cuban people and the Soviet technicians at these sites, the hazards to all concerned of continuing this threat will be recognized.

Third: It shall be the policy of this nation to regard any nuclear missile launched from Cuba against any nation in the Western Hemisphere as an attack by the Soviet Union on the United States requiring a full retaliatory response upon the Soviet Union.

Fourth: As a necessary military precaution, I have reinforced our base at Guantanamo, evacuated today the dependents of our personnel there and ordered additional military units to stand by on an alert basis.

Fifth: We are calling tonight for an immediate meeting of the organ of consultation under the Organization of American States, to consider this threat to hemispheric security and to invoke Articles 6 and 8 of the Rio treaty in support of all necessary action. The United Nations Charter allows for regional security arrangements— and the nations of this hemisphere decided long ago against the military presence of outside powers. Our other allies around the world have also been alerted.

Sixth: Under the Charter of the United Nations, we are asking tonight that an emergency meeting of the Security Council be convoked without delay to take action against this latest Soviet threat to world peace. Our resolution will call for the prompt dismantling and withdrawal of all offensive weapons in Cuba, under the supervision of UN observers, before the quarantine can be lifted.

Seventh and finally: I call upon chairman Khrushchev to halt and eliminate this clandestine, reckless, and provocative threat to world peace and to stable relations between our two nations. I call upon him further to abandon this course of world domination, and to join in an historic effort to end the perilous arms race and transform the history of man.

✓ ✓ ✓ ✓ ✓

Finally, I want to say a few words to the captive people of Cuba, to whom this speech is being directly carried by special radio facilities.

I speak to you as a friend, as one who knows of your deep attachment to your fatherland, as one who shares your aspirations for liberty and justice for all. And I have watched with sorrow how your nationalist revolution was betrayed—and how your fatherland fell under foreign domination.

Now your leaders are no longer Cuban leaders inspired by Cuban ideals. They are puppets and agents of an international conspiracy which has turned Cuba against your friends and neighbors in the Americas—and turned it into the first Latin-American country to become a target for nuclear war—the first Latin-American country to have these weapons on its soil.

These new weapons are not in your interest. They can only undermine it. But this country has no wish to cause you to suffer or to impose any system upon you. We know your lives and land are being used as pawns by those who deny you freedom.

Many times in the past, the Cuban people have risen to throw out tyrants who destroyed their liberty, and I have no doubt that most Cubans today look forward to the time when they will be truly free—free from foreign domination. Free to choose their own leaders. Free to select their own system. Free to own their own land. Free to speak and write and worship without fear or degradation. And then shall Cuba be welcomed back to the society of free nations and to the associations of this hemisphere.

Our goal is not the victory of might but the vindication of right—not peace at the expense of freedom, but both peace and freedom, here in this hemisphere, and, we hope, around the world. God willing, that goal will be achieved.

NOTES

CHAPTER I

EXPANSION, COMMERCE, AND THE
"NATURAL LAW OF POLITICAL GRAVITATION"
(1783–1878)

1. Term meaning "no further."

2. Joel Poinsett was an expansionist-minded diplomat who was sent as a secret agent to Cuba by President Monroe. He later became Minister to Mexico.

3. The French invasion of Spain was sanctioned by the Congress of Verona in order to restore Ferdinand VII to full power.

4. The proposal made by George Canning (British Foreign Secretary) to Richard Rush (United States Minister to England) that the United States and Great Britain join in a mutual declaration warning the continental powers against interference in Latin America.

5. Daniel Webster, *Speeches and Forensic Arguments* (2 vols.; 8th ed., Boston, 1843), I: 330.

6. This selection, and others from this work in this chapter, are reprinted by permission of the publisher, The Carnegie Endowment for International Peace.

7. This selection, and others from this work in this chapter, are reprinted by permission of the publisher, the David McKay Company.

8. O'Sullivan was a leader of the "Young America" group, and an ardent advocate of Manifest Destiny in all of its aspects.

9. The Belize is the present-day British Honduras, and the Kingdom of the Mosquito was located along the east coast of Nicaragua and the extreme southeastern coast of Honduras.

10. Articles 7 and 8 of the Treaty of 1803 with France concerned commercial relations in the ceded area. France was given special privileges in the port of New Orleans for a twelve-year period, to be followed by a most favored nation status.

11. Senator Yulee of Florida. The resolution was withdrawn prior to debate, but Yulee hoped that it would be considered at a later date.

12. The Family Compact linking the Bourbon monarchies of France and Spain.

13. The Elgin-Marcy Treaty was approved by the Senate on August 2, 1854. The negotiations were marked by shrewd politics rather than by bluster.

14. In 1853, Tsar Nicholas I of Russia sent Prince Menschikoff on a special mission to the Turkish government. The object of the mission was to give Russia greater influence within the Turkish Empire, but the truculent tactics of Menschikoff did not produce the desired results.

15. The Crimean War had started in October, 1853, when Turkey declared war on Russia. England and France entered the war on the side of Turkey in March, 1854.

16. Reprinted by permission of the publisher, J. B. Lippincott Company.

CHAPTER II

EMPIRES IN CONFLICT AND THE CUBAN PROTECTORATE
(1879–1918)

1. Josiah Strong, Our Country: Its Possible Future and Its Present Crisis (rev. ed.; New York, 1891), p. 28.

2. Captain Alfred Thayer Mahan, "Possibilities of an Anglo-American Reunion," North American Review (July, 1894), as published in, The Interests of America in Sea Power, Present and Future (Boston 1898), pp. 118, 123.

3. George W. Auxier, "Middle Western Newspapers and the Spanish-American War," The Mississippi Valley Historical Review (March, 1940), pp. 523–34.

4. The Windward Passage is the channel between Cuba and Haiti.

5. This selection, and others from this work in this chapter, are reprinted by permission of the publisher, the Harvard University Press.

6. This account is possibly overdramatized, but it is valuable for the views presented; especially Ruben's account of the insurgent's attitude. This selection cannot be precisely dated, but it seems that the interview took place in January or early February, 1898. This is based on its location in the narrative and the attitude of the men involved. I believe that this discussion took place prior to the sinking of the Maine.

7. The insurgent General Calixto Garcia, who was given rather shabby treatment by General Shafter.

8. This selection, and others from this work in this chapter, are reprinted by permission of the publisher, the Harvard University Press.

9. General Enoch Crowder served in Cuba during the Second Intervention, and was sent to Cuba as the personal representative of President Woodrow Wilson on two occasions. He became the first Ambassador to Cuba in 1923. Henry P. Fletcher was a State Department official.

10. President Mario Menocal of Cuba.

CHAPTER III

THE NEW DOLLAR DIPLOMACY BETWEEN WAR AND DEPRESSION
(1919–1932)

1. *The Cuba Review* was published by the Munson Steamship Lines.
2. This was known as the "Foster Incident."
3. This figure indicates the discount rate. Cuba would receive 96.77 per cent of the face value of the bonds issued. This was quite high for bonds issued by Latin American governments during this period. Speyer and Company made a bid of 93.52 per cent.
4. Dwight Morrow, who later became Ambassador to Mexico.
5. Reprinted by permission of the publisher, *The Atlantic Monthly*.
6. Guantánamo Bay and Bahia Honda.
7. Colonel José Tarafa was a member of the Cuban Congress, and a prominent businessman allied with American interests.
8. Carlos Manuel de Céspedes was a cabinet member.
9. The plan was to have Governor Alfred E. Smith of New York and Mayor James Walker of New York City make speeches urging the abrogation of the Platt Amendment. Machado was unable to make the trip as scheduled, and the State Department found out about the plan before his visit in April, 1927. As a result, the plan did not materialize.
10. José Obregon was Machado's son-in-law.
11. The Warren Brothers Company was a construction firm that had been building the Central Highway in Cuba as part of the public works program. These bonds were deferred-payment public works certificates which the bank could either cash in at the Cuban Treasury as funds became available, or convert to serial certificates to be sold in the public bond market.
12. Henry Catlin was the president of the Santiago Electric company, and a business associate of the Cuban President.
13. Edwin P. Shattuck was a lawyer and a professional lobbyist. He worked for the Cuban sugar producers in 1922, and again (with Herbert C. Lakin) in 1929–30. He was also a personal friend of Herbert Hoover.
14. *Remolacheros*—Cuban name for the beet sugar producers.
15. President Calvin Coolidge refused to accept the recommendation of the Tariff Commission.
16. Lakin had reference to the members of the United States Sugar Association. The following sugar refining companies were members: W. J. McCahan, National, Hershey, Cuba Cane, Cuban-American, Cuban-Dominican, Czarnikow-Rionda, Fidelity, General Sugars, Lowry, Manati, Punta Alegre, Tuinucu, Atlantic Fruit and Sugar (subsidiary of United Fruit Co.).

CHAPTER IV

THE NEW DEAL DIPLOMACY AND THE CUBAN SETTLEMENT
(1933–1945)

1. Mrs. Phillips' husband was a correspondent for *The New York Times*. She later became a correspondent for the *Times* after the death of her husband. This diary account first appeared in Mrs. Phillips' book, *Cuban Sideshow*, published in 1935. This selection, and others from this work in this chapter, are reprinted by permission of the publisher, Ivan Obolensky Incorporated.

2. Reprinted by permission of the publisher, The Carnegie Endowment for International Peace.

3. The ABC was a secret political society organized to fight Machado. A number of university students were members.

4. The Drago Doctrine was enunciated by Luis Drago of Argentina in 1902. Its intent was to prohibit the use of armed force against any American nation for the collection of debts. The watered-down version adopted in 1907 at the Second Hague Conference was actually Elihu Root's modification of the doctrine. This version left an opening for intervention, and Drago voted against it.

5. The term "insular producers" refers to Hawaii, Puerto Rico, and the Philippine Islands.

6. W. H. Woodin was Secretary of the Treasury. He had important business links with the Cuban economy (The Cuba Company, the Cuban Chamber of Commerce in the United States), and had been President of the American Car and Foundry Company.

7. Rexford Guy Tugwell was Under-Secretary of Agriculture, and Adolph A. Berle, Jr. was in the State Department. Both men were officials of the American Molasses Company (which controlled a sugar refining company, The Sucrest Company). Dirksen brought out these connections in his speech. Mordecai Ezekiel was in the Department of Agriculture.

8. Federico Laredo Bru was the President of Cuba.

9. The claim of Fred A. Morris was for compensation for land seized by the Cuban Government. Warren Brothers Company held $9,800,000 in gold notes, and $1,050,000 in port notes, received in payment for constructing 481 miles of the Central Highway. The Purdy and Henderson Company had constructed the capitol building in Havana, and held $1,500,000 in public works bonds.

10. These discussions were held with Colonel Batista in Washington, D.C. A Ten-Point program was agreed upon, and tariff reform was one of the main items.

11. The monetary law made dollar accounts, with certain excep-

tions, payable in pesos. The credit moratorium was actually a moratorium on the collection of certain debts.

12. The legislation referred to was the bill authorizing a financial settlement with the remaining bondholders. It was introduced late in 1938, and shelved several times before it was finally passed.

13. A proposed tax of six per cent on money exported from Cuba was the most important complaint.

14. Under this law exporters of sugar were required to surrender 20 per cent of their proceeds to the Currency Stabilization Fund against payment in pesos at par. Other exporters were required to exchange 10 per cent of their proceeds, but this group was never required to comply with the law.

CHAPTER V

POSTWAR DRIFT AND THE CASTRO REVOLUTION
(1946–1962)

1. *Toward Our Common American Destiny* (Medford, Mass.: Fletcher School of Law and Diplomacy, Tufts University, 1955), p. 21; as quoted in, Edwin Lieuwen, *Arms and Politics in Latin America* (rev. ed., New York, 1961), p. 257.

2. U.S. Department of Commerce, *Investment in Cuba: Basic Information for United States Businessmen* (Washington, 1956), p. 10.

3. Jules Dubois, *Fidel Castro* (New York, Indianapolis, 1959), p. 181.

4. Teresa Casuso, *Cuba and Castro* (New York, 1961), p. 203. The version of Castro's speech used in this book includes the foreword that appeared in the 1954 edition, but the exact source for this reprint is not mentioned. Robert Taber, in his foreword to this 1961 edition, mentions the notes of the reporters in 1954 and also a version written in lime juice by Fidel Castro during his imprisonment. It appears that the Fair Play for Cuba Committee had access to both versions. Jules Dubois's book, *Fidel Castro*, contains a large excerpt from the speech which varies slightly in wording—but which is identical in meaning—from the version published by Lyle Stuart for the Fair Play for Cuba Committee.

5. Reprinted by permission of the publisher, Lyle Stuart.

6. Colonel Alberto del Rio Chaviano was the commander of the Regiment Maceo at Moncada Barracks, Santiago de Cuba, in 1953.

7. A caballería equals 33.1619 acres.

8. An arroba is twenty-five pounds.

9. This selection, and others from the same source in this chapter, are reprinted by permission of the publisher, *The New York Times*.

10. Reprinted by permission of the publisher, Ivan Obolensky Incorporated.

11. Cuba and the Soviet Union had negotiated a trade agreement on a barter basis in February, 1960.

12. This selection, and others from the same source in this chapter, are reprinted by permission of the publisher, the *International Review Service*.

13. Theodore Draper, *Cuba and U.S. Policy* (New York, 1961), p. 11. Peinado's booklet does not list the publisher. A friend was on the mailing list of the Frente Revolucionario Democratico (FRD) in 1961, and received this publication from Miami, Florida, during the period when he was also receiving the FRD newsletter.

14. This book was originally published by Harper & Brothers Publishing Company in 1960.

15. This selection, and others from the same source in this chapter, are reprinted by permission of the publisher, *The Wall Street Journal*.

16. Robert E. Light and Carl Marzani, *Cuba Versus the CIA* (New York, 1961), pp. 48–52.

17. Haya de la Torre is the founder and leading figure in the APRA party (also known as the *apristas*) in Peru.

18. In the interests of accuracy, Mr. Stewart Alsop has requested that the following corrections be indicated. "First, President Kennedy did not inherit from President Eisenhower anything so detailed that it could be rightly called 'a plan.' Also, President Eisenhower's intention to use the Cuban refugees in an operation against Castro was clear. Second, Secretary of the Treasury Douglas Dillon was not present at the critical April 4th meeting." This article is one of the best discussions of a subject which is beclouded by secrecy. Reprinted by permission of the author, Mr. Stewart Alsop; copyright 1961 by the Curtis Publishing Company.

19. Richard Bissell was the deputy for plans and operations in the Central Intelligence Agency.

20. McGeorge Bundy and Arthur M. Schlesinger, Jr. were presidential advisors.

BIBLIOGRAPHICAL ESSAY

The following list is provided for those readers who may wish to explore the subject, or any aspect of it, in more detail. This is not an exhaustive list, but it does include many of the major works written on the subject.

THE BASIC COLLECTION of documents for any study of American foreign policy is *Papers Relating to the Foreign Relations of the United States* (Washington, 1862–   ). The papers pertaining to Latin America have been published as a separate volume since 1932. Currently the volumes for 1941 and 1942 are being published. The State Department also publishes many separate documents in its various series. The Inter-American Series is especially useful ꞏfor study in this area.

The most valuable collection of diplomatic documents for a study of U.S.–Latin American relations between 1831 and 1860 is William R. Manning, ed., *Diplomatic Correspondence of the United States: Inter-American Affairs, 1831–1860* (12 vols., Washington, 1932–39). A useful work for an earlier period is William R. Manning, ed., *Diplomatic Correspondence of the United States Concerning the Independence of Latin-American Nations* (3 vols.; New York, 1925). Two useful collections of treaties and similar official documents are William M. Malloy, ed., *Treaties, Conventions, International Acts, Protocols, and Agreements between the United States of America and Other Powers* (4 vols.; Washington, 1910–38), and David Hunter Miller, ed., *Treaties and Other International Acts of the United States of America* (8 vols.; Washington, 1931–48).

The debates and proceedings of Congress contain much material which is valuable for foreign policy studies. These have been published in Worthington C. Ford, *et al*, eds., *Journals of the Continental Congress* (34 vols.; Washington, 1904–37), the *Annals of Congress* (1789–1828), the *Register of Debates in Congress* (1824–37), the *Congressional Globe* (1833–73), and the *Congressional Record* (1873–   ). Much valuable material also appears in the published hearings of Congressional committees, and in the documents published by both houses of Congress.

Several collections of selected documents with editorial commentary have been published in recent years. Robert A. Divine, ed., *American Foreign Policy* (New York, 1960), Dorothy Burne Goebel, ed., *American Foreign Policy: A Documentary Survey, 1776–1960* (New York, 1961), and Ruhl J. Bartlett, ed., *The Record of American Diplomacy* (3rd ed.; New York, 1954) are three useful volumes of this type. William A. Williams, ed., *The Shaping of American Diplomacy* (Chicago, 1956) is an extremely valuable collection of documents and interpretive articles. Many of the important official documents concerning the Latin American policy of the U.S. are published in James W. Gantenbein, ed., *The Evolution of Our Latin American Policy: A Documentary Record* (New York, 1950).

      ✻   ✻   ✻   ✻   ✻

The two standard surveys of the Latin American policy of the U.S. are Graham Stuart, *Latin America and the United States* (5th ed.; New York, 1955), and Samuel Flagg Bemis, *The Latin American Policy of the United States* (New York, 1943). Although not confined to U.S. policy, J. Fred Rippy, *Latin America in World Politics* (3rd ed.; New York, 1938) contains much information on this subject. Dexter Perkins, *A History of the Monroe Doctrine* (rev. ed., Boston, 1955) is the major work on the development of this policy. An interpretive analysis of the history of U.S. relations with Latin America is presented by Perkins in *The United States and Latin America* (Baton Rouge, 1961). A slightly different emphasis is given in John A. Logan, Jr., *No Transfer: An American Security Principle* (New Haven, 1961). Latin American reaction to U.S. policy from the 1930's to the late 1950's is the major theme of Donald Dozer, *Are We Good Neighbors?* (Gainesville, Fla., 1959). Dozer also stresses the decline of the Good Neighbor image. Thomas W. Palmer, *Search for a Latin American Policy* (Gainesville, Fla., 1957) presents U.S. policy since 1945 with emphasis on political factors. The best documented study of U.S. policy from the mid-1920's through the 1930's is Bryce Wood, *The Making of the Good Neighbor Policy* (New York, 1961). In certain respects Wood expands the thesis presented in Alexander De Conde, *Herbert Hoover's Latin American Policy* (Stanford, 1951). One of the most valuable interpretive studies of U.S. policy is Arthur P. Whitaker, *The Western Hemisphere Idea* (Ithaca, N.Y., 1954). Thomas F. McGann, *Argentina, the United States, and the Inter-American System, 1880–1914* (Cambridge, Mass., 1957) is the best study of this stage of the Pan-American Movement and the rivalry between Argentina and the U.S. A detailed survey of Pan-Americanism from the point of view of U. S. policy is provided in J. Lloyd Mecham, *The United States and Inter-American Security, 1889–1960* (Austin, Tex., 1961).

Dexter Perkins, *The United States and the Caribbean* (Cambridge, Mass., 1947) is a short survey with emphasis on the period since the 1890's. A more detailed survey with the same general emphasis is J. Fred Rippy, *The Caribbean Danger Zone* (New York, 1940). A work which is still useful for the early period is Dana Munro, *The United States and the Caribbean Area* (Boston, 1934). Wilfrid H. Callcott, *The Caribbean Policy of the United States, 1889–1920* (Baltimore, 1942) provides one of the best documented studies of this period. Howard C. Hill, *Roosevelt and the Caribbean* (Chicago, 1927) is also valuable for an understanding of Roosevelt's motives and actions. Chester Lloyd Jones, *The Caribbean Interests of the United States* (New York, 1916) is useful for the economic side of American policy, and is also valuable for understanding the motives behind this policy due to Jones's connections with the State Department. A broader study by the same author is *The Caribbean Since 1900* (Madison, Wis., 1936). One of the best studies of American investments in Latin America is Willy Feuerlein and Elizabeth Hannan, *Dollars in Latin America* (New York, 1941). A collection of articles which presents a critical evaluation of U.S. aid to Latin America since 1945, as well as various other facets of economic relations, is J. Fred Rippy, *Globe and Hemisphere: Latin America's Place in the Postwar Relations of the United States* (Chicago, 1958). Herbert Feis, *The Diplomacy of the Dollar: First Era, 1919–1932* (Baltimore, 1950) is an illuminating discussion of private loans to Latin America and the loan policy of the State Department. American military assistance to Latin America since 1940 is related to the chronic problems of militarism in Edwin Lieuwen, *Arms and Politics in Latin America* (New York, 1960).

✓   ✓   ✓   ✓   ✓

The basic work in the field of U.S.–Cuban relations from the Cuban point of view is Herminio Portell Vilá, *Historia de Cuba: en sus relaciones con los Estados Unidos y España* (4 vols.; Havana, 1938). Another useful work by thirty Cuban scholars is Ramiro Guerra y Sánchez, *et al.*, *Historia de la nación Cubana* (10 vols.; Havana, 1952). Charles E. Chapman, *A History of the Cuban Republic: A Study in Hispanic American Politics* (New York, 1927) is a general political survey which tends to be quite pro-U.S. Mixtures of history, travel literature, and valuable personal observations are presented in Irene A. Wright, *Cuba* (New York, 1912), and Erna Fergusson, *Cuba* (New York, 1946). A popular, well-written account of the historical development of Cuba is Hudson Strode, *The Pageant of Cuba* (New York, 1934). Volume I of a projected multi-volume history of Cuba from the Marxist point of view, covers the period from 1492 to 1845. The other volumes of Philip S. Foner, *Cuba: From Spanish Colony to American Colony to Independent Nation* (New York, 1961–   ) are in preparation.

✓   ✓   ✓   ✓   ✓

Except for certain periods, the area of U.S.–Cuban relations to the 1890's has not been covered in depth by recent scholarship. James M. Callahan, *Cuba and International Relations: A Historical Study in American Diplomacy* (Baltimore, 1899) is the most detailed and useful of the older works. It is out-of-date in certain respects and lacks either footnotes or bibliography. John H. Latane, *The Diplomacy of the U.S. in Regard to Cuba* (Washington, 1898), and James M. Callahan, *Cuba and Anglo-American Relations* (Washington, 1897) are shorter reports published by the American Historical Association. Several excellent works of more recent date have been published for the period 1848 to 1855. Robert G. Caldwell, *The López Expedition to Cuba: 1848–1851* (Princeton, 1915), is still a useful work, although Herminio Portell Vilá, *Narciso López y su época* (3 vols.; Havana, 1930–58) is one of the most scholarly and detailed studies of this era, and one which revises a number of older views. The scholarly, and perhaps definitive, work on U.S. diplomacy in the early 1850's is Amos Ettinger, *The Mission to Spain of Pierre Soulé* (New Haven, 1932). This work is based on a vast amount of multi-archival research and embodies Ettinger's earlier monograph *The Proposed Anglo-Franco-American Treaty of 1852 to Guarantee Cuba to Spain* (London, 1930). Basil Rauch, *American Interest in Cuba: 1848–1855* (New York, 1948) is an excellent study with emphasis on economic factors. Rauch also discusses the events preceding the period listed in the title. The story of the early attempts by little-known agents of the U.S. government to improve commercial relations with Cuba is related in Roy F. Nichols, *Advance Agents of American Destiny* (Philadelphia, 1956).

✓   ✓   ✓   ✓   ✓

One of the most detailed accounts of the military aspects of the Spanish-American War is French E. Chadwick, *Relations of the United States and Spain: The Spanish-American War* (2 vols.;

New York, 1909–11). A more recent survey in detail is Miguel Varona Guerro, *La guerra de la independencia de Cuba: 1895–1898* (3 vols.; Havana, 1946). Walter Millis, *The Martial Spirit: A Study of the War With Spain* (New York, 1931) is a vivid and interesting presentation. Frank Freidel, *The Splendid Little War* (Boston, 1958) is essentially a pictorial history, but the narrative does present some revised views on the subject. The motives behind the war and the theme of business opposition are given scholarly treatment in Julius Pratt, *Expansionists of 1898* (Baltimore, 1936). The activities of the Cuban Junta prior to the war are dramatically described by the former legal advisor to the Junta, in Horatio S. Rubens, *Liberty, the Story of Cuba* (New York, 1932). The legalistic approach to U.S.–Spanish diplomacy is presented in Horace E. Flack, *Spanish–American Diplomatic Relations Preceding the War of 1898* (Baltimore, 1906), and Elbert J. Benton, *International Law and Diplomacy of the Spanish–American War* (Baltimore, 1908).

The role of journalistic propaganda is presented in detail in Joseph E. Wisan, *The Cuban Crisis as Reflected in the New York Press: 1895–1898* (New York, 1934). An interesting study of popular pressure and war is M. M. Wilkerson, *Public Opinion and the Spanish–American War* (Baton Rouge, 1932). A number of speeches and documents are printed in Fitzhugh Lee, *Cuba's Struggle Against Spain* (New York, 1899). Albert G. Robinson, *Cuba and the Intervention* (New York, 1905) is a useful survey of the war and the occupation. The Cuban perspective can be found in Enrique Collazo, *Los Americanos en Cuba* (2 vols.; Havana, 1905). The generally neglected story of the part played by the Cubans during the war is presented in Herminio Portell Vilá, *Historia de la guerra de Cuba y los Estados Unidos contra España* (Havana, 1949). This book is a useful corrective to the studies which emphasize American participation. Orestes Ferrara, *The Last Spanish War* (New York, 1937), is a valuable, multi-archival treatment of the subject with primary emphasis on European diplomacy.

An illuminating source on American opinion prior to the war and on postwar conditions in Cuba is Robert P. Porter, *Report on the Commercial and Industrial Condition of the Island of Cuba* (Treasury Department Document No. 2072, Washington, 1898). A valuable source for the first year of the occupation is the *Civil Report of Major-General John R. Brooke, U.S. Army: Military Governor, Island of Cuba* (Washington, 1900). Several reports and speeches concerning the occupation are printed in Robert Bacon and James B. Scott, eds., *The Military and Colonial Policy of the United States: Addresses and Reports by Elihu Root* (Cambridge, Mass., 1916).

✓   ✓   ✓   ✓   ✓

Edwin F. Atkins, *Sixty Years in Cuba* (Cambridge, Mass., 1926), is a very useful volume of personal reminiscences written by a prominent American investor in Cuban sugar properties. The major emphasis of the volume is the period from the 1870's to about 1905. A detailed political survey of U.S.–Cuban relations is Russel H. Fitzgibbon, *Cuba and the United States: 1900–1935* (Menasha, Wis., 1935). Leland H. Jenks, *Our Cuban Colony* (New York, 1928) presents a critical analysis of economic imperialism in Cuba from the latter part of the nineteenth century to the mid-1920's. The pattern of U.S.–Cuban relations from 1917 to 1960 as this was affected by a variety of business interests is the major theme of Robert F. Smith, *The United States and Cuba: Business and Diplomacy, 1917–1960* (New York, 1961).

One of the most useful studies of the intervention of 1906–9 is D. A. Lockmiller, *Magoon in Cuba* (Chapel Hill, N.C., 1938). Two valuable sources for the Isle of Pines controversy are U.S. Senate, *Papers Relating to the Adjustment of Title to the Isle of Pines* (Document No. 166, Washington, 1924), and U.S. Senate, Committee on Foreign Relations, *Adjustment of Title to Isle of Pines* (Report No. 1, Washington, 1922). Cuban evaluations of the Platt Amendment are presented in three critical studies which also reveal a growing Cuban nationalism: these are Ambrosio Valentín Lopez Hidalgo, *Cuba y la Enmienda Platt* (Havana, 1921), Luis Machado y Ortega, *La Enmienda Platt: estudio de su alcance e interpretación y doctrina sobre su aplicación* (Havana, 1922), and Emilio Roig de Leuchsenring, *El intervencionismo, mal de males de Cuba republicana* (San Jose de Costa Rica, 1931). David A. Lockmiller, *Enoch H. Crowder, Soldier, Lawyer, and Statesman* (Columbia, Mo., 1955) is a laudatory study of a man who played an important role in U.S. relations with Cuba. An interesting and revealing examination of Cuban conditions in 1930 are presented in A. Hyatt Verrill, *Cuba of Today* (New York, 1931). M. Márquez Sterling, *Los Conferencias del Shoreham: El Cesarismo en Cuba* (Mexico DF, 1933), and Herminio Portell Vilá, *The Non-Intervention Pact of Montevideo and American Intervention in Cuba* (NP, 1935), are two rather polemic tracts attacking U.S. policy during the Machado era and the period of upheaval during 1933 and 1934. A former Ambassador to Cuba offers his version of the events from 1928 to mid-1933, and the role of American capital, in Harry F. Guggenheim, *The United States and Cuba* (New York, 1934).

One of the best studies of the economy, society, and government of Cuba in the 1930's is Raymond L. Buell, *et al.*, *Problems of the New Cuba* (New York, 1935). This book written by a committee of the Foreign Policy Association also presents a number of recommended approaches to the problems. Carleton Beals, *The Crime of Cuba* (Philadelphia, 1933) is an attack on U.S. policy toward Cuba, with emphasis on the Machado era. A short, but useful evaluation of the period of revolution in 1933–34 is Charles A. Thompson, *The Cuban Revolution: Reform and Reaction* (Foreign Policy Association Information Service, Vol. XI, No. 22, New York, 1936). A valuable eye-witness account of Cuba in the early 1930's is R. Hart Phillips, *Cuban Sideshow* (Havana, 1935), which was later embodied in an expanded treatment, *Cuba: Island of Paradox* (New York, 1959).

◆   ◆   ◆   ◆   ◆

The Cuban economy and its relationship to the economy of the United States is an important element in U.S.–Cuban relations. A valuable survey of these economic relations during the first three decades of the twentieth century is Phillip G. Wright, *The Cuban Situation and Our Treaty Relations* (Washington, 1931). Wright's earlier book *Sugar in Relation to the Tariff* (New York, 1924), is a detailed examination of U.S. tariff policy and Cuban sugar to 1923. The problems of the Cuban sugar economy are placed in the context of the international sugar problem in H. C. Prinsen Geerligs and R. J. Prinsen Geerligs, *Cane Sugar Production, 1912–1937* (London, 1938). Viriato Gutierrez, *The World Sugar Problem, 1926–1935* (London, 1935) is a well documented argument for some type of international production agreement. The U.S. sugar program during World War I is uncritically described in Joshua Bernhardt, *Government Control of the Sugar Industry in the United States* (New York, 1920). Bernhardt had been a member of the Sugar Equalization Board during this period. Somewhat later he wrote a general survey of the sugar programs enacted by the government between 1917 and 1947; *The Sugar Industry and the Federal Government: A Thirty Year Record, 1917–1947* (Washington, 1948) reproduces numerous documents dealing with these programs. A valuable collection of statistics mixed with propaganda is presented in United States Cuban Sugar Council, *Sugar-Facts and Figures, 1952* (Washington, 1952).

A most scholarly and detailed analysis of the monetary problems of Cuba is Henry C. Wallich, *Monetary Problems of an Export Economy: The Cuban Experience, 1914–1947* (Cambridge, Mass., 1950). Lowry Nelson, *Rural Cuba* (Minneapolis, 1950) is the most significant examination of all aspects of rural society in Cuba which has been produced. Emphasis on the historical aspect of Cuban economic development is presented in Gustavo Gutierrez, *El dessarrollo economico de Cuba* (Havana, 1952), and Julián Alienes y Urosa, *Caracteristicas fundementales de la economica Cubana* (Havana, 1950). A similar study, and one that is highly critical of the role of the U.S. is Raul Lorenzo, *El empleo en Cuba* (Havana, 1955). Useful statistical information and economic analyses are published in U.S. Department of Commerce, *Cuban Readjustment to Current Economic Forces* (Trade Information Bulletin No. 725, Washington, 1930), and *Investment in Cuba: Basic Information for United States Businessmen* (Washington, 1956). Tariff Commission, *The Effects of the Cuban Reciprocity Treaty of 1902* (Washington, 1929) is a valuable source for documents concerning the history of the treaty, but it is also an argument against revising the treaty in Cuba's favor.

✓   ✓   ✓   ✓   ✓

The revolution of Fidel Castro has already produced a bibliography of some magnitude, and the end is not in sight. These books are mainly attempts to explain, evaluate, and otherwise interpret the situation in Cuba. Most can be classified as "current events" rather than as history, but some are documents in themselves because of the authors. Many of these contain valuable information, and thoughtful interpretations that are useful to anyone interested in the current situation.

Reporters for news media have written most of the documentary works. Jules Dubois, *Fidel Castro* (New York, 1959) is a combination biography-eye witness description. Although this book is very complimentary to Castro, the author has since changed his opinion. Herbert L. Matthews, *The Cuban Story* (New York, 1961) is a thought-provoking analysis of developments in Cuba by *The New York Times* editor who first interviewed Castro in 1957. An extremely sympathetic account of the revolution is Robert Taber, *M-26: Biography of a Revolution* (New York, 1961). Taber was a CBS reporter who became one of the leaders of the Fair Play for Cuba Committee, and who went to work for the Castro Government in 1961. A valuable personal account of the changes in the revolution is presented in Teresa Casuso, *Cuba and Castro* (New

York, 1961). Miss Casuso has written a moderate analysis based on her contacts with Castro in Mexico, and later as an official of the Cuban Government.

The best analysis of the revolution to date by a rather impartial student is Irving P. Pflaum, *Tragic Island: How Communism Came to Cuba* (New York, 1961). Part of the research for this book was done for the American Universities Field Staff. The Communist interpretation is presented in Joseph North, *Cuba—Hope of a Hemisphere* (New York, 1961), and Blas Roca, *The Cuban Revolution* (New York, 1961). The latter was the general secretary of the Cuban Communist Party. Leo Huberman and Paul M. Sweezy, *Cuba, Anatomy of a Revolution* (New York, 1960) is an interesting evaluation from a general Marxist viewpoint. A highly polemic view from the extreme right is Nathaniel Weyl, *Red Star Over Cuba* (New York, 1961). Daniel James, *Cuba: The First Soviet Satellite in the Americas* (New York, 1961) takes the same general view, but is better documented and less emotional. C. Wright Mills, *Listen Yankee: The Revolution in Cuba* (New York, 1960), and Jean-Paul Sartre, *Sartre on Cuba* (New York, 1960) are short, pro-Castro statements based on limited observations in Cuba. Both are critical of the U.S., but Mills is far ahead in this race. Warren Miller, *90 Miles From Home: The Face of Cuba Today* (New York, 1961) is a disorganized set of observations which generally portrays an impressionistic, friendly evaluation of Castro's Cuba. A penerating analysis of the April, 1961, invasion fiasco and Castro's drift to Communism is Theodore Draper, *Cuba and U.S. Policy* (New York, 1961). A contrasting view of U.S. policy and the invasion is presented in Robert E. Light and Carl Marzani, *Cuba Versus the C I A* (New York, 1961). Luis Conte Aguero, *Los dos Rostros de Fidel Castro* (Mexico, 1960), Alberto Baeza Flores, *Las cadena vienen de lejos* (Mexico, 1960), and Manuel Artime Buesa, *Traicion!* (Mexico, 1960) present the viewpoint of the Cuban exiles. Theodore Draper, *Castro's Revolution: Myths and Realities* (New York, 1962) is a well-balanced, critical analysis of three years of Castro rule.

✓ ✓ ✓ ✓ ✓

Those readers interested in Latin American affairs should also consult the following journals. The best source for contemporary events is the *Hispanic American Report*, published monthly by the Institute of Hispanic American and Luso-Brazilian Studies. The *Hispanic American Historical Review* is an excellent source for articles of a historical nature, and is published quarterly. A publication of more recent origin, the *Journal of Inter-American Studies,* is a very valuable source for articles covering a variety of areas. It is published quarterly by the School of Inter-American Studies of the University of Florida. *Inter-American Economic Affairs* is most useful for current economic matters, but it also includes historical material. The magazine *Americas* is primarily devoted to current developments and is more popular in nature. It is issued by the Pan American Union. The *Revista de Historia de América* is a valuable historical review published semiannually by the Commission on History of the Pan American Institute of Geography and History.

Addendum. Several recently published works merit inclusion in this essay for varying reasons. The most comprehensive work on the April, 1961, invasion is Karl Meyer and Tad Szulc, *The Cuban Invasion: The Chronicle of a Disaster* (New York, 1962). Nicolas Rivero, *Castro's Cuba: An American Dilemma* (Washington, D. C., 1962), represents the views of a moderate exile, but with little new information. Two apologetic polemics recently issued are, Fulgencio Batista, *Cuba Betrayed* (New York, 1962), and Earl E. T. Smith, *The Fourth Floor. An Account of the Castro Communist Revolution* (New York, 1962). Three interesting interpretations dealing with United States policy and the Cold War in Latin America are; Salvador de Madariaga, *Latin America Between the Eagle and the Bear* (London, New York, 1962); Adolph A. Berle, Jr., *Latin America: Diplomacy and Reality* (New York, 1962); and, Frank Tannenbaum, *Ten Keys to Latin America* (New York, 1962).